+H61 .M42 1985

Y0-AIO-803
H61 .M42 1985 C.1 STACKS

AUDREY COHEN COLLEGE

H
61
M42
1985

Madge, John
　　The tools of social
　science

H
61
M42
1985

Madge, John
　　The tools of social
　　science

DATE	ISSUED TO
NOV 2 0 1999	

DEMCO

HISTORY
AND
HISTORIOGRAPHY

A THIRTY-ONE-VOLUME FACSIMILE SERIES
OF CLASSIC BOOKS FOR BOTH HISTORIANS AND STUDENTS
ON THE NATURE OF HISTORY,
HOW HISTORY IS COMMUNICATED,
AND HOW TO DO HISTORICAL RESEARCH

EDITED BY
ROBIN WINKS
YALE UNIVERSITY

COLLEGE FOR HUMAN SERVICES
LIBRARY
345 HUDSON STREET
NEW YORK, N.Y. 10014

A GARLAND SERIES

THE TOOLS OF SOCIAL SCIENCE

John Madge

Garland Publishing, Inc., New York & London
1985

29013

For a complete list of the titles in this
series see the final pages of this volume.

First published 1953 by Longmans, Green and
Co., Ltd.
Reprinted by permission of Longman Group Ltd.

Library of Congress Cataloging in Publication Data
Madge, John, 1914–
   The tools of social science.

  (History and historiography)
  Reprint. Originally published:
London ; New York : Longmans, Green, 1953.
  Bibliography: p.
  Includes index.
   1. Social sciences—Methodology.
2. Social sciences—Field work.
3. Interviewing. 4. Social sciences—
Language. I. Title. II. Series.
H61.M42   1985   300'.72   83-49160
ISBN 0-8240-6369-4 (alk. paper)

The volumes in this series are printed
on acid-free, 250-year-life paper.

Printed in the United States of America

THE TOOLS OF SOCIAL SCIENCE

THE TOOLS OF
SOCIAL SCIENCE

JOHN MADGE

LONGMANS, GREEN AND CO
LONDON · NEW YORK · TORONTO

LONGMANS, GREEN AND CO LTD
6 & 7 CLIFFORD STREET LONDON WI
ALSO AT MELBOURNE AND CAPE TOWN

LONGMANS, GREEN AND CO INC
55 FIFTH AVENUE NEW YORK 3

LONGMANS, GREEN AND CO
215 VICTORIA STREET TORONTO I

ORIENT LONGMANS LTD
BOMBAY CALCUTTA MADRAS

First published 1953

Printed in Great Britain by Richard Clay and Company, Ltd.,
Bungay, Suffolk

ACKNOWLEDGEMENTS

I should like to affirm my debt to the many pioneers in the social sciences, on whose wisdom and experience I have drawn so heavily in preparing this book. I also wish to thank those who have given their time to the tedious business of reading through and commenting on my successive drafts. My hope is that their guidance has eliminated some of its grosser imperfections.

Finally I must express my gratitude to my wife Janet—herself a social scientist, even though temporarily domesticated—for her very practical help in piloting the book through all its stages.

J. H. M.

CONTENTS

INTRODUCTION 1

Chapter 1
THE METHOD OF SOCIAL SCIENCE

1. INTRODUCTION 19
2. GENERAL ORIENTATIONS 21
3. LANGUAGE
    (a) The Search for a Distinctive Language . . . 38
    (b) The Taxonomic Solution 44
    (c) The Operational Solution 46
    (d) Some Attempts at Definition 50
    (e) Summary and Conclusions 57
4. LOGIC
    (a) The Emergence of Empirical Logic 58
    (b) Mill's Logic Introduced 61
    (c) Limits to Applicability 65
    (d) The Inverse Deductive Method 67
    (e) The Guidance of Statistics 72
    (f) Accounting for Results 76
    (g) Conclusions 79

Chapter 2
DOCUMENTS

1. DOCUMENTS AND SOCIAL SCIENCE 80
2. THE PERSONAL DOCUMENT
    (a) Establishment as a Reputable Source of Information . 81
    (b) Possibilities of Distortion by the Informant . . 85
    (c) Distortion Introduced by the Investigator . . . 89
    (d) Personal Document Material as a Basis for Generalisation 90

		PAGE
3. Documents of Other Kinds		91
(a) Records		92
(b) Reports		93
(c) Availability of Documents		95
(d) The Value of Generalisations Based on Documents		98
(e) 'Case-history' Material		100
4. Problems of Authentication		
(a) Authenticity and Meaning		103
(b) The Interpretation of Statistics		105
5. Interpretation		108

Chapter 3

OBSERVATION

1. The Importance of First-hand Observation		117
2. Principal Difficulties in Observation		119
(a) Inadequacies of Our Sense-organs		120
(b) Observation and Inference		122
(c) Effects of Interaction between Observer and Observed		127
Attempts at neutralisation		
Participant observation		
3. Some Practical Applications		131
(a) Functional Anthropology		132
(b) Industrial Sociology		133
(c) Mass-Observation		135
(d) Action Research		136
(e) Overheards		137
4. Observational Schedules and Other Means of Recording		
(a) Social Behaviour		139
(b) Observing the Inanimate		139
5. Conclusions		141

Chapter 4

THE INTERVIEW

Part A—TYPES OF INTERVIEW		144
1. Influencing Potentates		145

Contents

2. EXAMINING EXPERTS 148
3. INTERVIEWING PEOPLE 150

Part B—THE FORMATIVE INTERVIEW

1. THE NON-DIRECTIVE INTERVIEW 153
2. THE FOCUSED INTERVIEW 164
3. LIFE-HISTORIES 167
4. THE INFORMAL INTERVIEW 173

Part C—THE MASS INTERVIEW 177

1. SUBJECTS SUITABLY EXPLORED BY THE USE OF MASS INTERVIEWS
   (a) The Ideal of Objectivity 178
   (b) Election Forecasts 181
   (c) Other Opinion Polls 184
   (d) Attitude Measurements 187
   (e) Latent Structure Analysis 191
   (f) Scalogram Analysis 194
   (g) Inherent Limitations of Attitude Measurement . 198
   (h) Conclusions 203
2. SAMPLING 205
   (a) Background 206
   (b) Mathematical Considerations 207
   (c) Practical Considerations 210
   (d) Size of Sample 213
3. THE PILOT SURVEY 216
4. APPROACH TECHNIQUES 217
5. THE SETTING AND CONDUCT OF THE INTERVIEW . 218
6. NOTE-TAKING AND CARDING 220
7. HOW TO MINIMISE BIAS 233
   (a) Verification by Use of a Second Source of Information 236
   (b) Statistical Tests for Internal Verification . . 237
   (c) Assessment of Plausibility 237
   (d) Optimum Conditions for Truth . . . 241

Contents

8. The Problem of Non-response 248
9. Summary and Conclusions 252

Chapter 5
EXPERIMENT

1. The Scope of Experiment 254
2. The Controlled Experiment
   - (a) The Model 261
   - (b) An Experiment in Electioneering Techniques . . 263
   - (c) Rural Hygiene in Syria 265
   - (d) Social Effects of Good Housing 266
   - (e) Comment and Conclusions 267
3. Modifications of the Controlled Experiment Design
   - (a) The Limits of Post-factum Analysis . . . 271
   - (b) Comparison of Intelligence of Own and Foster Children 278
   - (c) Who Shall Survive? 278
4. The Experiment in Time
   - (a) Merits and Weaknesses 280
   - (b) Frustration and Regression in Children . . . 281
   - (c) The Hawthorne Experiment 282
   - (d) Conclusions 286

Chapter 6
THE LIMITS OF SOCIAL SCIENCE   290

INDEX OF REFERENCES 295

GENERAL INDEX 305

INTRODUCTION

It is now over a hundred years since Auguste Comte heralded the new positive science of man which, he believed, would complete the pyramid of knowledge and put an end to metaphysical speculation. Comte's prophecy has been only partly fulfilled. There have been many attempts to provide a means of superseding speculation about the unknown and the unknowable, but all have been unsuccessful.

Meanwhile, knowledge has been expanding magnificently, and has been gradually lapping over into the domain of human behaviour. We have witnessed, particularly in the last half-century, an impressive growth in the practical applications of social science. Its underlying principles are only precariously established, but this has not deterred thoughtful and active men from developing methods that have been increasingly well adapted to the answering and resolving of practical problems.

It has been my aim in this book to concentrate attention on the practical techniques developed by social scientists. After an examination of some aspects of language and logic, attention will be given in turn to the use of documents, to observational methods, to the interview and questionnaire, and to the rôle and prospects of social experimentation. There will inevitably be diversions from time to time, caused by some point of principle that has a direct bearing on the choice of method, but the emphasis is throughout on practice rather than on theory.

There are some who will feel that this is putting the cart before the horse, and that it is impossible either to act effectively ourselves or to evaluate the actions of others without having previously secured our theoretical base. In my more cautiously logical moments I find their argument almost entirely convincing. But it is a fact that science has gone forward without, and even in spite of, its methodologists and logicians. Moreover, this divorce is reflected in the teaching of all sciences, in which the theory of knowledge is taught, if at all, in strict isolation from the practical training in how to win scientific knowledge. So it is not strange to find, on the one hand, philosophers relying on distorted and obsolete scraps of science, and on the other hand scientists rushing in on the most delicate and ageless controversies and freely distributing their logically outrageous solutions.

This sense of disappointment at the fragility of first principles is no new thing.

> If we open any book, [wrote John Stuart Mill in 1836 at the age of thirty] it is impossible not to be struck with the mistiness of what we find represented as preliminary and fundamental notions, and the very insufficient manner in which the propositions which are palmed upon us as first principles seem to be made out, contrasted with the lucidity of the explanation and the conclusiveness of the proofs as soon as the writer enters upon the details of his object. Whence comes this anomaly? Why is the admitted certainty of the results of those sciences in no way prejudiced by the want of solidity in their premises? How happens it that a firm superstructure has been erected upon an unstable foundation? The solution of the paradox is that what are called first principles are in truth *last* principles. Instead of being the fixed point from whence the chain of proof which supports all the rest of the science hangs suspended, they are themselves the remotest links of the chain. Though presented as if all other truths were to be deduced from them, they are the truths which are last arrived at.[1]

This is a very penetrating passage, one of the earliest rediscoveries that accumulation of knowledge may not necessarily be the primary function of science. Mill's statement may lead us to infer that we are equally free to regard scientific activity as containing its own rewards, with knowledge as a residue rather than as an end. But if we adopt this belief, as I think we should, we must do so with our eyes open, and be prepared to defend it. For it is anything but uncontroversial, and its implications have been far from completely worked out. It is in direct conflict with the classical, and still widely held, theory that the function of all science is to accumulate a corpus of exact knowledge. And yet, strangely enough, in field after field scientists have openly sought out the answers to practical problems, and have regarded knowledge in the classical sense as little more than a by-product of their search. And for reasons which we shall next briefly consider, in no science is the pursuit of objective knowledge more futile than in social science.

---

[1] MILL, J. S. (1836), *On the Definition of Political Economy and on the Method of Investigation Proper to It*, reprinted in NAGEL, E. (1950), *J. S. Mill's Philosophy of Scientific Method*, pp. 408–9.

OBJECTIVITY

Every philosopher today agrees that we cannot learn about the world without enlisting the help of our senses. But all philosophers, except for a few fanatics, are by now also reconciled to the fact that we cannot make use of our sense experiences without adopting certain presuppositions—or *a priori* truths—which can never be verified by appeal to the senses, and accept the view that ultimately therefore empirical truth itself rests on these presuppositions.

Now clearly for there to be one truth and one alone, these presuppositions must be completely predetermined and immutable. If different individuals are free to choose different presuppositions, then the conclusions which they will derive from their observations will also differ. When this point was grasped in the late eighteenth century, it became a matter of honour among philosophers to discover a list of presuppositions which could be defended as unique and immutable. Thus, Immanuel Kant laid great store on the concepts of space and time, both in his discussion of causality and in his method of defining objects (two objects cannot occupy the same space at the same time), and for some time his solution seemed an acceptable one. Unfortunately, the uniqueness of Euclidean geometry and of Newtonian motion have since been shown to be illusory.

Another line of approach was adopted by J. S. Mill, who suggested that these presuppositions are not necessary or certain, but are, in a special sense, hypotheses about the real world arrived at by generalisation from previous successful experiences. A little later, Herbert Spencer proposed somewhat to broaden the basis by postulating that they derive from the accumulated experiences of countless generations.

The earlier philosophers who had thundered out their necessary truths, justifying them by appeal to the ' natural laws ' given by pure intuitive reason, at least had the courage of their convictions. These watered-down and uncertain latter-day grounds for the choice of prior beliefs were sorry and unconvincing substitutes. The fact was that no one could any longer find any solid justification for the certainty of truth. In this climate and with the first stirrings of modern psychology, it is easy to understand the insidious emergence of the view that all knowledge is relative, and that the search for absolute truth is without hope.

This view took independent root in various soils. In the United States in 1878, Charles Peirce first formulated the pragmatic theory of belief which was later to be enthusiastically adopted by William James. This theory abandoned the search for 'first things, principles, "categories", supposed necessities', and looked instead towards 'last things, fruits, consequences, facts'.[1] Thought was thus to be regarded as an instrument of life, designed to overcome whatever thwarts the impulse to action; beliefs were to be regarded as rules for action; the sole test of truth was expediency. In this way William James set out to extend the doctrine of utilitarianism to embrace truth as well as morals. To him, truth and goodness were, in fact, different aspects of the same thing.

A generation before Peirce, in the very different climate of mid-nineteenth-century Europe, there had arisen the immensely influential thesis of Marx and Engels. Through their practical immersion in the intellectual and political struggles of the day, these two men came to recognise the—to them—false perspective which distorted the beliefs of their political opponents, the bourgeoisie. It seemed to them a matter of urgency to unmask these false ideologies, and to substitute the grasp of objective reality which they claimed as a prerogative of the working classes.

It is a startling thought that from these rival theories, which have so much in common, there should have emerged the active principles that underwrite the two great world powers of our day. Their similarities are undeniable. Both admit the uncertainty of truth and set up instead the criterion of utility in thinking. But, also for both, this criterion has shown itself liable to degenerate into a method of undermining alien falsehoods rather than of establishing useful truths.

Karl Mannheim has in recent decades helped to bridge the gap by developing the more constructive theory which has become known as the 'sociology of knowledge'. He renounces the abstract concept of objective knowledge, but shows that in given circumstances it is possible to arrive at reliable decisions in factual disputes. These decisions are limited by the observers' incom-

[1] JAMES, W. (1907), *Pragmatism*, pp. 54-5.

plete perspective, but when members of a group have aims in common, they will also tend to reach agreement on questions of fact.

This theory, here ruthlessly abridged into two sentences, provides us with a tidy framework within which we may understand the wide discrepancies between different views which, as our observations tell us, are honestly held by people in different circumstances. It helps us to understand why natural scientists, whose subject-matter is basically uncontroversial, seldom find it difficult in the long run to decide the relative merits of different scientific statements. In the short run, personal or even national implications may distort truth in natural science, but there has generally been enough basic international agreement on aims and enough practical disadvantage in maintaining a 'false' view to make such differences short-lived and to ensure a steady line of development.

There is a striking contrast in the domain of human relations. Here radically different systems of belief, and hence radically different views of truth, live precariously side by side. The only apparently effective means of 'converting' an individual or a group from one system of beliefs to another are the employment of force or of concentrated special pleading. This medley of co-existent truths can be accounted for in only two ways. One is that I—each I of us—have uniquely hit upon the true presuppositions and so have access to the only truth, while all the others are misled by false ideologies. The other, and to my mind the only tenable, view is Mannheim's perspectivist view of many truths, each shared only by those who have shared experiences and have agreed between themselves on social aims.

It is easy to apply this to the individuals and the groups that provide the subject matter of social science. The first lesson in human relations tells us that clashes in belief and conflicting interpretations of truth are universally to be found in and among societies. But how about the social scientist himself? Has he a means of immunising himself against the infectious emotions of his fellow-men? When the rest of the world is incapable of attaining an unbiased objectivity, what special power does he possess that is able to single him out from all humanity?

This is a central question in social science, and one which recurs in various forms throughout this book. The conclusion will be reached that social scientists can reduce the extent to which they themselves are infected by the societies that they study, but that they cannot eliminate infection. However expert and however conscientious the scientists, some variety of truths is therefore to be expected, and can be actually found, in every social issue.

Even the palpable disagreements should not, however, lead us to ignore the considerable areas of social knowledge in which a far-flung community of aims is possible. Human societies as a whole have a common interest in humanity's struggles against illness. Hence there is no ultimate discrepancy between the fund of medical truth acceptable to widely differing cultures. Quite large groups of nations can persuade themselves that they have a common stake in the defence or propagation of one way of life or another. On other points, sharp differences in aim between individual nations will be recognised in different systems of belief. Furthermore, within one country, what is acceptable will vary according to age, maturity, class and so on. Each family, and even each individual, will have to some extent a personal definition of truth.

Thus it is that, while the natural scientists can approach the ideal of objectivity without sacrificing a concrete aim, to postulate an objective social science is to ask for something which is probably unattainable, and may even be undesirable. If we assign a functional rôle to science, we may require social scientists not as detached referees basing their judgments on a set of universal theories, but as active engineers of social change in directions freely chosen by each community of interests; in this case, their ability to help will be partly determined by their own identification with their adopted community and with its aims.

KINDS OF PRESUPPOSITION

Let us consider very briefly the kinds of presupposition on which any individual must adopt a stand.

The most universally accepted are the symbols of mathematics. These are the systems of conventions (e.g. $0, 1, \ldots +, -, =, \times \ldots$) and the rules of formal logic that have been built up into an internally consistent whole. These are not necessary truths, for other systems could be devised, but long experience and constant adaptation have made them convenient in use; hence they are the common heritage of all nations sufficiently civilised to need them.[1]

The next kind of presuppositions are those embedded in our language system. Apart from the verbal synonyms for mathematical and other similar symbols, these are directly concerned with the world we know—broadly speaking, descriptions of objects and of relations between objects; they then imply a certain regularity and causality in the world of experience. As we shall see later, the attempt to attach necessary meanings to words and thus to frame exact definitions is somewhat stultifying. But, again, any like-minded group can agree on the meanings of the set of words that they need to carry out their purposes.

These two forms of symbolism are entailed in all orderly thought and communication. They are the bricks that individuals and groups pile up in order to express themselves. But the form of the structure that they may build is also to a great extent safeguarded by society. The artist has his æsthetic code which, as history shows, may change its emphasis from time to time and in different cultures. Closely parallel, there are present in all thought, and most explicitly in the case of scientific thought, what have been called *preference rules*.[2] These may be regarded as a kind of scientific code of behaviour, as a series of ideals towards which scientists are expected to strain. Examples are the ideal of simplicity (Occam's razor) and the ideal of precision (e.g. by measurement). Such ideals tend to be elusive, and are sometimes contradictory; if so, disagreements on which to emphasise often conceal underlying differences as to aim.

Next we must take into account the general orientations which are peculiar to a given science. The elaboration of a distinctive general orientation may be the signal for the establishment of a fresh discipline. Even so it will almost certainly contain some elements openly borrowed from established sciences. A case in point was Durkheim's hypothesis that ' the determining cause of

---

[1] The quality of convenience, which is inherent in mathematical and logical symbols, perhaps underlies Poincaré's more general criterion of convenience which he felt should be applied to all concepts, empirical or otherwise. One plausible explanation of the extraordinary pervasiveness of number is suggested by Craik, who sees in it (*The Nature of Explanation*, p. 53), a ' proof of the extreme flexibility of the neural model or calculating machine '. A similar view is contained in the theory of cybernetics.

[2] See e.g. KAUFMANN, F. (1944), *Methodology of the Social Sciences*, pp. 41, 71 seq. etc.

a social fact should be sought among the social facts preceding it', which explicitly echoes the concept of causality, a basic tenet of nineteenth-century physical science. As Merton has pointed out, the investigator can seldom afford to ignore such general orientations, even though they in no way prescribe for him the *specific* hypotheses that it will be his task to pursue.[1]

The initial development of specific hypotheses is a distinct and crucial step. In natural science many of the most fruitful hypotheses have been drawn by analogy or by deduction from a fresh corner of a previously established theory. The dilemma of social science—viewed as a corpus of knowledge—is that there is no generally acceptable theory, and even if there were such a thing it could not be regarded as established before it had been tested empirically at all important points. An adequate system of social laws has to be both internally consistent and proof against confutation by external evidence. The first requirement is easily satisfied in comparison with the second. Without the interdependence of fact and theory, we are liable, on the one hand, to be served with a meaningless array of isolated correlations and with causal 'explanations' unattached to any general theory, while on the other hand we are being asked to accept general theories built on a foundation of casual observation and of popular science.

This dilemma offers a fair excuse for doing little, so long as we believe that the function of social science is merely to build up a body of established knowledge on the subject of human relations. After a point, the motive of curiosity which is said to inform pure seekers after truth may be insufficient to break the circularity of the defences against social understanding. But even those who are most abstractly inclined are compelled to admit not only that social science, like other sciences, benefits by contact with practical problems, but also that human relations require some insight from those participating, and that to some extent this insight can be transmitted as well as experienced. By any analysis, social science—like all science—is more than merely the residue of experience. It is the doing as well as the knowing. And provided the doer proceeds with awareness he will not only solve his immediate problem but will also be able to contribute a fragment

[1] MERTON, R. K. (1945), 'Sociological Theory', *Am. Journ. Soc.*, 50, 464. Reprinted (1949) in the author's *Social Theory and Social Structure*, pp. 83–96.

to the residue of experience from which substantive and communicable theory may be built.

If we revert in our minds to concrete instances, it will be found that the suggested conflict between a theoretical and an empirical approach to social science is almost entirely illusory. All theory requires some empirical foundation, however distant, and virtually all empirical inquiry is based on some theoretical grounds, however naïve these may be. With the world of phenomena to choose from, selection in a purely random manner of what may be relevant would be irresponsible and absurd.

The only occasional exception is in the case of experiment. It is a matter of history that many of the most fruitful discoveries in experimental science have been made apparently by chance, and quite in advance of the explicit theoretical systems in which one day they find their place. It is widely believed that this ability to soar is the mark of the intuitive genius, but a similar experience occurs at more pedestrian levels. To this day, many practices—in medicine, for example—are retained because they have a desired effect, even though it is not known why they work in the way that they do. There is a comparable practice in social relations. All the time, and at all levels, social arrangements are being changed by administrative decisions. In normal life, the consequences of these changes are not mapped out; sometimes they are even deliberately distorted by interested parties. Social science, with its gift of heightened awareness, can become a refined instrument of social change: but it need not and cannot wait upon the completion of an authoritative social theory.

To vary a social phenomenon experimentally the experimenter has to take hold of all essential factors even if he is not yet able to analyse them satisfactorily. A major omission or misjudgment on this point makes the experiment fail. In social research the experimenter has to take into consideration such factors as the personality of individual members, the group structure, ideology and cultural values, and economic factors. Group experimentation is a form of social management. To be successful it, like social management, has to take into account all of the various factors that happen to be important for the case in hand.[1]

Time and again we are driven to recognise the relevance and the unique and irreplaceable merits of experimentation.

[1] LEWIN, K. (1947), 'Frontiers in Group Dynamics', *Hum. Rel.*, 1, 9. Reprinted (1952) in his *Field Theory in Social Science*, p. 193.

THE PERILS OF OBSERVATION

I must here briefly introduce the subject of observation, which is more fully dealt with in the body of this book.

Knowledge is acquired by combining our sense-experiences, but the form of knowledge is governed by the kinds of presupposition that we are prepared to adopt. It must also be recognised that the process of sense-experiencing is itself very intimately connected with these presuppositions. It is simply not true that our senses provide a set of mechanical instruments by which all relevant aspects of a situation are noted. There are two unanswerable objections to this view. The first is that our individual senses are selective. This alone is an important enough limitation on the completeness of our record, but it must also be recognised that our senses are better than any record of them can be; what we actually experience is an integral reaction, and the more we attempt to analyse this experience into its constitutent parts, the more incomplete and atomistic our record becomes.

Nevertheless, if we are to make our total sensations available to others—and to some extent if we are to retain them for our own recall—we cannot avoid analysis, with its consequent simplifications. The question is what to record, and what to omit from the record. To the layman this decision is almost entirely unconscious; if he is naturally or consciously skilful in deciding, a man may be an artist. Scientists are largely ruled by the code of ' objectivity ' and by the standards of competence laid down for them, but the scientist who breaks fresh ground may often possess the more positive skill of recognising the unexpected.

It is necessary that the scientist should be conscious of the basis of his selection, and part of the observational skill that he must develop is skill in perceiving his own experiences. Objectivity in this sense is wholly desirable. But self-awareness by itself, although it helps him to avoid paying too much attention to the bizarre and the conspicuous, does not positively guide him to a realistically-based judgment of what is relevant and what irrelevant. His objective sustains him when dependence on objectivity would let him down.

He also requires some grounds for selecting an appropriate method of observation from the considerable variety concurrently in use in social science. His choice of method will be influenced by his peculiar capacity, as a human being, of insight into the unexpressed thoughts and feelings of fellow-humans; it will be restricted by the corresponding difficulty of detached observation of situations which cannot leave him emotionally untouched. While it would be too radical to claim that he is barred from all objective observation, it is in fact impossible to evade the question of relevance, and we must again recognise the insidious control of our perceptions by our purposes. To the theoretician, the criterion is relevance to a particular hypothesis and hence to the general theory of which this hypothesis forms a part. If the aim is social accounting, the relevance of observations will be predetermined by the nature of the account that it has been decided to present. If the aim is social engineering, relevance will be gauged by the insight and mastery offered by a given series of observations.

I think that we can reconcile this variety of methods and of aims if we bring into our appreciation a sense of the very different levels at which any science, and not least social science, must operate. In a crude way, we are sometimes taught to conceive of science as comprising three almost mechanical stages, namely observation—hypothesis—verification. This is almost wholly misleading. For although observation is anything but a mechanical process, and what is observed is ruled by a whole series of prior considerations, it must equally be admitted that observation has its technical side, and that how we observe is subject to great variation. The everyday observer develops a rough-and-ready technique that enables him to cope with everyday needs. But in virtually every scientific discipline there have been developed a series of aids and accessories to observation, that help the scientist to observe with greater clarity, to compare with greater precision and to record with greater reliability. Parallel with these are the emergent experimental techniques which permit the social scientist to manipulate his raw material, to speed up natural processes or to introduce artificial ones.

No such improvements can be won without some corresponding loss. In almost every case the loss is a certain restriction on the freedom of observation. As the magnification of a telescope is increased, so is the field of vision restricted. The limited choices available to a rat in an experimental maze are paid for in the range of rat behaviour that the experimenter can explore. Thus the aid to observation inevitably circumscribes the degree to which an hypothesis reflects the total situation.

In most scientific fields, this progressive concentration onto a narrow area restricts the problem without distorting it. It is on the whole an efficient means of approaching precision. Let me take a simple illustration. An experienced geologist is prospecting for copper, and after consulting maps and other documents he sets off for a likely spot; as he clambers over the rocks he comes across a patch of greenish colour, which his experience tells him may indicate a copper-bearing ore. He hacks off a bit, and handles it. It seems to be about the right weight and has a familiar-looking structure. So he puts it in his bag, and when he returns to camp carries out a simple test, dissolving a little of his ore in nitric acid. The result is promising, for the liquid turns the expected blue-green. He labels his specimen and sends it back to a laboratory. Here scientists analyse it carefully, confirm that it contains copper and discover its other constituents. If this is satisfactory a larger expedition will return to the site, bore trial holes and so on. Finally, chemists will undertake a full quantitative analysis, so that mining engineers and financiers may determine whether the ore is rich enough in copper to merit extraction.

The procedure is simple in the example chosen, particularly as it is an instance of applied science in which those taking part know from the start exactly what they are looking for. But the principle is clear. An entrepreneur would be regarded as foolish if he set up expensive machinery for extracting copper at a spot indicated merely by the prospector's findings: conversely it would be just as absurd for him to collect samples of ore at random from every part of the world and then to analyse them all in an elaborate laboratory in the hope that one sample might lead extractors to the most suitable site for their operations. And in any such instance, the same inevitable economy follows from using different techniques at different stages of inquiry.

In most sciences there is an intrinsically efficient order of succession for bringing the different techniques into play; provided the objective of the search has been firmly decided, a positive result at one stage of precision will justify an advance to a more exact, narrower, hypothesis. Conversely, if an hypothesis has at any stage to be abandoned or if an unexpected result has to be accounted for, it will regularly be necessary to regress to an earlier, less precise, stage. The whole procedure can be an orderly one.

As a corollary of this, the more precise techniques are most easily employed when the probing required is at its minimum, because the subject has become familiar to the investigator and the situation has been relieved of its tension. Quantitative methods are thus customarily found in use at what has by then become a superficial level of inquiry; the fact that they can be used at all implies that the process of penetration, the baring of the problem, has already taken place.

In the case of social science, in some respects the parallel is close. The logic of procedure in social science is the logic that is common to all scientific method, and provides a similar safeguard against absurd conclusions. Again, there is beyond doubt a place for prospectors in social science. As in all sciences, it is wasteful to invent and apply elaborate devices to detect and measure human phenomena if these phenomena remain figments of the imaginations of chair-borne thinkers. Fictions created by the exercise of pure reason are never effective substitutes for concepts derived in familiarity with living events.

But it is an inescapable fact that the social scientist who goes out into the social field must be prepared for a convergence of his aims and interests with those of his human material. He himself is bound to be changed by his experience, and his aims will be changed in keeping, but his intervention will similarly lead to changes. This latter effect is now being encountered in microphysics, but it dominates social science. Furthermore, the distortions increase in importance as the situation in which the study takes place becomes more artificial, and hence more suitable for exact measurement.

In these respects, observation in social science must always differ profoundly from that in natural science. In both, the aim is a progressive increase in precision, in knowledge and control. But in the case of the latter it is fairly safe to presuppose that the final result will be within the range indicated by the preliminary surveys: when a prospector was supposed to be looking for copper, we would refer him to his terms of reference, if not to a psychiatrist, if he returned joyfully with a sample of juicy oranges. In social science there is a much greater risk that the prospector will set out in search of one thing and come back with something entirely different, which he has learned to regard as far more significant and important. The fact is merely noted here, and a judgment on it is deferred until the final chapter of this book.

VALUES

It is now appropriate to allude in a more mature form to the question of value-judgments in social science. This intrusive question has been answered in a great variety of ways. At one extreme is the stand taken by those who might be called naïve behaviourists, who are determined that all science is value-free, with the result that they not only deny the existence of their own intrinsic evaluations but are even very reluctant to admit that the feelings and beliefs of their human subjects are of concern to them, except when these are expressed in the form of overt acts.[1]

Behaviourists appear to have allowed themselves some relaxation of the sanction on attitudinal studies,[2] and in this respect the attempt to equate the social sciences with natural science seems almost to have been abandoned. In contrast, however, the ideal of the value-free social scientist reaches far beyond behaviourist circles, and is still widely held.

This standpoint was advocated with particular subtlety by Max

---

[1] The paradigm of the value-free social scientist was expressed by one of the leading exponents of this standpoint in the following words :
' A more common and less conscious source of error is the tendency of scientists, and especially of social scientists, to permit the current code of morals of the community or their own personal notions of ethics to influence them in their collection and manipulation of data. The findings of science are *per se* non-ethical. It is not the business of a chemist who invents a high explosive to be influenced in his task as a scientist by consideration as to whether his product will be used to blow up cathedrals or to build tunnels through the mountains. Nor is it the business of the social scientist in arriving at laws of group behaviour, to permit himself to be influenced by considerations of how his conclusions coincide with existing notions, or what the effects of his findings on the social order will be. For his purpose *as a scientist*, science must be an end in itself . . . As a scientist his only ethical responsibility lies in seeing that the rules of scientific procedure have been complied with.'—LUNDBERG, G. A. (1929 ed.), *Social Research*, pp. 35–6.
A recent statement of preference for " overt act " material was made by Kinsey et al. ' We do not have much confidence in verbalizations of attitudes which each subject thinks are his own, when they are, in actuality, little more than reflections of the attitudes which prevail in the particular culture in which he was raised. Often the expressed attitudes are in striking contradiction to the actual behaviour, and then they are significant because they indicate the existence of psychic conflict and they throw light on the extent to which community attitudes may influence an individual.'—KINSEY, A. C. et al. (1948), *Sexual Behavior in the Human Male*, p. 58.
See also pp. 33 seq. and 125 seq. of this book.
[2] This point is discussed by NADEL, S. F. (1951), *Foundations of Social Anthropology*, pp. 57 seq.

Weber, who more than a generation ago undertook an important analysis of the implications of a value-free social science. His analysis was provoked by opposition to the 'professorial prophets' who flourished in Germany up to the end of the First World War, and who used their Chairs for bringing political influence to bear on their students. To counter them, Weber proposed a self-discipline aimed at 'ethical neutrality'. He regarded this as an unattainable ideal, but nevertheless one which should guide the social scientist away from the determination of ends and towards the examination of socially formulated aims in order to assess their rationality, implications and internal coherence.[1]

There is indeed no logical inconsistency in believing that, while values are a legitimate object of study, the social scientist as such has no justification for intruding his own assessment of the relative value of alternative value systems. There are, however, practical grounds for doubting whether any human being is capable of the detachment that would be required of the true neutral.

In recent years there has tended to emerge a fresh point of view. This begins with the conclusion that pure value-free social science is unattainable, and that the inevitable bias of the investigator is less dangerous if fully exposed. But it has gone further than that, and it is now suggested that the social scientist *ought* to have a standpoint on social issues in order to ensure that he has 'an actively selective point of view'. It is claimed, by R. S. Lynd for example, that without this active concern with the point at issue the investigator will lapse into the random collection of pointless facts and will claim immunity from the need to organise these facts *and to act upon them* until some unattainable time when all the data are safely gathered in.[2]

Sponsorship of value-drained research can provide a similar mock solution for the troubled administrator.

> There may be an uneasy recognition of the existence of major problems, indeed problems closely related to the subject of the research, but considerable anxiety associated with the task of tackling them. The advent of the research worker is hailed as providing an apparently painless way out of this conflict: executive authority may be under pressure to do something about problems that can no

[1] See WEBER, M. (trans. E. A. Shils, 1949), *The Methodology of the Social Sciences*, pp. 1-47; BLUM, F. H. (1944), 'Max Weber's Postulate of "Freedom from Value Judgments"', *Am. Journ. Soc.*, 50, 46. For a critique of Weber's position, see KAUFMANN, F. (1944), pp. 202 seq.
[2] LYND, R. S. (1939), *Knowledge for What?*, pp. 183 seq.

longer be avoided; it accepts research, therefore, in the hope that this will postpone indefinitely the need for action. Research, then, may be used as a neurotic escape from the need for facing up to problems.[1]

But if a social scientist adopts an actively and openly selective point of view, he has the duty of choosing one which is at least reconcilable with the values of the society that he serves. As an abstract problem of choice, this is by no means straightforward, but its difficulties have not deterred a succession of social scientists from attempting an ideal solution.

These solutions have ranged from Durkheim's application, by analogy with physical health, of the joint criteria of normality and utility,[2] through various biological and evolutionary analogies, through dependence on 'rational' belief in such universals as liberty and justice,[3] to acceptance of the irrevocably subjective nature of ethics.[4] All such positions are unassailable in principle, for they can seldom be shown theoretically to be wrong. In practice they tend to disappoint, for they seldom offer useful guidance as to which particular norm or ethical principle should be emphasised in given circumstances. The conflict of interests recurs constantly in some form or another, and it is just on such occasions that human ingenuity is able to justify—on rationalist and relativist grounds—practically any policy put forward by a sectional interest. This appears to be why the exposure of specific ideologies has been such a common feature of both Marxist and pragmatic doctrines, and why a general analysis of the function of ideology occupies such a prominent position in modern psychoanalytic thought.[5]

But to undermine the beliefs of others is rather ineffective as a positive remedy. All living organisms appear to exhibit vague generalised aims of survival and change, whether evolutionary or involuntary.[6] Aims are canalised by circumstances in different

[1] COOK, P. H. (1951), 'Methods of Field Research', *Austral. Journ. Psychol.*, 3 (2), 90.
[2] See DURKHEIM, E. (1895—trans. 1938), *Rules of Sociological Method*, pp. 47 seq.
[3] Professor Ginsberg writes: 'I find it difficult to believe that the striving for justice, for example, has no basis in reason or cannot be subjected to rational tests'.—*Brit. Journ. Soc.*, 2, 9.
[4] For example, 'The ethical ideal must remain as rich and concrete and inner *and as inexpressible* as life itself, at whatever cost to the completeness of our theories'.—MACIVER, R. M. (1924 ed.), *Community*, p. 174.
[5] See, for example, FROMM, E. (1942), *The Fear of Freedom*, pp. 239 seq.
[6] Cf. FREUD, S. (1950 ed.), *Beyond the Pleasure Principle*, pp. 47 etc.

directions at different times. Somewhere, however deeply embedded, there lurks in every value system some reflection of the fact that alternative aims, and alternative means of achieving them, vary in the satisfactions that they promise to interested groups. And in spite of all prophets, this kind of satisfaction, which is what men mean by efficiency, cannot be assessed without trial.

Thus there emerges in a new form the conclusion that the social scientist cannot rise above the aspirations of his social environment, and that he will be misled if he attempts to do so. Freedom from value-judgment is an unreal imperative because it is unrealisable. Instead of aiming to become the objective value-free theorist, the social scientist may without shame take on the job of social engineer, in which he may use his experience and special skills in the service of his chosen community. In this capacity he can goad his fellow citizens on to discontent with those social institutions whose efficiency is inadequate or dwindling, can help them to choose by experiment between different ways forward, and can guide them towards making better use of what social and material resources are available to them by attaining greater self-awareness and cohesion.

This is not some strange new idea, but one that has impelled a large proportion of the most memorable social scientists of the past century. Their results have been uneven, but there is a strangely neglected uniformity in the aspirations of these great men. Comte's altruism, Le Play's paternalism, Booth's genuine concern for the relief of poverty, the fervid ecological propaganda of Geddes, for each one of them the stimulus of social curiosity would by itself have been patently inadequate. Furthermore, it is significant how frequently the social survey has been regarded by its protagonists not merely as a preliminary to social action [1] but as itself a form of social action. One important, and regularly stressed, feature of the well-run social survey has been that it has enlisted the enthusiasm of members of the community being studied, and enhanced their sense of belonging to the community, their pride in its achievements and their urge to remedy its faults. The social survey is a movement as well as a fact-finding expedition.

[1] A recent discussion of the relation between social survey and government will be found in ABRAMS, M. (1951), *Social Surveys and Social Action*, pp. 124 seq.

For historical reasons, those forms of social investigation which have been imbued with this spirit of amelioration and reform have been allotted a rather depressed status. They appear as neither hard-headed enough for the practical business of government nor scholarly enough for full acceptance in academic circles. It has to be faced that this depressed status is reflected in the amateur and obsolete techniques on which they still too often depend. But in the long run, and under experienced and conceptually sophisticated guidance, these practical and cooperative enterprises in social experimentation—in material and institutional planning, in industry and education, in physical and moral reablement—may well contribute more to human well-being and to the resolution of social tensions than any other of the varied activities subsumed under the title of social science.

Chapter 1

THE METHOD OF SOCIAL SCIENCE

1. INTRODUCTION

SOCIAL science in action is full of confusion for a spectator. He will soon be struck by the great variety of methods in actual use; and he will later come to realise that these methods reflect a bewildering diversity of ideas, concurrently maintained by different groups of social scientists, as to what it is that they are trying to do.

It is a little as though this same spectator found himself beside a playing-field, on which a strange assortment of players were assembled. Gradually as he watched he would begin to discern that several games were being simultaneously played on the same pitch, and that the incidents of contact between—say—a hockey player and a rugby-football player were, at least early in the games, due to chance rather than to design.

After some pondering, he might conclude that—whatever the participants may have believed—the proximate aims of their activity were of no great relevance. The common effect of their ritualistic behaviour had been to exercise their muscles, to increase their appetites, to give them something to think about, in some cases to strengthen their friendships and their self-confidence. If the function of the different games could be distinguished at all, it would be in the degree to which these different purposes, and their components, were fulfilled.

This analogy is a dream within a dream, symbolising social science as a microcosm of social life. It cannot, however, be pursued much further. The rules by which each pair of teams conduct themselves are designed to satisfy the requirements of a good, clean and exhilarating game. Except in minor matters, the rules are complete and the objective—i.e. the manner of winning—is exactly specified.

This is not altogether the case in the field of social science. It is true that you will find teams of busy observers who claim to be motivated primarily by curiosity. But many of the players are bent, not on recreation, but on the discovery of answers to what seem to them to be urgent problems of social policy and social engineering. Their rules are designed not so much to constitute an artificial and equitable system of play as to provide the means of finding effective solutions to oppressive social problems. In some form or another, each one of the many empirical approaches to the domain of social science is related to a distinctive view of social processes, and the great majority are aimed ultimately at tightening man's grip on these processes.

In the long run, it is reasonable to expect that a conceptual standpoint will tend to lose its appeal if it consistently fails to provide the foundation for this enhanced mastery. In the natural sciences, in spite of some phenomenal delays, discredited concepts have ultimately been discarded, and others are on the wane. Even psychology is mature enough to have outgrown some of its infantile outfit. But in the social sciences this process of discrimination has hardly begun.

On the other hand, if we are to be guided by experience in the natural and biological sciences, techniques tend to be more persistent than the theories that originally called them into play. Alchemists, for example, appear to our minds to have had rather misguided ideas about the nature of matter, but the experimental techniques which they evolved in pursuit of their goal of transmutation, and the incidental knowledge which they gained of the behaviour of matter, are still of great importance to chemistry. Modern chemical techniques have been enormously refined and elaborated, but they are still recognisably the offspring of alchemy.

In social science, therefore, we are at present in no position to condemn any method which avoids conflict with the basic rules and orientations of all science, and which in any respect enhances man's understanding of and insight into social affairs. Individuals will continue to prefer one theory or another, and one technique or another, but it is important for each one of us to place all available techniques in their proper perspective and to try to understand the appropriate context for each.

In practice we shall learn that no single technique is adequate for the grasp of a situation of any depth and complexity, and in time we shall learn that these methods can most effectively and most economically be combined in a more or less regular sequence. This sequence, as foreshadowed in the Introduction, is one which

General Orientations

guides the investigator towards a progressively narrower and more exact hypothesis, and which concomitantly demands both of himself and of his experimental subjects an increasingly restricted freedom of action. It is a thread on which the different techniques available may be strung in a logically graded order, even though in any particular inquiry only a proportion of them have to be called into service.[1]

Subsequent chapters are devoted to a detailed examination of certain techniques. Before we embark on this, however, some preparation is needed, and the present chapter is designed to assist in such a preparation. I have therefore included first a brief general survey and evaluation of those orientations which appear likely to dominate the next phases of empirical social science. This is followed by an examination of the twin problems of language and logic, which together haunt the designer of social scientific investigations.

2. GENERAL ORIENTATIONS

One point on which all social scientists from Comte and Spencer to the present day have been agreed is that human behaviour is less predictable than the events with which most previous scientists have had to deal. This has been interpreted to mean either of two things. Some people conclude that human and social behaviour is not wholly subject to determining factors, but that every individual has some capacity of choice which enables him to vary his conduct in partial independence of the forces operating upon him. Others believe that, although human behaviour is fully determined by circumstances, these circumstances in all their ramifications are so numerous and so unknowable that we

[1] 'It begins with a problem or a group of problems that are real in the experiences of daily life. As a first step toward the solution an attempt is made to define them more precisely, to explore their boundaries, to spot their essential facts, to formulate a system of concepts about these facts—in short, to develop a tentative theory or hypothesis that is based on the available data. This hypothesis is then used as a guide to further inquiries which are more precise and detailed and which yield data that are more systematic and closely interrelated. These data, in turn, are used for the further revision and refinement of the hypothesis. When this procedure of induction-deduction has been carried far enough it has been found, especially in the physical sciences, that the theory or hypothesis can be stated in mathematical terms. At this point the precision and power of mathematical methods may be employed and the theory approaches its fullest predictive value.'—Mark A. May in Foreword to DOLLARD, J. et al. (Eng. ed., 1944), *Frustration and Aggression*, pp. vii-viii.

can never hope to predict how any individual or any group will respond to a given situation.

As it is impossible to devise a test which will discriminate between these two views, there appears to be little point, at least in the present context, in further speculating on them, or in trying to decide whether or not the individual possesses free-will, or the power of existential choice, or whether his actions are fully determined.[1] The scientist sets out to distinguish and recognise causal associations when they occur, and it will be generally agreed that some such associations can be discerned in the sphere of human relations as well as in other natural phenomena,[2] and furthermore that knowledge of these associations makes possible some measure of prediction and control of human behaviour. Whether or not full knowledge of all the circumstances could be used to make exact predictions of the behaviour of individuals is an empty and meaningless question, for it is perfectly clear that we can never hope to possess sufficient knowledge to make this kind of prediction possible. But that limitation neither proves nor disproves the doctrine of free-will.

In just the same way, the fact that we cannot, and never shall be able to, predict exactly when a particular leaf will fall off a tree or where it will land does not help us to prove or disprove a theory that the leaf launches itself when it feels like it; but this does not prevent us from predicting that most leaves will fall in autumn, or that the rate of defoliation will be higher in windy weather.[3]

Some people, scientists among them, are inclined to equate chance with choice, and to elevate our own uncertainty into a principle of nature. But this is a matter of temperament, and leaves us as far as ever from a final decision on the question of free-will. All that can be said, as a matter of history, is that animistic explanations of natural phenomena have fairly steadily been

---

[1] 'Sociology does not need to choose between the great hypotheses which divide metaphysicians. It needs to embrace free will no more than determinism. All that it asks is that the principle of causality be applied to social phenomena.'—DURKHEIM, E. (1938 ed.), *The Rules of Sociological Method*, p. 141.
[2] See, for example, MILL, J. S. (1842), *A System of Logic*; 8th ed., p. 608. LUNDBERG, G. A. (1939), *Foundations of Sociology*, pp. 141-2.
[3] John A. Clausen, in a chapter contributed by him to STOUFFER, S. A. et al. (1950), *Measurement and Prediction*, catalogues (p. 574) the various types of prediction made in social science. He divides these into 'Predictions for the Individual Case' and 'Predictions for Groups of Individuals'. His examination shows that quite a substantial proportion of predictive studies do in fact fall into the former category.

abandoned, and that increasing knowledge has generally improved reliability in prediction. The history of this increasing success in prophecy has been the history of science.

Most unartificial events within the province of natural science take place in the presence of a considerable number of simultaneous influences. They also tend to occur sporadically. It is thus a matter of considerable convenience to the natural scientist to be able to bring these events about experimentally, under controlled conditions. But it must be recognised that this convenience is won at the cost of imparting to results a somewhat spurious simplicity. By a straightforward experiment, Boyle was able to show that, *other things being equal*, the volume occupied by a gas varies inversely with the pressure being exerted upon it. He would have been hard put to it to build up his law by the systematic observation of different amounts of different kinds of gas in different containers under changing conditions of pressure and temperature, such as he might accidentally have come across in a search for suitable cases.

Boyle's law is regularly quoted because of its apparent simplicity and universality. It is, however, hardly characteristic of most natural scientific statements. It is common, for example, to find that a 'natural' process will not take place without the simultaneous fulfilment of a number of conditions. A chemical reaction may only take place in the presence of specified constituents, and at a given temperature and pressure; the reaction itself may generate heat, but will only continue if this heat is conducted away so that the required temperature is not exceeded. Although the circumstances demanded may be 'fed in' separately, when they have been brought together they constitute an interacting system, and can no longer be manipulated as isolated elements.

At a certain degree of complexity it may become desirable to treat what is happening, not only physically but also mentally, as one complex situation or process rather than as a number of different things reacting with each other to produce further sets of things. This certainly makes it easier for us to grasp as a whole whatever we may be observing, and is in line with our customary mode of experiencing things in everyday life.[1]

[1] At the risk of dogmatism, we may claim that the total grasp of an experience is universally natural, and is only later succeeded by a more sophisticated

There have been endless arguments among scientists and philosophers as to whether the reaction, or process, or situation is ' real ' in the same sense that the separate elements which together make it up are real. This is not the place to discuss the arguments put forward both for and against their ' reality '. Even if they only correspond with a peculiar mental way of looking at the outside world, such concepts, as evolved by Gestalt and field theorists, have definitely provided the means for increased mastery, particularly in some areas of psychology and of physics. It also seems likely that they will play an important, though not an exclusive, part in the further development of social science. As Lewin wrote, ' In the social as in the physical field the structural properties of a dynamic whole are different from the structural properties of subparts. Both sets of properties have to be investigated. When one, and when the other, is important depends upon the question to be answered. But there is no difference of reality between them.' [1]

The best vindication of the Gestalt and field approach is empirical rather than theoretical, and rests on firm scientific achievement. Moreover, formal and mathematical instruments are being forged to further their advance. So far in the social sciences its achievements, though valid, have not been as spectacular as in some other areas. It is very noticeable, however, how pervasive the influence of Gestalt thinking is becoming in a variety of fields of social science. This may signalise an important first step in the mental re-equipment of the social scientist.[2]

An ambitious form of diagram has been evolved by Kurt Lewin and his colleagues. These diagrams are designed to be pictorial representations of empirical situations as they appear when

---

analytical approach. Margaret Mead, on the other hand, contrasts ' the way in which we (Americans) think in single sequences, each unit quite simple and clear, while you (British, etc.) seem to think in units which are so very complex that it would be quite impossible to put all of their multiple dimensions into words '.—MEAD, M. (1944), *The American Character*, p. x.

[1] LEWIN, K. (1947), ' Frontiers in Group Dynamics ', *Hum. Rel.*, **1**, 8. Reprinted (1952) in his *Field Theory in Social Science*, p. 192. As an example of the opposite viewpoint see P. W. BRIDGMAN (1951), ' The Nature of Some of our Physical Concepts ', *Brit. Journ. Phil. Sc.*, **1**, 264. Bridgman's objection is that the existence of a field of force cannot be detected except by introducing some object upon which it can act. The ' scientific ' approach is therefore via the object rather than via the field.

[2] If so, it will confirm Spencer's dictum on the subject of social sciences, that a scientist trained in simpler subjects may actually have to unlearn part of his training before being able to deal successfully with this most involved class of facts.

organised in terms of field theory. Because this theory is derived from topological concepts, the diagrams are multi-dimensional, and convey a strong sense of direction. There is little doubt that field theorists find them valuable aids to conceptual insight, even though they do not directly portray the empirical data from which they have been abstracted.

In the larger sphere we are beginning to recognise how dependent we are on synthesis.

> The scientific temperament feels much more comfortable when it is breaking down a complex phenomenon into simpler parts than when it is trying to pull together a series of diverse facts into a unity of relationship. For a solution of the ultimate riddles, however, synthesis is more important than analysis. . . . It is not an understanding of units which we now seek, but of unity.[1]

Up to a point, the progress of science has depended on increasing specialisation—that is, on the mental ability to concentrate on some particular feature of our environment and to regard it as an isolated feature. This centripetal tendency, although it continues, shows signs of spending itself, and may even be gradually replaced through the centrifugal demand for the unification of knowledge. The specialisms of medicine, geography, psychology —to take three striking examples—are being re-embedded in their social matrix, and in the process are demanding a transformed mental outlook of their proponents.

Among the social sciences, the development of an integrated approach has been most marked in the case of anthropology. This is not difficult to explain. Owing to the conditions under which anthropologists undertake their field-work, narrow specialisation is precluded. Every professional student of the subject has been forced to acquire some competence in the means available for learning about different features in man's environment. Furthermore, the relative smallness and isolation of communities studied,[2] and the strangeness of their customs to the western observer, have made it relatively easy for him to take a total, and unpreconceived, view.

What first occurred as a limiting condition of work can, in the

---

[1] From an address by the botanist Edmund W. Sinnott, quoted by LYND, R. S. (1939), *Knowledge for What ?*, p. 245.
[2] A. I. Richards gives (BARTLETT, F. C. et al.—Eds. (1939), *The Study of Society*, p. 293 fn.) the size of communities studied by various famous expeditions. Outside Africa, these have regularly had less than 2,000 inhabitants.

view of some anthropologists, be transformed into an asset. As a result, there has evolved in the United States a school of 'cultural anthropology' whose adherents set out to study the culture—that is, the total local pattern—of social behaviour and man-made environment. Social customs, kinship systems, artifacts are no longer regarded by them as individual features to be torn from their cultural context.

> A culture, like an individual, is a more or less consistent pattern of thought and action. Within each culture there come into being characteristic purposes not necessarily shared by other types of society. In obedience to these purposes, each people further and further consolidates its experience, and in proportion to the urgency of these drives the heterogeneous items of behaviour take more and more congruous shape. Taken up by a well-integrated culture, the most ill-assorted acts become characteristic of its peculiar goals, often by the most unlikely metamorphoses. The form that these acts take we can understand only by understanding first the emotional and intellectual mainsprings of that society.[1]

This is a powerful argument which it would be futile to neglect. Moreover, there is ample evidence that those who approach the study of human relations from this standpoint gain very greatly in richness of understanding. The culture concept is a tool of the utmost importance.

In a revealing passage, Beatrice Webb describes what she as a young woman felt was lacking from psychology as it existed in her youth.

> What roused and absorbed my curiosity were men and women, regarded—if I may use an old-fashioned word—as 'souls', their past and present conditions of life, their thoughts and feelings and their constantly changing behaviour. This field of inquiry was not, as yet, recognised in the laboratories of the universities, or in other disciplined explorations of the varieties of human experience. . . . What turned me away from psychology, even the 'psychology' to be found in books, was what seemed to me the barren futility of the text-books then current—I am afraid that, in my haste, I regarded the manipulation of these psychological abstractions as yielding no more accurate information about the world around me than did the syllogisms of formal logic. For any detailed description of the complexity of human nature, of the variety and mixture in human motive, of the insurgence of instinct in the garb of reason, of the

[1] BENEDICT, R. (1935), *Patterns of Culture*, p. 33.

multifarious play of the social environment on the individual ego and of the individual ego on the social environment, I had to turn to novelists and poets, to Fielding and Flaubert, to Balzac and Browning, to Thackeray and Goethe.[1]

But what delighted her as an inquisitive person also disturbed her as a would-be scientist. For, she goes on, '*In all this range of truth-telling fiction the verification of the facts and of the conclusions drawn from the facts was impracticable*'.[2]

It is difficult to avoid a similar attitude of ambivalence towards much of the work so far produced by cultural anthropologists. Are they the modern scientific counterpart to the novelists whose 'truth-telling fiction' so delighted Beatrice Webb, even while they stirred in her the desire to verify their facts and the conclusions drawn from them ? Are their facts and generalisations presented to us after a rigorous attempt at objective verification, or do they represent the first sketch drawn to portray the cultural unity of the communities studied ? Again, what kind of hypotheses are they able to test, except that the culture-patterns of these different communities are internally consistent and comprehensible as wholes, and also that each is, as far as is known, virtually unique ?

It may be unfair to put such questions to those who are developing a way of scientific thinking and fact-finding that is still in its infancy. But sooner or later it will be necessary to determine the inherent value and limitations of this line of approach.

Perhaps the first point to recognise is that there is a genuine affinity between this newly forged 'scientific' method and the treatment of human relations as it has been practised for so long by writers. In many areas of knowledge it has been possible to distinguish art from science fairly clearly. As has often been pointed out,[3] a work of art is normally evaluated by its impact on the recipient, without reference to the means by which it is produced, while what is ultimately significant for science is a combination of the result and the process of arriving at it. Both the artist and the scientist rely at some stage on their feelings to test the ideas created by them, but the rules of proof are more exactly codified for the scientist.

[1] WEBB, B. (1926), *My Apprenticeship*, pp. 137-8.
[2] *ibid.* (my italics).
[3] For example by LEVY, H. (1932), *The Universe of Science*, p. 194.

The main difference [writes Craik] is that the scientist should not regard his feelings as proof that his hypothesis is right; he must be thankful for whatever inarticulate thoughts and emotions have suggested a new hypothesis, but he must test it by experiment. The artist does not do this; he relies on the fullness of this inner feeling of satisfaction, and the acceptance or rejection of his work by other men, to establish the truth or falsity of his expression of reality; and the greater artist he is, the greater will be the field of thought and experience from which these inarticulate feelings and purposes arise, and the greater their chance of expressing ideas and facts that are fundamental in general experience.[1]

It may be believed that the social scientist will never, like the natural scientist, be able to confirm or confute his hypotheses by objective tests or to construct a form of proof which is indifferent to 'these inarticulate feelings and purposes'. As we shall see, proof generally waits on experimental testing, but it may well be impossible to devise a valid experimental method in social science unless it is designed to accommodate this essential subjective element.

Whatever may be the position in other sciences, experimental social science may thus inevitably contain an important element of art. But it should not be inferred that in social science the process of arriving at results is immaterial. In point of fact, greater demands in this respect are made on the social scientist than on the natural scientist. The former is obliged in a unique way to enlist and to retain the co-operation of his subject-matter, and this requires of him a sensitivity and a social skill that in some circumstances may make the process of arriving at a result even more important than the 'scientific' recording of his results. The function of the record is to impress those not directly involved in the particular experience, and this may potentially be less influential than the expanding ripples emanating from an experience that has given satisfaction to those taking part.

While, however, the development of adequate social skill may be seen in theory as a condition of advance in social science, there appears to be a serious chasm between the actual practice of social science and the practical guidance of human relations.

One of the most consistent critics of the unbalanced development of social science is Elton Mayo. He writes:

[1] CRAIK, K. J. W. (1943), *The Nature of Explanation*, p. 86.

The so-called social sciences encourage students to talk endlessly about alleged social problems. They do not seem to equip students with a single social skill that is usable in ordinary human situations. Sociology is highly developed, but mainly as an exercise in the acquisition of scholarship. Students are taught to write books about each other's books. Of the psychology of normal adaptation, little is said, and, of sociology in the living instance, sociology of the intimate, nothing at all. Indeed, in respect of those social personal studies that are becoming more important year by year, no continuous and direct contact with the social facts is contrived for the student. He learns from books, spending endless hours in libraries; he reconsiders ancient formulæ, uncontrolled by the steady development of experimental skill; the equivalent of the clinic, or indeed of the laboratory, is still to seek. . . .

The result is that those graduates of brilliant achievement who lead the procession out of the universities are not well equipped for the task of bringing order into social chaos. Their standard of intellectual achievement is high; their knowledge-of-acquaintance of actual human situations is exceedingly low. They dwell apart from humanity in certain cities of the mind—remote, intellectual; preoccupied with highly articulate thinking. They have developed capacity for dealing with complex logic, they have not acquired any skill in handling complicated facts. And such a student of society is encouraged to develop an elaborate social philosophy and to ignore his need of simple social skills.[1]

It may at least be agreed that the aim of the cultural anthropologists is consonant with Professor Mayo's plea for a form of skill which permits the handling of complex facts. What is more controversial is whether these methods are capable of transmitting the knowledge thus acquired.

One basic difficulty seems to lie in the fact that although the observer is assisted both by his direct experience and by his conceptual equipment to grasp as a whole the culture being studied, he can communicate this understanding in itemised form only by presenting in turn the traits selected as significant. Unless the reader can live in the observer's report just as the observer lived in the community, the grasp will be only imperfectly transmitted.

The second point is that the desire to transmit a vivid picture

[1] MAYO, E. (Eng. ed. 1949), *The Social Problems of an Industrial Civilisation*, pp. 19–20. BERTRAND RUSSELL, who similarly stresses the importance of what he calls ' sensitivity ', comments (*Outline of Philosophy* (1927), p. 97) ' The learned man who is helpless in practical affairs is analogous to the miser, in that he has become absorbed in a means '.

has on occasion led the observer to be lax in distinguishing observation from inference. It is as though it were feared that too rigorous an objectivity when applied to the parts might undermine insight into the whole.[1]

The third limitation arises from a fact already mentioned—namely, that one characteristic of every community studied is its uniqueness. If the units of study are such that no discernible uniformities link them, there is little scope for the generalisations which it is the traditional function of the scientist to formulate.

Even if we admit the seriousness of these obstacles, much of value in the culture concept remains unscarred. Outstandingly, there is the depth of understanding attained by an observer who has allowed himself to regard his separate observations not in isolation but as temporary abstractions from a cultural whole. Again, and deriving from this understanding, is a rich source of more exact and localised hypotheses, which can be tested by other methods. Finally, there is the personal, and not objectively scientific, predictive skill developed through long experience, as for example the skill which enabled Ruth Benedict to understand at a distance the fundamental assumptions of Japanese culture, and to predict the behaviour of the Japanese people, both in the closing stages of the war and under the United States occupation forces.[2]

Furthermore, within the perspective of the culture concept, various features commonly found in social life can be isolated, observed and treated experimentally. Although social groups, when considered as a whole, may be unique—just as no two individual men are identical—they and their interactions do tend to contain some recurring characteristics. Leaders emerge and disappear, states of competition and co-operation manifest themselves, frustration provokes aggression, codes of behaviour are crystallised and dissolved. Leadership forms, competition and co-operation, group ethics, when concretely and realistically defined, may thus justifiably be studied and compared, provided that, while manipulations and observations take place, they are allowed to lie where they are, embedded in their total culture.

[1] For an elaboration of this point, see pp. 122 seq.
[2] See BENEDICT, R. (1946), *The Chrysanthemum and the Sword*. It is of course a common occurrence for concepts developed in the course of scientific investigation to find direct application in practical situations.
  The development of personal skill based on the systematic use of experience is well illustrated in medicine, in which the *syndrome*, or configuration of symptoms, can equally well be grasped and with equal difficulty be described.

Just as 'real' are social processes and their products, such as learning, manufacture and consumption, which can be observed either as processes or in terms of their products.

The translation of the approach of cultural anthropology to civilised societies involves the study of communities which are both more complex and less isolated than most primitive societies. A tribal village may generally without undue distortion be regarded as a closed system, but this is quite unrealistic in the case of a modern community. Again, a tribal structure is characteristically based on some form of hierarchical caste system, in which individuals accept the rôle into which they are born, and this will clearly have a simpler and more stereotyped pattern of inter-relationships than is found in a modern adaptive community, in which the rôles of only a handful of individuals are rigidly predetermined or completely secure.

These and other added complications impose upon the social scientist who desires to study contemporary societies, the need to forego the study of the total culture of a social group in order to concentrate on some particular feature of the group's behaviour. He may well also find it necessary to isolate, at least mentally, a particular group which he will then treat for the time being as constituting a closed system.

As the size of an interactive group increases, there is an extremely rapid increase in the number of inter-relationships, and hence of the complexity of the group as a whole. It is fortunate for the social scientist that this rise in complexity which harasses his attempt to grasp the whole also appears to limit the 'natural' size of such a group. It is a matter of common experience, for example, that a committee whose members are expected to contribute to decisions cannot satisfactorily number more than—say—a dozen, and will often work more smoothly and decisively with far fewer members. There is a similar 'natural' limit to the effective size of a group in large-scale industrial or military organisations. As soon as the members of any group are expected to do more than blindly obey orders or rubber-stamp decisions, the proper multiple at each level in such hierarchical systems appears to average not more than ten. With increasing democratisation, a corresponding decrease in group size can be expected.[1]

[1] See, for example, BARNARD, C. I. (1938), *The Functions of the Executive*, pp. 105 seq., etc. Again, in didactic education, the size of class can be

It is thus not surprising that some of the most penetrating examples of social research have been devoted to the study of small groups as such. Concentration on the small group, in circumstances as normal as possible for such a group, has also provided valuable opportunities for social experiment.[1]

There seems little doubt that rigidly localised studies along such lines as these provide some of the most promising avenues for future exploration. The objection to this form of study, that it is not sufficiently cosmic, appears to be based on a misapprehension as to the means by which advances have been won in other sciences. Recently, attention has been called to ' the outstanding and inexplicable fact of scientific discovery, that in order to discover the most fundamental mysteries of the universe and to acquire power over the greatest forces of nature, man has had to examine not the majesty of sea or mountain, not even the thunderbolt of Zeus (though Franklin tried) but the dancing of pieces of straw under an amber rod and the twitching of frogs' legs outside an Italian butcher's shop—not the majestic but the trivial '.[2]

As we shall see, J. S. Mill was in two minds about social experimentation. On the one hand, he regarded experiment as the only safe path to proof, and, on the other hand, he despaired of the possibility of experimenting in social science. This was largely because the type of experiment that he envisaged was too ambitious. He took as his example an imaginary experiment which would be designed to test the hypothesis that a protective tariff benefits a nation.

> If two nations can be found which are alike in all natural advantages and disadvantages; whose people resemble each other in every quality, physical and moral, spontaneous and acquired; whose habits, usages, opinions, laws and institutions are the same in all respects, except that one of them has a more protective tariff, or in other respects interferes more with the freedom of industry; if one of these nations is found to be rich and the other poor, or one richer than the other, this will be an *experimentum crucis*—a real proof by

---

larger than in the informal methods increasingly favoured today. There may even be an illustration in the contrast between the authoritarian structure of the large Victorian family and the more democratic structure of the small modern family.
[1] See Chapter 5 on ' Experiment '.
[2] THOMPSON, G. P., review in *New Statesman and Nation* (Nov. 1950), **40**, 466; cf. STOUFFER, S. A. (1950), ' Afterthoughts of a Contributor ', in MERTON, R. K., and LAZARSFELD, P. F., *Continuities in Social Research*, p. 203.

experience which of the two systems is most favourable to national riches.[1]

Mill clearly chose his case because he knew it to be impossible.[2] But constantly in empirical social research we find a similar tendency to dash into some broad superficial inquiry—often chosen because of its topical interest—only to recoil from its complexity. Of course social processes are complex. But it is surely right to build up from relatively simple situations which we can hope to grasp and handle as a whole before attempting to fathom the profundities of those larger aggregates which for the time being lie outside the range of our equipment and our authority.

We may safely conclude that group studies in which the group as such is the object of study offer potentially one major avenue to empirical social science. But although such methods may ultimately supersede the methods evolved and elaborated, principally by social psychologists, to probe into the behaviour and attitudes of individuals in society, it is to the latter that we have to look so far for the greater contribution to the development of social science.

The scope and methods of psychology have matured beyond recognition in the past century. A hundred years ago psychological truths were principally sought introspectively, by the psychologist examining the recesses of his own mind. But today the pendulum has swung, perhaps to the other extreme, and to all those who take their lead, directly or indirectly, from the behaviourist school of psychology, the truth about human beings lies not at the back of the mind, but in the muscles.

If the practice of cultural anthropology is at times closely akin to the novelist's art, behaviourist psychology is uncompromisingly grounded on the methods of natural science. Once we accept the belief that the task before the social scientist is to establish a science of human and social behaviour in extension of classical physics and chemistry, the argument as to procedure is a com-

---

[1] MILL, J. S., *A System of Logic*, p. 575.
[2] Strangely enough, Mill's *experimentum crucis* did virtually take place. Between 1866 and 1901 Victoria and New South Wales were both self-governing Colonies, with closely comparable populations, climate, natural resources, national income, etc. One adopted a Protectionist policy, while the other adhered to Free Trade. No significant divergence of their economic circumstances seems to have resulted.

pelling one. Science, it is claimed, is organised knowledge, built up of what we have learned by the use of our sense-organs. In the same way we can only derive knowledge of human beings by observing them, just as other scientists observe comets, bacteria or white mice. We can see what a man does, and we can hear what he says or read what he writes. If he has any feelings which he does not reveal by overt behaviour, we have to accept the fact that these feelings are hidden from us and not try to make up for our ignorance of them by inferring that he is feeling what we would be feeling if we were in his shoes. The only safe source of knowledge about human beings is what we can see and hear, and everything else is guesswork.

Moreover, the logic of this argument is reinforced by the practical results of adopting it, which have so far been of much greater value and consequence than those achieved by any other method yet devised by social science. Although the behaviourist viewpoint is not so logically simple as may at first appear, the methods based on it still dominate empirical social science, and the greater proportion of the distinct techniques described in this book have therefore an ostensibly behaviourist foundation.

If we undertake, as detached observers, to report on the activities of a group of human beings, it is clearly convenient for us to isolate each human being in turn and to describe his actions. This need not imply that we regard him as a body in a vacuum, but that we observe, not the interactions and inter-relations themselves, but the overt behaviour of each individual, produced—we may assume—by the total of the influences to which he is or has been exposed. The primary unit of study is thus the individual man and not, as in earlier examples, the primitive community, the small group, or some recurring feature of social life such as leadership or competition.

It is also convenient, by some judicious priming, to speed up the rate at which observations can take place. This is most frequently done in the case of 'verbal behaviour'. Theoretically, if one waited long enough one would expect each individual to express his opinion on teetotalism and totalitarianism, but it is clearly a time-saving device to ask him for his views on these burning topics.

The decision to adopt the individual man, woman or child as the unit of study does not preclude a form of analysis in which the atomised data are recombined in such a way as to provide a total picture of a group situation. The conceptual gap between the human group and the human individual has been bridged with some success by a few diagrammatic aids to understanding, notable among which is the sociogram.[1] Unlike the field theory diagrams already mentioned, sociograms are normally derived directly from empirical data relating to individuals, and records not only the ostensible pattern of relationships in the group portrayed but also the nature of the relationships enjoyed by any particular member of the group.

It appears likely that graphic and other methods of representing group behaviour will in the course of time be still further developed. Meanwhile, the collection of data on individuals clearly favours description in numerical terms. Owing to the variability of social phenomena, numerical and quantitative descriptions and the inferences based on them are predominantly statistical.

The use of statistics, and specifically of statistical sampling, has the advantage of allowing the investigator to make general statements on the basis of representative observations. If you set out to study a group or community as a whole, your results will not hang together unless you have included all the interactions taking place in that group, and this means taking account of every member of it. If your labours are successful, you will at the end have a pretty complete picture of one group but no means of gauging its typicality. For the same amount of effort you can pick out a large number of individuals of given characteristics from different groups, observe how each behaves within his own particular environment, and generalise statistically as to how people of that type tend to behave. But although you may be able to describe the characteristic behaviour of individuals, you will have foregone the attempt to describe the behaviour of societies as such.

It must also be accepted that, in spite of modern developments such as factor analysis, the adoption of statistical techniques involves considerable restrictions in the use of material. There is at times a distinct conflict between the *statistical* ideal of material that can be readily analysed into simple manipulable components, and the *descriptive* ideal of material that presents precisely, but without loss of unity, the essential and unique characteristics of

[1] For a brief description, see pp. 231 seq.

each individual or group. At one end of the scale we have, for example, the kind of data provided by the mass-questionnaire—a large sample, snappy answers (preferably yes, no or don't know), and just enough of them to give scope for a few correlations. The other end of the scale is represented by the spontaneous autobiography, richly illuminating about the individual, packed with hints for further investigation, but in itself extremely difficult to analyse or use ' objectively '.

Social science was, if not the parent, at least the earliest patron of statistical method, and with biology has continued to be its most influential patron. For some time, however, the statistical infant has been showing signs of outstripping its early sponsors in the precision, power and elaboration of its techniques. It is not difficult to collect material suitable for statistical analysis, but there is a constant danger that the ease with which certain statistics can be collected will beguile social scientists into describing things in terms of what can conveniently be counted and measured rather than in terms of what it is really useful for us to know about them.

This danger has been regularly stressed. Hogben, for example, writes:

> Nothing but confusion has resulted, and can result, when mathematics is used before we are quite clear about the sort of things with which we are dealing and what sort of measurements it is useful to make. Only then can we decide what sort of mathematics is a useful instrument for increasing knowledge. The immense success which has resulted from applying mathematics to the study of the world when some of its features have been clearly delineated by careful observation has fostered a blind reverence which is precipitating a real crisis in our own culture, especially in the field of psychology where the amount of arithmetic devoted to intelligence-testing is out of all proportion to its substantial basis of enduring fact.[1]

To Hogben's example of the intelligence test we may add that of the public opinion poll, whose practitioners and sponsors are often

---

[1] HOGBEN, L. (2nd ed., 1937), *Mathematics for the Million*, pp. 224–5.
Similarly Elton Mayo wrote: ' It is much easier to measure non-significant factors than to be content with developing a first approximation to the significant.' (Quoted by K. Mannheim in his Foreword to KLEIN, V. (1946), *Feminine Character*, p. xii.)
More recently, Stouffer has taken up the cudgels, by warning against the blind and indiscriminate use of scales. He fears (*Measurement and Prediction*, pp. 479–80) that ' there may be a temptation for future students to become so devoted to the application of scaling that they may fail in the vitally important task of analyzing fully the situation in which they want to apply their scales '.

unable to convince us what exactly it is that they are measuring, although appropriate statistical techniques are highly developed.[1]

While, however, it is proper to guard against the misuse of quantification, it cannot be implied that there is very much choice in the matter if we aim at empirical generalisation. At their very least, statistical techniques expose the principal assumptions underlying the generalisations arrived at and provide some stable measure of the degree of confidence with which it is reasonable to accept them. The statistical method gives precision and system to the more or less unconscious inductive processes constantly used in everyday life. When a man attempts to generalise from his own unrepresentative selection of data, and perhaps even openly rejects statistical method, you may at best regard his generalisation as a brilliant and illuminating piece of guesswork. He may have lighted on an inspired hypothesis, but he has certainly proved nothing.

We have suggested that it is necessary to regard the various phases of scientific inquiry as selected points along a continuous process, during which a hypothesis is progressively both narrowed and verified. If this model is borne in mind, there is no difficulty in finding a place for all the methods available to social science, in spite of the vivid differences between the synoptic sketch of the cultural anthropologist and the most precise manipulation of the social statistician. What is more, the multiple approach is not merely permissible but is obligatory. The domain has not been adequately explored unless the line of proof has been made as continuous and as complete as social scientific techniques permit. Conclusions reached without exact validating methods are unsatisfactory termini because of the uncertainty attached to them, but conclusions reached by confining attention to those factors that it is easy to enumerate or measure can be either trivial, meaningless or both.[2]

[1] See pp. 180 seq.
[2] It is made clear elsewhere that, although the most frequent progression is from the broad hypothesis to the exact test, a move in the opposite direction (e.g. when tabulated results show some unexpected feature) is by no means rare. See, e.g. MERTON, R. K., and KENDALL P. L. (1946), "The Focused Interview"; *Am. Journ. Soc.*, **51**, 541–57.

3. LANGUAGE

> In the inductive sciences a definition does not form the basis of reasoning, but points out the course of investigation.
> —Sir William Whewell.
>
> If there are five empty seats and I say the bus is full, the bus is full.
> —Conductor of a No. 96 'bus (*This England*, 28. vii. 1951).

(a) *The Search for a Distinctive Language*

The process of investigation consists very largely of what, to the investigator, appear to be flashes of insight, sudden glimpses of connections between things and sudden awareness of distinctions and differences. These, in order to be retained, have to be symbolised, if, indeed, they do not, as is most often the case, originally occur in an already symbolised state.[1]

The symbols referred to are the symbols of language, and it is natural that we should start our practical discussion of method with a brief consideration of language and of its function in life and in science. Social scientists have a twofold interest in language. Not only do they, like other scientists, need a set of verbal symbols in order to explore and describe their area of knowledge, but they also rely on the 'verbal behaviour' of fellow humans for much of their evidence of human relations. In both these uses words have to be taken seriously; indeed, it has been suggested by the pioneer of semiotics that the concept of sign may prove as fundamental to the sciences of men as the concept of cell for the biological sciences.[2]

The scientific use of language is in the main an extension of the everyday use of language. But while all scientific vocabularies borrow in part from the phraseology and grammar of everyday life, most established sciences have found it desirable, for reasons that will be discussed, to construct a set of terms which are initially distinct from those in common use.

In contrast with practice in other sciences, we find that the majority of words in use among social scientists have been borrowed from current popular terminology, even when the meanings attached to them have been narrowed or adapted to serve their more exacting use. Some fresh words have been coined, but many of these, while laying their users open to the charge of making a mystery of their science, have added little to the clarity

---
[1] Ogden, C. K., and Richards, I. A. (3rd ed., 1930), *The Meaning of Meaning*, pp. 131-2.
[2] Morris, C. W. (quoted by Lundberg, G. A. (1939), p. 44).

or precision of observation. Very often we find the same word being used in a different sense by different social scientists, or different words being used to describe indistinguishable concepts. This state of affairs is more than adequately recognised by social scientists. From time to time the proposal is made that those concerned should join together and thrash out an agreed set of definitions. There have been attempts to construct a special technical dictionary of words used in the social sciences.[1] Various enthusiasts have tried to build systems of words so logically irrefutable and so appealing in other respects as to win over the profession *en bloc*. It is clear that all such efforts have failed. Social scientists do habitually borrow from their predecessors and from their colleagues, but they borrow eclectically. And if we look at the kinds of word that have stuck, we find that they have predominantly been fresh amalgams of familiar words. In-groups, folkways, patterns of behaviour or of culture, these are typical survivors, while more pretentious conceits—such as *plurel* or *socius*—have been far less widely adopted.

The failure of social scientists to mend their ways, and their inability to emulate the ' exact ' definitions of natural science, are often regarded as yet further signs of the backwardness of social science. According to this view, no more than time and effort are required to enable social scientists to catch up; when experience has accumulated, we shall have a water-tight system of words which, however unintelligible to the lay public, will enable at least us professionals to understand each other and to translate the words and concepts of everyday life into a consistent and rarefied scientific language. Just as doctors are reputed to huddle round the patient and mysteriously murmur of *strabismus* and *aphagia*, so we shall put the objects of our study in their place by exchanging comments on *group dissociation* or *parasymbiosis*. Language could thus become a weapon of authority as well as a means of communication between equals.

---

[1] G. A. LUNDBERG (1st ed. 1929), *Social Research*, pp. 57–8), refers to early attempts in the United States to compile a sociological glossary. In 1905, Small listed 48 terms and concepts which at that time, in his opinion, constituted the terminology of sociology. In 1927, Eubank extracted 276 terms from current sociological literature, but found them ambiguous and overlapping. When he invited ten leading sociologists to give lists of major concepts employed by them, he found a complete absence of unanimity in their replies.
More recently, a ' Dictionary of Sociology ' has been published, but has been equally criticised on these now familiar grounds.

But perhaps, after all, the straining after scientific precision may not be as important and rewarding as at first appears. Would we really benefit by a distinctive professional language? Should we not first pause to wonder a little how it is that the popular usage of words, for all its lack of precision, does on the whole work so satisfactorily in everyday life?

Scientists tend to criticise everyday words because such words fail to achieve the idea of objectivity. But can it be avoided that every word is more than just a cold objective description of something? Because the word has to be understood it has to hook meanings on to itself, and these meanings are acquired in one way only—namely, by use in actual situations. The individual learns the meaning of a word in this way, and the word itself gains in power and precision as an instrument of communication [1] through being used. Russell reminds us, ' A word is intended to describe something in the world; at first it does so very badly, but afterwards it gradually improves '.[2] At no time in this process must it necessarily be defined; all that is required of correct usage is that the word in question should fit the situation in which it is used in a way that satisfies both its user and those to whom he is speaking.

> The use of such inarticulate guidance from feelings is another argument for the view that popular usage of words is not merely loose and inaccurate, but indicates something very profound about the way in which we are led to use certain words to describe particular situations.[3]

People with common backgrounds and shared experiences undoubtedly understand each other's use of language. Insofar as the social scientist wants to share their meanings he must at least get to know their words. And he can only do this by making himself familiar with the full contexts in which the words in question are habitually used. In history this may be done by comparing documentary passages. ' The meaning of a word is to be determined by bringing together the passages where it is employed.' [4] In direct experience it is done intuitively as a result of repeated instances, ' arrived at by a process of abstraction

---

[1] OGDEN, C. K., and RICHARDS, I. A. (1930 ed.), p. 98.
[2] RUSSELL, B. (1927), p. 267.
[3] CRAIK, K. J. W. (1943), p. 103.
[4] LANGLOIS, Ch. V., and SEIGNOBOS, Ch. (1898), *Introduction to the Study of History*, p. 147.

from a hundred current modes of speaking on the subject '.[1] The very fact that any such word has repeatedly been needed suggests that it refers to something which is significant to those who use it.

They that wish to enter into the spirit of social relations cannot therefore be justly criticised if they try to model their language on that of everyday life. But this does not mean that the perfection of finality has been reached in the common tongue. It has to be recognised that everyday language, like workaday commonsense, is capable of being greatly improved, as a tool both of life and of knowledge. The possibilities of improvement, and the need for it, are particularly evident in two directions. Everyday language is, in unfavourable circumstances, too imprecise for rigorous use. Even more serious, sometimes it is downright ambiguous.

Take a 'billion'. This is a word in general use on both sides of the Atlantic. As an arithmetical symbol, it is supposed to belong to one of the groups in which exactness may be taken for granted. But consider the statement, 'A billion equals a thousand million'. Is this statement true or false?

Of course the answer depends on who you are, and on who will be prepared to agree with you. If you are an unsullied American the statement is true, and if an uncontaminated Englishman it is false. If, like many modern souls, you have imbibed a bit of both cultures, you will remain undecided until you have weighed the internal or contextual evidence, or perhaps until you have put it to experimental test.

This dual meaning of billion is a single illustration of the discrepancies between two very similar languages. It is undeniable that any such discrepancy is a nuisance, a barrier to perfect communication. In this case there may not be any very compelling reason to choose one meaning rather than the other, but no one doubts that in the long run two peoples who want to share the instrument of language will have to agree between themselves which usage to adopt.

This example can be generalised by saying that people with fully common aims—that is, with the impulse to co-operate in all projects—and aware of their community, tend gradually to

[1] MILL, J. S. (1836), *On the Definition of Political Economy*; reprinted in NAGEL, E. (1950), *J. S. Mill's Philosophy of Scientific Method*, p. 409.

eliminate their language conflicts, retaining only decorative and immaterial distinctions. Convergence in language may in fact be an important indication of intensifying community.

The language of the group is the badge of its unity. Every collection of human beings who have to live or work together must produce a language for themselves, if their social relationship is to be sound. Every school has its own slang. The R.A.F. made itself a grammar and a dictionary, but unless the situation is understood, the language cannot be understood.[1]

Of course, the purpose of language is to arrange with others how we shall act in the world.[2]

But even if we grant the kind of goodwill which roots out ambiguities and, so to speak, accept a majority ruling on words and their meanings, we still have to allow for the existence of certain highly developed interests. For these, social scientists, like all scientists, need a ' universe of discourse ' that the layman will probably not be sufficiently keen to explore, at least without a time lag. In similar circumstances the established sciences have undertaken the long process of building a specialised vocabulary. Many words have flashed across the scientific firmament and spent themselves without a trace, but an agreed language has gradually accumulated in each branch of science and has become the badge of its unity, which no man can counterfeit. ' With the strictly scientific words, writers have not the power to decide whether they shall accept them or not; they must be content to take submissively what the men of science choose to give them.'[3] The linguistic purity of any new word is of secondary importance. Provided the coiners can persuade their colleagues of the value of the new concepts, they are ' as much within their rights in naming what they have discovered or invented as an explorer in naming a new mountain, or an American founder a new city '.[4]

It has of course often been a difficult task to persuade even professional colleagues to adopt new words, however convinced the proposer may be that they will help to clarify concepts. Part of this difficulty is due to a reasonable reluctance to attach a new label to an old idea. Part is due to an instinctive recognition,

---

[1] DAUNT, M. (1951), ' Language is a Branch of Literature ', *Universities Quarterly*, 5, 242.
[2] BRONOWSKI, J. (1951), *The Common Sense of Science*, p. 79.
[3] FOWLER, H. W. and F. G. (1931 ed.), *The King's English*, p. 32.
[4] *ibid.*

sometimes denied to the inventor of a new concept, that logical grounds alone do not justify an addition to the language; a new word will only be of value if it does get widely adopted, and its proposer may therefore be required both to create and to satisfy a real demand. But a universality of demand, even within the profession, in turn depends upon unanimity as to the aims and methods of the science, and this kind of unanimity among social scientists is still out of sight.

In the social sciences, moreover, we are constantly up against the fact that it is next to impossible for one human being to maintain a completely detached attitude towards the activities of other human beings. This has a bearing on the difficulty of compiling a technical language of social science. ' With sciences in their initial stages, before they have developed into affairs for specialists, and while they are still public concerns, the resistance to new terms is very great. Probably the explanation of this is to be found in the lack of emotive power which is a peculiarity of all technicalities.' [1] If we believe that the science of man probably cannot, and certainly should not, develop solely into an affair for specialists isolated from public concern, then we must reconcile ourselves to placing a limit on the spread of unemotive technicalities. Empson has posed a dilemma about ' the wicked scientific words; either they are simple though dead, and then at least they are safe tools, or else they are full of delusive suggestions, and then . . . they are primitive total meanings'. He plumped for the practical English of the artisan, which was safe and simple, but also made active suggestions. ' The common words were not only clear but widely applicable, that is easily extended, in fact they had a looseness of their own, which was of a useful kind.' [2]

We must also consider a third alternative. Language is a shared experience, and the social scientist is required to share both with his public and with his professional colleagues. Perhaps we can envisage a man with enough social skill and sensitivity to

[1] OGDEN, C. K., and RICHARDS, I. A. (1930), p. 131.
[2] EMPSON, W. (1951), *The Structure of Complex Words*, p. 380. MARSHALL, T. H. (1947), *Sociology at the Cross Roads*, p. 18, also discusses this dilemma. While pressing for simplification rather than elaboration of sociological concepts, he discards the possibility that sociology can be content to use the simple language of ordinary speech. He reminds us of ' the peculiar difficulties of a science that deals with the familiar objects of daily experience around which cluster a host of ambiguities and unconscious assumptions embedded in the language of the many in the street. The words have been spoiled for scientific use and one is forced to look for something better.'

adjust his language to that of the group with which he is communicating. It is a *sine qua non* that he should be able to make himself clear in conversation with the groups that he is studying, and to extract the full meaning from their replies. But why, it may still be asked, could he not be versatile, and equip himself to converse with his fellow specialists on an altogether higher plane of abstraction and precision ?

Before we can answer this we have to probe a little deeper into the meaning and implications of scientific precision.

(b) *The Taxonomic Solution*

We are sometimes inclined to assume that the only kind of precision is mathematical exactness, which requires that in measuring or in counting something we should keep within a certain margin of error. This is an important kind of precision, but it is not the only—or even the most important—safeguard against inaccuracies. Before we can measure or count, we have to choose a definition of the thing that we are concerned with. To be useful, this should be not only consistent with—and distinguishable from—other accepted definitions, but should also have relevance to some real experience. Internal consistency has its place, but it is not enough.[1]

In the world of experience the kind of thing that the scientific linguist is asked to do is to set up a category—e.g. of object, quality, relation or process—in such a way that it is possible to diagnose without serious doubt whether or not some particular case fits the category in question.

In many ways the simplest kind of category is one that relates to an object. Philosophers have expended much ingenuity in the attempt to devise rigid methods of classifying objects and foolproof methods of identifying them. One long-favoured method has been definition by minute description. Thus if you want to define a tree you list its characteristics—that it is a perennial plant which does not die down each year, etc., etc. But when is a bush not a tree ? And what of a tree that survives the winter in a temperate zone but elsewhere is cut down by frost, shooting

---

[1] 'There will always remain the opportunity for investigating the nature of principles, and the meaning of such ideas as that of principles "working" or " holding true ", but the final road to progress will lie not on the search for analytical exactitude in verbal definition but in the self-validatory procedure of experiment and hypothesis. The important feature of a concept is that it should be exact *in the right way*—i.e. true, not just internally precise.'
—CRAIK, K. J. W. (1943), p. 5.

again from its roots, like a herbaceous plant? Clearly, however minute the description, there will always be examples whose suitability for inclusion under the category ' tree ' will have to be judged ' on its merits '—i.e. by reference to common usage. Your tree is a tree when it is also a tree to your friends.

Even in a close-knit circle, vagueness such as this may have costly results when the definition is needed as a guide to action. Suppose that you tell a man to clear a wood by cutting down the undergrowth and leaving the trees. He may be lazy, and leave standing a lot of spindly saplings that will never come to anything. But perhaps you have offered him the undergrowth as firewood, and he is short of fuel; then you may find that his interpretation has been far too liberal and that hardly any trees still stand. If this may happen, it is clearly prudent to define a tree in some arbitrary fashion, for example as having a stem at least six inches thick at a specified distance from the ground.

This is an extremely simple illustration of the procedure adopted by modern taxonomists. Taxonomic definition originated in systematic biology as a means of naming, describing and classifying plant and animal species and so on. As the science has developed it has become increasingly clear that the creation of categories (e.g. plum trees) and the placing of any given item into its correct category must be conducted in full awareness of the very wide range of variation around a biological norm. Both the norm and the range have to be established empirically, and this involves the modern taxonomist in the inspection of very large samples, sometimes running into tens of thousands. Furthermore, in order to compare the variations of individual items it is necessary to express these variations numerically. Taxonomy in its contemporary form is thus seen to be a highly sophisticated, quantitative version of the long-established principle of definition by minute description.

Some biologists who have entered the field of social science have expressed high hopes at the prospects of using social taxonomy for mapping the social habits as well as the physical features of biological specimens, including man. Kinsey et al., for example, remark :

> If individuals are collected in a fashion which eliminates all bias in their choosing, and in a fashion which includes material from every type of habitat and from the whole range of the species, it should be

possible to secure a sample which, after measurement and classification, will indicate the frequency with which each type of variant occurs in each local population, or in the species as a whole. If the sample is adequate, the generalisations should apply not only to the individuals which were actually measured, but to those which were never collected and which were never measured at all. Obviously, the correctness of such an extension of the observed data depends upon the size of the sample, and upon the quality of the sample; and the capacity of the taxonomist is to be measured by the skill he demonstrates in choosing and securing that sample.[1]

Ways of minimising the distortions inevitable in sampling will be discussed in a later section. Here we are concerned with the principle of taxonomic definition. It would be quite wrong to belittle the importance of examining adequate numbers both in arriving at facts and in extending definitions, but we must be clear that the taxonomist will be forced either to write his own subjectively chosen norms into his definitions, or to derive these norms from customary usage. If we want to know whether Anglo-Saxons have blue eyes, and if we want to discover the proportion of W.X. women in Manchester, our inquiries will be valueless until we get down to a properly conducted quantitative investigation. But lurking behind any such investigation are the initial questions of definition, which the taxonomic concept of normality cannot answer. Who counts as an Anglo-Saxon? What is the colour-range admissible as blue? What are W.X. dimensions? When does a girl become a woman? What are the boundaries of Manchester? In real life we will find that each of these empirical concepts has absorbed, and been shaped by, a tremendous stream of active administrative experience, and will be justified thus rather than by virtue of a demonstrable normal frequency distribution curve.[2]

(c) *The Operational Solution*
We find much the same problem throughout the social sciences. It is very noticeable that the heroic theoretical concepts, such as

[1] KINSEY, A. C. et al. (1948), *Sexual Behavior in the Human Male*, p. 17.
[2] As has already been mentioned, the concept of normality was central in Durkheim's theories. A wide chasm constantly occurs, however, between the idea of normality and any empirical attempt at demonstrating normative behaviour. Cf. STOUFFER, S. A., ' Afterthoughts of a Contributor ', in MERTON, R. K. & LAZARSFELD, P. F.—Eds. (1950), *Continuities in Social Research*, pp. 206–7, in which reference is made to ' quite new intensive work on this problem '.

Language

those attempting to classify different forms of human association —group, body, crowd, family, mob, community, corporation, clique, society, gang and so on—vary greatly in the exactness with which they can be defined. A group remains a tenuous concept. A crowd, though recognisable, has indistinct edges. A society, when formal, can be defined as exactly, though as arbitrarily, as the city of Manchester. A household is definable, and a family less so. A married couple can be defined almost as rigidly as a man or woman separately. Here again the real test is not the test of logic, but that of administrative experience. And unless we recognise and accept the momentum and direction imparted by real life, we shall remain bound up in the tangles of a hopeless circularity.

Similar difficulties are encountered in any attempt to define attributes or qualities. In spite of a persistent and widespread tendency to think otherwise, these attributes are not things-in-themselves, but come to life only in concrete instances. Intelligence, for example, in the everyday sense is a capacity shared by people whom we are prepared to label intelligent; we judge them by their acts. Similarly we attach other labels denoting greed, laziness and so on. In common usage we draw the line between greed and good appetite by implicit reference to some social norm which lays down broad rules of conduct in the matter of eating.

It is useful to compare this situation with an analogous issue in natural science, such as that of defining temperature. Temperature is a recognised ' property of matter ', in that objects can generally be said to be at a certain temperature at a given time. With unaided senses, the temperature of an object may be roughly described as hot, tepid, cold, etc. The scope for inaccuracy in such a description lies partly in the fact that the distinction between—say—hot and warm rests solely on the basis of agreement. The child learns to distinguish hot from warm by accumulating experience of particular hot and warm objects. He gets to know that ' hot ' feels hotter than ' warm ', and with some practice he and his teacher will agree in most circumstances on whether to classify an object as ' hot ' or ' warm '.

As is well known, however, if one of them has just been handling something hot he will be inclined to under-estimate the temperature of a second object handled. This admits another sort of unreliability—namely, that due to the personal circumstances of the tester.

The invention of the thermometer reduced the latter source of inaccuracy, as it transferred the perceptual process from that of feeling the hot object to that of watching the height of a column of fluid.[1] It also made it much easier to learn what was to be described as hot and what as warm. In practice it was found more convenient to replace, or at least to supplement, the attempts at verbal definition by an arithmetical scale.[2] This allows reasonably precise description of the temperature of a given object according to the agreed conventions governing the particular temperature scale in use. If, however, one attempts to define a temperature of 185° F., there is very little that can be said except in such terms as that 'if a reliable and suitable thermometer graduated in degrees Fahrenheit is immersed in an object at this temperature, then any observer, of adequate intelligence and capacity for observation and exercising reasonable care, will find that (subject to any necessary corrections to allow e.g. for the cooling effect of the thermometer) the appropriate point on the top surface of the fluid column will be level with the point graduated as 185° F.' A definition such as this is known as an 'operational definition'. Ultimately its validity depends on the empirical inference that any number of observers making any number of observations will, provided the safeguards mentioned are followed, take the same reading from the thermometer.[3] If an exceptional observer fails to do so, we will suspect his capacity to observe, or the accuracy of his thermometer, before revising our opinion of the temperature of the object in question.

The widespread adoption of 'operational definitions' is largely due to the mathematical physicist Professor P. W. Bridgman of Harvard University. His method is designed to avoid absolute

[1] The possibility of personal errors, though it can never be eliminated, can be still further banished, for example by arranging for the rising mercury to close an electrical circuit, and thus ring a bell, at a predetermined point. The point may not have been accurately predetermined, but any error will at least be more consistent.
[2] The power of survival of pre-scientific definitions is illustrated by the typical cookery book which continues to describe oven temperature according to a verbal scale (e.g. moderate, quick) even when the temperature of ovens is controlled thermostatically.
[3] 'A scientific observer is not expected to note his integral reaction to a situation, but only that part of it which experience leads him to regard as "objective", i.e. the same as the reaction of any other competent observer.'
—Russell, B. (1927), p. 177

concepts in favour of experimental or operational concepts which take account not only of what is to be defined but also of the person claiming to define it. According to his view, 'the true meaning of a term is to be found by observing what a man does with it, not by what he says about it'.[1]

Just as taxonomic definitions have been of great value in biology, so also operational definitions have facilitated the practice of physics. But of course, to the logician, the definition of temperature given above is riddled with weep-holes. All the words like 'reliable', 'suitable', 'adequate', 'reasonable care' permit, and in fact demand, that the observer should exercise his personal judgment. In the last analysis, if not earlier, as much subjective skill—or social sensitivity—is required of the operational definer as of the taxonomist.

But we must be careful not to attach too much significance to the particular sequence of operations specified. A definition which strictly relates only to one set of circumstances is too narrowly based to be of much succour to communication. If we are to have a socially acceptable definition we must presuppose a socially natural or inculcated sequence of operations. Weiss, for example, sets out to devise operational definitions for the major physical concepts. He starts with *Motion*:

> In developing a definition of motion . . . a demonstrator A points to an object on the table and arbitrarily declares to another individual B that this object (as it lies motionless) is in zero motion. A moves it towards the right and then defines this act as a *movement towards the right*. A then demonstrates movements towards the left, forward, back, etc. With ever increasing complexity A demonstrates movements that are long, short, up, down, regular, irregular, circular, elliptic, parabolic, sinusoidal, centrifugal, etc. All of this can be demonstrated without recourse to definition, or rather the definitions can be created *de novo* as new forms of behaviour from the demonstration. A may now ask B to repeat the demonstration to another individual C; C then demonstrates to D, etc. The adequacy of the method as to uniformity is attested when successive individuals in turn take the place of demonstrator and the last individual repeats the demonstration to A exactly as A originally presented it to B. To the extent that the demonstration has gained or lost during transfer from one individual to another, has it been faulty, and to that extent is there what is known as a lack of understanding. Assuming that

[1] BRIDGMAN, P. W. (1928), *The Logic of Modern Physics*, p. 7.

the above demonstration has been repeated until all the individuals involved respond similarly when asked to demonstrate sinusoidal movements, pendular movements, fast movements, etc., we can then by the extension of the principle arrive at a definition of movement which gives it the properties of *rate* and *direction*.[1]

When thus elaborated *ad absurdum*, the operational definition may appear as something very special and very new. But when we strip it of its finery, we observe that the class learning the meaning of motion is being trained in the same way as the other class learning the technique of the differential calculus or as the baby who is learning the meaning of the verb ' to run '.

On the other hand, although this procedure may contain no very fresh element, it fulfils a useful function if it provides a satisfyingly rigorous ' proof ' of the meaning of motion, time, temperature and so on.[2] An operational definition is at its best when applied to uncomplex basic concepts of this nature. In such circumstances it can offer a high level of precision. But it fails us at the very moment when we are in most need of clarity.

The vagueness of a concept is equivalent to a difficulty in observing clearly the thing to which the concept is presumed to refer; indeed this difficulty—knowing what to observe, being able to observe it, and knowing how to observe it—is the crucial obstacle in bringing the concept into touch with empirical experience.[3]

And two rather general characteristics of social science limit the area in which we can hope for much help from operational definition in the search for conceptual precision.

(d) *Some Attempts at Definition*

The limitations can best be studied by considering a class of characteristics that have no serious counterpart in the natural sciences. These are the attributes with which we label human beings and social behaviour. It is not impossible to describe in strictly physical terms the speed of an athlete or the tone of a

[1] WEISS, A. P. (1929), *A Theoretical Basis of Human Behavior*, pp. 21-2, quoted by LUNDBERG, G. A. (1939), p. 235.
[2] Somewhat similarly, Professor Moore sets out to prove that external objects exist, by waving his hands in the air. He proves that his two hands exist by holding them up, saying as he makes a certain gesture with the right hand, ' Here is one hand ', and adding, as he makes a certain gesture with the left, ' and here is another '.—MOORE, G. E. (1939), *Proof of an External World*, p. 25.
[3] BLUMER, H. (1940), " The Problem of the Concept in Social Psychology." *Am. Journ. Soc.*, **45**, 713-14.

singer, but difficulties multiply when we require to describe an individual as brave or jealous, or the actions of a group as aggressive or respectful. The behaviourist framer of operational definitions is somewhat at a loss when faced with the need not only to define and describe overt acts, but also to interpret their meaning. Operational descriptions can only pin down dissected aspects of such behaviour; they can report in terms of bared teeth, stiffened sinews or cap in hand. But, for all their symbolism, these isolated scraps of behaviour may be misleading. The first man may be about to clean his teeth, the second may have cramp and the third an itchy scalp. On the other hand, inventories which list simultaneously observed items of behaviour very soon become too unwieldy to handle. In everyday practice we would mentally classify a man as behaving respectfully or bravely, according to the norms of our society, by a general awareness of his response to a sequence of situations rather than by itemisation, and in many instances the social observer who wishes to extract the most from his opportunity will be impelled to do the same.

Hovering uncomfortably between behavioural qualities such as speed and socially weighted qualities such as bravery or jealousy, we find the bitterly contested concept of intelligence which has become something of a rallying point for controverters.

Common-sense lay judgment as to intelligence is based on implicit, though undefined, reference to norms of behaviour, by which a certain informal importance is attached to speed of response, facility in solving puzzles, verbal skill, memory and so on. Intelligence testing as a ' scientific ' technique has grown up on the assumption that norms such as these do derive from an ' innate general cognitive factor ' which can be made explicit and standardised; a variety of tests have consequently been devised which, if properly conducted, faithfully record the actual performance under test of individuals subjected to them. Furthermore, the development of ' factor analysis '[1] has provided a method of detecting a consistent, and probably hereditary, element in the individual's responses to a variety of tests. The existence of this element, sometimes known as the general factor of intelligence, has on occasion persuaded its proponents to claim not only that their tests are valid but also that they can be used for predicting how those tested will perform in the outside world.

[1] See pp. 191 seq.

The basis for the first claim, being mathematical, is quite strong,[1] while that for the second claim is rather weak. It has so far seldom proved possible to make reliable forecasts of an individual's real-life performance by reference to his intelligence-test performances. At present a behavioural—i.e. operational—technique of intelligence testing may, for all its precision, offer a less socially useful, and thus less exact, predictive tool than the informal insight of an experienced and worldly selection committee. This may be a bitter pill for social science, but it is one that only ostriches can refuse.

Let us take another example of perilous definition—namely, that of 'social class'. The term calls to our mind a definite phenomenon in most developed societies. We are prepared to agree that few societies are 'classless'. We accept the concept of class, but that is only the first step in an attempt to allot different individuals to one or another social class. In practice, various investigators have adopted entirely different criteria for social classification, such as income, occupation, housing standards, social behaviour, social affiliations, self-placing and so on.

While one would expect some correspondence between the results of classifying people according to these varying criteria, it is useless to pretend that they are all describing the same thing. The attempt to classify any population into graded categories of social class encounters not only all the difficulties met in attempting to define temperatures, but also the further difficulties introduced by the partial identification of man with man.

The simplest mode of procedure is to adopt some 'objective' test, such as that of income, and to assume that variations in income—which we can determine—are correlated with variations in social class. Income is then adopted as an index of social class.

The belief that social class is directly related to economic status became prominent with the Marxist theory of the class struggle, and it appears undeniable that—in the long run, at least—an adequate economic status is necessary to support a given social status. On the other hand, even crude observation will convince us that the possession of wealth does not automatically convey social standing. Other objective facts—such as type of occupation or parentage or housing standard or area of residence

---

[1] For a valuable brief survey see BURT, C. (1950), 'The Trend of National Intelligence' (Review Article), *Brit. Journ. Soc.*, I, 154 seq.

—can similarly be used to give a broad indication of social class. The fact that a family goes to live in a superior residential district at least suggests some aspiration to membership of the class which inhabits that district.

But these broad tendencies are not sufficient to fix the class of an individual, or even to eliminate regular inconsistencies which attempts at correlation will reveal. It is known, for example, that many office workers have lower incomes than many manual workers, but that this does not deter them claiming, and acting up to, a superior class status. Other barriers, such as that of race, may preclude a man from rising to the social status indicated by his economic position.

With such cases in mind there have been many attempts to substitute openly subjective criteria for ' objective ' facts such as those mentioned above.

> Class . . . can well be regarded as a *psychological* phenomenon in the fullest sense of the term. That is, a man's class is a part of his ego, *a feeling on his part of belongingness to some thing* ; an *identification* with something larger than himself.[1]

Following this theory, it is clearly reasonable to question the people themselves, to ask them to what class they belong and how they would place other people that they know. One of the most ambitious of such attempts was that made by Warner and his colleagues in the Yankee City Studies, in which apparently all the residents in the town of 17,000 inhabitants were placed socially on information provided by other inhabitants.[2]

Also available are various documentary and observational methods, such as the collection and analysis of club membership lists, the noting of informal groupings when people acquainted with one another jointly attend some gathering, or the determination of socio-economic status by making an inventory of possessions.

As with the isolated tests of intelligence, any of these tells us something about the individuals concerned. But none is free from practical defects and from some theoretical naïveté. Thus they are commonly divided into objective and subjective methods.

[1] CENTERS, R. (1949), *The Psychology of Social Classes*, p. 27.
[2] WARNER, W. L., and LUNT, P. S. (1941), *The Social Life of a Modern Community*, further developed and documented in their (1942) *The Status System of a Modern Community*. The methods used have been strongly criticised on a variety of grounds.

This leads to absurd results; for example, the district in which a man lives is labelled as an objective fact, whereas the club which he joins is regarded as subjective.[1] It is obvious that the qualifying adjectives 'objective' and 'subjective' are almost meaningless in this context. Even economic status, apparently an 'objective' fact, depends ultimately on the rewards that a given society is prepared to allow to a particular individual who follows a given calling, and is thus a reflection of society's subjective mood.

When we ask ourselves why, as social scientists, we want to know the social class of certain individuals or the class composition of certain groups, we are likely to find the answer in terms of a mass of specific inquiries into which questions of class enter. In the past thirty years research in social medicine has aimed to discover whether some classes are more prone than others to certain diseases; in this case, for the practical reason of availability, decisions on the class of families have been made according to an initially [2] arbitrary scale derived from the occupation of the chief earner. The existence of statistics on housing and overcrowding standards, levels of unemployment and so on has led many British research workers interested in comparing the class structure of different areas to presume that these are suitable indices. In the United States, as we have seen, field-work investigators have had greater opportunities for the collection of fresh material, but, even so, considerations of time will have strongly influenced the choice of class criteria, and have generally precluded all but informal attempts at determining the social status of individuals. As must so often be the case, convenience takes precedence over suitability.

It is clear that the most direct, if not the only ultimate, function of the intelligence test is that it should tell us something about an individual's real-life performance. If we adopt a similar criterion for the test of social status, the emphasis of our inquiry will fall on the social meaning of class to the participants in a community and on the kinds of attitude and behaviour induced by this social meaning. This excludes no factor that the community and the investigator together accept as having a bearing on

---

[1] See also LIPSET, S. M., and BENDIX, R. (1951), *Brit. Journ. Soc.* **2**, 150–68.
[2] A recent attempt to prepare a less arbitrary scale has been reported. See HALL, J., and CARADOG JONES, D. (1950), 'Social Grading of Occupations', *Brit. Journ. Soc.*, **1**, 31–55.

such behaviour. But the single, universal definition of social class determined once for all societies by the authoritarian and omniscient scientist has melted in our hands.

Finally, let us briefly examine the batch of words that have been sporadically adopted by social scientists intent to pin down the features of human aggregation and interaction. It was for long assumed that a clear-cut system of definitions of these words was an essential prerequisite of social science, and a tremendous amount of work and thought has gone into the attempt to devise a nomenclature which would win general assent through its clarity, theoretical consistency and practical utility. It would be absurd to say that this effort has been wasted, because out of it has come a greatly enriched understanding of the nature and complexity of human association. It must be admitted, however, that an agreed nomenclature is still lacking.

If it were reasonably easy to conceptualise into a single scheme the different forms and causes of social grouping, we may be fairly sure that it would have been done before now. In practice all that has emerged is a set of attributes which any given group may or may not possess. Examples of such attributes are origin, size, cohesion, permanence, function, tolerance. Few of these offer clear-cut dichotomies. As Mess, following MacIver, has pointed out, for example, the well-favoured word *community*, used to connote a general agreement on interests rather than a specific functional bond, is a matter of degree; it is better to speak of groups as being more or less communal.[1]

The identification of any one type of group thus becomes an exercise in taxonomy, in which the investigator himself seizes the significant attributes, scales them according to what appears to him to be a reasonable metric, and arrives at a personal—and possibly ephemeral—definition.

This is not very good, but again the immediate alternative is to revert to the haphazard vocabulary of the human beings whose activities are being observed. This would represent something of a catastrophe for certain types of social theory. But in social action it is remarkable how little names matter, particularly in the early uninhibited stages of an engineered change. Two or three persons, intent on some purpose, gather together and cry, ' Let's

[1] Mess, H. A. (1942), *Social Structure*, p. 78. Cf. MacIver, R. M. (3rd ed. 1924), *Community*, p. 291. ' All community is a matter of degree.'

form an association: let's form a society, a club, a movement '. It is in the doing of something that the unity resides, and not in the names given to the act. Social groups are to be seen in still-pictures taken from the reel of human activity; when the film is run through you will notice that each of them is living out its process of formation, growth and dissolution. Some are institutionalised and linger more persistently than others, but all are subject to change and decay. With this recognition that what is centrally important is process and change rather than mere existence, comes the demand which can be increasingly heard—not only in psychology but also in natural science—that we should in our thinking and in our definitions substitute verbs for nouns.[1]

We are thus led towards a new vision of the operational definition. Unlike those framed by natural science, the operations on which these new definitions depend are chosen for their social significance and carried out by the joint determination of the social scientist and of his subjects.

[1] BRENTANO, F. (1874) states that the true subject matter of psychology is not, for example, ' red ' but the process of ' experiencing red ', the act which the mind carries out when it, so to speak, ' reddens '. We should perhaps substitute verbs instead of the nouns heretofore characteristic of psychology. See MURPHY, G. (1949 ed.), *An Historical Introduction to Modern Psychology*, pp. 225–6.

' We must consider whether the language of philosophy and psychology is not unsuitable for expressing their problems. It uses nouns freely to designate immutable substances, incapable of coming out of nowhere or of changing into one another or ceasing to exist; and these substances are in consequence sharply delimited from one another.... When we examine physical reality, as now understood, we find that very few of the " things " which we denominate by nouns show these properties.'—CRAIK, K. J. W. (1943), pp. 19–20.

' In every concept, in every concrete meaning, there is contained a crystallization of the experiences of a certain group. When someone says " kingdom " he is using the term in the sense in which it has meaning for a certain group. Another for whom the kingdom is only an organization, as for instance an administrative organization such as is involved in a postal system, is not participating in those collective actions of the group in which the former meaning is taken for granted. In every concept, however, there is not only a fixation of individuals with reference to a definite group of a certain kind and its action, but every source from which we derive meaning and interpretation acts also as a stabilizing factor on the possibilities of experiencing and knowing objects with reference to the central goal of action which directs us. The world of external objects and of psychic experience appears to be in a continuous flux. Verbs are more adequate symbols for this situation than nouns.'—MANNHEIM, K. (1936), *Ideology and Utopia*, pp. 19–20.

' I would almost suggest that " culture " is not a noun but a verb, indicating the action carried out by the peoples as they move forward under the urge to rise, take shape and mould their characters.'—ARCINIEGAS, G., " Culture—a Human Right ", in *Freedom and Culture* (1951).

' Considerable difficulty in reasoning about values might be averted if the verb form " to value " were used instead of the noun " value ".—HADER, J. J., and LINDEMAN, E. C. (1933), *Dynamic Social Research*, p. 102.

(e) *Summary and Conclusions*

This is a vista, but one for which we are perhaps not yet ready. For the present, our needs can be summarised thus. Initially, we should aim wherever possible to make use of the everyday language of practical affairs, for it is only when we do so that we can hope to capture what those whom we are studying feel to be the meaning of their behaviour and environment. However, because as social scientists our interests are concentrated on one face of nature, we will need to expand everyday language, just as all enthusiasts expand the common language. Precise words are to be preferred to vague ones, but the ultimate proof of precision is given by what people do with the word, or by what it makes them do, and not by its tightness of fit into any previously conceived theory.

The ultimate function of the social scientist's vocabulary is to understand, promote and assist in the control of social change. For this to be possible in a democratic community, the scientist's words must have achieved a meaning in the minds of those whom he aims to influence. In the long run this does not entail over-simplification, provided that the scientist's aims are shared with them. As the growing vocabulary of football pools is at present illustrating, techniques and terminology of considerable complexity will be mastered if the need is felt.

At an immature stage of the scientist's intervention it is generally necessary for him to depend on a somewhat theoretically orientated system of hypotheses. In order to conceptualise his theories, he may have to increase his personal store of words. Some will be borrowed by analogy from other branches of activity, and others may be coined. In mastering a difficult art, the social scientist must pass through a self-conscious stage in which he gains support from the panoply of theory and concept mustered by his predecessors. At this stage it is impossible to criticise his methods or the language that he harnesses to them, because they are his own and for him alone. But sooner or later it will be his task to spread the influence of what he is learning, both to his fellow scientists and to the public. Then he will realise that his power to disseminate the lessons that he has learned will greatly depend on how far he meets these others, on how far he catches and echoes their tune. Like the poet who sings of how he feels, the scientist wishes to spread the excitement of what he has discovered. Both are driven by their feelings, but neither finds consummation without sharing. And the novelty of new discovery is not easily assimilated by those who have not taken part in it.

The Germans have a word *Bedeutung*,[1] which has no exact English equivalent. It combines the sense of 'symbolic meaning' with that of 'general importance'; and it thus hints at a bridge between meaning and purpose that we are in our language liable to ignore. Quite literally, an unimportant concept fails to stimulate us into the frame of mind in which we can be bothered to attach meaning to it. In physics or in botany the scientist has no need to win over his raw materials. Some human scientists have assumed a correspondingly arrogant attitude towards their living subject-matter. In the interest of science it has been felt justifiable to patronise, and even to cheat. This conscious perpetuation of the two worlds—of the intellectual theorist and of the ordinary man—is the source and symbol of much of the pseudo-science which we have not yet learned to discipline or to discard. And nowhere is the chasm between life and theory more evident than in the attempt to sustain the arid mysteries of a separate language.

4. LOGIC

(a) *The Emergence of Empirical Logic*

Closely linked with the problem of language is the problem of logic. And just as there is an everyday language, so also there is a common-sense intuitive logic on which we normally rely. In many circumstances it is not only sufficient but also desirable to leave the process of logical inference to the ingrained unconscious; the attempt to be more rigorous can be as disastrous to thought as the attempt to run by the conscious control of our leg-muscles can be to our powers of movement.

It can be readily observed, however, that people are liable at times to reach contradictory and even absurd conclusions from any given starting point. In the majority of such cases the error in inference, when pointed out, will be recognised by the person

---

[1] Cf. HODGES, H. A. (1944), *Wilhelm Dilthey: an Introduction*, pp. 20, 159 (Definition), etc.

committing it, however unpalatable the truth may be to him. The scientist himself is sometimes misled into inconsistencies, but however much he may desire to justify one conclusion, he will sooner or later be compelled to renounce that conclusion if he cannot support it by the logical and mathematical processes which he has been trained to accept.

There is little reason to suppose that the logician or the scientist, however highly trained, actually employs the recognised methods of thought in his initial inferences. But these methods provide him with the independent and steady safeguard that his conclusions will be acceptable to others. ' The syllogism is not the form in which we necessarily reason, but a test of reasoning: a form into which we may translate any reasoning, with the effect of exposing all the points at which any unwarranted inference can have got in.' [1]

If we then regard the procedures of logic and mathematics as formal tests of the validity of any piece of reasoning, we next have to satisfy ourselves—at least in an elementary way—that these tests are themselves valid. If necessary, we must specify the sense in which their validity is assured.

This aim has customarily been pursued since the time of Aristotle by assuming a clear-cut distinction between the two forms of inference known as deduction and induction. The process of deduction consists of drawing particular conclusions from initial postulates. The simplest example takes the form: All men are mortal; Socrates is a man; therefore, Socrates is mortal.[2] In contrast, the process of induction is a method of deriving generalisations or *laws* by combining a number of isolated facts.

Although Aristotle had perceived this distinction and the necessary rôle of induction, the inductive form of logic was neglected for over 2,000 years. Throughout that period the only science known was formal science, as typified by Euclidean geometry, in which theorems were derived from initial postulates. The methods of mathematics, which make no demands on empirical knowledge, remained almost unchallenged as the

---

[1] MILL, J. S. (1867), *Examination of Sir W. Hamilton's Philosophy*, p. 487. (Quoted by NAGEL, E. (1950), p. xl.)
[2] As might have been predicted, the methods of mathematics and of deductive logic have steadily converged, and the gap between them has been bridged, initially by Russell and Whitehead, in the present century. Modern symbolic logic has become extremely elaborate, and progressively more rarefied.

scientific ideal until the seventeenth century, and the hope was sustained that all the truths of science could be ascertained from established first principles, just as Euclid had derived his theorems of geometry from his postulates. Only one difficulty remained, and that was to discover these obstinately concealed first principles of nature.

In due course, with the renaissance and with Europe's resurgent confidence in man's power to master nature, there came a reawakened delight in purposeful observation and in control of the tangible facts of life. The leaders of the new science did not drift into their reliance on observation and the empirical techniques, but embraced these methods deliberately and with a sense of superiority. Francis Bacon (1561-1626) wrote: 'It cannot be that axioms discovered by argumentations should avail for the discovery of new works. . . . We must lead men to the particulars themselves, while men on their side must force themselves for a while to lay their notions by and begin to familiarise themselves with the facts.' William Harvey (1578-1657), who discovered the circulation of the blood, likewise wrote: ' I profess to learn and to teach anatomy not from books but from dissections, not from the positions of philosophers but from the fabric of nature.'

This *empirical* approach to knowledge was given coherence by John Locke (1632-1704), who was persuaded not only that knowledge should be confined to what was immediately given through the senses, but also that no other ingredient was needed. For him, the facts amassed could be integrated intuitively and irrefutably to form generalisations.

The philosophical grounds for empirical knowledge were critically and somewhat destructively explored by Hume (1711-1776). Later they were restated by Immanuel Kant (1724-1804) in a subtler form which took account of the presuppositions that underlie all knowledge derived from sense experiences, and without which these experiences would remain incoherent. Kant represented such presuppositions as the 'transcendental' contributions of the mind to knowledge.

In the history of European philosophy the doctrines of Kant and of his successors are of primary importance. But their direct influence on the development of scientific technique and on the growth of scientific territory has not been decisive.

(b) Mill's Logic Introduced

It was, in fact, left to one of the pioneers of social science, John Stuart Mill, to examine in detail the technical—as opposed to the theoretical—process by which the mind justifies generalisations derived from empirical facts. In his *System of Logic*, first published in 1842, Mill set out to devise rules of inductive inference that would bear comparison with the well-established laws of deductive, or formal, logic. To him, formal logic was merely ' the smaller Logic, which only concerns itself with the conditions of consistency ' ; what he sought was a ' larger Logic, which embraces all the general conditions of the ascertainment of truth '.[1]

As with deductive thinking, Mill's aim was not so much to guide and confine the process of thought as to provide a chart by which the ground, once covered, could be retraced. What he tried to do was to provide the means by which a scientist could systematise in retrospect his intuitive processes, and so could reassure himself that his conclusions had obeyed the rules of inductive thought.

Mill's labours resulted in the formulation of four ' Methods of Experimental Inquiry ', namely, the Method of Agreement, the Method of Difference, the Method of Residues and the Method of Concomitant Variations.[2] These are briefly described in the next few pages.

FIRST CANON—METHOD OF AGREEMENT

If two or more instances of the phenomenon under investigation have only one circumstance in common, the circumstance in which alone all the instances agree is the cause (or effect) of the given phenomenon.

SECOND CANON—METHOD OF DIFFERENCE

If an instance in which the phenomenon under investigation occurs, and an instance in which it does not occur, have every circumstance in common save one, that one occurring only in the former ; the circumstance in which alone the two instances differ is the effect, or the cause, or an indispensable part of the cause, of the phenomenon.

---

[1] See NAGEL, E. (1950), pp. xxxi–ii. Mill's debt to Sir John Herschel must not, however, be minimised.

[2] It is a little confusing that Mill uses *five* Canons to state his *four* Methods. This is because the Third Canon relates to a combination of the Methods described in the previous two Canons.

These are Mill's two basic methods of inquiry. As he points out, they have many features of resemblance. In particular, both are methods of *elimination*. 'The Method of Agreement stands on the ground that whatever can be eliminated is not connected with the phenomenon by any law. The Method of Difference has for its foundation, that whatever cannot be eliminated is connected with the phenomenon by a law.'[1]

But although they both rest on elimination, they are very different in their practical applications. The Method of Difference is, where it can be applied, a method of great power, which Mill described as 'the most perfect of the methods of experimental inquiry'.[2] But the conditions for exercising it are correspondingly stringent: it is rare that an opportunity to compare two occasions identical in all respects except one will occur except under the control of an active experimenter. Such occasions as do conform are essentially experimental situations.

The conditions for applying the Method of Agreement are very much less rigorous and, unfortunately, any conclusions drawn must be correspondingly tentative. If I have a headache on two different days, and not otherwise, and if I have noticed that both these days have been exceptionally sunny, then I may begin to believe that the sun caused my headache. But my grounds for believing so are clearly insecure. The headache might have had different causes on the two days, or alternatively the actual cause of my headache—e.g. what I had for breakfast—though present on both occasions, might not have been recorded. Mill himself concludes that the method of agreement is chiefly to be resorted to as a means of suggesting applications of the method of difference, or as an inferior substitute for it when experimentation is ruled out. If I am able to try the effect of wearing dark glasses on a sunny day, and find that my headache has abated, I shall have exploited both methods in discovering that the sun has been straining my eyes.

The essentially preliminary nature of all non-experimental methods, which Mill thus asserts, represents one of the themes underlined in the present book. Meanwhile, Mill's Third Canon shows that a shadow of the Method of Difference may be preserved even when experimental conditions are unattainable.

[1] MILL, J. S., *A System of Logic*, p. 256.
[2] *ibid.*, p. 575.

THIRD CANON—JOINT METHOD OF AGREEMENT AND DIFFERENCE
If two or more instances in which the phenomenon occurs have only one circumstance in common, while two or more instances in which it does not occur have nothing in common save the absence of that circumstance, the circumstance in which alone the two sets of instances differ is the effect, or the cause, or an indispensable part of the cause, of the phenomenon.

Mill takes as an example the conditions for the formation of dew.

. . . the instances in which much dew is deposited, which are very varied, agree in this, and, so far as we are able to observe, in this only, that they either radiate heat rapidly or conduct it slowly : qualities between which there is no other circumstance of agreement than that, by virtue of either, the body tends to lose heat from the surface more rapidly than it can be restored from within. The instances, on the contrary, in which no dew, or but a small quantity of it, is formed, and which are also extremely various, agree (as far as we can observe) in nothing except in *not* having this same property.[1]

This joint method is put forward as some kind of a substitute when direct experimentation is ruled out. The two sets of facts, compiled according to the Method of Agreement, are independent of each other, and yet when compared with each other tend to corroborate a single explanation. But the force of any conclusions reached cannot be compared with that of conclusions reached by experiment, for everything depends on the correct mental choice by the observer of the unique circumstance which is to be shown as universally present in the first group of observations and universally absent in the second group. In practice we can never be sure that we have chosen correctly. If we could be sure, either set of instances alone would suffice for proof. As we cannot, ' this indirect method, therefore, can only be regarded as a great extension and improvement of the Method of Agreement, but not as participating in the more cogent nature of the Method of Difference '.[2]

It is particularly necessary for the social scientist to recognise the inferiority of the Joint Method, if only because it is frequently invoked by social scientists as an adequate substitute for social experiment. This question is discussed in a later chapter,[3] and we must now pass on to Mill's two remaining methods.

[1] MILL, J. S., *A System of Logic*, pp. 273-4.
[2] *ibid.*, p. 259.   [3] Chapter 5—Experiment.

FOURTH CANON—METHOD OF RESIDUES

Subduct from any phenomenon such part as is known by previous inductions to be the effect of certain antecedents, and the residue of the phenomenon is the effect of the remaining antecedents.

This method was first formulated by Sir John Herschel, the eighteenth-century empirical astronomer. Its practical application in the natural sciences has led to a number of important discoveries. For example, the presence of argon in the atmosphere was detected because of the observed difference between the residual density of atmospheric nitrogen and the density of nitrogen obtained by other means. Again, the planet Neptune was discovered through the observation of previously unexplained aberrations in the orbit of Uranus.

It will be clear that the Method of Residues rests on previous knowledge of the relevant laws of Nature, and can only be applied when an aberration from these laws is noted. Logicians are therefore inclined to classify it as a Deductive rather than as an Inductive method. What is more important to us is that its use in social science is limited by the dearth of established exact laws of social relations.

FIFTH CANON—METHOD OF CONCOMITANT VARIATIONS

Whatever phenomenon varies in any manner whenever another phenomenon varies in some particular manner, is either a cause or an effect of that phenomenon, or is connected with it through some fact of causation.

This Method represents Mill's way of recognising the growing importance to science of measurement and quantitative differences. In modern terminology, two qualitative characters are said to be *associated* if a relation exists between them; a relation between qualitative and quantitative characters is called a *contingency*, while when two sets of quantitative characters are related to each other they are said to be *correlated*.[1] Today science of all kinds is dependent on measurement of variables and on consequent correlation analysis, and the initial logical basis for all such analyses is stated in this Fifth Canon.

---

[1] See, for example, FLORENCE, P. S. (1929), *The Statistical Method in Economics and Political Science*, pp. 124 seq.

(c) *Limits to Applicability*

Mill's four Methods of Experimental Inquiry were an important landmark in the development of empirical science. As he himself stated, however, they were deliberate simplifications of the inductive problems actually encountered by scientists. Before assessing their adaptability to our own problems in social science we must therefore follow Mill a little further in his examination of the gaps in the formulation that he himself had proposed.

The practical difficulties that oppressed Mill were due to two circumstances, which he described as ' plurality of causes ' and ' intermixture of effects '.

By *plurality of causes* he was referring to the fact that it is often impossible to distinguish the particular cause responsible for a given effect. ' Many causes may produce mechanical motion : many causes may produce some kinds of sensation : many causes may produce death. A given effect may really be produced by a certain cause and yet be perfectly capable of being produced without it.' [1]

It is this fact which so greatly diminishes the value of the Method of Agreement when based on a small number of instances. It is only when the instances are considerable in number and varied in general circumstances that the conclusions achieve any high degree of independent value. Conversely, to base assurance merely on the *mass* of evidence is wrong. According to Mill, *the plurality of causes is the only reason why mere number is of any importance, and a single application of the Method of Difference, by eliminating some possible cause of the observed effect, is of more value than the greatest multitude of instances which are reckoned by their number alone.*

Even more universal an experience is the *intermixture of effects* resulting from the simultaneous operation of two or more causes. This may lead to a compound effect whose constituent elements, while still present, disappear into one total, just as two different mechanical forces are resolved into a third force. Alternatively, the initial effects may cease entirely, to be succeeded by phenomena altogether different and governed by different laws ; this often

---

[1] MILL, J. S., *A System of Logic*, p. 286. DURKHEIM, F. (*Method*, pp. 127 seq.), disputes Mill's argument as to the plurality of causes ; in his view, when the proximate cause has been discovered, it alone will be found to have produced a given effect. Thus, ' A given effect has always a single corresponding cause '. But this is essentially a verbal quibble ; cf. pp. 72, 272.

F

results, for example, from a chemical reaction, and—when the chemical change is reversible—can be studied by the type of experimentation known as chemical analysis.

Contrary to first impressions, the former type of intermixture of effects is much the harder to analyse, and the problem of discovering causes is in such circumstances generally insoluble. If our only data are the actual movements of an object, we cannot in any valid sense infer the direction and magnitude of the forces that persuaded it to move as it did; there are, in fact, an infinite number of sets of forces which could have produced the observed effect, and we have no means of choosing between them.

How can we escape from this dilemma? The classical escape is by means of the *a priori* law. If appropriate laws covering the separate causes have already been established, all that we have to do is to deduce from these laws what the compound effect will be of a number of simultaneous forces. In fact we will only bother to observe what actually happens if we are not too sure of our *a priori* laws.

On the other hand, our inquiry may necessarily be empirical and inductive if, as in social science, there are no adequate previously established laws. In this case we still have the choice of approaches, one dependent on the Method of Agreement and the other on the Method of Difference. 'If it merely collates instances of the effect, it is a method of pure observation. If it operates upon the causes, and tries different combinations of them, in hopes of ultimately hitting the precise combination which will produce the given total effect, it is a method of experiment.' [1]

To assist comparison between the methods of deduction, observation and experiment, Mill chooses a case from medicine, and considers how the efficacy of a mercury compound in the treatment of a particular disease would be examined.

The deductive method would set out from the known properties of mercury and the known laws of the human body, and would thereby estimate the effect of mercury on the disease in question. The pure experimental method would simply administer mercury in as many cases as possible, noting the attendant circumstances and remarking its effect in each instance. The method of simple observation would collate instances of recovery to see whether mercury had been administered, or would compare instances of

[1] MILL, J. S., *A System of Logic*, p. 294.

recovery with instances of failure to determine whether the only point of difference lay in the dosing or non-dosing with mercury.

Complete reliance on this last method—that of observation—was, according to Mill, clearly impossible, if only because many patients were likely to recover whatever their treatment (plurality of causes). Mill also believed the purely experimental method to be inapplicable, primarily because he could see no way of ensuring that the control and experimental sample should be identical in character before the experimental change was introduced. Statistical control of observations and the control of experiments by randomisation and replication, were still undiscovered devices, and he was thus driven back to the method of deduction as offering the one hope of primary assistance.[1]

This same conclusion was developed by Mill in Book VI of his *System of Logic*, which he devoted specifically to the logic of social science. He here set up as an ideal that the social sciences should adopt the methods of natural science, even though he recognised that their innate imperfections would for ever prevent them from being comparably exact. He believed that it would in due course become feasible to ' lay down general propositions which will be true in the main, and on which, with allowance for the degree of their probable inaccuracy, we may safely ground our expectations and our conduct '.[2]

(d) *The Inverse Deductive Method*

And how did he hope that this would be achieved? He was certain, even more so than in the case of medicine, that it would be impossible either to conduct social experiments or to arrive at empirical generalisations by the observations of social behaviour. If, therefore, there was to be a social science at all, it would have to lean heavily on deduction from known social laws, making use of empirical inductive methods only to check the accuracy of predictions made by deduction from these laws. To this procedure he gave the name *Inverse Deductive Method*.[3]

---

[1] See Chapter 5, 'Experiment'. Subsequent experience has shown that Mill was too pessimistic even in his own chosen example, for controlled medical experiments are now of course commonly undertaken.

[2] *ibid.*, p. 553.

[3] ' In such cases the inductive and deductive methods of inquiry may be said to go hand in hand, the one verifying the conclusions deduced by the other; and the combination of experiment and theory, which may thus be brought to bear in such cases, forms an engine of discovery infinitely more powerful than either taken separately '—SIR JOHN HERSCHEL.

His conclusion hinged entirely on the possibility of discovering and establishing the basic laws of human behaviour. By a train of argument, Mill concluded that all such laws would prove to be laws relating to individual character. Moreover, they would be not mere empirical laws, like those of psychology, but the fundamental causal laws which explain observable psychological behaviour. Mill thus suggested the need for a new discipline concerned not with human character but with the formation of character, and proposed for it the name *ethology*.[1]

For much of his life Mill continued his fruitless search for these deductive laws governing the formation of character. The failure of Mill and his successors to find them has been regarded by some as tantamount to a demonstration that ethology, and the Inverse Deductive Method which depends on it, was a figment of his imagination. Alternatively, it may be regarded merely as a sign that psychology, from which the propositions of ethology were to be derived, is still too immature to provide what is asked of it. Whatever the answer, the history of social science has shown a persistent demand for some comprehensive system of basic laws against which the reasonableness of empirical findings may be judged. Mill's own search was abortive, but his explicit recognition of the need for such a search is still today of far more than mere historical importance.

What, though, is the position today? Social facts are no less complex and no less disjointed today than they were a hundred years ago. The orthodox aims of social science, to generalise and to predict, remain unchanged. Where stands the Inverse Deductive Method, and have we now the basic laws from which behaviour may be predicted?

A few years ago Professor Ginsberg classified under six heads the types of generalisations so far attempted by social scientists. He assumed general agreement for the view that sociological investigations should be carried out in accordance with the Inverse Deductive Method. When, however, he considered the logical procedures ostensibly used, he found that in every class except one the generalisations attempted were predominantly reached inductively, even though in some cases inherent plausi-

---

[1] From the Greek word ' ethos ', ' a word more nearly corresponding to the term "character" as I here use it, than any other word in the same language '.— MILL, J. S., *A System of Logic*, p. 567.

bility was claimed by appeal to the theories of popular psychology. Generalisations of only one type—namely, those of economic theory—are reached deductively from assumptions regarding human behaviour, and they do so by leaving to further inquiry the problem of how far the assumptions correspond to fact.[1]

This is a depressing, but incontrovertible, analysis. It confirms once more that the search for basic laws has not yet been rewarded. Successive failures have not, meanwhile, deterred some celebrated social scientists from their attempts to develop comprehensive and encyclopædic social theories. In all cases these general theories remain unverified, and owe little to the rigorous discipline that the same social scientists have in mundane moments imposed upon themselves and upon others. Sometimes the form of presentation effectively rules out any chance of verification.

Impatience of this sort has undoubtedly diverted energies from empirical advance. No long ago, Professor Burgess commented:

> Conceptual systems, as formulated by sociologists, were at first not oriented to empirical research but had as their objective the interpretation of society. Many early and even some contemporary social scientists appear to consider a conceptual analysis of society as if it were a substitute for research. This survival of the tradition of the social philosopher has retarded the development of sociological research.[2]

Professor Marshall has wittily added:

> Concepts are made for use, not for show. There was a compelling persuasiveness about the famous cry—' Give us the tools and we will finish the job '. One may be forgiven for responding less eagerly to the scholar, be he sociologist or anything else, who says—' Give me a job, and I will spend the rest of my life polishing the tools '.[3]

The danger with the scholar's conceptual theory is that it suffers a constant tendency to abstraction, to remoteness from real life. The material on which the theory is based may originally be derived from living experience, but—as time goes by—the inherent logic of internal consistency is liable to become more important than correspondence with the facts. Even when a

---
[1] GINSBERG, M., ' The Problems and Methods of Sociology ', in BARTLETT, F. C. et al—Eds. (1939), p. 473. Reprinted (1947) in *Reason and Unreason in Society*, pp. 35 seq. See also *Reason and Unreason*, p. 125.
[2] BURGESS, E. W. (1945), ' Sociological Research Methods ', *Am. Journ. Soc.*, 50, 475.
[3] MARSHALL, T. H. (1947), p. 19.

theory offers an adequate basis for explaining a particular sequence of experiences or for solving a particular set of problems, there is an unfortunate tendency to abstract and to generalise any such theory far beyond the area of inquiry in which it has been validated and found useful.

On the other hand, we must equally be on our guard against the belief, implicit in much empirically guided work, that it is possible to collect and make use of facts, and even to organise them, in a conceptual vacuum. The problem constantly before the social scientist is how to cultivate the necessary awareness of his own predispositions and beliefs without allowing this self-knowledge to inhibit his purposes.

It is arguable that those who pin their faith too exclusively on the Inverse Deductive Method are in reality reflecting a certain confusion in their own aims. There are two reasons why this should be so. One is the almost universal instruction that knowledge is in some way superior to activity; this is bound to encourage the belief that the search for truths and generalisations is in itself a sufficient aim. The other reason is that social scientists—or at least respectable ones—have traditionally been shuttered off from contact with their raw material; this is true by definition of historians, and has until fairly recently been true by force of circumstance of other academically recognised social scientists. It has been very characteristic of all such scholars to make do with other people's data.

As we have seen, in facts collected for administrative purposes, the definitions will have been polished in use, but the considerations which lead an administrator to ask that certain data should be connected will—we may assume—be predominantly practical and immediate in their application. A census of population or production, even in most cases a social survey, will appear justifiable to its sponsors only insofar as it provides useful answers to real-life questions. The practical questions that empirical social research tends to explore are practical in the sense that they relate to immediate problems of social adjustment rather than to the study and elaboration of social theory. In comparison, although the bulk of research in natural science is practical in the sense that it involves the collection of fresh data, the hypotheses to be tested may belong to 'pure' science as easily as to 'applied' science. In principle, the techniques and the apparatus used may be indistinguishable, but each will nevertheless reflect a distinctive dominant motive—i.e. the elaboration of theory in the former case, and in the latter the solution of practical problems within an existing conceptual framework.

It is still a matter of debate whether time will provide an integrated system of social theory in which 'pure' science can flourish; reasons given elsewhere in this book suggest this to be improbable. No one, however, can claim that any such integrated system is yet in being.

> Our thinking is rarely far enough progressed to enable us to start out with a sharply formulated hypothesis; most studies are exploratory, directed towards the general examination of a field in order to develop theoretical formulations. Furthermore, even if the original problem was well thought through, the actual study often has new and unanticipated implications. In other cases, the situation is even more complicated. Many studies grow out of practical needs. Only after they have served their pragmatic purposes can they be explored for whatever theoretical content they contain.[1]

The authors of this extract suggest that the time has arrived to make much greater use of existing survey material, and they support their belief by reference to the varied secondary uses to which the vast amount of data collected by the Research Branch, Information and Education Division of the United States War Department has been put.[2] The initial collection of these data was often dictated by highly practical needs, such as the desire to know the numbers of different kinds of individuals or items present in specific units. Once collected, the material was available for analysis at very varied levels of abstraction. The first development was the use of the records to determine the extent of the relationship between one characteristic and another.[3] The

---

[1] KENDALL, P., and LAZARSFELD, P. F., 'Problems of Survey Analysis', in MERTON, R. K., and LAZARSFELD, P. F.—Eds. (1950), pp. 133-4.

[2] The material referred to here is published as *The American Soldier*, Vols. I and II (1949).
Vol. I, STOUFFER, S. A. et al. *Adjustment During Army Life*.
Vol. II, STOUFFER, S. A. et al. *Combat and its Aftermath*.
Measurement and Prediction, discussed on pp. 192 seq., is the methodological volume in the same series.

[3] In one example cited a survey primarily designed as a study of 'attitudes towards redeployment and demobilisation' was subsequently used to examine such varied questions as: level of adjustment according to combat experience and service overseas; feelings of personal commitment according to combat

next stage was to 'account for' any such relationships by the methods of secondary analysis, which are summarised later in this chapter.

A still more sophisticated level is reached when the same material is used to test general hypotheses and concepts, such as that of the 'primary group'[1] and that of 'relative deprivation'.[2] When built on a rigorous foundation, concepts such as the above, which have the modest aim of organising empirical data, can, if validated, have our unreserved confidence. If in a variety of circumstances the same concepts appear to fit the facts, we may regard them as providing one element that is constant enough to be isolated and handled. The theorist appraises such concepts for their potential contribution to a more inclusive general system. The observer values their guidance on what to look out for in the field. The experimenter incorporates them in his design as entities to be disseminated among his subjects and jointly manipulated by himself and them.

(e) *The Guidance of Statistics*

Some impatient readers may be inclined to think that the present discussion has been rendered obsolete and valueless by the vast development of statistical techniques. Inspection shows that this belief is hardly justified, but that when used in appropriate situations the methods of statistics do have an important function.

It will be remembered that Mill was disturbed that his Methods were unsatisfactory when a simple and direct causal relationship was replaced by what he called a 'plurality of causes' and an 'intermixture of effects'. These complications were to be suspected when the Methods of Agreement and of Concomitant Variations yielded only partially positive results, and experience showed such occasions to be very common. Mill could not say with clarity much more on the subject than that the results

---

experience, overseas service, length of time in the Army and various demographic factors; willingness to fight the Japanese according to race and theatre of present service; attitudes towards civilians in the United States according to closeness to the front-lines; combat-men's resentment of rear-area troops; self-appraisal of health by rotational returnees; willingness of returnees for further overseas service.

[1] SHILS, E. A., 'Primary Groups in the American Army', in MERTON, R. K. and LAZARSFELD, P. F.—Eds. (1950), *Continuities in Social Research*, pp. 16–39.
[2] MERTON, R. K., and KITT, A. S. (1950), 'Contributions to the Theory of Reference Group Behaviour', in *ibid.*, pp. 40–105.

obtained were connected with the laws of probability, and that the investigator's confidence in his conclusions could reasonably increase with the number of confirmatory cases.

Since then the growing use of statistics has led to a thorough examination of the conditions under which, and the extent to which, it is reasonable to infer relationships between two or more variables. This examination may be regarded as having supplemented Mill's initial study of the basis on which empirical inference rests; in some spheres it may be regarded as having provided the means to transform a weak method of inference into a powerful one. 'Statistics . . . must accept for analysis data subject to the influence of a host of causes, and must try to discover from the data themselves which causes are the important ones and how much of the observed effect is due to the operation of each.' [1]

The first function of statistics in this field is to ensure that cases studied are representative of the larger universe from which they are taken, and to calculate the margin of accuracy of results obtained. *Sampling* is most widely used in the design of mass interview surveys, and the subject is consequently discussed in the chapter devoted to that subject.[2]

The second function of statistics is to assess an investigator's grounds for confidence in maintaining that two variables found in his empirical material are causally connected. It might be asked, to take an example from *The American Soldier*, whether the attitude of troops towards civilians was genuinely different according to the theatre of operations in which they were stationed. The idea that there may be some such difference would have been suggested by previous knowledge, by the investigator's personal experience or by his initial examination of the survey material. The alternative hypothesis would be that such differences as were revealed by the survey were due to chance, admitted by random sampling.

Modern methods of deciding between these hypotheses date from 1900, when Karl Pearson first formulated his χ^2 test for significance. The value of this quantity in a suitable instance is readily calculated, and it is today possible in many cases to use a χ^2 Table which will reveal, with sufficient accuracy for ordinary

---

[1] YULE, G. U., and KENDALL, M. G. (14th ed., 1950), *An Introduction to the Theory of Statistics*, p. xv.
[2] pp. 205 seq.

purposes, whether or not a given difference is 'significant'.[1] This does not tell us how satisfactorily the hypothesis has been verified or how strongly the two factors are associated, nor of course does it in any way help to explain the reason for any significant difference identified. What it does do is to tell us whether or not our guess that there is an association between the two factors is justified by the information so far collected. It may thus protect us from the extravagant pastime of inventing explanations for non-existent relationships.

This test has the merit of being applicable to a great many circumstances, and the factors concerned need not necessarily be expressed in a numerical form. In the illustration given above, for example, there are no satisfactory means by which an army's various theatres of operations can be distinguished on a numerical scale. The usefulness of χ^2 tests is, however, limited by their inability to give any information as to the strength of the relationship which binds the different factors concerned. When the variables can be described numerically, the strength of this relationship can be calculated and described in terms of the *correlation coefficient*. This is a quantity whose value lies between $+1$ and -1. Either extreme value shows that each variable is completely associated with the other; if $+1$, the factors vary directly (if one increases, so does the other), while if it is -1, they vary inversely (if one increases, the other decreases). A correlation coefficient of 0 shows that the two factors are entirely independent, so that one can be varied without any influence on the other.

It is probable that if a direct causal link existed between any two factors, so that the correlation coefficient became either $+1$ or -1, this link would have been established in some other way. History shows, for example, that the classical problems of natural science were adequately handled without the need for probability calculations. In biology, on the other hand, and now in psychology and sociology, the impossibility of isolating full causal links has stimulated the demand for correlation analysis. Inevitably, therefore, full ± 1 coefficients are very rarely found in these

---

[1] See, for example, FISHER, R. A. (11th ed. 1950), *Statistical Methods for Research Workers*, pp. 78–113. A difference is described as 'significant' if it would not have occurred by chance in more than a small proportion of cases. This proportion is commonly $\frac{1}{20}$, but the research worker is entitled to adopt a more—or less—rigorous standard if he thinks it desirable, and can persuade others that he has acted justifiably.

fields, and quite a low value is often of interest, provided that the figure arrived at has been shown to be 'significant' and is thus not likely itself to have occurred by chance. In order to assess significance it is necessary to know not only the correlation coefficient but also the number of independent cases from which it is derived. Calculation is by formula or more conveniently by the use of an appropriate Table.[1]

The usefulness of correlation analysis has been greatly extended by the development of the technique of *partial correlation*. In the simplest case, when three factors are simultaneously operating and the correlation between each pair is known, it is possible to calculate what the correlation would have been in a population in which the third variable was fixed. The third variable is then said to have been 'partialled out'.

Another important extension has been made possible by the development of *rank correlation analysis*. This may be applied when factors can be placed in rank order but cannot be assigned a numerical value. In suitable cases, use of this form of analysis can be nearly as informative as the calculation of a correlation coefficient. Furthermore it has the great merit of requiring no assumptions as to the normality of distribution of the material provided.

Methods such as these, so briefly summarised here, may thus be regarded in the context of logic as techniques for regulating and refining human judgment as to the interconnectedness of different observations. In appropriate circumstances which do not involve the strait-lacing of material unsuitable for quantification,[2] the use of statistics provides an invaluable check on the more palpable distortion of facts by a wilful investigator. The popular war-cry that 'statistics can prove anything' is almost exactly untrue. Statistics, as a branch of mathematics, is as value-free as any manmade device can be. In practice, statistics is far more often called in to undermine conclusions that previously appeared undeniable to their intuitive author than to prove the significance of what he is inclined to discredit. It is other people's statistical results, and not our own, that turn us into sceptics.

On the other hand, it must be recognised that statistics provides

[1] FISHER, R. A. (11th ed. 1950), *Statistical Methods for Research Workers*, pp. 174, 209.
[2] This limitation is, unfortunately, not always observed. See this Chapter, pp. 36-7.

no more than a device to tell us, with mechanical regularity, what degree of confidence in any particular hypothesis is justified. Statistics cannot tell us how much we need an answer of sorts, however perilously based, nor how great a loss we risk by the incorrect acceptance of any particular answer.[1]

Ultimately, moreover, we cannot eliminate our desire to arrive at a particular answer, and the effect of this desire is irresistibly contained in our conclusions. The machinery of statistics is mathematical, but its use in concrete cases is indelibly coloured by the aims of its user. The investigator, who cannot fail to take sides in any social situation, can only arrive at the ' truth '—however generally acceptable or localised that may be—by giving rein to his will. The idea of probability as a measure of confidence is a fertile one, but unless we obstinately adhere to an unattainable ideal of objectivity, we have to admit that our confidence partakes of our own will. Exploration of the partial identity of will and possibility may in time be as revealing, if not as constructive, as the earlier reintegration of the concepts of mind and matter.

(f) *Accounting for Results*

The immediate purposes of a survey may be fulfilled if a relationship between two factors can be demonstrated or denied with a reasonable fund of certainty. It is very seldom, however, that an isolated result of this nature is of much value outside the context in which it was obtained. Before anything of general interest can be extracted, it is normally necessary to explore a little deeper in search of the link which connects any two associated factors.

In the paper already mentioned, Kendall and Lazarsfeld have very carefully examined what they describe as the ' secondary analysis ' of survey material. They show that this secondary analysis may have any one of three functions, which they describe as *explanation, interpretation* and *specification.*

Explanation is concerned with controlling what the authors describe as *spurious factors*. It can be shown, for example, that there is a high positive correlation between the number of fire engines present at a fire and the amount of damage resulting from

---

[1] 'The fundamental task is to determine the criteria of loss. Evidently, these criteria are not fundamentally statistical in nature, so that the criteria of correct inference from data do not lie solely within statistical research.'
—CHURCHMAN, C. W. (1948), *Theory of Experimental Inference,* p. 257.

it. A half-baked conclusion would be that the fire engines cause the damage, whereas in this particular case the true explanation is easily found. The spurious factor is the seriousness of the fire; as is characteristic, this precedes the other two factors, and affects them both in a related way. Until it has been eliminated, the statistical results are valueless, and are often highly misleading.

A celebrated instance from sociology occurs in Durkheim's classic study on suicide. Durkheim established the existence of a positive correlation between suicide and level of education, but he felt this correlation to be ' in contradiction to the laws of psychology '. He therefore sought the spurious factor which had misled him. He found this in the situation produced by the weakening of religious ties, which leads both to a search for new knowledge and to a tendency to discount the moral sanctions against suicide.

Interpretation is logically somewhat similar to explanation, although, as Kendall and Lazarsfeld point out, we respond psychologically to the two in a very different manner. If we explain away a result by exposing a spurious factor, we feel that we have saved ourselves from a mistaken conclusion, but no more. If, however, we are able to discover an *intervening* factor which is acting as a causal link between the two factors previously statistically to be correlated, we feel that we have definitely added something to our knowledge.

For example, practical experience in the early nineteenth century made it clear that epidemics were more likely to break out and spread in the more overcrowded parts of a town. Overcrowding could thus be said to cause epidemics. Florence Nightingale believed that epidemics were a ' natural ' function of overcrowding, and ridiculed the independent reality of such proximate causes as infection and contagion. It was only after the discovery of bacteria as an *intervening* factor that doctors were able to *interpret* the connection that had previously rested purely on an empirical basis.

It is important to note that in the case of *explanations* the spurious factor normally precedes the two correlated factors, while in the case of *interpretations* the additional factor is intermediate in time between the two primary factors. Sometimes the results of one survey are insufficient for a decision as to the order in which different observed effects occurred. Kendall and

Lazarsfeld quote several such cases, one of which was concerned with the relationship between attitudes towards one's officers and willingness for combat.[1] From the data provided it was impossible to say which of these attitudes developed or was acquired first. In other cases independent information provided the necessary clues. Thus, when it was found that married men were likely to have higher rank than single men of the same age and length of service in the army, it was not clear which came first, promotion or marriage. It was known, however, which soldiers had been married on joining the army and which had married since, and it was thus possible to infer that marriage was more often a consequence of promotion than a cause.

Other cases demonstrated the great value of ' panel ' techniques, by which the same sample of informants are interviewed on successive occasions, which can be quite widely spaced.[2] This device sometimes provided the only possible means of distinguishing spurious factors from intervening variables. Thus, when it was found that N.C.O.s were more inclined to conform to army discipline than privates, the question arose whether the attitude of conformity to authority increased a man's chances of promotion or whether this attitude was developed after promotion. A ' panel ' survey stretching over six months suggested very strongly that those temperamentally disinclined to conform had a rather poor chance of promotion.

The third type of secondary analysis to be outlined has been called *specification*. The function of this is to isolate and identify the conditions under which the relationship between the two primary factors is most pronounced. In an example cited, primary analysis had shown that better-educated soldiers tended to have higher rank. It occurred to the analysts that the relationship might be more emphatic if length of service were to be taken into account. Further analysis showed that this hunch was justified: the effect noted was found to be very definite in the case of soldiers who had been in the army for some time. On the other hand, by the time that later recruits joined the army the organisation was fairly completely manned, and prospects of promotion were bleak even for the better educated. When therefore a

---

[1] We are not here concerned with the validity of the means by which the information was collected. This question is discussed in Chapter 4.
[2] See Chapter 5.

certain minimum length of service was specified, the connection between education and rank was much more pronounced than it had been in the whole original sample.

As a matter of fact, *specification* in some form or another is a central and persistent feature in all scientific method. Constantly, as we try to use observed regularities for the establishment of causes, as we try to account for the association of phenomena or of events, we are driven to seek—step by step, if necessary—an acceptable and intelligible chain of causation. The plausibility of such a chain largely depends upon the success with which the process of specification has been employed in confirming proximate causes.

(g) *Conclusions*

We have to be constantly on our watch so that inferences based on observational material shall not slip past our logical defences and get themselves presented as tantamount to proofs. J. S. Mill, whose work still towers across a century of later logic, clearly recognised the supremacy of experiment, and of the Method of Difference on which all experimentation is based. Although his early fear that social experiment was permanently ruled out has proved to have been too pessimistic, the scope for experiment remains limited by both real and illusory difficulties. In many cases the only material we have is that based on documentary evidence, on observation and on questioning, and the lack of conclusiveness inherent in results based on these sorts of material should not blind us to their progressively improving preparatory value. In many fields the information to be won by such methods is adequate for the object in view, and the collection of information frequently merges into the complementary administrative action. In other fields provisional information must remain uninterpreted and un-acted-upon. We can only deplore this, and search for ways of putting such information to experimental test. Stouffer, the director of the United States Research Branch already alluded to, was responsible for one of the most massive increments of attitude study material in the history of social science; and yet he concludes, ' I would trade a half dozen Army-wide surveys on attitudes towards officers for one good controlled experiment '.

Chapter 2
DOCUMENTS

1. DOCUMENTS AND SOCIAL SCIENCE

THE social scientist has one important asset, in that the events and processes which concern him leave their own traces in the form of documents. Such documents not only describe contemporary events, but also help to reveal how these events have appeared to those living through them. Written evidence thus has the straightforward function of providing facts and figures, and the indirect function of helping us to project our understanding into other times and other places.

Documents preserved from the past fall naturally within the province of the historian and are indispensable to him. 'Pas de documents, pas d'histoire.'[1] Some historians concern themselves with current events, but even when they do so they normally concentrate on documentary material, and eschew the other techniques used by social scientists. This concentration on a single technique may help to explain the frequently found statement that history is a method and not a science.[2]

There is no sense in an attempt to exclude historians from the ranks of social science, and only foolish social scientists renounce the use of documents, whether these are contemporary or preserved. Thus overlapping is inevitable. 'There are signs', writes Lynd, 'that the other social sciences, instead of waiting for history to give them what they require, are themselves going to the past and writing their own history around the need to know specific things about the past in relation to current institutional problems.'[3] This may be an accurate picture of what is happen-

---
[1] Dictum by Langlois and Seignobos. The version in English reads: 'For there is no substitute for documents: no documents, no history'. LANGLOIS, Ch. V. and SEIGNOBOS, Ch. (1898), *Introduction to the Study of History*, p. 17.
[2] E.g. SEIGNOBOS, Ch. (1901), *Méthode historique appliquée aux sciences sociales*, Paris. On p. 3 he writes: 'History is not a science; it is a method (procédé de connaissance).'
[3] LYND, R. S. (1939), *Knowledge for What?*, p. 138.

ing in the United States, but in Europe a partnership between social science and the historical method was set up long ago. Historians have not only made significant contributions to our understanding of social processes, but have also evolved a most careful technique for the verification and analysis of documentary material.

Like Comte himself, the early British social scientists leaned heavily on historical documentary evidence. The Webbs, for example, gave perhaps as much emphasis to the history and evolution of the institutions that they were studying as they did to their contemporary forms and problems. To them, and rightly so, the present functions and structure of these institutions could only be comprehended by a full study of the way in which they had grown up. To view an institution in isolation without reference to its past is as artificial as to consider it without regard to the wider social setting in which it has its place. Similarly, in the case of a contemporary institution, to rely exclusively on what the investigator and his colleagues can personally observe or directly elicit by means of interviewing and other modern techniques is to neglect the richness and spontaneity of existing documentary sources.

What, then, are these documents, and how can the investigator gain access to them? For convenience, they can be broadly divided into two groups. The first of these groups includes all so-called personal documents, the authors of which describe events in which they participated, or indicate their personal beliefs and attitudes. Such personal documents are essentially subjective, and are generally distinguishable without difficulty from the second group, which comprises the public or official written documentation of social activity.

2. THE PERSONAL DOCUMENT

(a) *Establishment as a Reputable Source of Information*

We are safe in saying that personal life-records, as complete as possible, constitute the *perfect* type of sociological material, and if social science has to use other materials at all it is only because of the practical difficulty of obtaining at the moment a sufficient number of such records to cover the totality of sociological problems, and of the enormous amount of work demanded for an adequate analysis of all the personal materials necessary to characterise the life of a social group.[1]

This challenging claim by Thomas and Znaniecki in presenting *The Polish Peasant* was made thirty years ago, when the personal document, although it had already been used sporadically in psychology, in anthropology and in historical research, was still a novel source of raw material for sociological analysis. It is necessary to examine briefly how far their claim has since been accepted by social scientists and substantiated by the results of research based on the use of personal documents.

First, what classes of material are to be included in the terms ' personal document ' and ' life history ' ? In its narrow sense the *personal document* is a spontaneous first-person description by an individual of his own actions, experiences and beliefs. This definition does not require that the document should be entirely unsolicited, or even that the choice of topics should be left entirely to the discretion of the subject. It does, however, exclude the interview, and particularly the structured interview, in which the influence of the interviewer on the subject's responses is too direct to be ignored.

The wide range of personal document material not excluded by this definition comprises autobiographies—whether comprehensive or limited to one particular topic—diaries and letters and other artistic and projective documents which describe the subject's experiences and his beliefs, or which give insight into his cultural background.

The term ' life-history ' in its strict sense relates to the comprehensive autobiography. Its common usage appears, however, to be fairly loose, and a ' life-history ' may prove to be almost any kind of biographical material.[2]

We must next consider how it is that the claim made by Thomas and Znaniecki on behalf of such material proved ultimately to have constituted a turning-point in the development of social science.

At the time of the publication of *The Polish Peasant* the principal

[1] THOMAS, W. I., and ZNANIECKI, F. (1919), *The Polish Peasant in Europe and America*, pp. 1832 seq.
Cf. DILTHEY, W., *Gesammelte Schriften*, 7, 199 : ' Autobiography is the highest and most instructive form in which the understanding of life comes before us.' (HODGES, H. A. (1944), *Wilhelm Dilthey: an Introduction*, p. 29.)
[2] See Chapter 4 for a description of life histories and other personal documents compiled by means of interview (pp. 167 seq.).

aim of almost all social scientists was to discover means of making their discipline comparable in objectivity with natural science. Under the influence of the behaviourist school of psychology, attention had concentrated upon overt behaviour, and there was little concern in, or even belief in the reality of, the inner subjective values and attitudes of the human beings under observation. From this viewpoint, private documents, being essentially subjective, were regarded as of restricted scientific value.[1] It is not surprising, therefore, that although the subject-matter of *The Polish Peasant* aroused considerable interest, less attention appears to have been paid at first to the question of the authors' choice of raw material.

However, the sociological use of personal documents, though out of the main stream of development, at no stage entirely disappeared. Its persistence was partly, perhaps, due to the growing acceptance by social science of the whole range of psychological concepts and methods, and not merely of those proposed by the behaviourists. Traditionally, the introspective conclusions of the individual psychologist had been the initial and classical source of knowledge on the workings of the mind. This 'dogmatic phenomenology' wilted for a time under the forceful empirical and behaviourist objection that the introspective findings of one man, however intuitively gifted, failed to encompass the tremendous diversities in human behaviour and beliefs. But it did not follow from this that the subjective world was meaningless or non-existent. Indeed, the revelation by Freud and others that it is possible to conceptualise human beliefs and actions in terms of private, and even unconscious, motives and influences showed that the subjective world is not necessarily inaccessible to scientific probing.

But although it can be accepted that under proper conditions the individual may be able to disclose his private beliefs, and even to some extent the motives which lie behind them, these separate disclosures are to the social scientist only of local and limited interest; he must still survey the range of beliefs found in the

---

[1] In illustration of this standpoint is Professor G. A. Lundberg's behaviourist comment (*Social Research*, 1st Ed., 1929, p. 207). 'Life-history documents such as autobiographies, case histories, letters, diaries, etc. must therefore be regarded as the crudest form of scientific social data. They become useful for scientific purposes only to the extent that they become expressed in objective terminology, and become subject to quantitative classification.'

body of people with whom he is concerned so that he may discern their common cultural component. The new phenomenology is thus forced, in its search for valid generalisation, to concern itself with this range, and not to linger with the unique introspections of individuals.

This very briefly is the background to the remarkable recrudescence of interest in subjective phenomena which has been taking place during recent years. In volume, perhaps the most impressive developments have been in opinion and market research,[1] but personal documents have been extensively employed, and the uses to which they can be put have also been exhaustively reviewed.

When the Committee on Appraisal of Research was set up by the U.S. Social Science Research Council, one of its first decisions was to sponsor the writing of critical appraisals of certain outstanding published works selected from the different social science disciplines. From sociological literature, the choice fell on *The Polish Peasant*, and Blumer was asked to report on the methods used by its authors. His report was published in 1939,[2] and led to keen controversy. Blumer was critical of the use of letters, autobiographies and other personal documents which the authors had used in their work, by then twenty years old; he found that, while these documents had been highly illuminating and tended to strengthen or support the plausibility of hypotheses put forward, there was no sense in which they could be claimed as proving these hypotheses. In subsequent discussions the majority of other leading social scientists agreed with his conclusions.

The Committee consequently invited four authorities, drawn from different social scientific disciplines, to develop their views on the validity and limitations of personal documents as tools of social science. The authorities were Professor G. W. Allport, psychologist; Professor Louis Gottschalk, historian; Professor Clyde Kluckhohn, anthropologist; and Professor Robert Angell, sociologist.[3]

[1] The characteristic techniques of opinion and attitude research aim at minimising the spontaneity of informants, and do not therefore fit into the present section. They are discussed in Chapter 4.
[2] BLUMER, H. (1939), *Critiques of Research in the Social Sciences. I: An Appraisal of Thomas and Znaniecki's ' The Polish Peasant '.*
[3] ALLPORT, G. W. (1942), *The Use of Personal Documents in Psychological Science.* GOTTSCHALK, L., KLUCKHOHN, C., and ANGELL, R. (1945), *The Use of Personal Documents in History, Anthropology and Sociology.*

The two volumes in which their papers are published are of absorbing interest. The authors have adopted a wider definition of personal documents than is here used, but most of the material and methodological issues that they discuss fall within the narrower definition.

While they reached the common conclusion that, subject to the necessary safeguards, the use of personal documents is not only permissible but indispensable, their systematic analyses of the attendant hazards remain of lasting value. In particular, two crucial issues have to be faced. The first is the methodological question of how far distortions enter during the process of translating private thoughts into permanent records. The second is a more practical problem—namely, how to amass and analyse the number of personal documents needed for the derivation of general laws or hypotheses.

(b) *Possibilities of Distortion by the Informant*

An initial step is to consider the various motives that may induce individuals to record details about themselves. Allport,[2] after surveying earlier classifications, distinguishes thirteen underlying motives, several of which may operate in any particular case: self-justification by special pleading; exhibitionism (e.g. Rousseau's *Confessions*); desire, sometimes compulsive, for order (e.g. Pepys' *Diaries*); literary delight, ' wherein personal experience is revealed in a delicate and pleasing way '; securing personal perspective (e.g. H. G. Wells' *Experiment in Autobiography*); relief from tension, or catharsis; monetary gain; assignment, such as satisfaction of the request to a class of students to write brief autobiographies; assisting in therapy, as for a psychiatric patient; confession as a means to absolution; scientific interest; public service and example, ' manifestly written to achieve a reform, to offer a model or a warning, to help others through their difficulties '; desire for immortality (the motive explicit in Marie Bashkirtseff's journal).[1]

It is clear that some of these motives are of interest only when it is for some reason necessary to explain why the individual decided to produce a personal document. But in the case of others the underlying motive is liable to have influenced the

[1] ALLPORT, G. W. (1942), pp. 67–75, etc.

document's content. Some authors, for example, have a deliberately propagadist intention—the desire to justify, or obversely to accentuate the wickedness of, past conduct, or the urge to call attention to some public evil to which the writer has been subjected. In such documents distortion is inevitable; even so, it may often be useless, if not meaningless, to attempt to distinguish the conscious intention from what is unconscious or compulsive.[1]

Literary dishonesty, which compels the writer to idealise his experiences to form an æsthetically structured whole, may similarly either be deliberate or result unconsciously from the tricks of memory; this motive may lead to suppression of unpalatable or undramatic sequences, to an over-emphasis of the continuity of a career or of the common themes linking different life experiences and to a displacement of the moments of climax.

It must also never be forgotten that every contributor is a prisoner of his own particular culture. It cannot be helped that his thought-processes are largely determined by the society in which he lives; indeed, this may not matter, because it may well be that it is his society that concerns us more than the man himself.[2] But we must be on the alert for polite omissions. It is understandable that the writer should find some subjects too offensive to contemplate, but it is serious if, having once admitted them to his thoughts, he refuses to commit them to paper on grounds of propriety and convention.

In this context the three main forms of personal document—namely, autobiographies, diaries and letters—may be distinguished. *Autobiographies*, which are at least edited, if not written, some time after the events recorded in them, and which are almost invariably intended for publication, can be expected to suffer from conscious stylisation, from propagandist intentions, and from the tendency to rationalise; on the other hand, the

[1] Cf. ALLPORT, G. W. (1942), pp. 131–2.
[2] 'Of the attitudes which life-histories reveal the most important for the sociologist are those of which the individual is, or was until his attention was called to them, quite unconscious. Men know themselves as they know and are known by other men about them. They are keen for what is unique and different, but the things in which one man seems like another do not interest them. The individual's opinions, for example, of which he is always keenly so conscious, are usually the least important of his personal attitudes. It is things which people take for granted which reveal at once the person and the society in which he lives. The naïve behaviour of the individual is therefore an unfailing index of the society of which he is a member.'—PARK, R. E., in GEE, W. (Ed.) (1929), *Research in the Social Sciences*, p. 42.

The Personal Document

perspective view enables the author to select and display those of his experiences and actions that subsequently proved to be significant features in his life-history.

Diaries are often the most revealing, especially when they are ' intimate journals ', both because they are seldom constricted by the fear of public showing and because they reveal with the greatest clarity what experiences and actions seemed most significant at the time of their occurrence. As a general rule, if they are ever published, they make fascinating reading. As source material, however, they can often disappoint. They may exaggerate the conflicts and dramatic phases of life while leaving gaps, often of several months, during calm and happy periods. They are liable to ' take much for granted, often failing to describe persons or situations whose existence and character the diarist merely *assumes* '.[1] Finally they are not free from pose, induced by secret or open plans for future publication.

Letters have been extensively used by historians, and particularly by biographers, though sociologists have made little use of them. Most letters have some propagandist intention, in that they are designed by the writer to convey to the recipient some impression more telling than mere facts. As with diaries, they often lack continuity and assume much of which any third party must be ignorant. It has been pointed out that both the artificialities of letter-writing and the effects of distance between writer and recipient must be explored before correspondence can be taken as a true measure of interpersonal relationships.[2]

This survey shows the extent to which personal documents by their nature admit the possibilities of distortion. How far is it possible in individual cases to detect and correct such distortion?

This is a recurrent problem, which has to be met not only in the personal document but also in any report whose accuracy depends on the truthfulness of witnesses. It must be admitted that no internal test exists which without support permits the analyst to adjust his material. The only satisfactory corrective tests are external ones, such as the degree of correspondence with

[1] Cf. ALLPORT, G. W. (1942), p. 98.
[2] ALLPORT (*ibid*, p. 109), describes an investigation made in 1931 by Kahle into letters written and received by 200 girl inmates in a protective institution. He comments on the amusing contrast which ' sometimes exists between the idyllic and sentimental letters written by a mother to an inmate daughter and the wrathful letters written to the institution after the girl's parole home demanding her immediate return to custody '.

other sources of information or with observed behaviour, and the success of predictions based on the original material.

In lieu of corroboration, we have to be content with the inherent plausibility of certain types of statement. Thus Gottschalk has been able to list five kinds of circumstances which may be allowed to predispose the investigator to believe that the informant's statement is truthful.

(1) When the truth of a statement is a matter of *indifference* to the witness, he is likely to be unbiased. (On the other hand, the fact that he is not particularly interested may have impaired his observation or his memory of the point at issue.)

(2) When a statement is *prejudicial* to the informant or his interests, it is likely to be unusually truthful. If the statement is in the nature of a confession, however, the investigator must satisfy himself that the informant is not boasting of his own depravity or cunning.

(3) When the facts at issue are so much *matters of common knowledge* that the informant would be unlikely to be mistaken or to lie about them.

This form of indirect confirmation is probably of more value in historical than in contemporaneous research. In the case of the latter, if the information is indeed common knowledge it will already be known to the investigator.

(4) When the part of the statement of primary interest to the investigator is both *incidental* and intrinsically *probable*. Gottschalk cites as one example a typical advertisement, such as ' A & B coffee may be bought at any reliable grocer's at the unusual price of fifty cents a pound ', and points out that ' all the words and inferences of the advertisement may well be doubted without corroboration except that there is a brand of coffee on the market called A & B coffee '.

(5) When the informant makes statements which are *contrary to* his expectations and anticipations as assessed by the investigator's knowledge of his thought-patterns and preconceptions.[1]

It will be recognised that if an informant sets out to mislead the investigator he may be skilful enough to exploit those conditions which are favourable to credibility.

[1] GOTTSCHALK, L. (1945), pp. 43-4.

One is also forced to admit that in very few instances will the investigator be in a position to apply these tests to written statements obtained by him, as they presuppose an impossibly extensive knowledge of the informant's backgrounds, beliefs and interests.

(c) *Distortion Introduced by the Investigator*
Many of the personal documents which have actually been used in social science have been recorded not by the informant but by the investigator. This has sometimes been necessary because the informant was illiterate, sometimes—as in anthropological studies —because of language difficulties, and very generally because the investigator has had definite preconceptions as to the form and content of the document that would suit his purpose.[1]

More sophisticated informants are sometimes given a schedule of suitable topics as a guide to compilation. The manner in which these topics shall be treated is left to the informant, but this guidance is bound to some extent to canalise his approach. The effect is to increase the documents' relevance to the concepts and hypotheses of the investigator, while their relevance to the informant's standpoint may be correspondingly reduced.

While he can justly claim to be playing a useful rôle in prompting the memories of his informants,[2] the investigator who moulds personal documents into predetermined form should recognise that by doing so he has taken the first step along the path towards the definition and isolation of his hypothesis. It is a step similar to that which his interviewer colleague takes in discarding the non-directive technique in favour of the focused interview. His informants are now beginning to be blinkered and polarised by his own interests and line of approach. Although distortions are also liable to be introduced in the course of interpreting spontaneous material, these are different in kind. The guided informant is not only led to introduce topics which may seem to him personally as of little interest, but he may even adopt attitudes and pretend to beliefs which he would not have expressed if he had been free of the investigator's influence. In contrast, there

---

[1] The decision to compile life histories by interview sometimes contains an additional ulterior motive. See, for example, Dollard's technique, discussed in Chapter 4, which was designed partly to give the investigator contact with the normal activities of his informants.
[2] Some psychoanalytical problems may be created if forgetfulness, whether conscious or unconscious, is purposeful.

is less danger of reading into unprompted documents meanings that their authors did not intend.

(d) *Personal Document Material as a Basis for Generalisation*

Objections to the validity of generalisations founded on personal document material are generally aimed at the representativeness or the size of the sample.

How can we be sure that the authors of the documents analysed are typical of the population about which it is desired to generalise?

A list has already been given of the kinds of motive believed to have prompted different people to write about their lives and thoughts. There is a more general belief that those people whose personal documents become available tend to be suffering from frustrated emotional lives.[1] If this is a fair surmise, generalisations based on personal documents clearly refer to such people, and not to the population as a whole.

One means of overcoming this objection is to solicit the co-operation of a more representative cross-section, such as a class of students. While, however, it may be possible in these circumstances to persuade a fairly high proportion of the class to prepare and hand over documents, there is little doubt that the fact that they have been solicited will affect both the matter presented and the manner of presentation. The offer of payment coupled with the promise of anonymity is also shown by experience to induce otherwise reluctant people to provide personal documents, but representativeness is equally prejudiced by this device.

Even if the problem of typicality can be solved, it still remains difficult to obtain a sample of documents large enough to permit fine analysis. As the raw material is by its nature discursive, suggesting more lines of study than it elaborates, an adequate statistical analysis would demand an exceptionally large sample.

In favourable circumstances, however, investigators have been able to obtain large samples. Thus Thomas and Znaniecki used not only the full autobiography of the Polish immigrant Vladek but also a number of fragmentary autobiographies and over seven

---

[1] E.g. MURPHY, G., MURPHY, L. B., and NEWCOMB, T. M. (1937 ed.), *Experimental Social Psychology*, p. 841.

' There are, in fact, many reasons for believing that among those who keep diaries there are an undue proportion whose contacts are unsatisfactory and whose need to " talk out " their emotional problems can be satisfied in no other way.'

hundred letters. Prizes were offered to co-operative immigrants. In addition, the authors had access to a considerable collection of third-person documents, such as Polish newspaper accounts, records of societies and social agencies and court records.[1]

Thrasher in his study *The Gang* succeeded in supplementing his main techniques by persuading a number of boy members of gangs to write their own life stories.[2]

A characteristic English example of the use of personal documents occurs in the Cambridge Evacuation Survey, in the course of which essays were collected from children evacuated to Cambridge from Tottenham and Islington schools. Each child was asked to write two essays, one on ' What I Like in Cambridge ' and the other on ' What I Miss in Cambridge '. In the report nine sets of essays were reproduced in full with psychological vignettes of their authors, aged 15-16. In addition, twelve pages are printed of unrepresentative quotations from other essays.[3]

3. DOCUMENTS OF OTHER KINDS

In England, social scientists have traditionally regarded documentary material as their principal source of data. Although some use has been made—principally by historians—of personal documents, the material used has been mainly concerned with the description of events.

But even when the search is for objective descriptions rather than subjective responses of individuals, it is still necessary to distinguish between *primary* sources, which comprise the testimony of eye-witnesses of the events described, and *secondary* sources, which are made up of hearsay or indirect evidence.

The purist will accept as evidence only primary sources. As the Webbs put it :

. . . we can say with confidence that, for our own speciality—the analytical history of the evolution of particular forms of social

[1] THOMAS, W. I., and ZNANIECKI, F. (1919).
[2] THRASHER, F. (1927), *The Gang*. No detailed account is given of the techniques used in this pioneer study, but passing reference is made to ' boys' own stories ', as well as to documents, interviews and observation. Life-history material was in any case used informally, and not as the basis for any kind of statistical generalisation.
[3] ISAACS, S.—Ed. (1941), *The Cambridge Evacuation Survey*, Ch. V. (pp. 63-87), ' What the Children Say '. Results were not entirely free from distortion. It is reported, for example (p. 64), that the person who asked the children to write the essays mentioned in illustration that they might most have missed fish and chips. In a large number of cases they wrote that they had.

organization—an actual handling of the documents themselves must form the very foundation of any reconstruction or representation of events, whether of preceding periods or of the immediate past. . . . In our view the only safe place for summaries and abstracts is the waste-paper basket.[1]

It is natural that every investigator should want to return to primary source material, so that he may select and interpret the documents that seem important and significant to him. This is, however, a counsel of perfection, which if followed would lead to the exclusion not only of all researches making use of documentary sources, but also of many of the documents which are themselves compiled from primary data. To take an absurd example, we might be forced into the position of accepting the individual census enumeration forms, while rejecting the published census tables; in this case the compilation, as far as it goes, has virtually both the reliability and the flaws of the original enumerations.

The classification which follows therefore includes documents from both primary and secondary sources. The latter will be recognised as acceptable, though intrinsically less reliable because of the added opportunities which they give for distorted selection and interpretation.

(a) *Records*

The most satisfactory type of documents are those technically known as *records*, which have been defined as ' documents intended to convey instructions regarding a transaction or to aid the memory of the persons involved in the transaction '.[2] Of records, the most credible is the instruction or command, which, being itself an instrument in the transaction, gives little scope for error.[3]

Second in order of credibility are verbatim records of proceedings in Parliament, committees, courts, societies and so on. More exact than a written record is the gramophone recording, which preserves not only what was said, but also how it was said;

---

[1] WEBB, S. and B. (1932), *Methods of Social Study*, pp. 105, 107.
[2] GOTTSCHALK, L. (1945), p. 17.
[3] A note in confirmation of a verbal command is naturally less reliable than a note which itself constitutes an order. Even so, the existence of a written note of command provides no proof either that the command was ever obeyed, or that the commander intended that it should be. In our time, a discrepancy of this sort is probably most common in Eastern countries.

an unedited sound-film should be even better. Records of most such proceedings are, however, compressed and otherwise edited. When they are agreed versions they will have become somewhat idealised, as they will be abstracts of what speakers meant to say— or even subsequently wished that they had said—rather than what actually transpired. However, the opportunities for correcting false initial transcription give them on the whole a high level of credibility.

Business and legal papers constitute a third class of records. The reliability of these is also high, partly because of their nature. A Parliamentary Act or the constitution of a society is a datum designed to define and circumscribe a certain kind of social activity. The inventory, the balance-sheet and the invoice are useful accessories to business transactions, and there are often penalties for false statements. Official statistics, although the data on which they are based may be imperfect or imperfectly relevant to the investigator's interests, are again in most instances designed to inform rather than to deceive.[1] These types of record also benefit from the fact that they are normally prepared by experts.

(b) *Reports*

Reports differ from records ' in that they are usually written after the event, they are often intended to create an impression rather than merely to aid memory, and they are less intimate '.[2]

Reports are intrinsically less reliable than records. Even the most reliable among them, such as military and diplomatic dispatches or scientific papers, contain some intention of justifying the actions and minimising the failures of the general, ambassador or scientist concerned. They often suggest a greater tidiness in the sequence of events than was actually experienced.

Newspaper reports are also frequently part propagandist in intention. Even when editorial policy is not involved, the reporter is often led to inaccuracy through being in a hurry; or, again, he may be tempted to distort his story in search of news value. On the other hand, these reports have the great virtue of contemporaneity, and are often of value not only for their content of

[1] See pp. 105 seq., later in this chapter, for a discussion on how to avoid misuse of statistical material.
[2] GOTTSCHALK, L. (1945), p. 18.

truth, but also as revealing the attitudes of a possibly influential body of opinion.[1]

Official histories have qualities and functions which place them somewhere between official statistics and communiqués. Although the official historian generally has unrestricted access to records and to individuals concerned in the events being reported on, his work is sometimes disowned by historical circles, on the grounds that his closeness to these events precludes impartiality or perspective, and that even if he wishes to be impartial he will be circumscribed by the need to respect the reputations of the living and to honour the policies of the recent past.

These factors must undoubtedly restrict the contemporary historian, but, as has been shown by at least one recent official war history,[2] it is possible to transcend such restrictions. Every epoch is interpreted differently by different generations, but in this case the fact that we are still living through a rapid evolution of social policy, and one that the war greatly accelerated, gives to the historian's interpretation a content and immediacy that histories of the more remote past can never share.

[1] The reader will be reminded of a weekly feature in the *New Statesman and Nation* which for some time gave amusing current examples of the varied versions of the same events carried by different newspapers.

A classic example is given by Professor Hearnshaw,* who quotes four different newspaper reports of two foreign envoys' visit to the House of Commons some thirty years ago to hear a speech by Mr. Lloyd George.

Evening Standard	Star	Evening News	Pall Mall Gazette
In conversation they seemed to betray only a limited acquaintance with English; but every word of Mr. Lloyd George's utterance seemed intelligible to them. Not only did they follow him with eager interest, but often with animated comment.	Krassin could follow every word of Lloyd George. His colleague does not speak or understand English; so Krassin every few minutes leaned over and whispered a translation into the other's ear.	The two did not exchange a single remark during the whole of the Premier's speech.	The Soviet envoys, especially M. Krassin, seemed somewhat restless, and appeared to take more interest in the scene than in the speech, but this I heard attributed to their difficulty in following the words of the Prime Minister.

* ROSE, W.—Ed. (1931), *Outline of Modern Knowledge*, p. 806.

See also p. 113 fn., in which mention is made of the *Content Analysis* undertaken on behalf of the Royal Commission on the Press. The purpose of this analysis was to determine whether the treatment of certain controversial issues varied markedly with the political complexion of the newspapers studied.

[2] TITMUSS, R. M. (1950), *Problems of Social Policy*.

Documents of Other Kinds

Apart from records and reports, a variety of other existing documents can be put to use. *Editorials, speeches, pamphlets, letters to the editor* and so on help to reveal the clashing climates of opinion. Works of art and other projections of individuals' personality may also be regarded as public documents. The popularity of certain songs and writings, the survival of certain parts of the inherited folklore and the disappearance of others, are phenomena of direct concern to the social scientist. Folklore is one of the principal interests of the social anthropologist, but in spite of the increasing recognition over the last half-century [1] of the theoretical importance of popular behaviour, very little practical work has been done to exploit this source of knowledge, except in the study of primitive peoples or unacculturated racial minorities. Folklore has become identified with such 'folksy' activities as folk-song and folk-dance.[2] While it is of undoubted value that ancient popular arts should be recorded and preserved, we should not be deluded into ignoring the innumerable contemporary manifestations of popular taste, whose topicality and immediacy give them a peculiar fascination.

The nearest approach to such studies in Great Britain is contained in some marginal, and perhaps dwindling, work undertaken by Mass-Observation.[3] The various surveys of reading habits, radio listening, box-office appeal and so on, although providing interesting comparative and historical material, are in most cases too mechanically quantitative, too narrow and superficial in their approach, to be of more than technical value.[4]

(c) *Availability of Documents*

In spite of the loss of documents through various causes, there must remain in existence an enormous store of unstudied material. It is difficult to conceive of any subject of interest to social scientists for which there is no primary documentation.

The problem therefore centres around the means of getting to

[1] Dating largely from W. G. Sumner's classic *Folkways*, published in 1907.
[2] See, for example, LINDGREN, E. J. (1939), 'The Collection and Analysis of Folklore', in BARTLETT, F. C. et al—Eds., *The Study of Society*, pp. 328 seq.
[3] A somewhat similar interest was displayed in the Yankee City Studies. See WARNER, W. L., and LUNT, P. S. (1941), *The Social Life of a Modern Community*, pp. 378-421. But their analysis approximates to market research, as exemplified in Great Britain by the Hulton Readership Survey.
[4] But see BERELSON, B. (1952), *Content Analysis in Communication Research*, especially pp. 92-8; and MERTON, R. K. (1949), *Social Theory and Social Structure*, pp. 199-216.

know where relevant material can be found, of getting permission to study it, and of ruthlessly confining attention to those documents whose analysis seems likely to repay the labour of doing so.

Except in totally unexplored areas, the first search is for relevant secondary documents—that is, for reports made by previous investigators in the same or related fields. On most topics this itself proves to be something of a snowball process, as a properly annotated report will lead the reader, unless he is careful, further and further from the core of his particular problem.[1] It will be found, however, that in most subjects the number of original contributions is small, and that the name of any previous author who has had something constructive to add, or has himself examined significant and original sources, tends to recur.

If this author's original material is central to the current problem it may be thought desirable, after consideration and assessment of the use to which he has put it, to return to his sources. Generally, however, the subject-matter of the inquiry will suggest its own appropriate sources. The majority of social institutions possess official records—in minute-books, annual reports, records of proceedings and so on—of their inauguration and subsequent development. These provide not only the formal—and sometimes formalised—account of the institution's history, but also indicate the names of its leading characters and the dates around which controversial issues or changes of policy occurred. The investigator will thus be led to further sources, such as biographies and newspaper reports.

Many issues of particular interest to the social scientist are centred primarily around recent events. During the present century, for example, some institutions of major importance to us today have either been created or have been so transformed that their earlier history is of minor relevance. Although, as the Webbs put it, the present may be ' a mere point between two eternities ', it is also the point which we are most capable of understanding and the point of departure for a future that we may most usefully try to influence. While, therefore, it is disastrous to lose sight of the continuity of social phenomena, of the extent to which our

---

[1] 'The difficulty lies in keeping off by-ways: mastering the leading facts thoroughly, and not attempting to study all the excrescences, often the most fascinating part of the whole.'—WEBB, B. (1926), *My Apprenticeship*, p. 286 (from MS. Diary 17 iv. 1886).

present and future are bound up with past processes and events, it is equally necessary that social scientists, as indeed some historians do, should regard history in terms of its relevance to our own problems rather than for the intrinsic fascination which it shares with literature and the liberal arts.

Those who are prepared to accept the test of relevance will be led to consider knowledge of the early origins and growth of our present institutions as a means to broad perspective. The distant eminences can be sketched in, but every detail of the hillocks in the foreground must be carefully portrayed from the contemporary viewpoint. ' If the record of the past is to be usable in the present, it is not enough to " re-create the past " ; it must be re-created in sharp orientation to the specific intricacies of present problems.'[1] If these intricacies remain as entangled as before, we can derive no benefit from the lessons of the past.

Advantage may also be taken of the fact that it is considerably easier to concentrate attention on contemporary documents. In their case the evidence of the written word can be checked by direct observation or by interrogating participants and witnesses.

The importance and value of this can be shown by a simple example. A recent colleague of mine had occasion to study the procedure by which certain hospitals admit their in-patients. In this case the documentary evidence was of three types: a set of printed letters or postcards used by the hospitals concerned to inform patients that a bed would be available for them on a specified date; booklets giving the patient information about the hospital, its regulations and other arrangements; and a scattered and not very representative or reliable selection of 'personal documents' prepared by ex-patients to describe their experiences while in hospital. There seemed to be available no standing orders to hospital staffs. Documents from secondary sources were scanty, but included a few earlier descriptive reports and recommendations for the organisation of certain aspects of admission procedure.

Now, if the corresponding documents of a hundred years ago had come into the investigator's hands, two sorts of question would probably have remained largely unanswered. The first would have been: 'How far do these formal descriptions of the machinery of admission correspond with the actual experiences of

[1] LYND, R. S. (1939), p. 133.

patients when they arrive at the hospital, and how far do they represent the pious hopes of the management committee as to what should happen?' The second question would have been: 'What is the reason for the noticeable variation in tone as between admission cards sent out by different hospitals? Do they correspond with the variations in the warmth and humanity with which the different hospitals greeted their patients on admission?'

In contrast with the virtually unsupported evidence with which the historian would have to content himself, the student of contemporary institutions can see for himself. He can post himself in the hospital and follow discreetly what actually happens when a patient arrives. He can question the hospital secretary, the records officer, the hall porter, the ward sisters, the medical staff and the patients. He can ask why things are done in a certain way. He can even join the staff. He can clothe the narrow formal framework with the substance of organisation.

At the same time he will be alert for signs of change. He will note with interest that one hospital last year re-organised its admissions procedure and that another hospital is engaged in preparing a friendlier admission card.

This is but one instance of the practical advantage that the analyst of contemporary documents has over the historian of the past. It also illustrates a case in which the rejection of existing documentary evidence would have added greatly to the labour of learning about the procedure in question and would quite clearly have retarded the formulation of hypotheses about its essential functions.

(d) *The Value of Generalisations Based on Documents*

Studies such as the one just described are often undertaken in order to generalise about present practice, and sometimes in order to make general recommendations as to how this practice or that should be revised in the interests of greater efficiency or of greater humanity. Any conclusions can only be safely extended, even in the form of general guidance, to all similar places if those closely studied were typical. In the earlier stages of an investigation, moreover, it is probable that neither information nor hypothesis will be clear enough to justify an attempt at generalisation. It is first necessary to discover the range of possible features, and only later is it reasonable to attempt to determine how often they occur.

Documents can be a very useful source of information about what has happened, and their value for this purpose is enhanced by the fact that their content is independent of the investigator's selective processes. On the other hand, they are not so satisfactory for purposes of statistical inference, as they inevitably suffer from lack of homogeneity and from somewhat erratic availability. While, therefore, documents provide one invaluable aid to the exploration and initial classification of data, they can seldom by themselves be relied on to decide whether any particular feature is of common occurrence. On occasion, the existence of documents (e.g. police-court records) may itself point to unrepresentative events.

If we accept this limitation, the question still remains as to the most convenient means of seeking out the range of possible features. Even if the documents to be studied need no longer be regarded as representative, some basis of selection remains necessary. The Webbs, in discussing this question in the light of their experience, rejected any principle of random selection. They found the mere arithmetic of sampling too laborious, and ' had usually to fall back on indirect methods of sampling according to indications afforded either by the documents of the national government or by contemporaneous literature '.[1]

It must be remembered that the Webbs were principally concerned with describing characteristic institutions—such as trade unions or local government—rather than with statistical analysis of the relative frequency of occurrence of any particular features of them; moreover, that they did in fact consciously stratify that sample by dates, if not by places. It also appears that, owing to the way in which these particular institutions had imitated each other, there was considerable uniformity between them. In some other fields of social investigation it would, however, be unsafe, or at least uneconomical, to rely on such indirect methods of sampling. It is a recognisable fact that some places, like some people, tend to get into the news, and are mentioned in every possible context. Others, whose character may be intrinsically as interesting and important, attract little attention. While, therefore, the publicised institutions should not be neglected, it is

[1] WEBB, S. and B. (1932), p. 112.

fair to assume that a number of other interesting features will be brought to light by adding to the list a selection of other institutions which are less in the public eye. If no numerical generalisations are aimed at, the selection of this latter group need not necessarily be by strict random sampling, though it will often be desirable that it should be. Moreover, there is always some prospect that the results will exceed expectations and provide a basis for generalisation, in which case initial random sampling will minimise the need for a second stage investigation.

(e) ' *Case-history* ' *material*

Before leaving the question of availability of material, some special mention must be made of the status of the ' case-history ' records collected in the course of welfare work. This brings us in turn to the problem of the relation between the twin subjects of *social studies* and *social science*. Largely for historical reasons, and because of some similarity in subject-matter, an uneasy and confused relationship continues between ' social studies ' and ' social science '. Many British Universities subscribe to this confusion by overlapping the curricula for the two subjects.

There is, to the normal way of thinking, a clear distinction between the ultimate purpose of the two. The ' training ' in *social studies* is designed to prepare students for the practical tasks of welfare work, which is concerned with the relief of social maladjustment and with helping to adapt individuals to their given, and generally immutable, environment; on the other hand, the ' discipline ' of *social science* has come to be regarded primarily as a branch of rather theoretical knowledge concerned with the dissection and analysis of social environment, and only secondarily, and in a somewhat inferior form, interested in the use of such analysis for the purposes of social adjustment.

There are two main ways in which social studies and social science overlap. First, it can be assumed that the ' *social studies* ' student and the case-worker are better able to do their work if they have access to such knowledge of the workings of society as social scientists have been able to amass. Secondly, case-workers in the course of their duties collect a large amount of descriptive material on the individuals and families that they have been called in to assist.

Social scientists have for a long time cast envious eyes on this mass of social data. 'Case-workers', writes Lundberg, 'are the great observers of first hand social behaviour, and the great collectors of social data. Unless we can utilise their material for a science of sociology, the development of that science will be unnecessarily delayed.'[1]

When, however, social scientists attempt to make use of case-history material, its inadequacies for this secondary purpose soon become apparent. Case-workers tend to record their observations in an impressionistic way; although they may pay attention to such aspects as personality, social relationships, material conditions of family life and neighbourhood conditions,[2] their descriptions are subjective, based on general personal experience, with little regulated attempt at classification within an integrated conceptual framework. Moreover, as the sample of cases covered is more or less arbitrary, with a bias towards the socially pathological, and as the case-records have little uniformity, statistical generalisation is often difficult, if not impossible.

On the other hand, perhaps because of the unstructured and individually conceived nature of case-histories, they can possess more richness and evocative quality than the schedule, however efficiently the latter may have been designed and filled in. Case-records are, in fact, often revealing documents, with virtues and weaknesses very similar to those of other kinds of document that have already been discussed.

It is arguable that they should be accepted as such, and used as the stuff from which hypotheses can be derived but not tested. Social scientists themselves are increasingly depending on their own rigorously conducted individual case-studies as the source for fruitful hypotheses. But it seems particularly tantalising that the large and increasing body of case-workers, with experience of various forms of social pathology, with intimate knowledge of the families among whom they work and with acquired skill in interviewing and observing, should remain independent and unable to contribute more directly to social research.

Not only does this represent a serious loss of potential assistance to social science, but also it deprives case-workers of the guidance which would help them to locate their practical work more clearly

[1] LUNDBERG, G. A. (1929), p. 187.
[2] BROWN, S. C. (1939), in BARTLETT, F. C. et al.—Eds., *The Study of Society*, p. 387.

within its social context.[1] Lundberg noted that 'many of the abler social workers are today oppressed with a sense of the futility of working on an endless series of cases without some attempt to generalise the cases and their treatment so that in time scientific laws and principles of treatment might be formulated'.[2] It is clearly a matter of general concern that this gap between theory and practice should be bridged.

There are, and have for long been, various means available for doing so. Booth, for example, enlisted the help of school attendance officers for his survey of poverty in East London, making use of their—at that date—unparalleled knowledge of the homes and families in the districts entrusted to them. He and his colleagues extracted and codified this knowledge by prolonged questioning of the welfare workers; this method, though inferior to a direct survey, clearly gave results of considerable value.[3] A more recent example is given by the Maternity Survey,[4] a particularly well-conducted investigation, in which the field-work, although undertaken *ad hoc*, was carried out by Health Visitors; in this case initial familiarity with the district and its inhabitants must have considerably simplified their task.

Again, probably the majority of 'social studies' students undertake some survey work during their course. While this can be a good introduction to the methods of social science, and has in certain instances led to valuable results, it also has its dangers. The existence of the techniques of social investigation, and particularly of the mass interview and questionnaire technique, is common knowledge, but their practical and theoretical implications and the safeguards that their use entails too often are either not recognised or are neglected. In the absence of experienced guidance many such surveys are undertaken—and even printed—

[1] One danger that has to be recognised is that case-workers will, through inexperience, be even more liable than the professional social scientist to write causal hypotheses into their case-records. Thus, for example, if the idea is put about that delinquency is associated with broken homes, we can expect records on delinquency cases to make the most of the 'broken home' factor.
That this is not an imaginary danger is suggested by experience of the fashion element in medical diagnosis, of which medical and demographic research workers are well aware.
[2] LUNDBERG, G. A. (1929), p. 187.
[3] BOOTH, C. (1889-1903), *Life and Labour of the People of London*, 17 vols. Altogether a million London families were included in the Survey.
[4] *Maternity in Great Britain* (1948). A survey directed by Dr. J. W. B. Douglas on behalf of the Population Investigation Committee and the Royal College of Obstetricians and Gynæcologists.

in such a manner as neither to add to the corpus of social knowledge nor to initiate the students taking part into the proper methods of social science. There is normally no assurance that the benefit to be derived from such inquiries has compensated for the inconvenience, if not pain, suffered by those subjected to unskilled and sometimes unsympathetic questioning.

It is hoped that the standard and value of these training surveys will progressively improve. Meanwhile, even more important are the prospects of a convergence of social science and social studies, which is likely to take place progressively as the experimental rôle of social science becomes better recognised. If we accept the thesis that observation and fact-eliciting cannot take place without permanently influencing those who are being studied, and that the pursuit of knowledge is a residual function of action rather than a worth-while activity in its own right, the implications of this viewpoint must be faced, and social science's dual objective—research and therapy—can be recognised. If social science is to become a form of doing, instead of a form of contemplation, the traditional distinction between 'social science' and 'social studies' will disappear, to be replaced by a mild difference in approach between those whose principal interest is in immediate amelioration and those to whom the principal value of an experiment is in the lessons to be derived from it. But when this synthesis has occurred, neither subject will be like the thing we know.

4. PROBLEMS OF AUTHENTICATION

(a) *Authenticity and Meaning*

Several stages are often necessary in the interpretation and analysis of documents which have come into the hands of the investigator.

The first step is to ensure that these documents are authentic. This involves the attempt to determine both whether the document is what it purports to be and whether its author was as well-placed as he claimed to describe the facts contained in it. Some circumstances which improve the *plausibility* of informants' statements have already been outlined (p. 88).

Tests for authenticity are more important in the case of historical documents than in the case of contemporary documents, if only because it is easier to falsify the former. Fresh forgeries of both types are undoubtedly, however, still fabricated.

Authenticity can sometimes be discounted by external evidence, such as a preponderance of reports that conflict with the document in question. The production of a document which directly benefits its possessor—either financially or politically—also gives ground for question.[1] There are also internal tests, such as of the handwriting, writing materials, or anachronisms as to the events described, or the use of uncharacteristic language and concepts. It may also be necessary to discover how the document came to be found.

As Gottschalk [2] points out, garbled and edited versions of a document can sometimes cause more trouble than wholly forged documents. Interpretation or compression by an unknown intermediary can destroy the value of any document. This is perhaps why the Webbs, as already mentioned, condemned the use of any but primary documents. ' The value of extracts from documents ', they wrote, ' depends, it is obvious, on the accuracy, intelligence, and exact purpose of the extractor. When these factors are unknown, quotations from documents . . . are worthless for the main purpose of research, that is, the discovery, *in their right proportion*, of all the facts about the constitution and activities of a particular type of organisation.' [3] This passage suggests that what they feared was the *unknown*, and probably inexpert, intermediary editor.

The next problem is to determine the meaning which the author of any document intended to convey. This problem is a serious one for historians, who have to be on the alert for words whose meaning has changed in the passage of time, and for anthropologists, who have to explain their findings to their fellow-countrymen and who are thus forced to attempt the impossible task of translating primitive concepts into Western language. But even in our own time and our own country, faults in interpretation can occur if insufficient attention is paid to the differences in meaning attached by different social groups to the same word, or

---

[1] ALLPORT, G. W. (1942), mentions (p. 130) another possible motive for hoaxing : ' The story is told that school boys delighted in fabricating lurid sexual autobiographies for Krafft-Ebing who innocently published them in his books.'
[2] GOTTSCHALK, L. (1945), pp. 30 seq.
[3] WEBB, S. and B. (1932), p. 107 (their italics).

to cultural variations in emphasis. The 'perfectly marvellous' of one social set may correspond with the 'not bad' of another set. Such differences are subtle and not easily codified. Although some straightforward safeguards can be insisted upon, the power to interpret meanings is a highly individual gift, involving the investigator's capacity to project himself into the circumstances of the document's author.

(b) *The Interpretation of Statistics*

Apart from the need to discern the meaning which the author of the document intended to convey, special attention must be paid to more formal and precise documents or statements. This is most clearly to be recognised in the interpretation of statistics, when, owing to variations in definitions, two sets of figures may not be comparable.

A brilliant outline on this subject has been given by Professor Bowley, who writes:

> It is never safe to take published statistics at their face value, without knowing their meaning and limitations, and it is always necessary to criticise arguments that are based on them, unless one is able to trust implicitly the knowledge and good faith of the persons bringing them forward. It is extremely easy to falsify the lessons which numerical statements should teach. The actual use and appreciation of statistics are ultimately a matter of intelligence, special knowledge and common sense; but the following nine rules suggest the lines of study and criticism.[1]

The nine rules which he lays down may be summarised as follows:

> 1. Find the exact definition of the units which go to make the total—e.g. What is a soldier? What one pound's worth of exports? What a registered birth? What a member of the population, a case of fever, a bushel of wheat?... The apparent meaning of a total is seldom its real meaning, but generally results from an artificial definition, necessitated by the process of collection.... Generally expert knowledge is needed; sometimes the report on the statistics contains sufficient explanation and definition; sometimes the whole can

[1] BOWLEY, A. L. (6th. Ed., 1945), *An Elementary Manual of Statistics*, pp. 75–81.

be worked out from a study of the blank forms of inquiry (with instructions) on which the original data are obtained.

2. Consider how far the persons or things grouped together in a total or sub-total are similar; in other words, how far the group is homogeneous.

Whether the group or sub-group is sufficiently homogeneous depends entirely on the purpose for which the figures are used. . . . But we must never assume either homogeneity or similarity of division without knowledge.

3. Having defined and analysed the totals, the next question is, What is the relation of the quantity they measure to the quantity as to which we want knowledge? . . .

The statistical totals and averages are at best indices, not actual measurements, of the more subtle and often incommensurable quantity or quality, which is essentially the object of the investigation. In order that indices may be useful they must at least move up and down with the quantity they represent, as the thermometer moves with heat and the barometer with pressure, and they should further make great or small oscillations with great or small movements; but many of them have less relation to the complete phenomena than the thermometer has to sensation of heat (which depends also on moisture and physiological conditions), and may be as remotely connected as the fall of the index of a barometer with the fall of rain.

If experience shows that the indices are sensitive and trustworthy, they may be used to bridge over the gap between one more complete measurement and the next.[1]

4. Before trusting or even reading a statistical account, it is well to sit down and think quietly what statistics ought to have been collected, if possible, for the purpose in hand, and what sources of information exist, or should exist. . . .

We can thus decide as to whether the information is sufficient

---

[1] This need to study certain facts indirectly by the use of indices may be compared with the concept of intervening variables, first formulated by Durkheim, ' It is necessary . . . to substitute for the internal fact which escapes us an external fact that symbolises it, and to study the former through the latter.' See MERTON, R. K. (1945), ' Sociological Theory ', *Am. Journ. Soc.*, **50**, 467. One of Durkheim's treatments of the subject is in *The Rules of Sociological Method*, Chapter 2, in which the author, making a virtue of a common necessity, declares a preference for the indirect index, by reason of its greater constancy and objectivity.

for solving any assigned problem; in too many cases we find that it is not.

Further, if there is any suspicion of bias, of the intention to support any preconceived view, the criticism of method must be particularly rigid, and the maximum possible effect of the unconsidered factors must be allowed for.

5. When we have to deal with averages, rates and percentages, we must carry our second rule of criticism farther. Not only must we consider whether the numerators and denominators are homogeneous in themselves, but whether the terms of the denominator have a reasonable relation to those of the numerator.

Should the production of coal per head be reckoned with respect to the population of a nation, or to those engaged in the coal trade, or only to the coal-hewers? The general answer is that the denominator should be limited to those who have a direct relation to the numerator; the legitimate birth-rate (e.g.) should be in relation to married couples with some restriction of age.

6. When two quantities are compared we must consider whether they are strictly comparable, and for this purpose most of the foregoing rules are necessary. Comparisons are made between two similar measurements at different dates (e.g. population, death-rate, average wage), or between two similar measurements relating to different places (e.g. trade, consumption of meat or wheat per head, amount of taxation per head). We must test whether the two measurements are made on the same basis, so as to be indices of the same kind of phenomena considered, so as to cover the same ground and suffer from similar ' error of bias '. Having ascertained this, and so used rules 1 and 3, we then apply rules 2, 4 and 5 if necessary.

By such means we shall readily realise the difficulty of minute comparisons over long periods, during which relations have continually changed, and the extreme roughness of comparisons between such measurements as the indices of prosperity of two nations. Accurate comparisons can only be made between closely similar things or over quite short periods.

7. Closely connected with the last is the measurement of accuracy. . . . In all statistics we must decide whether the

data and methods will yield results accurate enough for the arguments based on them. . . . The less the groups satisfy the stringent conditions of the first six rules laid down, the greater must be the margin allowed for error. Where possible, the greatest possible error arising from imperfection of data or processes should be worked out.

8. We must not depend on figures relating to single days, months or years, or on comparisons relating to short isolated periods.

Every measurement must be viewed in the light given by a series of similar measurements stretching back over a long period; otherwise temporary fluctuations will be taken for permanent changes, as if a cold summer were regarded as proving a change in climate.

Where a sufficient record cannot be obtained, judgment must be suspended.

9. Having determined as far as possible the exact purport and limitations of the statistics, consider (without reference to the printed report) to what conclusions they lead, or whether they are so imperfect that no conclusions can be reached without further investigation. There is often a great gap between the statistical table and the non-statistical conclusions that are fathered on to it, especially if the statistics were obtained in order to support a preconceived theory. Statistical work properly ends with such a dull, matter-of-fact report as is customary in the publications of the British Government. As a separate process such results are to be taken in conjunction with non-statistical knowledge. Inferences are suggested and tested by the reported facts, and a severely critical and logical analysis is necessary before the whole investigation leads on to some reasoned action.

5. INTERPRETATION

Before closing the subject of documents, it is necessary to pay particular note to the question of how far documentary evidence, even when properly selected and checked for authenticity, can be used as proof. In other words, is there a fully reliable procedure for interpretation? This is a point of particular importance, not only because a large part of social evidence is still entirely derived at second hand from documentary sources, but also because there are reasons for supposing that the user of documents, being remote from the objects of his study, is uniquely tempted to stretch his material to suit his imaginative thesis and has unique opportunities for doing so.

This is not the place to recount the historians' battles, which culminated in the nineteenth century. Briefly, these were fought out between those who felt that their duty lay in the unprejudiced and objective presentation of bygone events, as they actually happened, and those who conceived their task to be that of interpreting past ages and of explaining their significance to contemporary readers even at the risk of substituting fiction for fact. Correspondingly, the *objective* school claimed to be studying history for its own sake, for the sake of obtaining true information about another time and place; they accused their opponents either of being absorbed in some romantic dream, as of the Middle Ages, or of distorting the lessons of the past in the pursuit of some practical aim or in the interests of some political platform.[1]

The struggle was bitter, and ended ostensibly in victory for the objective ' scientific ' school. Guided by some all-embracing frame, such as that provided by evolution, the victors foresaw their task as the collection and authentication of an ever greater mass of evidence, and discovered—almost too late—that they were driving themselves towards the narrowest forms of monographic specialisation.

The later ' scientific ' historians, such as Buckle in England and Taine in France, regarded their viewpoint as consistent with Auguste Comte's historical positivism. In the second half of the nineteenth century, belief in the universality of the methods of natural science was perhaps at its peak. But this had not been Comte's belief. He had always held the sciences to be hierarchical, with sociology near the summit; each new science brought in new features and demanded new methods. The characteristic method of sociology was to him the method of history, and the feature which distinguished the transition from biology to sociology was the transformation of the common idea of development into the crowning concept of history. There was nothing in this to authorise the ambitious attempts made by his followers

[1] This standpoint, which has had some adherents among historians since the time of Thucydides, was branded by Croce as ' practicistical ', because it led to a form of rhetoric designed not so much to explain the past or present as to determine the course of the future.

to adopt uncritically the methods of natural science. Comte would possibly have felt more sympathy with the German historians such as Droysen and, perhaps even more, Dilthey. To them, the aim—which they regarded as no less scientific than Buckle's statistical inferences and Taine's syllogisms—was to achieve and to transmit an 'understanding' of the motives and activities of other generations.

Moreover, they recognised that historical material, though it could lead the student towards such an understanding, could by itself never provide full insight. Already in the mid-nineteenth century, Droysen was calling for the 'pluralism of methods', which—as this book describes—is only today becoming available to the social scientist.[1]

Furthermore, experience and controversy have today convinced all but a lagging minority of historians that the ideal of objectivity, however possible for the natural scientist, is beyond the power of any historian to attain. This does not mean that all facts are suspect. As Carr points out:

> Some facts undoubtedly exist, the exact date and place of William the Conqueror's landing in England, the number and fire-power of the ships that fought at Trafalgar or at Jutland, the statistics of population or industry or trade for a given country at a given period. These things have the same relation to history as bricks or steel or concrete have to architecture. They are facts which need to be established, tested and verified; the historian must not be caught out using shoddy material. But they are not in themselves 'facts of history'. It is only the decision of the historian to use them, the conviction of the historian that they are significant for his purpose, which makes them into the 'facts of history'. . . . His choice and arrangement of these facts, and the juxtapositions of them which indicate his view of cause and effect, must be dictated by presuppositions; and these presuppositions, whether he is conscious of them or not, will be closely related to the conclusion which he is seeking to establish. . . . History is therefore a process of interaction between the historian and the past of which he is writing. The facts help to mould the mind of the historian. But the mind of the historian also, and just as essentially, helps to mould the facts. History is a dialogue between past and present, not between dead past and living present, but between living present and a past which the historian makes live again by establishing its continuity with the present.[2]

[1] See CASSIRIR, E. (1950), *The Problem of Knowledge*, especially pp. 243-247, and 257.   [2] CARR, E. H. (1951), *The New Society*, pp. 9-10.

Interpretation

If we accept this, as I think we must, all that remains is to cast about for the source of the presuppositions that any historian has written into his facts. And here again we must conclude that what he has done has been to give substance to his aims. Curiosity and a sense of scholarship will have made their contributions, but above these may be traced the shadowy form of real and immediate problems.

An admission that the relevance of problems may have to be the basis of our selection is inconsistent with the abstract ideal of knowledge for its own sake. We must also concede that the social scientist who wishes to apply his science is committed to the study of problems on the practical outcome of which he is forced by circumstances to take sides. The alternative is to remain pure To the pure intellectual, as to the crossword solver, any problem is potentially as important (i.e. interesting) as any other; its relevance is irrelevant. The pure seeker after objectivity aims, even more stringently, to remain detached and non-committed. The pure social scientist is thus not even free to pick his problems according to their interest, but is forced into a dysgenic selection of the immaterial and the futile, because only then can he be assured of his own objectivity.

Meanwhile, how can those who wish to contribute to social adjustment exploit the documentary material with which we are at present concerned? How can they overcome their prejudices or absorb them into a valid scientific method?

The classical method, attributed to Socrates, is for the scientist to search his mind until he has exposed his own biases; the argument is that even if he cannot overcome them, at least he will be able to make some allowance for them.[1] Clearly any scientist should be prepared conscientiously to search his soul, and he should be required to do so and to publish the results. But the psychologically naïve belief that it is possible by introspection to unearth every secret interest and prejudice is no longer tenable.

[1] 'It has been recognised that social scientists who pretend to be able to ascertain values and prescribe social action out of pure fact-finding are just as much on the wrong track as social scientists who are so afraid of responsibility in the world of action that they hide behind an eternally insatiable need for collecting far more detailed knowledge before practical action can be wisely planned. . . . To make their position unmistakable, scientists should distinguish clearly between the factual relations they can establish and the value of judgments they will have to assume.'—MYRDAL, A. (1945), *Nation and Family*, p. 109.

The most persistent, 'obvious' and 'common-sense' of the individual's presuppositions may well be just those which are restricting his understanding, limiting the range of his hypotheses and preventing him from realising the significance of many of the facts available to him. If his access to the problem is by way of documents alone, these limitations are particularly likely to detract from the richness of his results.

Even within the circle of admissible ideas, the user of documents has ample scope for distortion. As long as his conclusions are based on his impressions, he is asking us to take a lot on trust. This leads to the argument that factual information is less slippery if some at least of it can be expressed in precise, preferably numerical, terms. Today we can hardly conceive of an account of the growth of a country or an industry which neglected available statistics of population or output.

A more recent development is the direct use of quantitative methods on documents themselves. This technique is known as *content analysis*, and has a brief and interesting history.[1]

A useful rule-of-thumb method of finding out how the author of a book has treated a subject is to look at the index. If the indexer has been in sympathy with the author, the number of references to a particular subject gives some indication of the importance attached to it by the author. Somewhat similarly, a publicity man's efficiency might be judged by the number of inches of free advertising copy that he has succeeded in placing.

This common-sense technique can clearly be made more precise, and in 1930 the first full analysis along these lines was published in New York. The topic happened to be the amount of space devoted to foreign news in American morning newspapers. Three years later the value of the technique was enhanced and confirmed in Hornell Hart's analysis of trends in the space devoted to various subjects in American periodicals and books; this report was published as part of the famous symposium, *Recent Social Trends in the United States*.[2]

The next important step was the adaptation in 1937 by Lasswell of the technique of content analysis for the systematic study of recorded psychoanalytical interviews. Subjects referred to in

[1] A book devoted to a description of the techniques and the achievements of content analysis, recently prepared by one of the most experienced practitioners in this field, has already been mentioned. See BERELSON, B. (1952).
[2] Vol. I (1933), pp. 382-442.

these interviews were systematically classified, and it was subsequently found that much the same system of categories could be used in a variety of other contexts. With the outbreak of war in Europe, Lasswell undertook the direction of an officially sponsored World Attention Survey, based on the content analysis of foreign newspapers. Apart from certain immediate functions, such as that of deflating the ego of Americans who assumed that British and German newspapers were full of references to the United States, this was soon found to provide an intelligence weapon of some importance. Analysis showed, for example, that in the last three months before the signing of the German-Soviet agreement of August 1939, significant changes were taking place in the number of references to Germany and the Soviet Union made in the newspapers of the other country.

> The amount of attention paid to Germany in the influential Russian newspaper *Pravda* remained steady during the summer. Not so the references to Russian in the *Volkischer Beobachter*. Here we see less and less attention paid to the Soviet Union, formerly a target of bitter hostility. This indicated that Germany was clearing the path for a sudden change in diplomatic orientation, as was learned when the pact was announced.[1]

An elaborate code of analysis, which retained traces of psychoanalytical concepts, was worked out and standardised. Regular tests were made on coders to make sure that their results remained comparable. Different indices of prominence were adopted: one was based on appearance in headlines, another on inches of space.

Subsequently, Leites and Pool used a similar technique to study changes in Comintern policy, and throughout the war students of Lasswell and Leites undertook analyses of United States foreign language press on behalf of the United States Department of Justice. Internal propaganda, the speeches of politicians, the content of radio and orchestral programmes, films, popular magazines and so on have come under similar scrutiny. Content analysis was used on the initial interviewing programme at the

[1] LASSWELL, H. (1941), 'The World Attention Survey', *Public Opinion Quarterly*, No. 3, 1941, reprinted in *The Analysis of Political Behaviour* (1948), pp. 296–303. Probably the most elaborate project in this field undertaken outside the United States is the analysis of the content of English newspapers, undertaken on behalf of the Royal Commission on the Press, Cmd. 7700 (1949), pp. 238–359.

I

Hawthorne works, and was included in the preparatory technique for the ' focused interviews ' undertaken by Merton and Kendall.[1]

Within the frame of reference adopted by the investigator, and accepted by his assistants, a high level of regularity of results has been confirmed in practice, particularly in the analysis of explicit symbols, such as single words or proper names. Even when the nature of material makes it impossible to undertake content analysis, advantage can still be taken of one intrinsic feature of documentary material. This is the fact that the same document can be scrutinised and assessed by a number of independent judges.

Personal documents, for example, while possessing the great virtue of spontaneity, are particularly hard to interpret systematically, for exactly the same reason. The fact that, in the limiting case, each contributor has chosen his own topics, and has expressed himself on these topics in his own words without guidance, implies a sacrifice of uniformity among documents, whether in subject-matter, in emphasis or in structure. Each contributor will have carried out his task in his own way and in defence of his own system of values, and this will be reflected in marked variations in the treatment of subjects.

But although such material will be difficult to handle, there is some compensation in the fact that the process of interpretation can be made entirely independent of the process of compilation.

The value of this asset has been tested on several occasions. Thus, Stouffer arranged for four judges to rate 238 topical autobiographies in terms of their authors' attitude towards prohibition, and found a very high level of agreement among the four judges.[2] Similar agreement was displayed by three judges who studied documents submitted by 600 college students, for the purpose of assessing the extent to which the parents of these students had influenced their childhood social development.[3]

It can well be imagined, however, that the task of reading through such a large number of autobiographies or other docu-

[1] See pp. 160–7. The method of content analysis used by Merton and Kendall is described in MERTON, R. K. (1949), *Social Theory and Social Structure*, pp. 268 seq.

[2] STOUFFER, S. A. Unpublished report, quoted by ALLPORT, G. W. (1942), p. 24.

[3] CAVAN, R. S., HAUSER, P. M., and STOUFFER, S. A. (1930), ' Note on the Statistical Treatment of Life History Material ', *Social Forces*, 9, 200–3 (quoted *ibid*, p. 25).

Interpretation

ments in order to assess the prevalence of some particular attitude in each author, is a time-consuming, if not tedious, business. Even if the judges are found to agree at the end of it all, the question remains whether the labour involved can be justified by the results obtained.

In his study of attitudes towards prohibition, mentioned above, Stouffer compared his case-history ratings with those obtained by an orthodox form of attitude measurement. In the college-student material the results of document analysis were compared with responses to a simple questionnaire. In these cases the two sets of results showed such close agreement that it seemed open to question whether the laborious analysis of personal documents had justified itself.

This similarity in results is understandable. Provided that the circumstances of collection of the two sets of data are equally favourable, the questionnaire may be regarded as little more than an elaborated guide to the topics that the investigator wishes his informant to cover. If the investigator has clearly in his mind the hypothesis that he wishes to test, and the material that he needs in order to test it, he has little to gain by using the more oblique approach of documentary analysis. By the time that he has formulated his problem as definitely and rigidly as this implies, the emphasis should properly be on the collection of easily handled representative material, suitable for quantitative analysis. Sometimes this alternative material is unobtainable, and then the simplifications and preconceptions inherent in documentary analysis have to be accepted. When he is able to pass on to more active techniques, it is entirely appropriate that the investigator should prepare himself for the next stage by reading all that he can get hold of, but it would still be wrong for him to become finally immersed in them.

The rich human material that so many documents contain is a fertile source of ideas. Spontaneous personal documents,[1]

[1] 'Life-histories, where it is possible to secure them, are almost always interesting, because they nearly always illuminate some aspect of social and moral life which we may have known hitherto only indirectly, through the medium of statistics or formal statements. In the one case we are like a man in the dark looking at the outside of the house and trying to guess what is going on within. In the other, we are like a man who opens the door and walks in, and has visible before him what previously he had merely guessed at.'—PARK, R. E. (1929), p. 47.

Sometimes, however, men find a corresponding satisfaction in being able to sense things that are undiscernible to untutored eyes. Cassirir mentions newspaper reports, committee minutes, business or official files—all these provide an invaluable preliminary to direct observation and to participation in social processes. They also supplement observation and participation in retrospect, by broadening the base of experience. But by themselves they tell an incomplete story, and it is clearly unwise to stretch their adoption into contexts in which they can offer neither economy nor satisfaction.

' a characteristic and remarkable passage in Niebuhr [the great nineteenth-century German historian] which is graphically expressive of this newly established ideal of knowledge. He likened the historian to a man in a dark room, whose eyes have gradually become so accustomed to the absence of light as to perceive objects that one who had just entered could not see and would even assert to be invisible. I have no doubt [continues Cassirir] that when Niebuhr wrote these lines he was thinking of Plato's allegory of the cave, though he gave it an exactly opposite turn. Plato was convinced that one who had left his cave and seen the light of day, who was no longer restricted to the sight of mere shadows but could attain to real knowledge, geometry, the knowledge of the eternal, would return only unwillingly and think it not worth while to discuss with his fellows the differences and meanings of the shadows.'—CASSIRIR, E. (1950), p. 229.

Our problem as seekers after science is to find grounds for believing a man who claims to have seen what is invisible to other men. Lord Acton once said, ' A historian has to be treated as a witness, and not believed unless his sincerity is established. The maxim that a man must be presumed innocent until his guilt is proved, is not made for him.'

Chapter 3

OBSERVATION

> The study of actual normal behaviour is the *greatest unmapped field of sociology* in all countries.—TOM HARRISSON

> The primary research instrument would seem to be the observing human intelligence trying to make sense out of the experience. . . . Perhaps it does not compare well with more objective-seeming instruments, such as a previously prepared set of questions, but as to this question the reader can judge for himself.—JOHN DOLLARD.

> Some social scientists will do any mad thing rather than study men at firsthand in their natural surroundings.—GEORGE C. HOMANS.

> One might safely assert that the reason so many people feel certain about the meaning of observation is that they know so little about it, just as in the pre-scientific ages so many knew what 'mass' and 'space' meant, simply because they knew so little about such concepts.—R. W. CHURCHMAN.

1. THE IMPORTANCE OF FIRST-HAND OBSERVATION

ALL modern science is rooted in observation and, as every scientist knows, observations at first hand are the most satisfactory. In practice, however, our knowledge of the world is built up principally of other people's observations, and not of our own. It is inevitable that we should admit second-hand knowledge, but we must recognise that in doing so we accept not only other investigators' careful observations, but also a whole mass of careless and casual popular impressions and legends whose reliability we have generally no means of checking.

It is clearly absurd to design an elaborate investigation on a groundwork of previous knowledge and ideas derived from such arbitrary sources. And yet far too often this is what in fact occurs. A detailed plan of campaign is worked out on a foundation almost purely of hearsay evidence.

First-hand preliminary observations are often dispensed with on grounds of lack of time, or through the mistaken belief that all the main features of the point at issue are already known. This is all very well if routine study only is contemplated, but it can be disastrous if a new area of knowledge is to be explored. It is not too much to say that the great majority of valuable original investigations, even those which end up in a strictly quantitative form, have sprung from careful initial first-hand observations.

The Webbs made it one of the principles of their inquiries to start with direct and unprejudiced observation:

> An indispensable part of the study of any social institution, wherever this can be obtained, is deliberate and sustained personal observation of its actual operation. Though the social institution itself may be, in its wholeness, as invisible and intangible as the biologist's species, yet the units, items, parts or particular manifestations of the institution will often be open, under one excuse or another, to close and prolonged inspection, from which the investigator may learn a lot. He clarifies his ideas, which gain in precision and discrimination. He revises his provisional classifications, and tests his tentative hypotheses. What is even more important, the student silently watching a town council or a trade union committee at work, or looking on at a conference of politicians and educationists, picks up hints that help him to new hypotheses, to be, in their turn, tried on other manifestations of his subject-matter.[1]

This process of initial observation described by the Webbs is for the social sciences what corresponds with the 'natural history' stage in the biological sciences. Though today the emphasis among biologists may be on controlled experiments in biochemistry and biophysics, it is not forgotten that the first stage in mastering the subject of living organisms was the painstaking observation and classification of living things, and that this absorbed generations of scientific work. As has been shown in a previous chapter, there have been many attempts to classify the subject-matter of the social sciences, but much of this classification cannot be applied empirically, because the categories are imprecise or are unrelated to the things that can be observed or to the purposes of the investigation.[2] In the same way, too many hypotheses are based on ideal and logically tidy considerations, instead of suggesting themselves to the investigator through his familiarity with actual phenomena. Direct personal knowledge is our only means of ensuring that our theories are grounded on empirical fact.

[1] WEBB, S. and B. (1932), *Methods of Social Study*, p. 158.
[2] Remember that whether objects or events are sufficiently homogeneous to be grouped together into one class depends entirely on the purpose for which the classification has been made.

2. PRINCIPAL DIFFICULTIES IN OBSERVATION

It is necessary to recognise frankly the obstacles to impartial observation. Probably the first social scientist explicitly to list and discuss these intrinsic difficulties was Herbert Spencer, who in one of his earlier books [1] devoted four chapters to the subject.

Spencer pointed out, for example, the procedural complications that result from the fact that many social phenomena, unlike the bulk of natural phenomena, are not directly perceptible, but often have to be established by putting together many details which are naturally dispersed in space and time. In consequence, a scientist trained in simpler subjects may actually have to unlearn part of his previous training before being able to deal successfully with this most-involved class of facts.

Spencer next commented on the barriers to correct observation and objective inference which result from the emotional entanglement of the social investigator in the subject of his study.

> For correct observation and correct drawing of inferences, [he writes] there needs the calmness that is ready to recognise or to infer one truth as readily as another. But it is next to impossible thus to deal with the truths of Sociology. In the search for them, each is moved by feelings, more or less strong, which make him eager to find this evidence, oblivious of that which is at variance with it, reluctant to draw any conclusion but that already drawn.[2]

He was also very conscious of the particular relationship between the sociological observer and the objects and events being observed. Characteristically, he likened this relationship to that existing between a single cell and a living body of which it formed a part.

> To cut himself off in thought from all his relationships of race, and country, and citizenship—to get rid of all those interests, prejudices, likings, superstitions, generated in him by the life of his own society and his own time—to look on all the changes societies have undergone and are undergoing, without reference to nationality, or creed, or personal welfare; is what the average man cannot do at all, and what the exceptional man can do very imperfectly.[3]

Social scientists have had nearly a century of practical experience to enable them to overcome difficulties such as these. In the event,

---

[1] SPENCER, H. (1873), *The Study of Sociology*, Chapters IV–VII.
[2] *ibid.*, p. 73. A remarkable fact about this quotation is that Spencer explicitly warns his readers against an error which many of his critics accused him of committing in his own scientific work.   [3] *ibid.*, p. 74.

the tendency has been to become more conscious of their implications, in all sciences, and not merely in social science, rather than to discover adequate means of overcoming them.

Of particular importance in this context is the fact of the interrelatedness of the observer and the situation being observed. Spencer stressed the influence of this on the 'objectivity' of the observer; perhaps because first-hand observation of social situations was not by then an established technique, he failed to mention a second and corresponding effect on the behaviour of those being observed. Careful and persistent examination of these two effects has led us to transform our approach not only to social science, but even to knowledge of all kinds.

We thus have to consider three main causes of distorted observation. These are: those due to the inadequacies of our sense-organs; those due to the interdependence of observation and inference; and those, constituting an especially acute problem in the social sciences, due to the impossibility of observing human beings without influencing their actions and being influenced by them.

(a) *Inadequacies of our Sense-organs*

Traditionally we tend to regard our sense-organs as reliable, though perhaps not as powerful as we would like them to be. 'If one's eyes are open, and one looks in a certain quarter, one cannot help seeing.' Although we are quite willing to accept the limitations in range and clarity of the 'naked eye', we are ready to accept that 'seeing is believing', at least as firmly as that 'the camera cannot lie'.

It is not at all difficult to show that this belief is entirely unjustified, and that in fact our sense-organs operate in a highly variable, erratic and selective manner.

Psychologists have conducted many experiments which have shown that what any man perceives on a particular occasion depends greatly on his state of mind and body at the time—his freshness, comfort, freedom from interruption, degree of confidence and so on.[1] Under favourable conditions he will be much more receptive to outside impressions than if he is, for example, tired or worried.

[1] For a valuable summary, see BLACKBURN, J. (1945), *Psychology and the Social Pattern*, pp. 15-28.

Apart from these subjective factors, certain things appear naturally to be more readily noticed than others, or tend to be perceived in a certain way. Common-sense and normal experience tell us that objects that are large or definite in form, or sounds which are repetitive, tend to catch our attention; less obvious are those structural features of objects which, as the Gestalt psychologists have shown, encourage us to perceive (i.e. interpret) them in certain ways.

Sense-organs are also inherently bad machines for the making of comparisons. Sometimes, as in the case of the pupil of the eye, which contracts in bright light, the organs are as though designed expressly to minimise contrasts. But other comparisons, such as between two different temperatures, are not directly derivable from our senses, whose natural way of functioning is to perceive subjective states (e.g. bodily comfort) on the two occasions; the analytical process of disentangling the temperature factor from the total sensation is sophisticated and artificial. As is well known, such 'observations' of temperature bear little relation to thermometer readings. It must, however, be realised that the thermometer, like all other 'objectifying' devices, gives us information about an abstracted feature of any environment. Such devices can be designed to improve on each separate sense organ at responding to some particular stimulus. But, as Russell has pointed out, there is as yet ' no way of combining a microscope, a microphone, a thermometer, a galvanometer, and so on, into a single organism which will react in an integral manner to the combination of all the different stimuli that affect its different " sense organs " '.[1] Quite often, 'subjective states' are what really concern us, and it is a waste of time to worry with a whole series of independent instruments; on these occasions our senses, although deficient by ideal 'scientific' standards, are more informative—and therefore more efficient—than the most accurate conceivable instrument.

[1] RUSSELL, B. (1927), *An Outline of Philosophy*, p. 63. HADER, J. J., and LINDEMAN, E. C. (1933), *Dynamic Social Research*, p. 165, make a similar point about communication. 'Technical methods for observing communication as verbal (symbolical) and as non-verbal (physiological) are still wanting. The chief difficulty lies in the fact that communication itself proceeds in wholes, not parts: the spoken word and the lifted arm, the threatening gesture, or the increased volume of tone happen as one, not two units of behaviour. When the observer separates the word from the gesture he is simply being arbitrary in analysis.'

There is, however, no justification for inferring that the quality of attention is unimportant. In particular, there is a wealth of evidence that it is thoroughly unsafe to rely on casual everyday observation. As early as 1895, Cattell reported a test on undergraduates at Columbia University, which showed that many things frequently seen had failed to make an impression definite enough to permit of recall. His findings have been confirmed by a number of psychologists, and would not be disputed by anyone concerned with the taking of evidence.[1]

(b) *Observation and Inference*

We have already abandoned the fiction that our sense-organs act like machines, which convey to us the sensations produced by external stimuli.

It has long been recognised that this pretence is untenable, and that pure, mechanically conveyed, sensations can only be realised in earliest infancy. The very passage of a sensation leaves traces, which are stored; a second, associated, stimulus no longer conveys a 'pure sensation', but sets up a process which combines the effect of the new stimulus with the stored effect of previous stimuli, and thus enables us to perceive. All perception, after the first weeks of life, is compounded of the immediate experience and of the stored experience. Anything that impinges on our senses conveys a meaning to us largely to the extent that we relate it to what we already know. Observation and inference are inseparable.

It is not easy to accept this undeniable fact that our responses to stimuli inevitably contain that part of our past experience which we need in order to explain or interpret what we have seen. Consider an example given by Russell:

> You say, 'What can you see on the horizon?' One man says, 'I see a ship.' Another says, 'I see a steamer with two funnels.' A third says, 'I see a Cunarder going from Southampton to New York.' How much of what these three people say is to count as perception? They may all three be perfectly right in what they say, and yet we should not concede that a man can 'perceive' that the ship is going from Southampton to New York. This, we should say, is inference. But it is by no means easy to draw the line; some

---

[1] See, e.g., MURPHY, G. (1949 ed.), *An Historical Introduction to Modern Psychology*, p. 245.

things which are, in an important sense, inferential, must be admitted to be perceptions. The man who says ' I see a ship ' is using inference. Apart from experience, he only sees a queerly shaped dark dot on a blue background. Experience has taught him that that sort of dot ' means ' a ship.[1]

This ubiquity of inference in the act of perceiving, and the consequent opening for false perception, has been confirmed by psychologists in a large number of experiments. Thus, for example, Bartlett exposed various drawings to a number of observers who were asked subsequently to draw on paper what they had just seen.

One complicated design showed a closed gate, a brick wall and a notice board. Although the letters on the notice board were too small and the length of exposure too short for the observers to be able to read what was written on it, yet 80% of them said it was ' Trespassers will be prosecuted ', thus indicating the influence of inference.[2]

Many tests of an observer's capacity to judge emotional expression have been reported.[3] In one experiment films were made of new-born babies' responses to different stimuli: some were hungry, others were pricked with a needle, and so on. The films were subsequently edited, so that the responses were shown without the stimuli, and it was found that observers were then very often unable to describe the emotion evoked. It was also found that '. . . the emotion designated for a certain reaction depends to some extent upon the interests and attitudes of the observer '. Other experiments have shown that the emotions of an acculturated child are more recognisable, and that the judgments of an observer can be greatly improved by experience.

A second, and equally important, consequence of the memory element in all perception is that what we observe is only a selection from what there is for us to observe. The annual critic from the *Tailor and Cutter* who reports on the clothing in portraits at Royal Academy Exhibitions is perceiving something in these portraits that the most eminent art critic may entirely fail to see. Each critic is able to see the features that interest him, and may be

---

[1] RUSSELL, B. (1927), p. 68.
[2] BLACKBURN, J. (1945), p. 17, referring to BARTLETT, F. C. (1932), *Remembering*. This fact is exploited in all visual projective tests.
[3] MURPHY, G., MURPHY, L. B., and NEWCOMB, T. M. (1937 ed.), *Experimental Social Psychology*, pp. 140-53, describe twenty-three such tests.

entirely unaware of the existence of other features, even though they are ' staring him in the face '. His past experience has given him an outlook, a frame of reference, into which some things fit neatly—and appear meaningful—but in which there is no place for other things which, appearing meaningless, are ignored.

Learning is the construction of a personal frame of reference. Without any frame, new experiences are isolated, unidentifiable, meaningless. But in time the frame is fully clad, and thus so complete that new experiences which do not immediately fit into it are liable to be rejected. We turn our blind eye towards them.

This is equally true of the kind of localised learning which we call research. The research worker with no frame of reference sees much, but identifies little. The research worker with too rigid a frame of reference sees only those things that confirm his preconceptions.

> The manner in which animals learn has been much studied in recent years, with a great deal of patient observation and experiment. Certain results have been obtained as regards the kinds of problems that have been investigated, but on general principles there is still much controversy. One may say broadly that all the animals that have been carefully observed have behaved so as to confirm the philosophy in which the observer believed before his observations began. Nay, more, they have all displayed the national characteristics of the observer. Animals studied by Americans rush about frantically, with an incredible display of hustle and pep, and at last achieve the desired result by chance. Animals observed by Germans sit still and think, and at last evolve the solution out of their inner consciousness. To the plain man, such as the present writer, this situation is discouraging. I observe, however, that the type of problem which a man naturally sets to an animal depends upon his own philosophy, and that this probably accounts for the differences in the results.[1]

This passage, in which Russell is comparing the claims of the behaviourist and Gestalt psychologists, is irresistible.

We are thus faced with the very awkward and serious difficulty that our senses are not, after all, even under the most favourable conditions, the means of providing us with ' objective knowledge ' about what we set out to observe.

There are various possible ways of responding to this difficulty.

[1] RUSSELL, B. (1927), pp. 32–3.

One way is to ignore it. Even if our observations are not very objective, it may be argued, at least they are able to prove to our personal satisfaction that what we see is true. If in everyday life we assumed anything else, our everyday life would become impossible. But is this science? Does it follow that we are justified in adopting everyday methods in the more meticulous pursuit of scientific knowledge? It is certainly rash to assume so. 'There is the danger that non-controlled observation is likely to give us the feeling that we know more than we actually do about what we have seen. The data are so real and vivid and therefore our feelings about them are so strong that we sometimes tend to mistake the strength of our emotions for extensiveness of knowledge.'[1]

Another, and more honest, way of facing the difficulty is to do all that can be done to objectify observations. There is no question that objectifying methods can greatly curtail the influence of the observer's personal equation, but they have only a limited field of application. In the pursuit of objectivity—

> the scientist becomes more and more an inventor of techniques which will do his observing for him and also a reader and interpreter and generaliser of the records which his instruments deposit. Anthropologists have found the camera and the sound recorder valuable tools for accurate observation. But so far the volume of observation objectively recorded is relatively small, and unfortunately the thing usually recorded—physical or material culture—is often the sort easiest to observe and report on objectively even without such instruments. Such phases of non-material culture as ritual, literature, songs, dances, etc., can also be observed and reported objectively either with or without instruments. But when the cultural anthropologist turns to methods, patterns, personality, temperament, structure and other intangibles, he cannot rely on instruments—at least he has not done so—and his observations are therefore subject to challenge by anyone who cares to disagree with him.[2]

The principal complaint in this passage can be interpreted to mean that objectifying devices are not used enough, or that they have not been applied to critical issues. But we have still to consider in what sense any device or technique can ensure the objectivity which is sought. Will not the scientist, by his choice

---

[1] BERNARD, J. 'The Sources and Methods of Social Psychology' in BERNARD, L. L.—Ed. (1934), *Fields and Methods of Sociology*, pp. 273-4.
[2] BERNARD, J. (1945), 'Observation and Generalisation in Cultural Anthropology', *Am. Journ. Soc.*, **50**, 284.

of those techniques which appear relevant to him, be writing his results into his observations? Moreover, may not the fact that the scientist has failed to devise an instrument for recording personality, or such aspects of social interaction as leadership, be due to the same basic cause as has made it impracticable so far to devise an instrument for recording and measuring those factors such as bodily comfort?

The answer to the first of these rhetorical questions is a qualified no, and to the second a qualified yes.

We have to remind ourselves again that the demand for objectivity is the demand for an abstract and unrealisable situation in which the observer is an unobtrusive, passive and passionless machine who records without discrimination whatever is put in front of him. The only things that any such machine, however elaborate, can record are events—that is to say, forms of overt behaviour.[1] In these circumstances the insights and interpretations injected into his material by the human observer represent imperfections in the material. As every human observer is subject to these lapses, an inanimate machine like a ciné-camera is clearly more appropriate. It is not distracted; it does not select; it is not subjected to quirks of distorted memory or actual forgetfulness; the same passage can be repeated. If the record has to be interpreted, it is clearly safer to multiply the judgments applied to it, by asking a number of separate investigators to carry out independent analyses. So if overt behaviour is our bedrock, we do right to extract what information we can as accurately and unchallengeably as the use of objectifying devices permits.

But we should also not be surprised if a decision to confine our observations to those abstracted features which can be recorded on the ciné-camera or the observation schedule, greatly narrows the range of social processes which it is possible to observe. In their progressively more ingenious and elaborate studies of child social behaviour, for example, Dorothy Swaine Thomas and her associates were compelled to reject those 'behaviour units' which were found not to lend themselves to accurate and consistent observation.[2] It was necessary to take the whole to pieces, and to treat—with appropriate reserve—the relatively few satisfactory

[1] The overt behaviour recorded may have been exteriorised by the machine, just as the electro-encephalogram reveals and records otherwise invisible electrical rhythms in the brain.
[2] THOMAS, D. S. et al. (1933), *Observational Studies of Social Behaviour.*

observations as a measure of the lost whole.[1] In this, as in other controlled observational studies, the most articulate and exact machine so far devised has proved no more capable of yielding insight into social behaviour than the thermometer reading can ' stand for ' bodily comfort.

(c) *Effects of Interaction between Observer and Observed*

We must next pay some attention to another critical problem in social science, which is that the fact of observation itself modifies the situation being observed. As has already been mentioned, the importance of this effect did not strike Herbert Spencer or other nineteenth-century social scientists, presumably because their methods seldom involved the open intervention of the investigator in situations under study. As long as social science remains a form of documentary research, in which the documents themselves are unsolicited, there is clearly no reason to fear that distortions will arise from this source.

Today the widespread use of active interventionist techniques demands very careful consideration of the effect of interaction between observer and observed. Any participation of the observer in social processes must lead to some modification of these processes; if it is agreed, as has been suggested, that the observer must participate in order to achieve insight, then the observed situation is bound to differ from the unobserved situation.

The possibility of distortion is even greater in the case of those techniques needed for the testing of more exact hypotheses. When an interviewer questions an informant, however self-effacing he may try to be, he clearly has to accept the consequences of choosing the topic of conversation. When an investigator introduces experimental changes into the situation, he not only cannot avoid reactions to his intervention, but is actually seeking them.

All such situations are thus made artificial, to the extent that they would not have happened in the normal course of events, and to the extent that awareness of this makes the participants behave

[1] ' Of course, if accuracy of record is the chief desideratum, this may be the thing to do; but if one is mainly concerned with the securing of significant results, then the laborious setting down of small units of behaviour of uncertain significance may well seem . . . like so much busy-work.' F. L. Goodenough (1937), on D. S. Thomas (quoted by GREENWOOD, E. (1945), *Experimental Sociology*, p. 93.)

in a self-conscious, and therefore abnormal, manner. But a change in external circumstances is a very common feature of social life. In the course of a day a man meets various people, and what he says to them—and how he says it—is greatly influenced by who they are. You are sent to school, conscripted into the army, transferred to a new housing estate—in each case you, like other people, adapt yourselves to an externally prescribed change in your situation without any vivid sense of artificiality.

Professor Wirth once said, 'A society is possible in the last analysis because the individuals in it carry around in their heads some sort of picture of that society'. Provided the change alluded to is regarded as normal by those whom it affects, it is normal, and not artificial. If, however, the participants regard the changed situation as an abnormal one which does not fit into their picture of the world, their self-consciousness will be aroused, their behaviour will be disturbed, and the situation will not adapt itself in a way enabling the investigator to predict a similar adaptation in 'natural' circumstances.

There are thus two distinct dangers to be watched in social science. One is the danger that self-consciousness will be aroused in the participants by the introduction, in however impersonal a manner, of changes which conflict with these participants' ideas of normality. The other is that the presence of an observer, even merely as one extra person in the interacting situation, will lead to distortion.

It is interesting to compare this with like experiences of natural science. It was for long assumed that the effects of intervention could be discounted in natural science, and that an experiment could constitute a genuine prototype of a normal process. This is partly true; if, for example, a chemical reaction can be induced in a retort it may be assumed that, after allowing for change of scale and so on, the same reaction can be produced in a commercial plant. There is in natural science, as far as we know, no effect corresponding with the effect of self-consciousness in social science, largely perhaps because few natural processes are self-generating in the sense that social processes are.

In the case of the other effect, however, some natural scientists are beginning to find themselves in the same dilemma as social scientists. Atomic physicists find that any apparatus used to detect the behaviour of atomic particles, being itself made of atoms, distorts their movements. Again, a beam of light used to determine visually the path of an electron introduces inevitable inaccuracies because the light itself alters the electron's position. ' We see,' says Max Born, ' that a necessary consequence of atomic physics is that we must abandon the idea that it is possible to observe the course of events in the universe without disturbing it.' [1]

Thus what is largely a psychological effect in social science is paralleled by a directly physical effect in natural science. Of the two, the latter is certainly no less intractable.

In the social sciences attempts to overcome these difficulties have been made along characteristically divergent paths. On the one hand we have an approach which is broadly consistent with the behaviourist version of psychology. According to this way of thought, as our only means of deriving knowledge of social processes is by observation of overt behaviour—which, of course, includes verbal behaviour—we must make the best of a bad job and carry on with our observations, making such corrections as we can.

The other line of thought accepts the fact that all situations are essentially dynamic and recognises that the intervention of an investigator will inevitably influence the social process. Investigation then assumes a dual function: the observer has the task of grasping the social process in all its complexity, but he is also required to ensure that the changes due to the fact of intervention will themselves give satisfaction to the participants. Let us consider these alternatives in a little more detail.

Attempts at Neutralisation. It is not without significance that a rather high proportion of controlled observational studies, such as that mentioned earlier, have been concerned with the behaviour of children. Children, like most animals, can soon be expected to lose their self-consciousness in the presence of unobtrusive observers, but adults are generally too self-aware for this to occur.

The behaviourist investigator must thus choose between two alternatives. One course is to confine study to children—which naturally limits the value and importance of any results achieved.

The other is to observe adults, making allowance for distortions

[1] BORN, M., *The Restless Universe*, p. 158 (quoted by GREENWOOD, E. (1945), p. 101 fn.).

caused by self-consciousness. Unfortunately, this is not as easy as might at first appear. It is not just a matter of adjusting certain figures, or of expunging certain forms of behaviour from the record. Except by analogy, there are no means of telling what the overt behaviour would have been under natural, unobserved conditions, and except on external or common-sense grounds, there is no reason for supposing that behaviour has not been entirely transformed through the presence of an observer.

Participant Observation. If we consider what causes the self-consciousness which is at the root of this particular difficulty, we can trace it to the fact that the situation in which observations take place has a different meaning for the observer and for those being observed. The observer, out for objectivity, has to concentrate on his scientific mission—while being sufficiently pleasant and human to avoid annoying the objects of his study. The observed are torn between the wish to co-operate, so as to make the inquiry a success, and the attempt to follow the injunction to behave normally. To neither party is the significance of the observational study quite straightforward—as straightforward to the observer, for example, as watching rats in mazes or to the observed as carrying on some everyday activity without eavesdroppers.

Nor is its meaning quite clear. The 'objective' observer sees, hears and records a series of overt acts of behaviour and speech. Because, as we have seen, observation and inference are inseparable, he will be forced into attempting some interpretation of what his senses convey to him. But because he is an outsider, he does not know what lies behind these acts, so that he not only misses much of their significance but also inevitably misinterprets much of what he does see. Lacking a common purpose and a common interpretation, observer and observed are thus liable to disagree about the 'truth' of what the observer records as having happened.[1]

As we have seen, the ambition of the objectivist is, by reducing inference to a minimum or by spreading the exercise of judgment

[1] For exactly the same reason, the records of two observers will not coincide if their aims and backgrounds differ. As Blumer has it, 'The observation of a social act . . . will hold up if the observers have the same grasp of the situation in which the behaviour is taking place and, by virtue of a common experience, attach the same meaning to certain gestures in behaviour'. BLUMER, H. (1940), 'The Problem of the Concept in Social Psychology', *Am. Journ. Soc.*, **45**, 715.

over a number of different observers, to achieve a satisfactory level of inter-observer agreement. This has been found to be difficult, but not entirely impossible. But there is plainly another course, which is to give up the unequal struggle to eliminate inference, and instead to do what can be done to ensure that the inferences, continually being made by the observer, shall be the right ones—in other words, that the overt acts shall have the same meaning for the observer as for the group being observed. And when the heart of the observer is made to beat as the heart of any other member of the group under observation, rather than as that of a detached emissary from some distant laboratory, then he has earned the title of *participant observer*.[1]

The primary task of the participant observer is to enter into the life of the community being studied. If this task is achieved, there will be two consequences: his subjects will learn to take him for granted and thus to behave almost as though he were not there, and he will learn to think almost as they think.[2]

3. SOME PRACTICAL APPLICATIONS

In case it should be imagined that this discussion is becoming theoretical, it is well to remember that entry into the normal life of a community has been a feature of social investigation from its beginnings. Le Play lived in the homes of the families whose budgets he was collecting, and Booth, in the course of his survey of London Life and Labour, lodged with various families in the East End, whose activities and conditions of life he vividly described in his notebooks.[3]

---

[1] The name was coined by E. C. Lindeman (see his *Social Discovery*, 1924). The later book—*Dynamic Social Research*, by HADER and LINDEMAN (1933)—contains the following near-definition (p. 148): 'Participant Observation is based on the theory that an interpretation of an event can only be approximately correct when it is a composite of the two points of view, the *outside* and the *inside*. Thus the view of the person who was a participant in the event, whose wishes and interests were in some way involved, and the view of the person who was not a participant but only an observer, or analyst, coalesce in one final synthesis.'

[2] However completely he allows himself to be absorbed into the present, he will never evade his past and future. Normally his presence will to some extent affect the community being studied. Occasionally, however, the opportunity arises to partake unobtrusively. As Lasswell points out, for example, 'a spectator who is buried in the grandstand does not modify the spectacle if he behaves like everyone else'.—LASSWELL, H. D. (1948), *The Analysis of Political Behaviour*, pp. 101–2.

[3] Some extracts are given in *Charles Booth: A Memoir*. (1918).

(a) *Functional Anthropology*

Similarly, anthropologists were in due course to learn the need to become accepted in and acclimatised to the primitive societies which they were studying. The great pioneer of this method was Bronislaw Malinowski, the creator of functional anthropology, who was the first man completely to face the difficulties encountered by a field investigator who attempts to bridge the cultural gap between his own Western civilisation and that of the primitive society which he is aiming to understand.

In *The Argonauts of the Western Pacific* he describes the relative ease with which he could codify the structural system of the Trobriand Islanders—their technology and kinship system. But this achievement left him dissatisfied.

> All this remained dead material, which led no further into the understanding of real native mentality or behaviour, since I could neither procure a good native interpretation of any of these items, nor get what could be called the hang of tribal life.[1]

He had collected his original information during working hours, while living with local Europeans. He began to suspect that this was a serious flaw in his technique and was preventing him from achieving the insight that he sought. So he determined to cut himself off from the company of other white men, and set up his camp in a native village. If you do so, he found, you quite naturally seek out the natives' society, this time as a relief from loneliness, just as you would any other companionship.

> And by means of this natural intercourse, you learn to know him, and you become familiar with his customs and beliefs far better than when he is a paid, and often bored, informant.[2]

By living in the village, Malinowski was able to see the customs, ceremonies and transactions of native life over and over again, and so achieved a grasp of what he called the *imponderabilia of actual life* which cannot possibly be recorded by questioning or consulting documents. At the same time he increasingly mastered the native language, at first well enough to converse freely, and later to understand their ritual and magical text.

In due course the absorption became even more complete.

---
[1] MALINOWSKI, B. (1922), *Argonauts of the Western Pacific*, p. 5.
[2] *ibid.*, p. 7.

I began to take part, in a way, in the village life, to look forward to the important or festive events, to take personal interest in the gossip and the developments of the small village occurrences. . . . Quarrels, jokes, family scenes, events usually trivial, sometimes dramatic but always significant, formed the atmosphere of my daily life, as of theirs.[1]

Meanwhile the natives as they saw him every day lost their self-consciousness at his presence. In such circumstances he found that he could gradually piece together a full picture of their lives, of their beliefs and superstitions, and of the unwritten laws which governed their actions.

Some degree of participation is, in fact, obligatory to anthropologists. As Firth puts it:

Conformity to their customs [the people] take not so much as a compliment as a natural adaptation; in a specific ceremony they can conceive only of participants, not of observers. At such a time one cannot be outside the group, one must be of it.[2]

Once the value of participation as a principle of social observation had been demonstrated, there was every reason to extend it from the social anthropology of primitive societies to the less difficult study of western communities. Several of the most indelible inquiries undertaken at the University of Chicago under the inspiration of Professor Robert E. Park made use of the participant observer technique.[3]

Participation, though with different degrees of identification with the community, was also a feature of many important urban studies, such as the Lynds' two surveys of 'Middletown', of John Dollard's studies in the Southern States, and of Warner and Lunt's 'Yankee City' investigations. It is no coincidence that these social scientists all consciously set out to apply the methods of social anthropology to contemporary communities.

(b) *Industrial Sociology*

Another instance of great significance is the story of the observations made, and of those detailed to make them, in the course of

[1] MALINOWSKI, B. (1922), *Argonauts of the Western Pacific*, p. 7.
[2] FIRTH, R. (1936), *We, the Tikopia*, p. 605.
[3] One classic, and regularly quoted, instance is that of Nels Anderson who, in order to compile the material used in his '*The Hobo*', himself lived for some time as a tramp.

the Hawthorne investigations.[1] The importance of this story in the present context lies in the fact that the participant observer method was not imposed on the investigation in deference to some preconceived theory, but nevertheless became an inevitable consequence of the course that the experiments followed.

In the case of the Relay Assembly Test Room, for example, initially the function of the observer appeared straightforward enough.

This position of test-room observer was given to the man who more than anyone else had been responsible for initiating and planning these new experimental studies. Not only had he participated in the illumination experiments . . . but also he was thoroughly familiar with shop practices and had had considerable experience in setting piece rates. As test-room observer, his function was twofold: (1) to keep accurate records of all that happened, and (2) to create and maintain a friendly atmosphere in the test room.[2]

Initially, 'his duties were to keep things running smoothly, to keep records of all the data, and to act to a certain extent in a supervisory capacity for the operators'.[3]

But as the investigation continued, these duties became incompatible with one another, and, as will be described elsewhere, the experiment was allowed to transform itself into a social situation in which the observer was accepted as a full participant.

This was in recognition of the fact that the investigators had been unable to maintain their fine spirit of scientific detachment in which the experiment had been launched. 'They were themselves human beings with feelings and sentiments. The observer in his daily association with the girls grew to be very much interested in them. Although he wanted them to be good human laboratory subjects (i.e. co-operative), he never treated them as non-human laboratory specimens. On many occasions . . . he displayed almost too great a sympathetic identification with the girls' feelings and sentiments',[4] in a way which was not 'strictly in conformance with the logic of the original experiment'.[5]

---

[1] See pp. 282 seq. for an account of this study, viewed from the experimental standpoint, which will help to place the present discussion in its proper context.
[2] ROETHLISBERGER, F. J., and DICKSON, W. J. (1939), *Management and the Worker*, p. 22.
[3] ibid., p. 180.   [4] ibid., p. 183.
[5] ibid., p. 72. The implications of these developments are discussed in Chapter 5 (pp. 286 seq.).

(c) *Mass-Observation*

In Britain little organised use has been made of the participant observer technique. The only important contributions have been made by Mass-Observation, which was founded in 1937 by Charles Madge and Tom Harrisson, and at least in its first years was greatly influenced by methods of anthropology. ' Anthropology begins at home ' was an early slogan, and Professor Malinowski was perhaps the most influential initial sponsor and guide.[1]

From the beginning the work of Mass-Observation was carried on in two ways : by a national panel of informants and by intensive studies undertaken by whole-time observers. A number of these ' participant observers ' were stationed in *Worktown*, a Lancashire cotton town, and others centred their field-work on a London borough, *Metrop*. ' Most of these observers ', it was reported of the latter in 1940, ' are living in separate families, so that they are in close touch with the feelings, rumours, behaviour in ordinary homes: there is no London headquarters where whole-time observers live together.' [2] ' Each . . . has been responsible for producing objective field-work, objective reportage. They are not themselves concerned with their *own* reactions, and the organisers of the research are only concerned with the reactions of the observers in so far as they may bias results qualitatively or quantitatively.' [3]

Since that date the emphasis of Mass-Observation has tended to switch more on to the investigation of specific problems by a team of outsiders, by means of more orthodox interview and questionnaire techniques. But the participant observer method has continued sporadically. For example, the study published as ' War Factory ' was ' made by one investigator moving about within the framework of the problem '.[4] The material used in ' Exmoor Village ' was collected by observers who ' lived for some time on the spot, inconspicuously and in varying rôles '.[5]

Mass-Observation started life as a ' movement ', aimed in somewhat shrill protest against the inactivity of British social

---
[1] See MALINOWSKI, B., ' A Nation-wide Intelligence Service ', in MADGE, C., and HARRISSON, T.—Eds. (1938), *First Years Work by Mass-Observation.*
[2] MASS-OBSERVATION (1940), *War Begins at Home*, p. 17.
[3] *ibid.*, p. 19. [4] MASS-OBSERVATION (1943), *War Factory.*
[5] TURNER, W. J., and MASS-OBSERVATION (1947), *Exmoor Village.*

science, and its early methods were correspondingly hit-and-miss. But that the idea of participation is a matter of principle is suggested by its initial bias towards functional anthropology, and is supported by the following quotation from a paper by Tom Harrisson in a quarterly edited by Charles Madge:

> Some penetration of the investigator into the environment is always necessary so that the problem may be understood at first hand and not formulated with unnecessary personal, class, intellectual or other bias or assumption. If results are to be 'realistic', investigators must penetrate and *live* in the communities they study. A major factor hindering fieldwork has been the separation—in physical and psychological terms—between the sociologist and his subject matter. Among the many subsidiary advantages of penetration is the effect it has in compelling the investigator to *experience* the problem practically and personally. This can often teach him elements in its innermost significance of conflict, thus enabling further study and analysis of points which might never have been recognized from a purely outside, objective position such as that of the interviewer or the observer of behaviour.[1]

(d) *Action Research*

Since the war other noteworthy experiments in observer participation have been planned and carried out in England. Adam Curle, of Exeter University College, and formerly on the staff of the Tavistock Institute of Human Relations, settled for several years in a small Devonshire village with the deliberate intention not only of studying the life and beliefs of the villagers, but also of finding and trying out ways of relieving the tensions, frictions and frustrations that might be found to exist.

An even more significant example is the work, also under the ægis of the Tavistock Institute of Human Relations, carried out by Elliott Jaques and others in collaboration with the Glacier Metal Company. The declared aims of this 'action research' project were: to study the psychological and social forces affecting the group life, morale and productivity of a single industrial community; to develop more effective ways of resolving social stresses; and to facilitate agreed and desired social change.[2]

As in industry there is a traditional chasm between management and workers, there appeared to be no single group with which the

[1] HARRISSON, T. (1947), 'What is Sociology?', *Pilot Papers*, 2 (1), 23.
[2] JAQUES, E. (1951), *The Changing Culture of a Factory*.

observers could identify themselves without arousing suspicions in another group. There was even a danger that, as newcomers, they would attract on to themselves open manifestations of the unresolved stresses in that community.

In such a situation, the social research worker must discover for himself a rôle in which he belongs to no special section of the community; and one in which as far as possible he may have independent and equal relations with all. On scientific as well as ethical grounds, therefore, the building up of an independent relation to the factory as a whole was taken as the first project task, and the management and the workers, through their representatives, were separately offered the opportunity to collaborate in the research, or alternatively, to turn the whole project down.[1]

One sensible solution is to draw a team partly from the community and partly from the ranks of social science. This was done successfully by the Tavistock Institute of Human Relations in a coalmine study in which one partner in a team of two was an ex-miner.[2]

(e) *Overheards*

It must be accepted that it is not always practicable, or justifiable in terms of time spent, for the observer to 'bury' himself in the community which he wishes to study. Particularly in Western countries, there are many opportunities of being, if not a participant observer, at least an unobtrusive one. In such circumstances it is not only desirable but perfectly possible that the behaviour noted, whether speech or action, should be spontaneous and unsolicited, 'in the natural context of their daily

---

[1] JAQUES, E. (1951), *The Changing Culture of a Factory*, p. 12. This declaration of independence, in accordance with which all personal relationships with factory personnel were banned, may have been inevitable in the study of a community which contains conflicting interests. Some loss of sympathy with each of the positions maintained would also appear inevitable.
It is of interest that the technique here adopted was deliberately taken from clinical medicine (pp. 15–16). This fact provides a link with an earlier study with a clinical slant, namely the famous Peckham Experiment. 'We now come to a very crucial question :—how can such an unfamiliar and objective factor as a scientist and observer be introduced into any social milieu without instantly shattering its spontaneity ? The answer seems to lie in the possibility that the scientist himself and his technicians should become one of the accepted groups forming the cultural diversity in the environment.'—PEARSE, I. H., and CROCKER, L. H. (1943), *The Peckham Experiment*, p. 46.
See also COOK, P. H. (1951), 'Methods of Field Research', *Austral. Journ. Psychol.*, 3 (2), 84–98.
[2] TRIST, E. L., and BAMFORTH, K. W. (1951), 'Some Social and Psychological Consequences of the Longwall Method of Coal-getting', *Hum. Rel.*, 4 (1), 3–38.

life '.[1] Harrisson describes unobtrusively collected 'verbal behaviour' as *overheards*, and writes:

> Systematic listening to umprompted conversations gets as near as the outsider can to the 'frank' level of opinion, and especially to spontaneous interest and to intensity of feeling. Hundreds of thousands of pounds have been spent on interview assessments of public opinion; no scientific study has been made of what people actually, naturally, do talk about. The omission is symptomatic.[2]

Overheards have proved a fruitful source of the kind of material in which Mass-Observation has always displayed interest. This material is rich in quality, and to the alert and experienced investigator provides a quick means of discerning the issues which will repay 'further studying and analysis'.[3] It is clear, however, that the chanciness of overhearing and the natural tendency of the observer to select, memorise and record the more bizarre conversations makes it rather rash to use such material as the basis of generalisations about current public interest or public attitudes.

It should not be concluded, however, that overheard conversations are valueless for statistical analysis. Several records of street conversations have been made, both in the United States (e.g. Broadway, New York) and in England (e.g. Regent Street, London), and certain tentative conclusions have been drawn from the results.[4]

It has not, of course, been shown that crowds in Broadway and Regent Street are typical of the two cities. On the other hand, it is quite possible to justify the view that an observer is in a position to overhear a sample of conversations which are representative of the street studied, at the time that the observations take place. This method of sampling is called by Yates the 'principle of the moving observer', and the main stipulations are that the observer should walk fast enough not to be often overtaken and that he should traverse the street in both directions at the same speed.[5]

---

[1] RICHARDS, A. I. (1939), in BARTLETT, F. C. et al.—Eds. p. 302.
[2] HARRISSON, T. (1947), p. 22.
[3] 'Undoubtedly a chance remark may put the statistician on the track of a causal relationship he could not have reached by computation or his own common sense, experience or introspection.'—FLORENCE, P. S. (1950), 'Patterns in Recent Social Research,' *Brit. Journ. Soc.*, 1, 231.
[4] See MURPHY, G., MURPHY, L. B., and NEWCOMB, T. M. (1937), pp. 693-4.
[5] YATES, F. (1949), *Sampling Methods for Censuses and Surveys*, pp. 43-4. This principle has been used for making population counts in streets and stores, as well as censuses of animals and insects.

4. OBSERVATIONAL SCHEDULES AND OTHER MEANS OF RECORDING

(a) *Social Behaviour*

Schedules normally come into their own when a rather precise and rather restricted hypothesis is to be tested. Insofar, therefore, as observation is a preliminary research activity, any schedules used will be purely informal and personal shorthand devices.

In contrast, the exact and painstaking analysis of social behaviour, largely of children, which has already been mentioned in passing, necessitates the use of ingenious schedules designed to simplify and expedite the recording of observational data. Much experience as to the form which such schedules should take has accumulated not only from pure research but also from practical inquiries, such as time and motion studies. Many such schedules consist of sheets of paper on which the minute-by-minute movements of those being observed can be plotted or symbolically recorded. Others, used to discover lay-outs which economise movement, make use of threads wound around pins to follow routes actually taken.

Ciné-camera records are also extensively used for the same purpose. Although naturally somewhat expensive, they make it possible to correct for variations in recording due to differences between individual observers and, perhaps even more important, provide a more or less permanent bank of observational material on which a succession of hypotheses can be tested.[1]

It is seldom that material initially collected in any of these ways is self-explanatory. Conversely, the sociometric and other diagrams developed for purposes of analysis and exposition are not necessarily suitable for direct use in the field.

(b) *Observing the Inanimate*

Just as the observational schedule finds many technical uses in industry, so the schedule, or weighted inventory, of objects is a common administrative device. Rating officers, tariff fixers and others measure up buildings or tot up the value of possessions for a variety of purposes.

[1] If it were not for the factor of self-consciousness, the effect of which is so difficult to gauge, one can envisage endless applications in social science for the ciné-film record. One possible development would be the combined use of the ciné-film, for a permanent record, and of the participant observer, who could interpret the record from personal experience.

Chapin has for nearly twenty years been advocating the use of an inventory of material possessions as an index of family social status.[1] He defines social status as 'the position the family occupies with reference to the average prevailing household possessions of other families in the community',[2] and this position is gauged by an observer, who notes the 'Material Equipment and Cultural Expression of the Living Room', and also the 'Condition of Articles in Living Room'. The presence of a bookcase gains so many points, while points are lost if an alarm clock can be spotted. Penalties are also exacted if articles are strewn about in disorder or if, in the observer's opinion, the decorations are 'bizarre, clashing, inharmonious or offensive'.

Points were originally awarded somewhat arbitrarily, but a more recent development has been the revision of the points scale by Guttmann, who applied factor analysis.[3] This had rather surprising results. Thus, while according to the original scale, a library table gained the possessor eight points, on the revised scale it lowered his social status by one point. Conversely, the presence of a sewing machine in the living-room was revealed as an asset worth two points, whereas it had led Chapin to deduct two points.[4]

This is an illustration of a somewhat fanciful and elaborate, though apparently widely used,[5] observational schedule applied to material possessions. If we are not drawn to the method, this is perhaps because it too glibly assumes a stereotype of family trappings which, although possibly valid, remains somewhat uncongenial and unmistakably foreign. But this should not blind us to the material evidence of social behaviour, past or present, which surrounds us, or to the knowledge which we should be able to derive from it. Farquharson has reminded us of the importance of studying material culture, and particularly its everyday things—'commonplace houses, furniture, ornaments, clothing, domestic

---

[1] See, for example, CHAPIN, F. S. (1947), *Experimental Designs in Sociological Research*, pp. 41–50, 191–4, etc.
[2] ibid., p. 47.
[3] GUTTMAN, L. (1942), 'A Revision of Chapin's Social Status Scale', *Am. Soc. Rev.*, 8, 362–9.
[4] CHAPIN, F. S. (1947), pp. 193–4. Surprise is tempered, however, by the revelation that Guttmann's scale was based on sixty-seven families, all of which were negroes living in Minneapolis and St. Paul in 1932 (*ibid.*, p. 162). In fact, not a very representative sample.
[5] According, for example, to YOUNG, P. V. (1949), *Scientific Social Surveys and Research*, p. 366.

Conclusions

appliances, tools, machines and so on '.[1] These are just the things that Chapin corralled into his schedule, but we shall still take a lot of convincing that he had broken them in and teamed them into a reliable index.

5. CONCLUSIONS

In one form or another, observations are inseparable from empirical science. The present chapter, while examining some of the obstacles to impartial observation, however and wherever used, has been particularly concerned with the question of how to observe social processes under natural conditions, with the minimum of intervention by the investigator. It is suggested that the most effective, and also the most promising, use of this kind of observation in social research is in the preliminary stages, when the investigator is more concerned with the correctness of his own orientation and insight than with the proof of any exact hypothesis.

It is unrealistic to expect the investigator to start his preliminary observations with a completely open mind as to what he is likely to see. In these initial observations, however, it remains advisable as far as possible to avoid preconceptions, and not to worry too much about the subjective and inaccurate nature of unaided sense impressions.

Above all, it is necessary to remember that the search is for an initial working hypothesis which, however plausible, is strictly for private consumption. It is very tempting to ignore this, just as the pioneers of social medicine did when they argued that smells cause disease.

Powers of observation can be developed by practice. With training, capacity to estimate time and distance can be improved. Improved receptivity to all sensory stimuli can be inculcated. This fact is not neglected in the natural sciences. From the

---

[1] FARQUHARSON, A., 'The Study of Material Culture' in DYMES, D. M. E.— Ed. (1943), *Sociology and Education*, p. 67.
   The localised validity of any material index is stressed by Margaret Mead. 'Where the advocate of better housing worries about the moral effects of a whole family living in a trailer, the anthropologist knows that it is not the small space, nor the poor sanitation, which is crucial. The anthropologist has seen people live with complete dignity and morality under conditions which would make a modern trailer look like a palace, or even a share-cropper's cabin look like a substantial and prosperous dwelling. Behind the small space of the trailer and its possible effect upon the morals of adolescent children is seen a system of family relationships which depend upon privacy, upon doors and upon bathroom keys.'—MEAD, M. (1944), *The American Character*, pp. 14-15.

beginning of their training, scientists spend a substantial share of their time in practical work, learning the arts and techniques of scientific observation and experiment. In due course their senses and their movements become as well co-ordinated as those of any craftsman, and even as those of a dancer or an athlete. Very few social scientists have undergone a comparable training in observation, and this although we are justified in ignoring far more in, say, the conduct of a chemical titration than in the observation of a social situation.[1]

It is in any case safe to ignore more when we know more.

One cannot observe everything closely, therefore one must discriminate and try to select the significant. When practising a branch of science, the 'trained' observer deliberately looks for specific things which his training has taught him are significant, but in research he often has to rely on his own discrimination, guided only by his general scientific knowledge, judgment and perhaps an hypothesis which he entertains.[2]

Many of the most successful scientific discoveries are due to those whose powers of observation enabled them to see simul-

[1] ' In order to be a competent observer, a long and rigid discipline of the muscular, sensory and central nervous systems is necessary, also their perfect co-ordination. Go into any physical or chemical laboratory and observe an observer at work : the skill of his movements, controlled by the activity of his brain, is comparable to the supreme artistry of a ballet dancer, a violinist or a sculptor. In all these pursuits, years of training are necessary, training in theory as well as in muscular practice. The " uninstructed sap " if let loose among the best microscopes, or placed in the finest astronomical observatory, would not be able to register a single fact in the scientific sense.'—B. MALINOWSKI (1938), p. 90.

[2] BEVERIDGE, W. I. B. (1950), *The Art of Scientific Investigation*, p. 99. A similar point is made by Roethlisberger and Dickson (1939), p. 389. ' The observer had to make some selection of material to record, but what should he select ? Of course, common sense determined part of the selection; for example, a heated argument between two operators or a clash between an operator and a supervisor would be noted by anyone. But the question goes much deeper. The point is that observation, if it is to be at all scientific, must be guided by a working hypothesis which enables the observer to make active discriminations in the complex interplay of factors before him. Without such guidance he is likely to miss much of significance and become lost in a welter of irrelevancies.'

The proper grounds for selection are more precisely specified by Mayo: ' A vivid awareness of context is the primary condition of effective attention. The skilled person ignores what is not immediately relevant to action, not because it is meaningless, but rather because it is in fact fulfilling the meaning he is actively assigning it.'—MAYO, E. (1948), *Some Notes on the Psychology of Pierre Janet*, p. 60.

Self-observation, as is demanded of the participant observer, requires even greater skill. As Koffka states, ' it should be noted that the method of perceiving experience is something that has to be learned and practised to an even higher degree than any other kind of scientific observation '.—KOFFKA, K. (1931 ed.), *The Growth of the Mind*, p. 11.

Conclusions

taneously more things, including unexpected things, than their less talented colleagues.

The close association between observation and memory has been mentioned in reference to the part that past experience plays in present perception. But while we see what we see because of what we remember, we are also liable to forget what we have seen unless we take the deliberate, and often rather distasteful, step of keeping full notes. Some fairly elaborate schedules and other forms of recording have been devised, but systematic note-taking is no less necessary at a stage of inquiry for which schedules are inappropriate.

Notes of this sort are personal possessions, and can seldom be shuffled and collated so as to verify or discredit an hypothesis. But observation, steeping oneself in the tangled currents of interest of any social situation, remains an indispensable part of the process of achieving insight that has been called ' discerning '.

Chapter 4
THE INTERVIEW

It is commonly supposed, although there is very little evidence to warrant such a supposition, that there exists a simple and logical relation between what a person says and what he thinks.—ROETHLISBERGER and DICKSON.

Practically nothing can be done by the student of primitive culture if he uses a pencil and a schedule and makes a hurried visit to a people to ask formal questions. He must live and observe and absorb their culture. Most of it cannot be stereotyped in question and answer form, and he will not get frank and true answers unless he has established confidence by long and sympathetic contacts ; and even then it is best to ask less and observe more.—L. L. BERNARD.

If the task were laid upon me of learning to know the minds of people in regard to their social actions by means of direct enquiry, my own experience would lead me to regard the prospects of success as greater among such people as the Melanesians than among the inhabitants of an English or Scottish village.—W. H. R. RIVERS.

Bear in mind that it is desirable to make the interview pleasing to the persons interviewed. It should seem to him or her an agreeable form of social intercourse.—S. and B. WEBB.

PART A—TYPES OF INTERVIEW

THE *interview* has been defined as ' a meeting of persons face to face, especially for the purpose of formal conference on some point '.[1] In other words, it is a purposive conversation, whose purpose may vary widely to include, for example, a meeting to select from candidates for a vacancy, a meeting to arrange for a certain course of action, or a meeting undertaken to collect information.

It will be found on examination that different forms of interview have more in common than would at first appear. As Oldfield has pointed out,[2] any interview is normally non-symmetrical in that the initiator plays a relatively active rôle while the other party—informant or candidate—plays a relatively passive rôle.

Furthermore, it is essentially a form of human interaction, of more significance than the mere oral exchange of information. Specifically, the interview gives the initiator a far better oppor-

---
[1] *Shorter Oxford English Dictionary.*
[2] OLDFIELD, R. C. (1941), *The Psychology of the Interview*, p. 6.

Influencing Potentates

tunity to gauge the truthfulness or other qualities of ...
or candidate than when he has to rely on documentary sou...

In spite of these common features, there is considerable variety in the interview situations encountered in social investigation.

The first form of differentiation is in the type of person who is to be interviewed. He may be selected because he is in a position of authority; or because he possesses special knowledge about other people or things; or because he is one of a class of people in whom the social scientist is interested. We can thus broadly classify interviewees into the *potentate*, the *expert* and the *people*.

The social scientist may wish to approach members of any of these three categories for either of several reasons. He may wish to enlist or retain their co-operation in, or at least consent to, a certain course of action. He may wish to gather facts or opinions or a combination of both. Or again, he may wish to instil in them the kind of confidence and insight that will help them to make appropriate decisions about their own future.

According to the foregoing classification we have three types of person who may be interviewed for three types of reason—making nine categories in all. Some are rarely met, but three stand out. We normally appeal to potentates for permissions, to experts for technical information, and to ordinary men and women for ordinary facts and feelings. And it is irrelevant that most men are potentates to some, and all are experts in something.

1. INFLUENCING POTENTATES

Most research projects require the prior consent of some authority or another, and even more depend on the active goodwill and co-operation of those involved. In many cases, particularly when there is a possibility of latent or open friction between the different parties to a social situation, it is necessary to explain the purpose of the project to all concerned who must be persuaded to agree on the desirability of carrying it out even though they may continue to differ on other issues. Some research bodies take this initial step so seriously that they refuse to come in unless they are actively invited by each of the different interests involved in the situation.[1]

---

[1] JAQUES, E. (1951), *The Changing Culture of a Factory*, pp. 7 seq., gives a description of the great pains taken in one instance to introduce the idea of research to management and workers.

L

The Interview

Most people with a modicum of social skill are generally able to get permission to initiate a research programme. An event which is probably commoner than initial failure is for the original goodwill towards the research project to be gradually dissipated in the course of research. This may happen for a variety of reasons, not all of which reflect on the value of the research being done. But support is more likely to be sustained if those in authority are not only asked to give their consent to the inquiry, but are also directly implicated in carrying it out.

Hader and Lindeman have given much attention to this function of the interview, as the result of experience in the course of a particular research programme. Their initial object had been to observe joint production committees in action, but the design was deliberately enlarged so as to ensure that the study would be sustained by the factory officials themselves even after the withdrawal of the investigators.[1] Thus a programme which started as a traditional research item—a ' method of external abstraction '—was deliberately transformed into a joint effort, and the search for facts was replaced by a self-perpetuating experiment in managerial techniques. The authors brought this change about by a regular sequence of ' motivating ' interviews with the management; in their opinion the transformation of emphasis thus brought about gives the interview a new function, in one sense more important than its traditional function.

The authors describe the technique which they evolved for this type of interview. It was found useful, before approaching the management, to attempt to forecast what their reaction would be to a request of the sort intended. For example, certain factors—such as concern for the success of the joint production committee and generalised interest in research—might be expected to dispose officials favourably to the project, while other factors—such as inertia and general suspicion towards outsiders—might tend to put them off. The success of the investigator could be gauged by his social skill in exploiting the favourable factors and overcoming the unfavourable ones.

The interview campaigns normally passed through three stages, each reflecting a distinct central purpose. The initial interview or interviews were designed primarily to ensure a favourable attitude

[1] HADER, J. J., and LINDEMAN, E. C., *Dynamic Social Research*, pp. 130 seq.

Influencing Potentates

to the investigators. At this stage the winning o
standing and sympathy with the objectives of the
took precedence over the eliciting or transmiss
was found that success or failure often depended (
introduction from an individual or body that
respect of the management. Without this initial advantage,
progress through the various stages of acquaintance to a sufficient
level of rapport might occupy several sessions.

In the second stage it became necessary to get down to details.
Here one major difficulty lay in the absence of a common language.
The investigators found that they were tending to express themselves in academic abstractions which were liable to fill practical-minded executives with misgivings; or the two parties were using what were ostensibly the same words in different senses. It became clear that unless the research worker was able to state his approach in language which could enlist the interest and curiosity of the executive, he might fail to gain the executive's consent to the study being made.

It was also shown that the investigator must be prepared to modify the details of his plan in the light of what he learns during these interviews. This is necessary not only to achieve maximum realism in his investigation but also to relate his postulates to the 'facts which the interviewee announces and in which he has faith '.[1]

Even after the research programme had been launched, it was found necessary to maintain regular contacts with the officials concerned. These contacts were used to test the facts which the investigators believed to have been discovered, to secure corroboration or correction, and also to give the officials an opportunity to share in the project. Wherever feasible, these co-operators were asked to perform some function allied with the project as a whole. The later interviews were thus ' conducted in an atmosphere of "working together ", as distinguished from the more orthodox method of research in which the investigators' facts were withheld until the time of a final report.'[2]

[1] HADER, J. J., and LINDEMAN, E. C. (1933), *Dynamic Social Research*, p. 134.
[2] *ibid.*, pp. 135–6. This emphasis on collaboration reveals an affinity with the psychoanalytic interview, the contribution of which to social science is discussed later in this Chapter.

See also JAQUES, E. (1951), for the description of a project in which collaboration was a cardinal rule, and in which great care was taken to define the rôle of the Research Team.

This co-operative technique applied to the 'motivating interviews' clearly makes a useful contribution towards bridging the gap between those who are contributing leadership to the situation under observation and those who have come to observe it. Not only does it stimulate and interest the participants and make allowance for the dynamic quality in social processes, but it also provides a very necessary corrective to the armchair planning and remote execution of which some social scientists are still excessively fond.

2. EXAMINING EXPERTS

During the past century there has been a spate of Royal Commissions and Parliamentary Committees, covering a vast range of subjects. They have gathered an enormous store of evidence from the most eminent of public figures. For a long time great prestige has been attached to them, and great changes have followed their reports. And yet, when we examine the basis of their authoritative conclusions, we find that seldom have they been able to do more than record a cross-section of authoritative opinions of the day. They have crystallised, and adjudicated between, the currents of opinion of their time, but they have seldom been able to adduce important new facts in support of these opinions.

The Webbs were entirely disillusioned as to the value of such Commissions.

> Of all recognised sources of information the oral 'evidence' given in the course of these inquiries has proved to be the least profitable. Considering the time spent in listening to it, or even in rapidly reading and analysing these interminable questions and answers—still more, the money spent over them—the yield of solid fact is absurdly small.[1]

[1] WEBB, S. and B. (1932), *Methods of Social Study*, p. 142.
The two Royal Commissions with which the Webbs were most closely connected were the Royal Commission on Labour (1892–4) and the Royal Commission on the Poor Law (1905–9). In both they were associated with a Minority Report.
In the former, the evidence 'consisted, for the most part, not of statements of fact, but of the answers to abstract conundrums put in cross-examination by the commissioners about every conceivable social or legislative reform. The greatest triumph was, by skilful questions, to lead the witnesses, especially the working-men witnesses, into some logical inconsistency. One or other of us attended some meetings of the commission; and it was certainly entertaining to watch the dialecticians "purring" at each other complacently when their little pounces came off. But this cat-and-mouse dialectic is not the way to discover new facts. Hence it is hardly surprising that the royal commission,

Examining Experts

Most professional social investigators would tend to a similar view. The truth is that we are whelmed by an unsupported array of opinion pressive, unless—as is sometimes the case ir example—no alternative basis for decision can be

If properly approached, however, these opinions are themselves of great interest, revealing as they do the main areas of conflict and obscurity. They are also, of course, highly informed opinions. The fact that an individual is prepared to give evidence probably implies that he will have taken the trouble to collect his thoughts on the subject, and may even have gathered, or caused to be gathered, factual material to support his case. But, as is generally recognised, the rôle of the normal informant in such circumstances is that of a party to the dispute, in which he is concerned to put forward as forcibly as possible the viewpoint which will justify his past actions, or the actions of those whom he supports, and facilitate future ones. The function of the committee of inquiry is essentially judicial, and its purpose to sort out or to reconcile the conflicting claims of its witnesses. And, as has often been pointed out, scientific truth is never attained by compromising between opposing views.

It is true that such committees subject their witnesses to fairly severe cross-examination, but the conclusions are nevertheless based on the aggregation of existing opinions—including those of the chairman and commissioners—rather than on the discovery of new truths.

The social scientist is not likely to fall into the trap of imagining that truth can be obtained by compiling expert opinions. He is more likely to succumb to the opposite fault of discounting expert

---

regarded as an instrument of investigation, drew a blank ' (*Methods of Social Study*, pp. 143–4; see also WEBB, B. (1948), *Our Partnership*, pp. 40–2.

In the latter, Beatrice Webb was herself a Commissioner, and entered fully into the spirit of the proceedings. In *Our Partnership* (p. 390 fn.), she quotes a ' kindly ' account by an ' accomplished journalist ' of one cross-examination conducted by herself. ' There is no cross-examiner at the bar more suave or subtle than Mrs. Webb. When I was called to give evidence before the Poor Law Commission I entered the room in the midst of her examination of Mr. Walter Long. The subject was the finance of the unemployed committees. Step by step she led him unconscious to his doom with gentle, innocent-seeming questions. Suddenly he saw that he was being made to admit that voluntary effort was a failure and that the rates must be used. But it was too late to retreat. With a quiet " Thank you, that is all ", she snapped the " bracelets " on his wrists, folded her hands, and sat back in her chair, the picture of demure, unexultant triumph.'

opinions altogether. Let us, then, recognise their legitimate contribution, which lies near the starting point for scientific inquiry rather than near its goal. Background material obtained by pumping 'experts' can seldom be relied on by itself, but if properly and critically amassed can provide invaluable checks, confirmations and corrections on the results of the field studies.

There should be no need to add a word of caution, which those with social skill will take for granted. The expert is almost certainly a very busy person, and probably one accustomed to authority, who expects his pronouncements to be treated with deference. It does no good to anyone, least of all to the investigator, to give an expert the impression that the interview is merely a formality or that his words of wisdom are to occupy a low position in the scale of scientific truth. If he really is an expert, steeped in his subject, he will probably have attained more insight into it than any outside investigator can ever hope to do.

The method of questioning experts is sometimes also used for a more restricted and factual purpose. Thus it is sometimes desirable to use outsiders as direct gatherers of specific information about families or places that they already know. A classic example, which has already been mentioned, is that of Charles Booth, who, in conducting his poverty survey, was able to tap the existing knowledge of hundreds of London School Board Visitors (the forerunners of our modern School Attendance Officers).

3. INTERVIEWING PEOPLE

We now come to the principal application of the interview in social science, that is its use for the purpose of making people talk about themselves.

The interview—and its half-brother, the questionnaire—is popularly regarded as the method *par excellence* of social science. After all, it is argued, what social scientists are interested in are people, and if you want to find out something about a person, surely the best way is to ask him or one of his friends.

In previous chapters we have briefly considered some of the assumptions underlying this forthright point of view. We have, for example, examined the grounds for believing that knowledge of groups and of group behaviour can be built up through knowledge of individuals and of individual behaviour. We have seen that there are even reservations to be made on the belief that there are such things as facts, and that a simple answer can be found to a simple question.

It is dangerously easy to dismiss such issues as the typically academic and metaphysical worries of men so scrupulous that they will never discover anything. Conversely, we may be tempted to exploit honest doubts on such points, using them as an excuse for repudiating the methods, and hence the functions, of social science.

As ever, if we are to steer between these false positions, we must abandon the abstract theoretical approach and concentrate instead on becoming familiar with the practical uses to which the interview and questionnaire have been put. The range of such uses is already immense. As will be shown, there is no clear line of demarcation between the course of psychotherapeutic sessions and the completion of a census form, between eliciting a deeply felt opinion and collecting a simple fact like the informant's age, between an interview which leads to confidence and insight and one which provides yet another batch of data to be marked up in the appropriate columns. But although dividing lines are arbitrary, the distinctions between one extreme use of the interview technique and another are in practice perfectly clear and of radical importance.

Of the many dimensions along which the various types of interview could if necessary be scaled, two appear to be of particular value. They also bear a very close relation to each other. These may hypothetically be called the ' richness-precision ' scale, and ' the degree of intervention ' scale.

Richness-Precision. As has already been pointed out, it is often necessary in science to choose at a given stage between an approach providing richness of impressions and an approach offering exact numerical data. Both techniques can often appropriately be used in succession in the course of one investigation. The former of these scales can thus be considered as offering an index of the stage reached in the inquiry—that is to say, the extent to which the investigator's hypothesis is already narrowed before the interview takes place.

If, as in the ordinary mass-interview or questionnaire survey, the questions put are prearranged and precise, delivered in standardised words and tone, richness is sacrificed in the interests of easily manipulated quantitative data. At the other extreme, in the counselling techniques the interviewer has no set questions, or even set subjects, and may make no record of the interview except a few notes to jog his memory in preparation for the informant's next visit; there may be no result, except a load off somebody's mind.

Degree of Intervention. The position on this continuum from precision to richness can be closely related to the extent of a certain type of intervention by the interviewer. An hypothesis is only narrowed because the investigator wishes it to be narrowed, and, like a sheepdog, constantly holds the informant on the track of relevancy. This speeds up progress, but rules out exploration.

The word intervention has to be qualified, because the psychoanalyst or counsellor may in fact be intervening as strenuously as the mass-interviewer; but he is intervening in a different way and for a different purpose. He is aiming to draw his informant out, and not to pin him down. He is intent on being a good listener, a 'feminine' flatterer, and not a drill-sergeant. Although he is on the job, he may well be changing his informant's thoughts and statements far less influentially than the ethereal investigator who has in some distant office designed a postal questionnaire.

Depth and Speed. A somewhat related scale could be devised to measure the extent of 'depth', or penetration, achieved by the interviewer. This is normally considered crudely in terms of the time devoted by the interviewer to each informant, and hence is taken as a measure of the rapport and intimacy of their relationship.

Although time spent is clearly not the sole criterion, limitations in time available are bound to restrict the possibilities of full rapport. We may at least say, therefore, that penetration is ruled out of a mass-interview survey and that the failure to achieve penetration in a counselling or psychotherapeutic situation reflects on the consultant or on his techniques.

Fact and Opinion. A common distinction is made between opinion questions and fact questions. According to our standpoint, the criterion of fact is confirmability, and some statements are clearly more readily confirmable than others. It may thus be convenient on *a priori* grounds to scale questions according to their factual content. The sex of an informant is normally confirmable at a glance, age confirmable within limits, income may be inferred from home circumstances or outward appearance. Reasons already adduced and examples to be given later show, however, that no such empirical guide can be trusted to be regularly true. Nor can any statement made be regarded as intrinsically more real in relation to the context in which it is made than an opinion statement such as ' I hate Stalin ' or ' I like cheese '.

The investigation of attitudes and opinions is increasing. Much time and ingenuity is being devoted to the development of mass techniques for the reliable measurement of public opinion. This is neither replacing nor yet assimilating the studies of group-attitude formation which are also beginning to accumulate. There appears to be nothing in the distinction between facts and attitudes to make one or the other more inherently suitable for quantitative study.[1]

PART B—THE FORMATIVE INTERVIEW

The following pages are devoted to a discussion and evaluation of a number of related interviewing techniques. These resemble each other, in that the informant is given some sort of freedom to choose the topics to be discussed and the way in which they are discussed. Correspondingly, the interviewer has the opportunity to enlarge his own understanding of the issues raised. In this sense all such interviews are *formative*, whereas mass interviews are not.

1. THE NON-DIRECTIVE INTERVIEW

An interview lacking any purposive element would be an idle conversation, and not an interview at all. So although there is a suggestion of planlessness in the title given to this type of interview by those who have developed it, this is merely because the normal reason why such interviews take place is not specified in it. In point of fact, their most usual function has been to help the informant to help himself rather than to collect from him any facts whatsoever.

The present-day non-directive, or counselling, interview is a not uncommon feature of American student and industrial life. In England we are only gradually becoming accustomed to a some-

---

[1] ' Opinion shades into knowledge, which is only that part of opinion socially certified by particular criteria of evidence '—MERTON, R. K. (1949), *Social Theory and Social Structure*, p. 201.
This point is more fully discussed in pp. 198 seq.

what similar, though generally less professional, procedure, which is being developed mainly for the promotion of family adjustment. All counselling of this sort may be said to stem ultimately in its modern form from Sigmund Freud's revolutionary recognition of the underlying importance of the unconscious element in regulating the individual's behaviour and beliefs, and by his discovery of means of access to the individual's unconscious. Freud was important not only as a craftsman who discovered how to heal by using intimate data supplied by the patient. He was also important as a scientist who formulated a theoretical system within which such data could be used, in association with pathological and other physical symptoms, to account for disease and to promote recovery.[1]

Freud's theories, especially as reinterpreted by his followers to take fuller account of the social component in the formation of character, have made an immense impact on social scientific thought. In the present context we are only concerned with the methods which he and his colleagues evolved in order to elicit the 'intimate data' that they sought. This has likewise greatly influenced contemporary interviewing techniques, particularly those of a more penetrating and less quantitative nature. Freud's form of psychotherapy generally entails a large number of separate sessions, sometimes spread over years, until all hidden places are exposed and all resistance conquered. During this long period, the rôle of the psychoanalyst in providing continuity and momentum to the probe is clearly of the utmost importance. In recognising and examining this fact, psychoanalysis has helped to clarify the technical groundwork of all interviewing.

Psychoanalysts have adopted widely varying views on the rôle proper to the analyst in the interview situation. Lasswell cites the psychoanalyst Sándor Ferenczi, who experimented widely with 'active' therapeutic methods, veering between an authoritative and an egalitarian rôle; he also points to the contrast between the relative prominence given by Alfred Adler and C. G. Jung to the part played by the physician, and the democratic group analysis of Trigant Burrow, 'supposed to take the leader off his authori-

[1] For an illuminating appreciation of Freud's importance to social science see LASSWELL, H. D. (1948), *The Analysis of Political Behaviour*, pp. 287 seq. See also the critical comments of GINSBERG, M. (1951), *Brit. Journ. Soc.*, 2, 76–8, and the sympathetic discussion by MANNHEIM, K. (n.d.), *Man and Society*, pp. 217 seq.

tative pedestal and to add the analysis of himself to the material furnished by the group'. He reminds us, however, that in no case is the analyst passive or mute, in spite of occasional claims to the contrary.[1]

While distortions introduced by the intervention of the analyst cannot be neglected, psychotherapy remains unique in its intention, which is to increase the patient's insight and skill in self-analysis rather than to indoctrinate him.[2]

In recent decades in the United States modifications of Freud's technique have begun to accumulate. Under the influence of Otto Rank and his colleagues, the practice of psychotherapy has been streamlined so as to curtail the number of sessions; this has sometimes involved concentrating attention on immediate, rather than on deep-seated, causes of maladjustment. Another departure, which has merits in addition to those of economy, is towards methods of group therapy.

Simultaneously, much attention is being given to the enlargement of psychoanalytic theory, so that the problems of the individual may be treated not in isolation, but as symptoms of social maladjustment.

It is out of these developments that the modern practice of counselling has emerged. At its best this is a highly-skilled procedure, conducted with self-awareness by experienced practitioners.

The theory and practice of counselling has been very well described by Carl Rogers. He distinguishes twelve characteristic

[1] LASSWELL, H. D. (1948), p. 289. Details of his procedures are given in FERENCZI, S. (1926), *Further Contributions to the Theory and Technique of Psychoanalysis*, pp. 198 seq. Trigant Burrow's creed is described in his highly stimulating *The Social Basis of Consciousness* (1927), and elaborated in his later books.

[2] ' The interviewer offers interpretations to the subject which are intended to assist him in recognising and avowing with serenity those aspects of himself which are concealed from full waking awareness, or which are recognised, if at all, with great perturbation of affect. . . . The interviewer systematically challenges the interpretation accepted by the subject (especially if these stem from the analyst). The interviewer knows that subjects are disposed to acquiesce in interpretations as a means of appeasing the anxieties of the moment; yet this may stand in the way of deeper insight.'—LASSWELL, H. D. (1948), pp. 289–90.

Cf. FREUD, S. (1924), *Collected Papers*. ' . . . he must bend his own unconscious like a receptive organ towards the emerging unconscious of the patient, be as the receiver of the telephone to the disc. As the receiver transmutes the electric vibrations induced by the sound-waves, so is the physician's unconscious mind able to reconstruct the patient's unconscious, which has directed his associations, from the communications derived from it.'

This passage is quoted and commented upon by HORNEY, K. (1939), *New Ways in Psychoanalysis*, pp. 285 seq.

steps in the therapeutic process. These begin with the important moment when the individual comes for help, and is met by a friendly and receptive but not didactic counsellor. In early sessions the patient gives vent to hostile, critical and destructive feelings, which the counsellor accepts, recognises and clarifies. In due course, and *invariably*, the antagonistic impulses are used up and give way to the first expressions of positive feeling. The counsellor accepts these, though without approbation, until suddenly and spontaneously ' insight and self-understanding come bubbling through '.[1]

With insight comes the first clarification of possible courses of action. The patient begins to realise that he has the power of decision. Next he actually exercises this power, until in a short while he is ready to emancipate himself from dependence on the counsellor.

There is an evident theoretical connection between this therapeutic technique and the interviewing techniques of social science. The counselling procedure has been evolved in order to ensure that the patient will progressively take over responsibility for his own actions. Correspondingly, the *raison d'être* of the non-directive interview is that the informant should decide for himself what topics are relevant to the interview situation, and how to treat any topic thus chosen.

As Rogers points out, the counsellor who conducts a non-directive interview ' needs to place upon himself the most unusual restraints and to develop a mode of discourse which is completely foreign to ordinary conversation '.[2] Whatever their situation, and however self-confident they may be, most people feel constrained to keep their end up in any conversation, to contribute remarks, witty or profound to taste, that will linger in their listeners' memories. It is a temptation that consultants and advisers can seldom resist. But the non-directive counsellor or interviewer must renounce all this. He must become a kind of colourless sounding-board whose echoes are only distinguishable because they are slightly clearer than the originals.

The counsellor endeavours to hold up to the client a verbal mirror which enables the latter to see himself more clearly and which at the

[1] ROGERS, C. R. (1942), *Counseling and Psychotherapy*, p. 40.
[2] ROGERS, C. R. (1945), ' The Non-directive Method as a Technique for Social Research ', *Am. Journ. Soc.*, **50**, 279.

The Non-directive Interview

same time indicates that he is deeply understood by a counsellor who is making no evaluation of him or his attitudes. It is this technique of reflection of emotional attitudes which has proved to have such surprising and unexpected value as a tool of social research.[1]

The interviewer techniques that have been adopted and their consequences can be satisfactorily described and evaluated because verbatim gramophone records have been made of complete interviews. From analysis of these records it has been possible to derive general rules as to which interviewer responses encourage the informant to self-expression and which tend to divert or block his train of thought.

The details of the technique are hard to summarise, and can clearly only be mastered by practice and subsequent criticism of the recorded version. A good initial idea of the procedure may be grasped by study of an annotated verbatim report of an eight-interview course of treatment of Herbert Bryan, a neurotic young intellectual, which occupies nearly 200 pages of *Counseling and Psychotherapy*.[2]

Rogers has also used elsewhere, by way of illustration, a condensed account of another sequence [3] recorded in a psychological clinic:

> A mother comes to the clinic for help with her two-and-a-half-year-old boy. At first her problem is the boy's fears; when this is accepted, it is his habit training; when this is reflected, it is the father's attachment to the boy which is so deep that it makes her jealous; when this is faced, she can admit that she never wanted the boy; finally, confronting this fact, she can gradually discuss her deeper problem—that she is afraid that she is losing the love of her husband.

This mother begins by telling that her son Buddy is fearful of other children:

> MRS. S. He is afraid of them, seems to be afraid that they will actually hurt him. And, having a small baby, I cannot go out and supervise him, so I let him play by himself.
>
> COUNSELLOR. You can't find time to supervise his play with other children, though you would prefer that.

Obviously, the counsellor is only rephrasing the attitude expressed by the mother. It enables her to go on talking about his fears and his fussiness, and she adds:

[1] ROGERS, C. R. (1945), p. 279.   [2] ROGERS, C. R. (1942), pp. 261 seq.
[3] ROGERS, C. R. (1945) pp. 279–80.

MRS. S. As long as you're with him, it's all right, but leave him alone, and he starts a violent screaming (*she pauses and laughs*). I see where I'm going to come out on this—back to myself.
COUNSELLOR. You feel that part of the problem may be in yourself.
MRS S. (*smiling*). Buddy developed a fear of everything—he used to like the rain, the wind. Now he wants to come in. He is afraid when planes go by.

The counsellor's response serves its purpose very nicely. He accepts the fact that the mother recognises her part in the problem, but he does not probe or question, which would almost certainly have aroused defensiveness. The mother is frightened herself by what she has admitted and retreats into conversation about Buddy's fear. As her attitudes are recognised, she talks of his habits.

MRS S. He is normal in physical functions, bowel movements and urination—almost completely trained. Once in a while he forgets on bowel movement. He is not too curious about sex. When he plays with himself, we just tell him 'Pattycake'. At night, urination is something of a problem, but not too much. He goes in cycles; we praise him when he doesn't wet the bed, but we don't blame him when he wets.
COUNSELLOR. You feel that you handle those things sensibly.

This is an excellent response which cuts through the content of the mother's statement and accurately reflects her attitude. Then she takes a new and deeper step, feeling more secure in the uncritical atmosphere which the counsellor is creating. She pauses, and then goes on:

MRS. S. I was just thinking, I could explain all this without coming to a psychologist.
COUNSELLOR. You feel that you really understand the situation.
MRS. S. Well, that's true and it isn't true.
COUNSELLOR. In a way you do and in a way you don't. (*Pause.*) Perhaps you would like to discuss what you feel about the situation.
Etc. etc.

This passage illustrates well the systematic good listening required of the counsellor. The reader can see that even in this brief exchange the counsellor must have been constantly fighting back the temptation to display his superior knowledge or understanding of the situation. The danger is the more emphatic because the counsellor's superior status in the interview relationship enables him to put forward his view with great authority. Members of this school of psychotherapy thus reject what they regard as the classical psychoanalytical device of explaining intellectually to the patient the basis of his maladjustment, and even refrain from attempting to evolve a rational statement of the underlying difficulty.[1] The work of the counsellor is done when the patient has recovered his self-reliance and alignment, and not when an intellectually neat diagnosis is ready to be added to the dossier, or when the patient has been dragooned into accepting the counsellor's advice.

It is demonstrable that a real difference in method distinguishes the followers of the non-directive school of counselling from those counsellors who retain the traditional directive techniques. Thus, for example, Rogers [2] quotes from an unpublished thesis by E. H. Porter which is devoted to a comparison between the results obtained by six counsellors favouring directive methods and five counsellors favouring non-directive methods. His material consisted of nineteen interviews on gramophone records.

Porter found that certain types of response were much more heavily used by the directive group and that certain others were predominantly used by the non-directive group:

3f. Counsellor expresses approval, disapproval, shock or other personal reaction in regard to client. *Ex.* ' Good! Grand! That's a nice start.' (Used 4 times as often by directive as by non-directive group.)

5a, b. Counsellor proposes client activity, directly, or through questioning technique, or in response to question of what to do. *Ex.* ' I think you ought to quit that job and put as much time in on your schoolwork as possible.' (Used 7–8 times as often by directive group.)

---

[1] To a layman, this criticism of classical Freudian psychotherapy does not appear to be firmly based. Freud and his followers have written extensively of the uncertain value of intellectual explanations. Thus, as early as 1922, Freud wrote: ' What then do we have to do in order to bring what is unconscious in the patient into consciousness ? At one time we thought that would be very simple; all we need do would be to identify this unconscious matter and then tell the patient what it was. However, we know already that that was a short-sighted mistake. Our knowledge of what is unconscious in him is not equivalent to his knowledge of it: when we tell him what we know he does not assimilate it *in place of* his own unconscious thoughts, but *alongside* of them, and very little has been changed.'—FREUD, S. (1929 ed.), *Introductory Lectures on Psychoanalysis*, p. 364.
[2] ROGERS, C. R. (1942), pp. 118 seq.

3b. Counsellor responds in such a way as to indicate recognition of expression of feeling or attitude in immediately preceding verbal response. *Ex.* ' And that makes you feel pretty low.' (Used 8–9 times as often by non-directive group.)

3c. Counsellor responds in such a way as to interpret or recognise feeling or attitude expressed in some way other than in the immediately preceding response. *Ex.* ' Maybe you didn't want to come this morning.' (Used 13+ times as often by non-directive group.)

The Hawthorne Interviews. It may properly be objected that a technique which is suitable for psychotherapy may have no relevance for social research. Some answer to this point is given by the experiences of the Hawthorne investigators, whose methods of interviewing and use of interview material evolved in a most interesting manner under the dictates of empirical, rather than of theoretical, considerations.

On the completion of the first stage of the Relay Assembly Test Room experiment, which is described elsewhere,[1] the research group decided to launch an interviewing programme which, for a time, overshadowed all other activities.[2]

The initial idea behind this programme was simple and, as events proved, over-simplified. Experience had shown that supervision was a weak point at the works, and the interviews were designed to provide material that could be used in supervisory training courses. This material was to comprise the essential facts about supervisor–employee relations, and was to be collected by approaching frankly the employees themselves and asking them to express their likes and dislikes about their working environment.

Plans were carefully laid, and a precise code of behaviour for the interviews was laid down. These were patterned on existing techniques of interviewing, such as that done in the course of their normal work by supervisors, employment departments and personnel people. The interviewer had certain topics to be explored, and if it was difficult to get the employee to talk, leading questions were put to him, such as: How does your boss treat you? Does your boss ever bawl you out? Has he any

---

[1] pp. 134 seq., and 283 seq.
[2] ROETHLISBERGER, F. J., and DICKSON, W. J. (1939), *Management and the Worker*, particularly Ch. IX (pp. 189–205) and Ch. XIII (pp. 270–91).

favourites ? Is your boss a slave-driver ? Do you consider your boss to be reasonable ?

The interviewer was also instructed to ask specifically for the employee's views on such things as the lighting system, heat, ventilation, drinking-water, toilets, safety devices and so on. Thus, throughout, the importance and relevancy of issues were decided by the interviewer. The interviewer led the conversation : the employee followed.

The deficiencies of this method were at last recognised. At a staff meeting one interviewer berated himself for being a poor interviewer because he could not keep an employee on the specified topics. Other interviewers confessed to similar experiences. After much discussion the interviewers began to wonder whether it was they who were at fault, or whether the fault lay in what they had been instructed to do.

It was finally decided to adopt a new interviewing technique, which was called the *indirect approach*. This was, probably unknown to its initiators, very similar to the counselling method that has already been described :

> After the interviewer had explained the program, the employee was to be allowed to choose his own topic. As long as the employee talked spontaneously, the interviewer was to follow the employee's ideas, displaying a real interest in what the employee had to say, and taking sufficient notes to enable him to recall the employee's various statements. While the employee continued to talk, no attempt was to be made to change the subject. The interviewer was not to interrupt or to try to change the topic to one he thought more important. He was to listen attentively to anything the worker had to say about any topic and take part in the conversation only in so far as it was necessary in order to keep the employee talking. If he did ask questions, they were to be phrased in a noncommittal manner, and certainly not in the form, previously used, which suggested the answers.[1]

These were the guiding lines of an extremely ambitious interview programme, under which in the two following years 20,000 interviews were conducted, each lasting on average one and a half hours. As the result of experience the initial directives were codified into five rules of conduct to which interviewers tried to adhere fairly closely. These were as follows : [2]

[1] ROETHLISBERGER, F. J., and DICKSON, W. J. (1939), p. 203.   [2] *ibid.*, p. 287.

1. The interviewer should listen to the speaker in a patient and friendly, but intelligently critical, manner.
2. The interviewer should not display any kind of authority.
3. The interviewer should not give advice or moral admonition.
4. The interviewer should not argue with the speaker.
5. The interviewer should talk or ask questions only under certain conditions.

   (*a*) To help the person talk.
   (*b*) To relieve any fears or anxieties on the part of the speaker which might be affecting his relation to the interviewer.
   (*c*) To praise the interviewee for reporting his thoughts and feelings accurately.
   (*d*) To veer the discussion to some topic which had been omitted or neglected.
   (*e*) To discuss implicit assumptions, if this were advisable.

While the rôle of the non-directive interviewer was thus becoming codified, there was a concurrent clarification of the use to which the interview material could be put. The questions in the original interviews had been designed to guide management to sources of employee irritation—such as draughts, dirty toilets and so on. One of the four departments of the Industrial Research Division had been devoted to the ' content analysis ' of favourable and unfavourable employee comments. As time went on, however, the need to make a clear distinction between the *manifest* and the *latent* content of complaints had begun to emerge. The notion that management could obtain an accurate and complete picture of industrial conditions by analysis of employee comments had to be abandoned. And yet at the same time the fact that an employee was moved to complain was often of great significance. Thenceforward, therefore, ' certain complaints were no longer treated as facts in themselves but as symptoms or indicators of personal or social situations which needed to be explored '.[1] A still later tendency was to regard the interview programme as providing a therapeutic service embedded in the factory and to play down even lower the factual value of material collected in interviews.

One feature of the non-directive interview is that the informant is much more articulate, and in fact talks much more, than in the directive interview. Porter, whose comparison of counsellor

---

[1] ROETHLISBERGER, F. J., and DICKSON, W. J. (1939), p. 269.

techniques has already been described, went on to compare the amount of talking done by counsellor and client. He found beyond dispute that the more directive counsellors do much more of the talking.

> In an analysis of word count in these interviews, Porter found that the ratio of counselor words to counselee words ranged from 0·15 to 4·02. In other words, at one extreme the client talked nearly seven times as much as the counselor. At the other extreme the counselor talked four times as much as the client—a statistical example of what it means to try to ' get a word in edgeways '. If we compare these two extreme counselors, the second talked more than twenty-five times as much as the first.
> There was a striking relationship between the ratio of words spoken by counselor and counselee and the degree of directiveness. In the ten directive interviews, the average ratio was 2·77, the counselor talking nearly three times as much as the client. In the nine non-directive interviews the average ratio was 0·47, the counselor talking less than half as much as the client. It will be noted from these two ratios that the directive counselors used on the average about six times as many words as the non-directive—one of the sharpest differences found in the whole study. This makes graphic the fact that in non-directive counseling the client comes ' to talk out his problems '. In a directive contact the counselor talks to the client.[1]

It is not surprising that in none of the cases given is the interviewer expected to be entirely passive. While he must not ask too many questions or lead the informant too much, he must also—as in psychotherapy—avoid the opposite error, which leaves the interview at the level of polite social conversation. He must retain control of the situation, but use it in such a way as to minimise the obtrusion of his own preconceptions. He must recognise that his primary duty is to help the informant to express what is in—or under the surface of—his own mind.

Such interviews also have the advantage, if properly conducted, of leaving a favourable effect on the informant, who will have acquired the elements of skill in self-analysis and will be in full sympathy both with the subject-matter and with the substance of the interview record. He will retain the memory of a psychologically significant incident, and perhaps of a distinctive social relationship.

[1] ROGERS, C. R. (1942), p. 122.

There are, however, serious limitations to the use of this technique for purposes of research rather than of therapy.

Firstly, the collection of material by such means is inevitably slow, and a rather small sample can thus normally be expected. Moreover, the unrestricted range of subjects which the informant may desire to discuss makes it almost impossible to bring records of different interviews into a single scheme. The investigator is left with a mass of fascinating and revealing individual case-histories which, owing to the difficulties of statistical tabulation and analysis, he is often unable to use as the safe basis for generalisation. While this type of interview is thus fruitful as a source of hypotheses, it may be an unsafe foundation for any but impressionistic conclusions.

Second, for the insight interview to be at all successful, great knowledge and skill are demanded of the interviewer. Interviewers in the United States sometimes help to equip themselves with this skill by undergoing a short course in personal psychoanalysis.[1]

Moreover, the interviewer must possess not only the general special skill demanded of any sympathetic listener, but also the specific ability to adopt temporarily the beliefs and attitudes of each in turn of his informants. It is only by doing so that he will be able adequately to help his informants to express themselves.

2. THE FOCUSED INTERVIEW

Now, it is clear that no interviewer can completely exorcise his own interests. In practice he is liable to impose his own hypotheses on the informant in an indirect way, without an open rational exposition—or even realisation—of what he is doing. From any sentence spoken to him he can select that part of the meaning that appears relevant to him; he can break the recurrent pauses by setting the ball rolling again in the direction of his choice. This will often be done unconsciously; as such a small proportion of interviews are recorded verbatim, it is impossible to gauge how much has been lost and how much distorted in this manner.

The normal ' depth ' interview can thus clearly never represent a state of perfect freedom from bias, which has to be preserved in

---

[1] See e.g. LASSWELL, H. D. (1948), p. 293.

The Focused Interview

all its purity against any modification in technique. The Hawthorne interviewers steered the informant on to particular topics but not away from others. If the informant responds to a topic towards which he is guided, it is fairly reasonable to infer that he would have reached that particular topic without guidance in the course of a long enough interview. The distortion is in the sectors represented, and not necessarily in the internal content of these sectors.

This viewpoint has found increasing support in recent years among those who wish to retain the good qualities of the non-directive technique and at the same time are keen to evolve a method that is economical and precise enough to leave a residue of results rather than merely a posse of cured souls.

One outstanding example is the programme reported by Merton and Kendall,[1] in which the *focused interview* was evolved. This procedure was designed to test specific morale-building devices used during the war, such as films, radio and pamphlets. Informants listen to the radio programme, for example, and the subsequent interview centres on their response to it.

The four canons of focused interview procedure are described as: non-direction, specificity, range, and depth and personal context.

Non-direction. The canon of *non-direction* closely follows the method already described. Examples are given of means of avoiding interviewer bias, the offering of suggestions and so on. Specific gambits are suggested, such that the interviewer should counter a question with a question, e.g. ' You mean it wasn't clear ? ', etc., etc.

The authors distinguish four degrees of guidance, or structuring, which can be imposed on the informant. There is the *unstructured question*, in which the stimulus and response are both left free, e.g. ' What stood out especially in this radio programme ? ' Any answer which refers to the radio programme is then relevant and acceptable.

We next have *semi-structured* questions, which can be of two types: those in which the response is structured and the stimulus left free even though the topic is indicated, e.g. ' What did you

---

[1] MERTON, R. K., and KENDALL, P. L. (1946), ' The Focused Interview ', *Am. Journ. Soc.*, 51, 541–57.

learn from this pamphlet that you hadn't known before?'; and those in which the stimulus is structured and the response left free, e.g. 'How did you feel about (a specific incident in the film)?'

Finally there is the *fully structured question*, as widely used in mass interviewing, in which the informant is presented with a stimulus and a few alternative responses. E.g. 'As you listened to Chamberlain's speech, did you feel it was propagandist or informative?'

In general, any questions in which the response is left free (i.e. two of the above) are legitimately used in a focused interview. The procedure is thus maintained as technically non-directive even if all the topics are selected by the investigator, but it is still wise to give some free scope to the informant.

Specificity. The second canon is *specificity*. The investigator is not interested in the informant's wide range of experiences and sentiments, but only in particular slices. In these chosen sectors the greatest possible vividness is desired, and vague impressions are to be deprecated. The interviewer's task is to encourage and bring out the informant's skill in 'retrospective introspection'. 'How did you feel . . ?' must be answered specifically, and if necessary the original stimulus (e.g. film sequence) is repeated in order to remind the subject of his original response.

Range. The criteria of *range* and *depth* are presented as tests by which the quality of a particular interview may be judged. The initial stimulus (film, radio or pamphlet) is subjected to *content analysis* by the investigator before any interviews begin, and when combined with any mass statistics that may be available provides an hypothesis as to what responses will occur. *Range* is achieved if the interview yields data which confirm or confute this hypothesis, and demonstrate that ample opportunities have been provided for the report of unanticipated responses.

Depth and Personal Context. *Depth* is achieved if the interview brings out the intensity of personal feeling aroused by the question. In achieving this, the skill of the interviewer is exercised to the full. If, for example, an informant moves to a new subject, is this because the former subject is peripheral to his interests, because he considers that the topic has been exhausted, or because it is a 'painful' subject which he does not wish to discuss? The interviewer must recognise that not every topic operates at the same psychological level, and his job is to expose and clarify the true intensity of the informant's feelings on each subject.[1]

3. LIFE-HISTORIES

It is implicit in the focused interview that the interviewer should be armed with an *interview guide*, or list of topics which it is desired should be explored in the course of the session. In this respect it is a close relation of a technique much used by anthropologists, which also originated in psychoanalysis. This is the method of eliciting life-histories by question and answer. As MacCurdy has said, ' Psycho-analysis in its primary meaning is . . . merely a special technique for gathering a history of the patient's life in a series of interviews '.[2] While it is true that ' the object of the psychoanalytical interview is primarily therapeutic, and to this scientific curiosity must always take second place ',[3] it is clearly legitimate to attempt a similar collection of life-histories for purposes of research rather than therapy.

There is no clear line of demarcation between the spontaneous autobiography, the volunteered self-record compiled by the informant to cover topics chosen by the investigator, and the life-history obtained in a series of interviews. The first two of these have been considered in the chapter on documents, but the third is discussed here as a form of interview material.

Whether the investigator desires it or not, he will be unable to keep the relationship between himself and his life-history informant on as cursory and simple a basis as it may be when other kinds of information are gathered in the field. The very fact that

---

[1] Cf. ROETHLISBERGER, F. J., and DICKSON, W. J. (1939), p. 276 :
' There is always the tendency to take one of two extreme attitudes, either completely believing or completely disbelieving everything a person says. In the first case the interviewer takes everything that is said at its face value. In the other case he disbelieves everything he hears. Both attitudes arise from the fallacy of assuming that everything that is being said during the interview is at the same psychological level. This is very seldom the case. Sometimes the speaker is bored and is just making conversation. Sometimes he is poking fun at the interviewer. Sometimes he is nervous and apprehensive and therefore he is guarded in the statements he makes. Sometimes he is trying to make a favorable impression on the interviewer. At other times he is more earnest, and is attending to and reflecting upon what is being said. Naturally, the meaning to be assigned to the speaker's remarks depends upon interpreting his responses in the light of the pyschological context in which they occur.'
[2] MACCURDY, J. T. (1939), ' The Relation of Psychopathology to Social Psychology ' from BARTLETT, F. C. et al.—Eds., p. 57.
[3] *ibid.*, p. 59.

interviews have to be prolonged and repeated in order to cover the ground, and the very nature of the material, are bound to lead to an affective relationship. The investigator is, however, at liberty to adopt either a free-association technique, in which the subject brings out material at his own speed and in his own order, or an active technique, in which the interviewer elicits the desired material by a process of direct questioning. Kluckhohn suggests that only the former should be accepted as giving a true autobiography, and proposes that the material collected by direct questioning should be called a ' semi-autobiography '.[1]

By analogy with the alternative forms of interview already discussed, we can also speak of a *focused autobiography* in which the focused interview technique is used to collect material on topics chosen by the investigator for their relevance to his hypotheses.

It would probably be agreed that most life-histories collected by psychotherapists are built up within the theoretical psychological structure favoured by the particular analyst. Similarly, if the purpose is social research, it is understandable that the ' ideal ' material tends to follow certain recognisable lines determined by the conceptual approach of the particular investigator. Let us consider what these lines should be.

The first point to clear is that the social scientist's interest in the responses of individuals will, except on rare occasions, centre more on what is typical about them than on their individual peculiarities.

In his fieldwork, which has already been discussed,[2] Professor Malinowski naturally engaged in numerous conversations with individuals. At the same time, although he singled out individuals, he did not forget that what he was studying was the community as a whole.

> . . . it has to be laid down that we have to study here stereotyped manners of thinking and feeling. As sociologists, we are not interested in what A or B may feel *qua* individuals, in the accidental course of their own personal experiences—we are interested only in what they feel and think *qua* members of a given community.[3]

[1] KLUCKHOHN, C. (1945), ' The Personal Document in Anthropological Science ' in GOTTSCHALK. L., et al., *The Use of Personal Documents in History, Anthropology and Sociology*, p. 125.
[2] See Chapter 3, pp. 132 seq.
[3] MALINOWSKI, B. (1922), *Argonauts of the Western Pacific*, p. 23. Cf. EVANS-PRITCHARD, E. E. (1951), *Social Anthropology*, pp. 44 seq.
It must be recognised, however, that in the study of modern adaptive societies

Most of the American social scientists who have followed Malinowski's field methods have trained both as psychologists and as anthropologists. This may have made them peculiarly suggestible to the interest-value of the individual. Whether for this or for some other reason, there appears to be a persistent inclination on their part to collect supplementary information about individual informants. Thus Kluckhohn suggests that, wherever possible, informants should be subjected to a physical examination—including analysis of blood and urine and basal metabolisms, should be photographed in the nude or near nude for the determination of the Sheldon somatotype, and should receive a battery of projective tests, such as the Rorschach and the Thematic Apperception Tests. It is claimed that by this examination it will be possible to penetrate beyond the communal components of the informant's personality, and thus to establish his strictly personal character.[1] What this means, how it can be done and why it would be desirable for the social scientist to be able to do so, are not explained. It is clear, however, that all such tests are meaningless unless norms for the community being studied have already been established.

But even if we frankly adapt the individual life-history as a sociological tool—that is, as a means of learning about the cultural milieu in which the individual concerned has lived—we still face the need for a systematic approach to the collection and presentation of the material. If the interviewer is able to influence the choice of facts to be recorded, he must have a clear idea of the purpose underlying his selection.

It is arguable that there is no general set of criteria that will fit all uses to which life-history material may be put. After careful thought, John Dollard arrived at the opposite view, and in *Criteria for the Life History* he has tabled a set of seven standards against which, in his opinion, the adequacy of any life-history compiled for the purposes of social science could be assessed.[2]

Dollard's seven criteria are introduced below:

I. *The subject must be viewed as a specimen in a cultural series.* This implies far more than the relevance of certain environmental

---

the investigator may have to construct a model of existing social structure and himself mentally assign individuals to the particular 'reference groups' from which they get their thoughts and feelings.
[1] KLUCKHOHN, C. (1945), pp. 129 seq.
[2] DOLLARD, J. (1935, 1949), *Criteria for the Life-History.*

facts. Suppose a child of a stated sex is born. Let us consider what we can say about what it will be like when it comes of age.

All of the facts we can predict about it, granted the continuity of the group, will define the culture into which it comes. Such facts can include the kind of clothes it will wear, the language it will speak, its theological ideas, its characteristic occupation, in some cases who its wife or husband is bound to be, how it can be insulted, what it will regard as wealth, what its theory of personality growth will be, etc. These and hundreds of other items are or may be standardized before the birth of the individual and be transmitted . . . with mechanical certainty.

II. *The organic motors of action ascribed must be socially relevant.* This means that the theory of motivation adopted must reconcile bodily activities with the social influences already described. The idea of a standard package of instincts given to every child will not explain the differences in behaviour between one group and another. Every act represents a response to a stimulus, but only within a social context. Conversely, culture is itself framed and confined by the capacities of the body itself and of the biological mechanisms which the body comprises.

III. *The peculiar rôle of the family group in transmitting the culture must be recognised.* This is self-explanatory, especially to disciples of Freud.

IV. *The specific method of elaboration of organic materials into social behaviour must be shown.*

The useful life history of the future will begin . . . with the organism; and it will show in detail how this organism slowly becomes capable of social life in its particular group. . . . This translation from the sheer ' socially relevant biological' to socialized motivational forces must be carefully delineated and formulated theoretically because it is of utmost importance to get this straight. Otherwise we will have our person fitted out as a mature individual with a set of attitudes corresponding to a culture but we will have no idea how he got this way and we are likely to miss altogether the initial and continuing importance of the biological substratum of the social life of the person.

V. *The continuous related character of experience from childhood through adulthood must be stressed.* ' The life-history document is a *Gestalt*, paralleling point by point the configurated experience of the individual.' Its intrinsic merit lies in its power to present continuity, configuration in time.

VI. *The 'social situation' must be carefully and continuously specified as a factor.* The point here is that, of the vast succession of situations which the individual experiences, certain ones will have for him a different meaning from that normally attached to them.

In the adequate life history we must constantly keep in mind the situation both as defined by others and by the subject; such a history will not only define both versions of the situation but let us see clearly the pressure of the formal situation and the force of the inner private definition of the situation.

VII. *The life-history material itself must be organised and conceptualised.* This criterion is inserted in protest against those who think that naïve material is pure, and hence automatically good. But ' life-history material does not speak for itself; the subject is unable to give us explanatory theoretical paragraphs making sense of the material. He may, on the contrary, and usually does, do the very best he can to disguise it. This fact makes it necessary that the life history worker play an active rôle over against his material; he must do the critical work of fashioning the necessary concepts, of making the required connections and of piecing the whole life history together to make sense plain and scientific communication easy.'

No one can deny that these criteria combine into a powerful conceptual system, and one which appears to avoid internal inconsistencies. One obtains a vivid picture of what their formulator regards as the central problem of social science. ' The important problem ', he writes, ' is . . . the problem of generation of attitudes ',[1] and his criteria support this viewpoint.

We can, however, rule out the possibility that any autobiographer will spontaneously, and without guidance, submit a document able to satisfy these stringent tests. It is evident that they require a high level of sophistication, and considerable specific familiarity with Dollard's adopted concepts and terminology.[2]

It is not surprising, therefore, that of the six documents chosen by him for analysis according to these criteria, only one—H. G. Wells' *Experiment in Autobiography*—was spontaneously presented

[1] DOLLARD, J. (1949 ed.), p. 204.
[2] ' Any stranger to this conceptual system will find it difficult to master, but we must stress that he can come by knowledge of its value only in the precise task of collecting and ordering life-history materials.'—*ibid.*, p. 36.

and organised. Of the other five, two were heavily edited and annotated self-records,[1] and the other three were psychoanalytical case-histories. Even so, the documents chosen for analysis did not emerge very satisfactorily from their tests:[2] only a case-history by Freud is highly rated on all criteria.

It seems therefore that the life-history with a rigidly pre-determined content is likely to be forthcoming only if it is directly elicited in a succession of interviews. In any case, Dollard arrived at his criteria as a result of personal experience in eliciting life-histories. His interest was aroused in the course of a survey of 'a Southern town'. His original aim was 'to study the personality of Negroes in the South, to get a few life histories, and to learn something about the manner in which the Negro person grows up'.[3] His interest aroused, and his criteria formulated, he took part in a subsequent investigation in which he set out to practise what he had preached.[4]

The life-histories were collected in the course of repeated interviews, based on psychoanalytic technique, adapted to the exigencies of the situation.

> The informant was invited to talk about his life in his own way, beginning where he chose and saying what he chose. It was stressed that the researcher would use the material in no way to the detriment of the informant and that communication of more than ordinary freedom would be appropriate. I explained that I would not ask set questions because I could not know in advance what questions would bring out the important information about the informant; surely that was something which only he could know, and I might spoil his chance to give an account of himself if I intruded with inappropriate questions.[5]

---

[1] Dollard (pp. 180, 218, etc.) significantly refers to the editors of these two documents as the authors. This is in line with Criterion VII, which assigned the active rôle to the 'life history worker' rather than to the subject.

[2] The greater part of *Criteria for the Life-History* is devoted to a point-by-point analysis of the performance of these six documents under test. This analysis has been ingeniously summarised by ALLPORT, G. W. (1942), *Use of Personal Documents in Psychological Science*, p. 27.

[3] DOLLARD, J. (1937, 2nd ed., 1949), *Caste and Class in a Southern Town*, p. 1. Although his report does not reproduce, even in part, any of the life-histories elicited, the author states that he found the material invaluable.

[4] DAVIS, A., and DOLLARD, J. (1940), *Children of Bondage*.

[5] DOLLARD, J., *Caste and Class*, p. 25. As a fully qualified psychoanalyst, the author was very conscious of the modifications introduced. He claims, however (p. 26 fn.), that his intelligent modifications could not be made by untrained analysts. If his claim is just, it greatly restricts the possibility of extending the use of this technique.

Dollard found that repeated interviews gave him a chance to observe the subject's bias in reporting on other people and their actions, to an extent that would have been impossible if the interview relationship had been superficial or defensive. Moreover, quite apart from the direct value of the biographic material, the interviews gave him direct insight on the social situation.

The use of the daily interview provided a wide-open window on the social life of Southerntown, although its alleged purpose was to study the mental life of the subject. One could not avoid hearing from each cooperator a report of the events and attitudes toward them which were shared by other people. This informal report was particularly valuable since the subject was not acting as a conscious informant but was merely talking about himself and what interested him: the result was that community processes could be seen with more intimacy and naturalness than if a method of formal questions had been used.[1]

4. THE INFORMAL INTERVIEW

The techniques so far discussed have not been much used by social scientists outside the United States. This may partly reflect the relative scale of applied social science in Europe and America, but it may also be partly traced to a reluctance of social scientists in other countries to adopt the deliberate and self-conscious approach which ' depth ' interviews demand.

More characteristic of this country has been the regular appearance of reports based on the inspired use of a series of informally organised interviews, which somehow remind us of the Englishman's passion for amateur status.

One early product of this method was Mayhew's celebrated serial report, *London Labour and the London Poor*, published in book form in four volumes from 1851 onwards. In his Preface, Mayhew showed himself to be very aware that he was breaking fresh ground:

> It surely may be considered curious as being the first attempt to publish the history of a people, from the lips of the people themselves —giving a literal description of their labour, their earnings, their trials, and their sufferings, in their own ' unvarnished ' language; and to pourtray the condition of their homes and their families by personal observation of the places, and direct communication with the individuals. . . .

[1] DOLLARD, J., *Caste and Class*, p. 485.

When the following leaves are turned over, and the two or three pages of information derived from books contrasted with the hundreds of pages of facts obtained by positive observation and investigation, surely some allowance will be made for the details which may still be left for others to supply.[1]

Since Mayhew's time there has been a large number of ' interview surveys ', which have similarly hovered on the frontier between social research and journalism.[2] In social science, informal interview material has regularly been used, both in the United States and in Europe, to illustrate conclusions reached by other means or to amplify the drier material extracted from case-record cards. Thus the American, E. Wight Bakke, produced in 1933 a once justly celebrated study of the effects of unemployment in England, in preparing which he at first deliberately adopted an informal method of interviewing. He writes:

> One of my first interviews gave me an example of the value of the indirect conversation as opposed to the quicker question and answer method. I was feeling my way in unknown territory, and, I admit, was a bit puzzled as to how to go about getting the more personal information concerning home life and religion. The visit was with a man and his wife in their home; the wife had gone to prepare coffee. I was feeling very keenly that what I was doing looked very much like prying into their personal affairs. These people are human beings, not rocks and trees. Furthermore, the fact that I was among people whose social environment was foreign to me and with whose attitudes I had not yet been able to become familiar, caused me to drop a remark to the man that I had some questions of a bit more personal nature to ask him. It was the worst thing that I could have done, of course. Just then his wife came in with the coffee and sandwiches invariably served about ten o'clock in the evening, and the conversation carried on. In our natural conversation over the coffee cups every question I had in mind was answered spontaneously and without the necessity of putting the questions. While the wife was taking out the cups, the man said, ' Now, Mr. Bakke, for those questions you were going to ask me '. I had to fumble around with some further question about birth control in order to prove that I had not merely been bluffing.[3]

[1] MAYHEW, H. (1851), *London Labour and the London Poor*, Vol. I, p. iii.
[2] Mayhew was a journalist, and it is of interest that the word ' interview ' was probably first used in connection with journalism. Its date of origin seems to have been about the time that Mayhew was writing.
[3] BAKKE, E. W. (1935 ed.), *The Unemployed Man*, pp. 296–7.

As the author gained experience of the problem of unemployment as seen through the eyes of the British unemployed, he was able to codify those points which seemed of significance to himself. He was thus able to revert to the ethnographic frame within which his work was planned, and then to go forward to a fairly highly structured form of interview, and even to the questionnaire. It is only recently, however, that informal interviews have been resurrected and claimed to provide an independently reliable foundation for scientific generalisation.

Professor Zweig, to whom this resurrection in England is perhaps due, has stated his informal methods to represent ' a new and unorthodox technique '. He goes on:

> I dropped the idea of a questionnaire or formal verbal questions put forward in the course of research; instead I had casual talks with working-class men on an absolutely equal footing and in friendly intercourse. These were not formal interviews but an exchange of views on life, labour and poverty.[1]

After one or two early rebuffs on revealing his credentials,

> I soon dropped all mention of my inquiry and developed a line of friendly informal intercourse. The enquiry became to me one of my greatest experiences in life. I learned more about life in the course of a few months than I had in many years before, sitting in libraries and lecturing at Universities. . . . For me, the inquiry was like a fascinating film of life, a new adventure and experiment in living.[2]

Altogether 400 cases were collected, of which 200 were ' what I consider to be representative cases ', and the others were unrepresentative, e.g. collected in public-houses, dog-racing stadiums and so on. Interview material was supplemented by what the author describes as ' mass-observation—i.e., by observing mass behaviour in all places of interest to my study and in workers' districts in London '.[3] Conclusions are, however, predominantly based on the interviews, seventy-five of which are included in condensed form in the printed report.

Professor Zweig vividly describes his own sensations and experiences in the course of his fact-finding.

> At the beginning it was an extremely painful and difficult process. You must observe and study people before you start to interview

[1] Zweig, F. (1948), *Labour, Life and Poverty*, p. 1.
[2] ibid., p. 2.
[3] ibid., p. 3.

them. You must already know quite a lot before you can put the right kind of questions in the right way. Your interlocutors must have the feeling that you already know something about their way of life before they are willing to say more about themselves. Soon I found out that the success of my interviews depended primarily on my own state of mind, my own flow of energy, sympathy and understanding. When my flow of energy was low, or when I was ignorant of the living or labour conditions, the interviews were a failure. Some interviews served me only as an introduction to other more comprehensive and satisfactory talks for which I was already prepared.[1]

In view of the author's obvious enthusiasm, in view of the insight into working-class behaviour which he attained and the apparent soundness of his conclusions, one is again tempted to feel that this is a method of approach of the first importance. It clearly avoids the crudities of mass-interview techniques and the tediousness and self-conscious laboratory atmosphere of some other methods already described. Professor Zweig admits the difficulty of achieving a random sample of informants, and was forced to accept a refusal rate of up to 10%, but he asks us to overlook these deficiencies in view of the greater truthfulness achieved by his method as compared with that given by a questionnaire survey.

In time our customary caution overtakes us. 'Where are the safeguards?' we ask ourselves. 'Are we not in effect being called, and willingly agreeing, to credit the man rather than his method? If he had produced a report which conflicted with what we already believed to be true, would we be so unanxious over his methods? Are we sanguine because his method is foolproof or because he is wise and manifestly so?'

This doubt is certainly liable to be proportionate to our sympathy with the author's conclusions. In a more recent survey in the same stream of development,[2] the authors' underlying assumptions were more open to dispute. Reactions varied: 'The

---

[1] ZWEIG, F. (1948), *Labour, Life and Poverty*, p. 4.
[2] ROWNTREE, B. S., and LAVERS, G. R. (1951), *English Life and Leisure*. The first quarter of this book comprises over 200 half-page case-histories collected by a system of indirect interviewing. 'This method consists of making the acquaintance of an individual—the excuses for doing so are immaterial—and developing the acquaintance until his or her confidence is gained and information required can be obtained in ordinary conversation, without the person concerned ever knowing that there has been an interview, or that any specific information was being sought. Such a method is laborious but effective' (p. xii). The case-histories are used sporadically and illustratively in the rest of the book.

broad accuracy of this picture is undeniable', stated a *Times* leader, thus surely implying that the survey was otiose; other authorities doubted the facts or the impressions created by them. For some reason this laborious undertaking failed to achieve authority, and the method of research should bear at least part of the blame.

It must be concluded that as a technique the informal interview falls between two stools. Neither does it guarantee deep penetration to the true attitudes and beliefs of a limited number of people, nor does it tell us of the manner in which typical people respond to a series of what may be somewhat ambiguous questions. Instead of either of these, essentially it gives us the story of how one or two men educated themselves to understand, and prepared themselves to pronounce on, a related series of problems. This story may be illustrated by selections and condensations from interviews, but these supply substance rather than proof. The principal gainer is the man who has had the opportunity to conduct the research. While his gain by itself may only imperceptibly expand the hard corpus of social scientific knowledge, he has helped to equip himself for the more precise methods of enquiry, and ultimately for the even more exacting experimental task of applying his learning to the solution of practical problems of social change.

Part C—The Mass Interview

In spite of their diversity, the methods so far discussed have had the common feature of demanding creative skill and sensitivity of the interviewer. In this lies both their strength and their weakness. Few would deny that more satisfactory answers on most topics can be obtained by 'depth' interviewing than by more rapid means. But it is also undeniable that the demands in skill and time for interviewing and analysis are such that statistically adequate results are often impossible to achieve.

It is consequently not surprising that the major effort in the design of interviews, throughout the world, has gone into the devising of means whereby interviewing can be transformed into a routine task, to be carried out by highly trained but not necessarily creative workers. For some purposes it can be fully 'mechanised', and is then known as a questionnaire. This is an attempt, so to speak, to transfer skill from the bench to the drawing-board. As in engineering, it can only be undertaken by rather drastic simplification of procedures and at the expense of enrichment. There is no scope in a mass interview for the idiosyncrasies of individual interviewers, and little opportunity for the development or elaboration of hypotheses in the course of the survey. Any change in design in the middle of a production run, such as might be suggested by growing experience, must normally be ruled out on grounds of cost. If, for example, certain questions are found to be imperfect, the number of interviews still to be done may be insufficient to justify introducing the improvement. Added to statistical objections there may be practical reasons for not interfering. The designer has set in motion a chain of events, and if this chain is tampered with, the smoothness of the whole process may be prejudiced.

There is no reason to be sentimental over the mechanisation of interview techniques. If mass methods give us our only means of achieving the level of confidence and generality which we need, we are not justified in condemning them because they are more a method of proof than a method of discovery, or because their ' results ' are sometimes mistaken as literally true. On the other hand, the mass-interview method has definite limitations which are not always self-evident, and it is necessary to construct proper safeguards against an attempt, conscious or unconscious, to evade or ignore them.

Many safeguards will be specific to particular inquiries, and others are such as can only be picked up by experience. There are, however, some pitfalls, and some devices to overcome them, that are common in greater or lesser degree to most surveys, and these are summarised in the pages which follow.

The discussion will be divided into eight sections: subjects suitable for mass interviews, sampling, pilot survey, approach techniques, the setting for and conduct of the interview, note taking and carding, how to minimise bias and how to allow for non-response.

1. SUBJECTS SUITABLY EXPLORED BY THE USE OF MASS INTERVIEWS

(a) *The Ideal of Objectivity*

Traditionally in England interviews, questionnaires and forms generally have been used for collecting ' factual ' information.

Although some answers may customarily be taken with a grain of salt, they are normally, and on the whole justifiably, taken at their face value. The Domesday Book, census forms, and Income-Tax returns have deliberately avoided opinion questions, and on the whole they are more valuable as a result.[1]

The 'objective' approach is admirably compressed into Professor Bowley's principles for the design of questionnaire forms. In his view [2] questions should:

(1) ask for the minimum information needed for the purpose in hand,

(2) be those which the informant is able to answer,

(3) require an answer of a 'yes' or 'no', or a simple number, or something equally definite and precise,[3]

(4) be such as will be answered truthfully and without bias,

(5) be not unnecessarily inquisitorial.

It is possible to apply these criteria to the great majority of question forms used in social investigation, particularly in England. Some questions will measure up to them better than others, and the avoidance of bias and of unnecessary inquisition may be a matter of dispute, but the use of simple, direct questions to discover 'objective' facts has been regarded as the procedural core of the interview and questionnaire method.

Until recently, in fact, it was felt to be inappropriate that opinions should be canvassed in a similar way. This view has been particularly persistent in England. Abrams, sweepingly but with some justification, suggests that Dicey, writing his *Law and Opinion in England* in 1905, still regarded public opinion as meaning ' little more than the views of the sharply limited class of

---

[1] Cf. Sir Sylvanus Vivian (sometime Registrar-General): 'Censuses are limited to facts which can be established by statements not involving any element of degree and unaffected (as far as possible) by personal bias. We have steadily ejected from the census programme things like personal disabilities which are liable to the " more or less " assessment according to the view of the person filling in the return, and have limited ourselves to matters capable of being more simply recorded.'—*J. Roy. Statist. Soc.* (1947), **110**, 317.

[2] BOWLEY, A. L. (1937 ed.), *Elements of Statistics*, pp. 20 seq.

[3] It is interesting to contrast this rule with the following advice from *Notes and Queries on Anthropology* (5th ed., 1929), p. 25: ' The danger of leading questions is obvious, and it is a good rule never to ask a question which is capable of being answered by a simple " yes " or " no ", but always to frame the question so that positive information has to be conveyed in the answer.' (*Notes and Queries on Anthropology* is the official guide to field techniques, published by the Royal Anthropological Institute.)

intellectuals whose writings directly influenced the minds of the nation's legislators '.[1] We have to admit that there is an element of paternalism in the British tradition of social surveys as there is in the British tradition of government. While overt opinions are not excluded from the former, these tend to be the opinions of the investigators, or of expert witnesses questioned by them, rather than of the ordinary people. The collection of facts is still regarded as a safer pursuit than the counting of opinions.

In contrast, Americans seem always to have had reservations about their legislators and administrators, and United States leadership is correspondingly sensitive to organised pressure; we should not therefore be surprised that the ' straw vote ', the rudimentary opinion survey, has already been in existence there for more than a century.

In America also the rigid distinction between fact and feeling was blurred, and even abandoned, at a comparatively early date. Much of the effort of advanced American social science is now concentrated on the exposure of beliefs, attitudes and opinions; and there has been a corresponding decline in what many regard, explicitly or implicitly, as the futile search for objective reality through subjective inquiry.

In terms of money and effort, the U.S. public opinion polls now absorb a large part of the expenditure on social investigation. These polls were mostly set up in 1935, and have by now virtually displaced the straw votes which had previously held the field.[2]

There are today in the United States a number of nation-wide public opinion polls. Perhaps the best known are Gallup's ' American Institute of Public Opinion ' and Roper's ' Fortune ' poll; both of these are run on a commercial basis, and much of their work—like that of other polling organisations—is devoted to market research on behalf of individual business clients. Their opinion polls may be regarded as public in two senses, in that they provide useful publicity as well as interesting information.

Offshoots, such as the ' British Institute of Public Opinion '

[1] ABRAMS, M. (1951), *Social Surveys and Social Action*, p. 63.
[2] The methods by which straw votes had been conducted were fantastically crude. For example, the Literary Digest, which collected its material by letter, based its sample on telephone directories and motor-car registration. The poor were thus effectively excluded. Analysis was based on the 20–25 per cent who bothered to answer. There was also evidence of deliberate manipulation of the results in order to influence the election (ROBINSON, C. E., *Straw Votes*, quoted by ALBIG, W. (1939), *Public Opinion*, pp. 228 seq.).

and market research organisations using polling methods, have been set up in the British Isles and in many other countries.

The emphasis of these polls is primarily on questions of opinion; this does not, naturally, rule out the inclusion of questions aimed at ascertaining whether the informant has at least a minimum knowledge of the subject at issue, and it leaves scope for the inclusion of a wide range of questions of all kinds. Indeed, the polling organisations are quite ready to devote themselves to facts about people's lives, if there is a demand for such facts.[1] Officially sponsored bodies, such as Listener Research for the British Broadcasting Corporation and the Social Survey Division of the Central Office of Information, whose function is to provide the basis for administrative action, may tend to include more factual inquiries. The latter is probably the most technically satisfactory of all mass-interview surveys.

(b) *Election Forecasts*

The prediction of election results is still an important function of most commercial organisations, and a function which they value for the public attention that it attracts. In another respect election forecasting is unusual, in that it is possible after a short interval either to confirm or to confute the accuracy of the survey. By this test the polling techniques of the better organisations appear by now to be adequate for forecasting election results except when, as in the 1948 U.S. Presidential Election, the candidates are rather evenly matched in popularity, or when, as in 1952, the pollsters lose their nerve and refuse to predict.

The failure of the polling organisations in the 1948 election shocked the American public not so much because forecasts had been hopelessly at fault as because the public had been beguiled into forgetting the inherently approximate nature of all such predictions. For this, over-confidence on the part of the organisations must take much of the blame, but there were signs that a similar over-confidence had also to some extent lulled the professional and academic guardians of this branch of social science.

The United States Social Science Research Committee immediately realised the critical situation which had arisen and, with the co-operation of other research bodies and of the polling organisations themselves, set up a special Committee on Analysis

[1] GALLUP, G. (1948), *A Guide to Public Opinion Polls*, p. 9.

of Pre-Election Polls and Forecasts. A strong technical staff was recruited, and less than two months after the election the Committee issued their Report. Their conclusions, together with the technical reports, have since been published.[1]

The chief of the technical staff, Frederic Mosteller, contributed an outstanding chapter on 'Measuring the Error'. He shows in this that the predictive value of polls, though not negligible, may in some circumstances be equalled by that of very much less elaborate analyses.

> One method used in weather forecasting to provide a base line or standard with which to compare excellence of forecasting methods is persistence. In other words, one predicts that tomorrow will be just like today. In weather forecasting, since the time intervals between prediction and event are rather short, such persistence forecasting does a very good job. We would not expect persistence to be very accurate in election forecasting because of the four-year interval involved. However, the persistence method has the advantage of being an essentially mechanical forecasting technique, requiring little intelligence. . . .
>
> Using the persistence method . . . we note that in the past (1900–1932) persistence forecasting has had large systematic errors and large standard deviations. In recent times (1936–1948), however, the systematic errors in forecasting by the persistence method have been of the same order of magnitude as those of the polling organisations. Indeed, they have been, if anything, a little smaller and certainly not always in the same direction. . . . Taken as a whole, it cannot be said that the polling forecasts in the past four presidential elections have a very distinguished record compared to persistence forecasts, which were as good or better in three out of four elections.[2]

It is also clear that errors have been reduced very little since 1936, and the forecasts are unlikely ever to achieve substantially higher accuracy than at present, except by chance. Sampling error cannot be eliminated, and cannot unfortunately even be estimated, owing to the almost universal use of quota sampling [3] by the commercial polling organisations. In addition, it may never be possible for forecasters to anticipate last-minute changes between the final pre-election poll and election day, or to predict accurately who will in the event vote, as this depends on various equally unpredictable factors, such as the weather.

[1] MOSTELLER, F., HYMAN H., et al. (1949), *The Pre-Election Polls of* 1948.
[2] ibid., pp. 65–7.   [3] See p. 212.

The survey material is, however, of more than ephemeral value. Political scientists have for long been accustomed to seek relations between the voting record of a district and the type of inhabitants that it contains. Information on the responses of individuals, some details of whose educational, class and other characteristics are known, makes it possible to narrow the limits within which the voting behaviour of an electorate of known composition may be predicted.

But although accuracy is thereby improved, it is still far from complete. There is a hard core of voters who can be relied on to behave consistently, but elections are often won by the candidate who succeeds in capturing the waverers. And cross-sectional surveys, however numerous, tell us nothing about who wavers and why.

In order to explore this point, Lazarsfeld and two colleagues in the Bureau of Applied Social Research at Columbia University undertook an intensive survey of Erie County, Ohio.[1] They used the so-called *panel technique* of sampling, in which the same people are repeatedly interviewed. Thus the main panel of 600 were interviewed at monthly intervals six times before the election, and once after the election to determine whether they actually voted and if so for whom. Control groups were interviewed less often.

The interviews themselves contained two portions. One portion was constructed of precisely worded questions with pre-coded answers. These are of a type which will be discussed later.[2]

In addition, the repeated interviews made it possible to secure voluminous information about each respondent's personal characteristics, social philosophy, political history, personality traits, relationships with other people, opinions on issues related to the election—in short, information on anything which might contribute to our knowledge of his political preferences.[3]

[1] LAZARSFELD, P. F., BERELSON, B., and GAUDET, H. (1944, 1948), *The People's Choice*.
[2] See pp. 226 seq.
[3] *ibid.*, p. 5. The claim to have collected voluminous, but apparently unusable, material on a variety of deep subjects occurs in research reports so often as to arouse suspicion. In this case the authors have extensively used their material for illustrative purposes; even so, they appear dissatisfied, for they state (p. 159) that ' a more sophisticated case study technique would be advisable to learn more about the background and the personality of the changers as well as the specific situations in which their changes of mind came about '.

The authors are very conscious of the need for further research before election forecasts can be made with much certainty. This work would appear to be well worth doing, not so much perhaps for the value of anticipating results by a few days or weeks as because of the unusual circumstances in which success or failure in opinion prediction can be reliably checked, and because of their contribution to an understanding of the dynamics of the political process.

(c) *Other Opinion Polls*

The use of mass-interview techniques for opinion surveys which are not similarly subject to confirmation is very much more tricky. Informants are no longer being asked merely to anticipate by one form of action (i.e. verbal behaviour) another form of action (i.e. voting) which is due to take place a few days later. In the streamlined mass interview the informant is asked to choose, from a small number of given alternatives, the answer which best fits his viewpoint.

Alternatively, there is the so-called *open-ended* interview. In this method the questions are put in a precise form, but the form of each answer is left to the discretion of the informant.[1] This gives the informant a chance to clarify his standpoint and to expose a little better the considerations that have influenced him in reaching it. On the other hand, the initially greater accuracy and sensitivity of the interview record are liable to be sacrificed in the coding process, without which statistical analysis cannot take place. The avoidance of pre-coded answers at the interview itself may be of no great advantage if all answers must subsequently be forced into one or other of a limited number of moulds.

It is in any case not easy to frame questions which give reliable scope to the intelligent informant and are at the same time readily understood by people of all educational levels. Professor Hadley Cantril of Princeton University has compiled a list which indicates eleven types of poor question. This list comprises: questions too vague to permit precise answers; questions obscure in meaning; questions getting at some stereotype or overtone implicit in the questions rather than at the meanings intended; questions misunderstood because they involve technical or unfamiliar words;

---

[1] This form of question is what Merton and Kendall call *semi-structured*; stimulus structured, response free. See p. 165.

Subjects Suitably Explored by the Use of Mass Interviews 185

questions presenting issues not circumscribed; questions where the alternatives provided for answers are not exhaustive; questions where the possibilities provided for the informant's selection are too many or too long; questions whose implications are not seen; questions concerned with the affairs of only a portion of the population and therefore meaningless to many other people; questions giving only surface rationalisations; questions getting only stereotype answers.[1]

It is also widely contended that the answers given are liable to be respectable public responses rather than those revealing inner feelings. If this is so, there may be wide discrepancies between attitudes expressed—which are ultimately forecasts of behaviour in hypothetical circumstances [2]—and actual observed behaviour in real circumstances. This is a persistent problem, but one which is clearly more prominent in the case of issues of high emotional content for the informant, if these emotions can be aroused in the course of a brief interview. While emotive questions need not necessarily be framed in terms of attitudes—they might sometimes appear to be strictly objective factual questions—it may be presumed that attitude surveys on the whole give greater scope for passions than, for example, a population census.

This last objection is essentially based on the belief that some issues are so important to the informant that one cannot expect him to remain truthful in answering them. An objection is made to some other questions on the precisely opposite grounds that certain informants are liable to be so indifferent to the issues involved, through ignorance or other cause, that any answers which they may give are of no value.

Objections such as these have for years rained steadily from the altitudes of higher learning upon the public-opinion pollsters. They have damped no ardour, nor apparently have they held off sponsors, but they have led to some attempts to put the polls on a more realistic footing. The Gallup poll, for example, makes some use of the *omnibus questionnaire* of 200–300 questions,

---

[1] CANTRIL, H. (1944), *Gauging Public Opinion*, pp. 3–22.
[2] ' It is probably safe to say that attitudes relate not primarily to the past, nor even primarily to the present, but as a rule to the future. " Do you believe in. . . . ? " is likely to mean " Would you like to have so-and-so happen ? " ',— MURPHY, G., MURPHY, L. B., and NEWCOMB, T. M. (1937), *Experimental Social Psychology*, p. 894.
See also Dollard's comments (pp. 202 seq.) on the relationship between the *origin* situation, the *test* situation and the *criterion* situation.

which 'may take a whole afternoon or evening to complete'[1] and which, it is claimed, is somehow used in the preparation of normal mass interviews. The *split-ballot* technique permits the measurement of the effect on answers of the form in which questions are framed, and presumably some attempt is made to use such measurements to adjust results.[2]

Finally, and most ambitiously of all, there is the device known as the Quintamensional Plan of Question-Design.[3] As its name distantly suggests, this comprises five stages, as follows:

>   1. The filter or information stage is aimed to find out whether the informant has thought about the issue. An affirmative answer is not necessarily accepted without further probing.
>   2. The 'free-answer' or 'open-ended' question. This enables the informant to reply in his own words.
>   3. The dichotomous or 'specific-answer' question, or system of questions. Ideally this restricts answers to Yes—No—Don't know, but if necessary '*multiple-choice*' or '*cafeteria*' questions may be substituted.
>   4. Questioning to elicit why the informant holds the views he does.
>   5. Questioning to find out how intensely the informant holds the views he does.

It must be admitted that neither the Quintamensional Plan nor any other device so far tried has convinced the doubters that polls can claim in any exact sense to disclose public opinions. On the whole, the approach to truth is a naïve one; for example, the test for intensity of belief (No. 5 above), which consists of a single straight question, 'How intensely do you believe . . . ?' is clearly too simple to stand.[4] On the other hand, there is not the slightest doubt that on a variety of vital issues—i.e. those manifestly affecting the lives of informants—the polls do provide a genuine index, at some level of understanding, of public attitudes and shifts in attitude. The pollsters' claim that they provide a measure of public opinion is thus irrefutable, but the trouble remains that polls are not a fine enough instrument to 'single out

---

[1] GALLUP, G. (1948 ed.), *A Guide to Public Opinion Polls*, p. 40.
[2] For a discussion of the *split-ballot* see also p. 243.   [3] *ibid.*, pp. 40–9.
[4] One interesting, and potentially important, product of scalogram analysis (described later in this chapter) is an empirical technique for measuring intensity. The whole question of how to map intensity of attitude is discussed in STOUFFER, S. A. et al. (1950), *Measurement and Prediction*, pp. 213–76, etc.

decisive aspects '[1] of public opinion, and hence to permit prediction of public actions. What they can do, and how they should set about doing it, are questions at present being earnestly explored in a number of academic Research Centres in the United States.

(d) *Attitude Measurements*

Meanwhile, the search has continued for a method which, while suitable for mass application, will more adequately pinpoint the distribution of opinions, measure their intensity and explore their origins. In the United States, during and since the last war, two methods of doing so have been evolved which, while not yet claimed as mature, are of great importance and promise.

These two methods were developed in parallel by social scientists attached to the Research Branch of the Information and Education Division of the United States War Department.[2] They represent the latest steps along a route which is entirely distinct from that which the public opinion polls have travelled.

It may be of value briefly to review the past history of this form of attitude measurement, which we owe to a succession of social psychologists.

To them, the attitudes of an individual are to be regarded as elements in his total personality, corresponding with his abilities or other qualities, such as ' intelligence ', which can be determined by testing. While it is true that an individual's attitude on some issues may be inferred from his actions—for example, a man who persistently gambles is unlikely to regard betting as immoral—it is often more convenient to elicit attitudes by verbal methods. The verbal methods used are generally direct, in that they entail point-blank questioning. Indirect methods, by which attitudes are explored without the knowledge of the informant, require more skill than is normally available for the conduct of mass interviews, and are therefore more suitable for the delicate techniques discussed earlier in this chapter than for large-scale attitude surveys.

---

[1] LAZARSFELD, P. F. (1944), " The Controversy Over Detailed Interviews : an Offer for Negotiation ", *P.O.Q.*, **8**, 38–60.
[2] This work was only part of that emanating from the Research Branch. For example, the development by Merton and Kendall of the ' focused interview ' already mentioned was also a Research Branch product.

The direct questioning technique is used by both the public-opinion pollster and the attitude surveyor. The question asked by a pollster elicits an answer that is taken to indicate the informant's opinion on a particular issue. In the attitude study, however, each topic is generally explored, not by a single question, but by a battery of related questions. Every such battery, made up of questions each of which varies a little in its implications, makes it possible to sort the informants out into some kind of order corresponding with the stand which they wish to take on the point at issue.

Multiple questioning has the added advantage of spreading the risk that the informant's response will be determined by some irrelevant consideration, such as a personal ambiguity in meaning or some specific and isolated preference or distaste. On the other hand, the extended data offered by the battery of questions are only acceptable if it can be shown that the questions, and the answers that they evoke, are related to each other, and that a 'Yes' answer to one question affects the chance of a 'Yes' answer to each other question. Specifically, it should be possible to place the questions in such an order that it is rare for an informant answering 'No' to a particular question to answer 'Yes' to other questions which are judged to imply a more extreme position.

This can best be illustrated by an example. One of the earliest attempts to use a scaling device for attitude measurements was the 'social distance' method proposed in 1928 by Emory Bogardus.[1] In its original form, informants were asked to state their first reactions to admitting members of certain specified races to different degrees of intimacy. The results obtained in one survey of 1,725 native-born white Americans are given below. The first five situations were chosen to represent decreasingly intimate relationships between the informant and members of the races listed.

This was clearly a very interesting and important exercise in method. On the whole it appears to support the conclusion that, for large samples at least, 'if a given group is not accepted in a given rôle, it will be refused in all " nearer " rôles '.[2]

[1] Quoted by MURPHY, G., MURPHY, L. B., and NEWCOMB, T. M. (1937 ed.), pp. 898 seq.
[2] ibid., p. 900.

Subjects Suitably Explored by the Use of Mass Interviews

In selecting the different degrees of intimacy tabled below, Bogardus had to assume that informants' reactions to them would be reflections of the same attitude complex—that is, that they were *unidimensional*; he must also have hoped that they would provide good scaling points along this single dimension. A

I would admit:	To close kinship by marriage.	To my club as personal chums.	To my street as neighbours.	To employment in my occupation in my country.	To citizenship in my country.	As visitors only to my country.	Would exclude from my country.
	%	%	%	%	%	%	%
English	94	97	97	95	96	2	0
American (native white)	90	92	93	92	91	1	0
Canadians	87	93	96	96	96	2	0
Scotch	78	89	91	93	93	2	0
Scotch-Irish	73	82	88	89	92	17	0
Irish	70	83	86	90	91	4	1
French	68	85	88	90	93	4	1
Welsh	61	72	80	81	86	5	0
Spaniards	28	50	55	58	82	8	2
Armenians	9	15	28	46	58	18	5
Japanese	2	12	13	27	29	39	3

glance at the table will show that these hopes were not consistently fulfilled. While the percentage of those willing to admit Welshmen increases fairly satisfactorily (from the scale-creation point of view) as the supposed degree of intimacy decreases, the scale does not work very well for English or Americans. Again, in none of the eight favoured nationalities is there any great differentiation between the percentage admitting these races ' to my street as neighbours ' and the percentage admitting them ' to employment in my occupation in my country '.

Defects such as these may be attributed to the necessarily arbitrary manner in which the categories were chosen. The next refinement was due to Thurstone, who evolved a less personal method of scale construction:

> Several groups of people are asked to write out their opinions on the issue in question, and the literature is searched for suitable brief statements that may serve the purpose of the scale. By editing such material a list of from 100 to 150 statements is prepared expressive of attitudes covering as far as possible all gradations from one end of the scale to the other. . . . When the original list has been edited . . . there will be perhaps 80 to 100 statements to be actually scaled. The statements are then mimeographed on small cards, one statement to each card. Two or three hundred subjects are asked to arrange

the statements in eleven piles ranging from opinions most strongly affirmative to those most strongly negative. . . . The task is essentially to sort out the small cards into eleven piles so that they *seem* to be fairly evenly spaced or graded.[1]

Statements whose placing by different judges varied widely were discarded, and each surviving statement was given a scale value such that the number of judges placing it in a higher category was balanced by the number of judges placing it lower on the scale.

Each of up to a hundred statements was thus given a position on the scale. Some such statements would be so close in ' meaning ' to each other, however, that the judges, as a whole, would be unable to discern the difference between them. When the difference is just noticeable, the two statements are taken to be separated by one unit of the scale. A final Thurstone scale, of which a wide variety has been published, consists of about twenty items, which are both adequately spaced and also cover the whole scale from one extreme to the other.

This method of scale construction is clearly an improvement on the earlier forms in which the ' meaning ' of individual items was virtually prejudged by one individual; it will be recognised, however, that it is necessary that the judges responsible for preparing the scale should have similar interests and attitudes, and a similar universe of discourse, to those on whom it is desired to carry out the test. This is regarded by some as a fatal defect. For example, it has been objected that the Thurstone type of scale building becomes ' increasingly difficult once we leave the classroom, the discussion club, and the other small, comparatively infrequent and highly selected groups that enjoy having experiments tried upon them. Such groups already have developed ways of making their attitudes articulate. It is the more numerous workaday groupings of society, which are inaccessible to his controlled measurements, about whose attitudes the social scientist is in the most need of information. Students may be required, good-natured academicians may be cajoled, and sundry needy persons may be paid to sort cards containing propositions into eleven piles. But it is difficult to imagine securing comparable judgments or satisfactory measurements in the final application

[1] THURSTONE, L. L. (1928), ' Attitudes can be Measured ', *Am. Journ. Soc.*, **33**, 544 seq.

Subjects Suitably Explored by the Use of Mass Interviews from bricklayers, business men, Italian-Americans, nuns, stevedores, or seamstresses. And, unless the scale itself is based upon equal-seeming differences to a random sample of the group which is to be measured, its validity—the degree to which it measures that which it purports to measure—becomes open to question.'[1]

It is thus not surprising that scores which should, according to the assumptions, correspond have been found to vary so seriously[2] as to detract greatly from the value of any results obtained.

(e) *Latent Structure Analysis*

The foregoing objections to Thurstone's method do not undermine his theoretical position. This is derived from the belief, first suggested by Spearman in 1904, that ' all branches of intellectual activity have in common one fundamental function (or group of functions) whereas the remaining or specific elements seem in every case to be different from that in all the others '.[3]

In order to justify this hypothesis, Spearman began the search for a mathematical procedure which would disentangle a primary or general factor from the other variable factors which surrounded or complicated it in any particular case. This search has culminated in the statistical technique known as *factor analysis*.[4] Thurstone was a leading figure in this development, and his work on attitudes may thus be regarded as one application of a very general approach to problems in which observational material can provide only indirect access to what we want to know. ' One might visualise the situation by saying that instead of measuring people's height

[1] FERGUSON, L. W. (1935), ' The Influence of Individual Attitudes on the Construction of an Attitude Scale ', *J. Soc. Psychol.*, 6, 115-17. The technique of interposing ' value judges ' between the investigator and his raw material has been regularly used in empirical social science. A recent English example was the empirical testing of a previously prepared Standard Classification of occupations into seven social classes. A list of thirty typical occupations was circulated to a large number of organisations and elicited about 1,400 returns, each of which recorded an individual's judgment on the appropriate class for each occupation listed. (HALL, J., and JONES, D. CARADOG (1950), ' Social Grading of Occupations ', *Brit. Journ. Soc.*, 1, 31-55.)
[2] MURPHY, G., MURPHY, L. B., and NEWCOMB, T. M. (1937), p. 905.
[3] Quoted by BLACKBURN, J. M. (1939), *Intelligence Tests*, in BARTLETT, F. C. et al.—Eds., p. 160. This is the so-called ' Theory of Two Factors '. Burt (*J. Roy. Statist. Soc.* (1950), B. 12, 87-88) claims the ' critical article ' for Pearson in 1901, when he was working on analogous problems to do with physical characteristics.
[4] For a treatment which minimises the demands on a reader's mathematical knowledge, see THOMSON, G. H. (1939), *The Factorial Analysis of Human Ability*.

and weight, one might be so unfortunate as to have to measure the length of their shadows. It is therefore necessary to rearrange the data so that they measure not shadows, but height.'[1]

This idea of Thurstone's has recently been developed further in the field of attitude survey, under the inspiration of Lazarsfeld, who has been at pains to eliminate the practical defects of the earlier attitude scales.

In this method, which has been named *Latent Structure Analysis*,[2] the investigator begins by assuming the existence of a continuous one-dimensional spectrum of basic attitudes on a particular issue. One such spectrum, for example, might cover the range of attitudes towards capital punishment. People are assumed to be arranged on this continuum, but in an unknown way. They are exposed to a series of *test items*, generally simple questions, to which they can answer yes or no, true or false, etc. The items are selected because it is believed that they are relevant to the problem, and will be useful in enabling the investigator to rank informants according to their position on the assumed continuum.

As an illustration, we may cite the three following *test items* which Lazarsfeld included in a survey in the belief that they had a bearing on a particular problem—i.e. the 'ethnocentrism' of American soldiers.[3]

1. I believe that our European allies are much superior to us in strategy and fighting morale. Yes —— No ——
2. The majority of all equipment used by all the allies comes from American lend lease shipment. True —— False ——
3. Neither we nor our allies could win the war if we didn't have each other's help. Agree —— Disagree ——

All these can reasonably be expected to relate to ethnocentrism. It is probable that only those informants with very low ethnocentrism would agree with the first statement, while the ethnocentric are most likely to believe the second. The third is a typical 'middle item' in any attitude test, for which the expecta-

---

[1] MURPHY, G. (1949 ed.), *An Historical Introduction to Modern Psychology*, p. 364. See also p. 77 of this book.
[2] STOUFFER, S. A. et al. (1950), Chapter 10, 'The Logical and Mathematical Foundation of Latent Structure Analysis' by Paul F. Lazarsfeld.
[3] *ibid.*, pp. 364 seq.
'By [ethnocentrism] we mean vaguely the extent to which they think that only Americans are of . . . value or importance for the war effort.'

Subjects Suitably Explored by the Use of Mass Interviews 193

tion is that it would be most favoured by those with neither very high nor very low enthnocentrism.

Now, in an ideal battery of test items suitable for latent structure analysis, *all* the relationship between responses to different test items should be explicable in terms of the assumed latent attitude continuum. This ideal is seldom realised, either because the test items are unsuitable, or because more than one latent attitude is affecting the responses—i.e. the hypothesis of a single attitude spectrum is incorrect. Cases have been found, however, in which virtually no association between the different test items, apart from that attributed to the latent attitude, can be detected. Furthermore, in a large number of tests it has been possible to state with considerable confidence that a certain group were likely to possess the hypothecated latent attitude and that another group were unlikely to possess it.

This technique has already been put to various practical uses in its first few years of existence. In the Research Branch itself various empirical studies were undertaken on attitude to the army, job satisfaction and so on, and surveys have also made use of the more generalised latent structure model in which the number of latent classes is unlimited. A survey of psychosomatic complaints in a sample of 1,000 soldiers was of this type.[1]

The method of latent structure analysis is of rather recent origin, and many of its details and implications have still to be worked out. So far the mathematical techniques associated with it are too complicated to encourage its general use, but this should not prove an insuperable objection. In the long run, its adoption may largely turn on the economies claimed for it in terms of the number of test items required as compared with attitude tests in which the underlying structure has not been explored. It has an especially interesting application to the problem of *shifts* in attitude.[2] On the theoretical side it sustains the age-long search for latent psychological constants which are more than mere statistical artifacts.

Since the war, work has continued at the Laboratory of Social Relations, Harvard University. For example, Stouffer and Toby report a latent structure analysis of ' pencil-and-paper material ' collected with the aim of discovering how a sample of informants

[1] STOUFFER, S. A. et al. (1950), pp. 441 seq.
[2] An example is given in *ibid.*, Chapter 11.

O

viewed the relationship existing between their personal and impersonal obligations. The material was somewhat unsatisfactory, comprising the 'what would you do?' responses of a group of undergraduates to a series of relevant mythical and somewhat roughly delineated situations. Even so, in the authors' claim, the ' study suggests that it is possible to classify people according to a predisposition to select one or the other horn of a dilemma in rôle conflict '.[1]

(f) *Scalogram Analysis*

In Lazarsfeld's analysis described above an attitude is defined as an *inference* as to latent classes which has to be tested by fitting to the manifest data an appropriate latent structure model. In contrast with this, the method developed by Guttman—who was also attached to the Research Branch during the war—deals only with the manifest relationship between attitude items, and *defines* an attitude directly as the observed responses to those items.[2]

Comparison has shown that theoretically the Guttmann scalogram procedure may be regarded as a special case of latent structure analysis. Empirically, however, the scalogram technique has the advantage of being defined solely in terms of manifest data, and hence of evading the need for any assumptions about the existence of latent classes. It also has the merit of practical simplicity at the stage of analysis.

The scalogram goes back to another idea implicit in early attitude scales. This is that it is possible to choose items so that persons who answer a given question affirmatively all have a higher affirmative score than persons who answer the same question negatively. Ideally, one can tell from an informant's score exactly which items he endorsed and which he rejected. Items in a scalogram analysis thus have a cumulative quality, like items in a height scale; if a man is over 6 ft. tall he is unquestionably over 5 ft. 6 in. tall.

The idea of an intrinsically cumulative list of items was present in Bogardus' 'social distance' scale, shown in the table on p. 189; as we have seen, however, this scale was somewhat

---

[1] STOUFFER, S. A., and TOBY, J. (1951), 'Role Conflict and Personality,' *Am. Journ. Soc.*, **56**, 395–406.
[2] STOUFFER, S. A. et al. (1950), pp. 6–7.

imperfect in practice. Similarly, scalogram items seldom scale perfectly, and one difficulty is to decide a reasonable standard of performance for them.

This standard is empirical, and is thus strictly related to the regularity of the responses obtained to the test items used (the so-called *coefficient of reproducibility*), rather than to any logical or abstract progression in these items. For example, it was desired to construct a scalogram from items relating to the different physical reactions to the dangers of battle, as reported by soldiers who had been under fire. Soldiers were asked whether or not they had experienced various symptoms, such as sinking feeling, feeling sick, cold sweat, vomiting, etc. As a result of the survey it was found that nine items formed a very satisfactory scale, but that ' cold sweat ', which had been tried as a tenth item, did not fit in and should be scrapped. For the others it was possible to say, for example, that in the great majority (92%) of cases a soldier who, according to his account, vomited also felt faint, felt stiff, shook and trembled, experienced a sinking feeling and a violent pounding of the heart; conversely, if he did not remember vomiting, he was very unlikely to have admitted the loss of control of his bowels or bladder.

Intrinsic cumulative characteristics have not been explored to any great extent, and may have a somewhat limited application. The cumulative effect may, however, be introduced artificially by using a series of multiple response questions and by choosing for each of these a *cutting point* which fixes a convenient position on the scale.

This may most easily be explained by an example. Thus, in an ' Attitude towards Officers' survey ',[1] two questions, and the corresponding choice of answers, were :

Q. 17. In general, how good would you say your officers were ?

       1. Very good.
       2. Fairly good.
       3. About average.

       4. Pretty poor.
       5. Very poor.

and

[1] STOUFFER, S. A. et al. (1950), pp. 123, 126 seq.

Q. 20. How much did you personally like your officers?

    1. Very much.
    ⎰2. Pretty much.
    ⎱3. Not so much.
     4. Not at all.

By use of a systematic procedure it was found convenient to combine some of the actual recorded responses so that each question allowed only a favourable or an unfavourable response. Answers 1, 2, 3 to Q. 17 were taken as favourable, and answers 4 and 5 as unfavourable. By a similar process, responses to Q. 20 were divided into two classes—namely, favourable (answer 1) and unfavourable (answers 2, 3, and 4). By the adoption of a different *cutting point* in each case, both items were enabled to pull their weight in the scalogram analysis.

It is important to recognise that this choice of cutting point, although at the discretion of the analyst, is not arbitrary or subject to prejudice, but arises empirically by analysis of the original responses.

In initial efforts to construct a battery of scalogram items, it is recommended that as many as ten or twelve separate items should be included. If 'scalability' is proved, it is considered quite justifiable to select a smaller number of items—say three or four—for the large-scale research programme. The selected items, being a sub-class of the accepted battery, will reproduce its pattern in a coarser profile. Ultimately it may be possible, as a result of a protest, to select a single item for large-scale use. It is claimed that, while repeating the economy of the conventional public opinion poll, this will differ radically in other respects, as the single item will be employed with full knowledge as to its place in the attitude structure.

One of the neatest features of scalogram analysis is the manual system developed to sort the material. This system depends on the use of two *scalogram boards*, which were specially designed and made for the purpose. Each board, which is 27 in. square, consists of a frame which takes 100 removable wooden slats: these slats can be clamped, but they can also be freed and handled separately. Every slat has 100 equidistant pockets, so that a board has a total of 10,000 pockets, each large enough to hold a silver-coated lead shot.

On the first board each slat is used to record the responses of one informant; this is done by dropping shot into the appropriate pockets, of which one is reserved for each possible answer. The slats are then placed by hand in rank order of—say—favourableness to the point at issue, corresponding with the responses recorded on them.

After thus shifting the individuals into the desired order, the next step is to shift responses into rank orders. This is done by placing the two scalogram boards face to face so that the sets of slats lie at right angles to each other. The boards are inverted, and the shot fall into the corresponding pockets in the other board; each slat on this second board thus now holds the shot corresponding with the range of responses to one question, and the slats can as before be ranked in the desired order.

For scalable material, at the end of this two-stage procedure, it is possible to observe at once the characteristic parallelogram pattern and to count without difficulty the number of misfits. The 'coefficient of reproducibility' of any arrangement, which describes the proportion of misfits, can then be calculated with ease. The same simple apparatus has been successfully used for many other problems involving an analysis of multivariate frequency distributions of qualitative data.

In view both of the practical simplicity of the scalogram procedure,[1] and of the freedom from restrictive assumptions, it is clear that a technique of great importance is being developed. In the earlier attitude tests the hypothesis that 'the symptoms come from a single universe and permit a rank ordering of respondents along a single continuum'[2] has had to be sustained without test, but in scalogram analysis this test is an inherent part of the procedure. If the material scales well, the hypothesis can be accepted with reasonable confidence.

What happens if the items cannot be used to construct a scale? There are various possible outcomes. It may be that re-examination of the original hypothesis will suggest that the idea of a single common variable should be replaced by a hypothesis introducing

[1] 'From a practical standpoint, the operational procedures developed in the Research Branch for swiftly evaluating a large number of questions simultaneously may rank as one of the major contributions of the Branch to social science technique. Work which would have required hundreds of hours of elaborate machine analysis can now be done in a few hours by one semi-skilled clerk.'—STOUFFER, S. A. et al. (1950), p. 16.
[2] ibid., p. 142.

several distinct variables. If so, these can then be isolated and tested independently. Alternatively, the appearance of unscalability may be found to be due to ambiguous, obscure or emotive (e.g. stereotyping) wording. If so, it is possible that the adjustment of wording may produce scalable material.

In practice, scales do occur fairly frequently, and the pioneers of this method believe that, given time, many abandoned projects could be re-defined into scalable form. They freely admit, however, that ' many attitudinal areas are so complex as to be non-scalable '.[1] Some such areas reveal a single dominant factor coupled with a very large number of small random factors; the misfits are thus randomly distributed. While an essential property of the true scale—i.e. reproducibility—is lacking, it is possible to construct a *quasi-scale* with such material. If the misfits are grouped together—i.e. not randomly distributed—it may be inferred that more than one strong variable is present, and the material is regarded as unscalable. The quasi-scale pattern was encountered in the case of personality inventories, information tests and measures of intensity of feeling. On the other hand, certain other areas, such as morale, were found to provide not even a quasi-scale and were regarded as unscalable. Although ' morale ' turned out to be a portmanteau phrase, however, several sub-universes—e.g. pride in one's outfit, satisfaction with one's job, and confidence in one's leaders—were found to be independently scalable. This in itself was an interesting piece of information.

(g) *Inherent Limitations of Attitude Measurement*

There is still one vital question to be considered. Even when we have conceded that the methods discussed above are far more accurate than the relatively crude techniques associated with public-opinion polling, in what sense do the results, however carefully compiled, reproduce attitudes? Is it safe to ignore the findings of those social scientists who have concentrated on ' depth ' interviewing techniques? What are the safeguards against confusing the manifest and the latent content of informants' responses, or against failing to distinguish the different psychological levels at which the informant may be operating even in a brief sequence of questions and answers?

[1] STOUFFER, S. A. et al. (1950), p. 159.

Subjects Suitably Explored by the Use of Mass Interviews 199

Professor Pear quotes G. W. Allport as indicating three inherent limitations of attitude measurement:

1. Measurement can deal only with common attitudes, and relatively few attitudes are common enough to be profitably scaled. By forcing attitudes into a scale, violence is done to the unique structure of man's mind.
2. Each person possesses many contradictory attitudes. For this reason his reaction when he is filling up a form may not be persistent.
3. Rationalization and deception inevitably occur, especially when the attitude studied pertains to the subject's moral life or social status. The difficulty of obtaining reliable information concerning attitudes towards sex is a case in point. Here anonymity is no guarantee. Lack of insight, ignorance, suspicion, fear, a neurotic sense of guilt, undue enthusiasm, or even a knowledge of the investigator's purpose, may invalidate an inquiry.[1]

The first of these points reflects the belief that *idiographic* description, without an attempt at *nomothetic* generalisation, is a legitimate activity of the scientist. In adopting this historical heresy, Allport is following the definition of science advocated by certain German historians, such as Rickert and Windelband. Most social scientists feel that a narrative description of unique characteristics, from which generalisations were specifically excluded, would fall outside the province of science even if a language could be coined which did not imply natural regularities.

The latent structure analysis and the scalogram have largely overcome Allport's second objection. Without violating the material, it is possible with their help to determine whether results are or are not scalable. The fact that a scale has been found to fit them demonstrates internal consistency; if informants regularly display complex attitudes by giving contradictory answers within a single test, this incoherence will be reflected in unscalable material.

If, however, consistent rationalisation and deception occur, it is quite conceivable that the answers, though false, will be scalable.

It is as well to consider further what is meant by truthful

[1] PEAR, T. H. (1939), *Contemporary Social Psychology* in BARTLETT, F. C. et al.—Eds., pp. 7–8.

attitudes. Let us take the following two questions, and the answers given to them (*ibid.*, p. 150):

	Q. 15. Which of the following best tells the way you feel about getting into the actual battle zone ?		
Q. 16. Do you feel you are now trained and ready for combat or do you need more training ?	(a) I want very much to get into it just as soon as possible *and* I'm ready to go anytime.	(b) Other replies	Total
	%	%	%
(a) I'm ready for combat now.	33	14	47
(b) I need a little (or a lot) more of some kinds of training.	14	39	53
TOTAL	47	53	100

Inspection shows that these two items do not fit at all well on to the same scale. Only 72% of answers are consistent indices of readiness for combat. As the authors suggest, ' the hypothesis for further testing would be that the desire for combat and the attitude towards adequacy of training are two separate areas each of which may be scalable separately '.

Although both are attitude questions, Q. 16 contains a substantial factual element; there is, in fact, no ultimate logical inconsistency in expressing both keenness to fight and belief that more training is needed. On the other hand, the investigators presumably included Q. 16 as a source of information on attitude. We may assume that keenness to get into battle is, during wartime, a socially favoured attitude. It is typically a public attitude. Conversely, some prudent men, however brave, want to avoid risking their lives; their private attitude is thus ' I don't want to fight '. These two can be combined in a socially acceptable form by saying ' I want to fight but I'm not quite ready '. Meanwhile the more honest, those less inclined to conform socially, will say ' I don't want to fight but I think I'm ready '.[1]

The authors suggest that two scales are necessary because the items relate to two different things. As has been shown, it can be

---

[1] This point is discussed by Kendall and Lazarsfeld in MERTON, R. K., and LAZARSFELD, P. F.—Eds. (1950), *Continuities in Social Research*, pp. 178–9. See also *ibid.*, pp. 172 seq.

at least plausibly argued that the items relate to the same thing (going to the wars), but that they have exposed a fairly common conflict in attitude to this question. And the principal difficulty is not that one answer is 'true' and the other 'false', but that one cannot forecast which attitude, and actions corresponding to it, will prevail in given circumstances.[1]

We are equally justified in wondering whether the replies given by soldiers as to their physical reactions to the dangers of battle (p. 195, *supra*), which scaled so satisfactorily, were entirely truthful replies. A plausible rival hypothesis would be that the symptoms most readily admitted were those regarded in the army as least shameful.

Prediction

It would be of great interest to be able to apply the ultimate test, of prediction, to other examples of scalogram analysis. Unfortunately, for various reasons,[2] the Research Branch was unable to make valid comparisons between predicted and actual performance. A clear link between the test situation and the future event is in any case likely to be rare. Forecasting is seldom as straightforward as that needed to predict the outcome of an election.

It is undeniable, however, that the administration of a set of tests such as have been described provides a very poor opportunity for sorting out the private and the public behaviour of an

[1] Actions, like attitudes, are socially conditioned. They 'are frequently designed to distort or conceal the "true" attitude quite as fully as verbal behaviour. When the politician kisses negro babies as an expression of his friendly attitude toward the negro race his action is probably a no more accurate index of his "true" attitude than is his impassioned utterances from the platform to that effect. Both are just as "true" attitudes *in their respective situations* as the views he expresses or the action he takes toward negroes after election.... How his responses in a hypothetical or symbolic situation correlate with his behaviour in a similar concrete situation involving complete overt adjustment can only be determined by a study of both kinds of behaviour in their respective situations'.—LUNDBERG, G. A. (1929), *Social Research*, p. 202.

[2] One elaborate investigation was designed for the screening of psychoneurotics at United States induction centres. The idea was to enable the limited number of psychiatrists available to concentrate their attentions on those recruits most likely to be rejected as psycho-neurotics. The test broke down, according to the authors, because psychiatrists' diagnoses were too erratic. 'Thus we have illustrated a central problem in social science—namely the difficulties of making predictions when the behavior to be predicted (in this case, actually, the behavior of psychiatrists with respect to the individual tested) is itself unstandardized and subject to great variation.'—STOUFFER, S. A. et al. (1950), p. 477.

informant. Nor do standardised personality tests appear to provide a better solution.[1]

As the authors point out, the capacity to predict and the conditions necessary for prediction are not yet established empirically. They quote, however, some 'modestly advanced preliminary thinking' about this problem which was contributed by John Dollard, while a Consultant in the Research Branch.[2]

Dollard's approach is to consider the relationship between three classes of situations. First there is the *origin situation*, in which the thought is first hit upon and rehearsed by the subject who is to be an informant. Next there is the *test situation*, in which the stream of thoughts is tapped by the interviewer. Lastly there is the *criterion situation*, the dilemma around which prediction is centred and in which the informant must proceed to a decision. Prediction is possible to the extent that these three situations correspond.

This favours prediction under such conditions as the following:

(*a*) If the informant is aware in the test situation of all elements relevant to his actual decision in the criterion situation—e.g. he might not be conscious of jealous feelings until they were actually aroused.

(*b*) If the informant is verbally and mentally equipped to forecast his behaviour. Those with poor verbal skills may be unable to do so.

(*c*) If there is a strong connection between thought and action. Dollard relates this to the fact of having received strong rewards during childhood learning. Those who have not been thus rewarded become day-dreamers.

(*d*) If the test situation stimulates only those verbal responses relevant to the criterion. For example, a man questioned under duress may well tell lies about his future actions.

(*e*) If the origin situation corresponds closely to the criterion situation. A man can best forecast his action if he knows from experience what it will be like, or if—as in election forecasts—origin and criterion situations are not essentially different.

---

[1] It was found (STOUFFER, S. A. et al. (1950), p. 479 fn.) that a multiple-choice form of Rorschach testing had no greater discriminating power in detecting psycho-neurosis than a single check-list item like 'Are you ever troubled with nervousness?'

[2] *ibid.*, pp. 483–5, which is derived from an article by DOLLARD, J. (1948), 'Under what conditions do opinions predict behaviour?', *P.O.Q.*, 12, 623–32.

(f) If no new dilemma intervenes between the test and the criterion situation. If a man moves to a fresh community he will absorb their different code of behaviour, and forecasts about his behaviour made before his move will be falsified. Similar falsification may occur by the so-called band-waggon effect, when actual voting is liable to be influenced by the publication of pre-election polling results.[1]

(g) If the test situation explicitly presents the conflict, i.e. anticipations of rewards and punishments, of the criterion dilemma.

A man will better predict what he will do in a future dilemma if he is told exactly what this dilemma will be. This condition cautions particular care in evoking the criterion situation vividly and specifying exactly the behaviour to be predicted.

This list of conditions is designed to apply primarily to cases in which the informant is asked directly to forecast his future action. It must be admitted that they will very seldom be operative. On the whole, the predictive value of direct questioning is limited, even in the case of straightforward issues with a low emotional content. But it would be naïve to presume that informants are regularly so unaware of the implications of indirect questions that they miss the connection between these questions and the real ' criterion dilemmas ' in which they may subsequently be placed.

(h) *Conclusions*

It is reasonable to conclude that the use of the opinion question in mass interviews has come to stay. We may also accept the belief that, although publicly expressed opinions may at some points

---

[1] ' The reading of our material gives a very strong impression that in political discussions the question of who will win is the most frequent topic among people. . . . This leads directly to a basic question : Was there a band-waggon effect ? The answer is yes. . . .

' The influence of expectation on vote intention is psychologically a rather complicated one. Probably some people had already half made up their minds for whom to vote, but it seemed less dangerous to put it in the form of an expectation rather than vote intention. In other cases, hearing about a candidate's chances might have activated a predisposition already existing. But in some cases respondents did not hesitate to say straight out that they were deliberately trying to vote for the winner.'—LAZARSFELD, P. F. et al. (1948 edition), *The People's Choice*, pp. 107-8.

D. G. MacRae (*Brit. Journ. Soc.* (1951), 2, 146) speculates on the possibility of adapting the type of feed-back analysis developed in cybernetics, and thus of adjusting social predictions to allow for the band-waggon effect.

differ from private opinions, they may correspond rather closely with public behaviour. Thus even when the privacy of voting is safeguarded by the secret ballot, the inevitably more public mass interviews used for election forecasting do lead to results of surprising reliability.

The opinion poll is an American invention, and has been slow to take root in England. It is still sometimes imagined that 'reputable' British organisations stick to facts, and leave opinions alone. This is not true; the official Social Survey, for example, has regularly included opinion questions in its inquiries.

The ultimate function of the opinion and attitude survey, and the precise meaning to be attached to its results, are still not clear. Two recent American techniques which have been described promise to reduce ambiguities in results. But internal consistency is not quite the same as truth, and it has yet to be demonstrated that any mass method can remove the need for the depth techniques described earlier in this chapter.

The problem thus becomes one of deciding when the mass interview may suitably be used, and when a more penetrating search for private opinions is indicated. Circumstances differ, but it may be supposed that representative members of a coherent and unified group of people should express public opinions which correspond fairly closely with their collective views and provide an adequate basis for predicting their future public behaviour. Conversely, when those questioned are misfits in their society or are members of a disjointed and diversified group, their public expressions of opinion may well so diverge from their private attitudes as to be of little informative and predictive value.[1]

Throughout, it must be remembered that there is no sharp dividing line between fact and opinion. Almost any answer, however objective and factual it may appear, is liable to distortion. The impulse to distort may be slight if the questions to be answered have a negligible personal emotive content to the informants, but the possibility can never be eliminated. Some

[1] 'Americans can poll Americans and understand the findings, but they can do this because of a prior step which is so obvious that no one mentions it: they know and take for granted the conduct of life in the United States. The results of polling tell more about what we already know. In trying to understand another country, systematic qualitative study of the habits and assumptions of its people is essential before a poll can serve to good advantage.'
—BENEDICT, R. (1946), *The Chrysanthemum and the Sword*, p. 18.

ways of minimising the risk of arriving at conclusions that are biased by unreliable information are mentioned in a later section.[1]

2. SAMPLING

Most of this book is concerned with the methods available for safeguarding the suitability and quality of social data. The present section is inserted as a reminder that, whenever generalisation is the aim, the selection of the sample must be made with corresponding care and rigour. While it may not be wise to imagine that science and measurement are synonymous, it is certainly foolish to imagine that social science presents many occasions on which generalisations are possible without the use of statistics. The alternative is to rely on insight or on informal subjective generalisations. This is a poor substitute, and it signifies nothing but the immaturity of social science that many informal generalisations should still be promulgated without statistical support.

In any inquiry of statistical importance it will be necessary to enlist the active help of an experienced statistician. In such cases close consultation and co-operation are essential at all stages of planning and execution. The occasions, which are not unknown even today, on which completed survey material is pushed on to a statistician for analysis are unfair both to him and to the investigators, much of whose work may prove to have been wasted.

The danger can be minimised by ensuring that every investigator is aware of the main statistical issues involved in the planning and execution of a survey. He will then at least know how little he knows of the statistical devices so far developed, of which sampling has perhaps proved of the greatest practical importance; it is on these grounds, and not in the attempt to contribute a condensed handbook on sampling, that the following pages have been included.

Today a number of books and papers on the subject of sampling are available. Of these the most complete and most useful is by Dr. F. Yates of Rothamsted Experimental Station, and is based on a manual originally prepared by him at the request of the United Nations Sub-Commission on Statistical Sampling. The reader

[1] pp. 233 seq.

who desires an exposition on sampling techniques is referred to Dr. Yates' book.[1] A valuable paper by Gray and Corlett, with a fund of practical information on methods used by the Government Social Survey, may also be consulted.[2]

(a) *Background*

Rule-of-thumb sampling is a common technique in everyday life. The tea-taster assesses the qualities of a consignment by sampling a pinch from the top of the chest; even were he physically capable, it would defeat his object if he had to drink the lot. Everyday experience has shown that in many circumstances it is safe, within limits, to generalise about the whole by studying a part. Statistical sampling is a methodical version of this procedure.

The pioneer of statistical sampling in social science was A. L. Bowley, and the occasion was his survey in 1912–13 of poverty in four English towns, of which the first was Reading.[3] Bowley, assisted by Burnett-Hurst, took a sample of roughly one family in twenty, and was able to gain data comparable in accuracy with previous surveys—e.g. the family surveys in Booth's *London Life and Labour* and Rowntree's York survey *Poverty*—for the expenditure of very much less time and money. The error due to sampling was discussed in the report on Bowley's initial survey, and was shown to be relatively unimportant.[4]

The use of sampling in social science continued sporadically for the next twenty years. Celebrated examples are John Hilton's Ministry of Labour *Survey of Unemployment* in 1923, Bowley's repeat survey in 1924 of the five towns and his sample survey of London, which formed a part of the *New Survey of London Life and Labour* conducted in 1928–35. It is only in

[1] YATES, F. (1949), *Sampling Methods for Censuses and Surveys*. This book also contains a bibliography with about 300 entries.
[2] GRAY, P. G., and CORLETT, T. (1950), ' Sampling for the Social Survey ', *J. Roy. Statist. Soc.*, 113, 150-206.
[3] BOWLEY, A. L., and BURNETT-HURST, A. R. (1915), *Livelihood and Poverty*, London. The other three towns were Northampton, Warrington and Stanley. Bolton was subsequetly surveyed in a similar way.
[4] In his second York survey, published in 1941 as *Poverty and Progress*, B. Seebohm Rowntree preferred again to conduct a census as opposed to a sample survey. However, as an interesting illustration of the effect of sampling he included a supplementary chapter (*ibid.*, pp. 478-92) showing in tabular form the errors which were actually introduced by taking at random different-sized samples of his complete survey material.
In his third survey, published as ROWNTREE, B. S., and LAVERS, G. R. (1951), *Poverty and the Welfare State*, a sampling method was finally adopted.

the last fifteen years, however, that sampling techniques have assumed their present importance.

Sampling was initially adopted for reasons of economy; and it is clear that many surveys carried out by the use of sampling methods could not have taken place if there had been no alternative to a full census.[1]

(b) *Mathematical Considerations*

It must be borne in mind that the social scientist has to accept imperfect accuracy in his results. Sampling further reduces accuracy, but if the sample is properly derived the error thus introduced can be readily assessed. In many cases sampling errors are probably far less important than the errors inherent in the methods of study.

Sampling techniques. The object of any sampling procedure is to secure a *sample* which will reproduce the characteristics of the *population*. This object is never completely attained, as two types of error are regularly encountered: those arising from biases in selection, etc., though avoidable, frequently occur, while those due to chance differences between the members of the population included and those not included are virtually certain to be present. The former type is termed the *error due to bias*, and the latter the *sampling error*; the former can be minimised by good craftsmanship, while the latter can be regulated by appropriate design.

Bias can be introduced either deliberately or by faulty techniques. An example of deliberate bias is the selection of members of a sample on the *a priori* grounds that they are ' representative '. Faulty techniques include: selection by some characteristic which happens to be correlated with properties of the unit which are of interest (e.g. United Kingdom citizens with surnames beginning with M would include an excessive proportion of Scotsmen); unauthorised substitution of one person for another by the field-worker or failure by the investigator to cover all the specified members of the sample.[2]

Random sampling. The simple way of avoiding bias is to draw the sample *at random*, and the most elementary method of random sampling is to draw lots—e.g. by picking marked cards out of a

[1] A complete census is not necessarily preferable to a sample survey, as it may itself give openings for inaccuracy, e.g. through the time elapsing in the course of data collection.
[2] See p. 212 seq.

container, in such a way as to avoid impugning the assumption that every unit has an equal chance of being picked. Although unexceptionable, this method is tedious, especially when the population is large. It is therefore customary to make use of a table of random numbers, which in effect lists the results of a previously conducted draw.

In many cases it is preferable to use the procedure known as *stratification*, which, while imposing restrictions on the randomness of the selection, does not necessarily introduce bias. In this procedure the population is divided into blocks or strata, according to certain principles, and each stratum is then sampled at random.

The population strata may be used for the extraction of a uniform *sampling fraction*. It is commoner, however, to vary the sampling fraction from each stratum according to need. For example, the proposed analysis may involve consideration of certain sub-groups whose numbers in the population are small, e.g. centenarians or millionaires. Random selection of units is unlikely to provide enough of such cases. The population is therefore stratified according to the characteristic in question [1] (e.g. wealth, or age). Sampling is carried out separately for each stratum and the strata of greater interest are sampled more extensively. Variable sampling fractions not only permit better analysis of sub-groups but also make it possible, after re-weighting the sample, to generalize more accurately about the total population.

Another useful device is *multi-stage sampling*: in two-stage sampling, for instance, the units finally constituting the sample are selected at random from first-stage units that have themselves been selected at random from the total population. Thus, for instance, a representative sample of British families might be selected by first taking a sample of all administrative areas in the British Isles and subsequently taking a sample of families from each administrative area thus selected.[2] Further sampling stages can be added if necessary.

[1] When necessary, it is legitimate to stratify the population simultaneously according to two or more characteristics.
H. J. Eysenck has described (e.g. *Brit. Journ. Soc.*, **1**, 57 seq.) a special case of the use of variable sampling fractions, in which the sample drawn from each group is made of equal size. He has called this 'analytical sampling'.
[2] This corresponds with the 'area sampling' of public-opinion polling and market research, though in their case the second stage may consist of quota sampling.

In multi-stage sampling more accurate results are obtained by selecting a relatively high first-stage sampling fraction and a correspondingly low second-stage sampling fraction; this fact has to be weighed against the increased convenience for fieldwork, etc.[1] of concentrating observations in relatively few areas.

Systematic sampling. Although random sampling is always preferable it is not always feasible, and use is very often made of *systematic sampling.* This may be permissible if proper precautions are taken.

The commonest form of systematic sampling is the selection of units at regular intervals from a list enumerating the population in question, e.g. every nth name. No such list is fully random, but alphabetical lists are generally adequate. The first name in the sample should be selected at random.

One serious objection to systematic sampling is that it is not possible to make a fully valid estimate of the sampling error, but this objection is frequently overruled. As a practical precaution it is important to ensure that there are no periodic features in the list, as these would naturally bias the sample.

Multi-phase sampling. It is sometimes convenient to confine certain questions to a fraction of the sample, while other information is collected from the whole sample. In the Maternity Survey,[2] for example, basic data were collected from the whole sample, while more detailed information, which it would have been too laborious to obtain for the whole sample, was only sought from certain individuals who were selected at random to form a sub-sample of the original sample. This procedure is known as *multi-phase sampling* (as distinct from multi-stage sampling).

The basic information recorded in the original sample makes it possible to compare certain characteristics of the sub-sample with that of the original list, and thus to test the representativeness of the former. It also facilitates stratification of the sub-sample, as the information collected in the first-phase sample can sometimes be gathered before the sub-sampling process takes place.

A limiting case of multi-phase sampling is the use of a census (or 100% sample) as the basis for sampling. In the case of the population census, this has heretofore been impossible in England,

---

[1] One important advantage of concentration is that the second-stage frame only has to be constructed for relatively few areas.
[2] *Maternity in Great Britain,* See also p. 102.

P

as the enumeration forms have only very rarely been made available outside the General Register Office.[1]

(c) *Practical Considerations*

From the statistical point of view, it is necessary to consider the purpose and nature of a survey before deciding on the method of sampling. Specifically, the categories of material, and the information which it is intended to collect on the subject, must be predetermined. It is also preferable to take a decision as early as possible on the method of collecting the data—e.g. by employing interviewers, or by postal questionnaire.

These considerations will help towards a decision on the most appropriate sampling unit—e.g. individuals, households, parishes —and the choice or construction of the corresponding *frame* (or list of such sampling units). It is also desirable that they should be borne in mind in deciding on the most suitable type of sample—e.g. stratified, multi-stage—on the size of sample required and on the method of selection.

Some initial field investigations will normally be required in order to ascertain the variability of the material, and hence how big the main sample should be. The need for this reinforces the value of a *pilot* survey, whose other principal merits are discussed elsewhere.[2]

Choice of sampling unit and frame. This may largely depend on availability. The limiting factor is generally the existence of, or the possibility of constructing, a suitable *sampling unit* and *frame*.[3]

For human populations, if the survey is concerned with individuals the commonest source is the *Electoral Register*, which lists all adults (21 +) and their addresses by electoral districts.[4] A better frame, while it was in being and for those who had access to it, was the *Maintenance Register*, which between 1939 and 1952 was kept in the National Registration Office of the 1,500 admini-

---

[1] Booth had the privilege of direct access to the 1881 and 1891 census material, and was also able to arrange for the insertion of certain special questions (number of rooms and number of domestic servants per household) into the 1891 census. See, for example, WEBB, B. (1926), *My Apprenticeship*, p. 226.
[2] pp. 216 seq.
[3] For an excellent discussion, see GRAY, P. G., and CORLETT, T. (1950), pp. 165–79.
[4] Since 1945, householders have not been distinguished from other adults on this register. For a full discussion on the use of the *Electoral Register*, see GRAY, P. G., CORLETT, T., and FRANKLAND, P. (Nov. 1950), *The Register of Electors as a Sampling Frame*.

strative districts in England and Wales;[1] its loss is felt by social surveyors as well as by administrators.

For families, there has never been a fully satisfactory frame. There is no list of biological families as such. Even households are not reliably listed, and so a third frame, based on the *Rating Records*, which list all separately rated dwellings, is often used. It will be appreciated that this is not equivalent to a list of households, as some separately rated dwellings contain more than one household.[2]

For some purposes the dwelling itself is the most suitable sampling unit; a dwelling is at least less mobile than its inhabitants.

When these sources are not available, or even when they are, it may be decided to use geographical areas as sampling units. Thus, for example, the map of a town can be divided into a number of areas, either about equal in size or estimated to contain an equal number of dwellings. Each such area would then constitute a first-stage sampling unit.[3]

For other purposes, other sampling units and frames will be called for. Thus a survey of insured workers might be based on the lists kept in Ministry of Labour Employment Exchanges, and a survey of factories might be based on the factory registers kept by the Board of Trade and other Regional authorities. When the survey is concerned with a single institution, such as a factory or a club, the frame is naturally provided by the list of employees or of members.

All such lists are subject to various types of defect. Information may be inaccurate owing to errors in recording, such as failure to record certain items and duplication of other items. Available lists may omit certain information, and very often will be out-of-date. The same defects are liable to occur in town plans and any

---

[1] And also, in duplicate for the whole country, in London. These Maintenance Registers were never freely available for non-official use.

[2] GRAY, P. G., and CORLETT, T. (1950, p. 173), quote the following figures, based on Social Survey experience, for separately rated dwellings in England and Wales: 94% contain one household only; 5% contain two households; 1% three or more.

[3] Many American ecological studies have been possible only because the United States Bureau of the Census has divided urban areas into relatively small ' census tracts '. The pioneer in this field was Professor E. W. Burgess of Chicago University.

It is interesting to recall that Charles Booth analysed much of his material by streets, and then by School Board Blocks, rather than by families; in his case, of course, the problem of sampling was not involved.

other sources of information. A careful examination, and revision where necessary, of any list that it is intended to use as a frame is therefore an essential preliminary to the survey. Practical experience reveals these defects with depressing regularity, and the injunction to revise existing data is no empty formula.

Quota Sampling. Many commercial survey organisations, such as the various national Institutes of Public Opinion, claim—with some empirical justification—that the time and trouble involved in preparing a frame are disproportionate to the degree of accuracy that is aimed at. For them the need for speed is often predominant, and speed may be incompatible with random sampling. The commonest substitute method is known as *quota sampling*. On the basis of aggregated census or other material, the planners of such surveys allot to each field-worker a quota of people to be interviewed, designed to contain the right proportion of people of given characteristics, e.g. social class, age, sex, urban or rural. *The selection of individuals to provide this right proportion is left to the field-worker*, who may pick the members of his sample on the street, at their homes, or even sometimes by telephone.[1]

The dangers in quota sampling are self-evident and inescapable. Field-workers' selection may be biased, for example, in favour of approachable individuals. Moreover, the representativeness of the quota is dependent on the characteristics (age, sex, etc.) used in its selection. If, then, some new and unforeseen alignment, such as type of occupation, becomes of importance or is revealed as important during analysis, there is no safeguard that the sample interviewed will represent it in the proper proportions. Finally no means can be devised for calculating sampling errors, and thus the limits of accuracy of the results cannot be assessed.

For these reasons, in spite of the obvious practical advantages of quota sampling, the method is seldom used by research workers or by non-commercial organisations.

Even less defensible are the instances in which an executive

[1] A discussion of the pros and cons of quota sampling, fortified with a description of the quota sampling practice of four leading British market research organisations, has been contributed by MOSER, C. A. (1952), ' Quota Sampling ', *J. Roy. Statist. Soc.*, **115**, 411–23.
It has been frequently suggested that the cost per interview with quota sampling is half that with random sampling. This economy may be dearly bought if the result is unreliable material.
Quota sampling has an analogue in experimental procedure known as frequency distribution control. See pp. 268 seq.

Sampling

—e.g. a headmaster, a factory manager or an army adjutant— volunteers to select the sample. However carefully the need for randomness is explained, such executives are liable to pick out those whom they think would answer questions well or those who can best be spared from their regular work. This is a recurrent difficulty which can only be met with tact and firmness.[1]

(d) *Size of Sample*

There is clearly a practical advantage in reducing field-work to a minimum, and one of the most important decisions in planning a survey is how large the sample must be.

There are various common misconceptions about the necessary size of sample. One is that the sample should be a regular proportion (often put at 5%) of the ' population ', and another is that the sample should total about 2,000. No such rule-of-thumb method is adequate. The size of the sample is properly fixed by deciding what level of accuracy is required, and hence how large a *sampling error* is acceptable. Great economies are often possible if a realistic attitude is adopted to the precision required.

A measure of the average magnitude of this sampling error is given by the *standard error*. The standard error, however, depends not only on the size of the sample, but also on the variability of the material. The investigator is thus placed in the predicament of having to know something about the results which his survey will bring in before he can complete his plans for carrying it out. Except in cases when this prior information already exists in reasonably accurate form, it is therefore desirable to conduct a pilot survey to get an indication of the material to be expected before launching the main investigation.

In straightforward cases, the purpose of the main survey will be to estimate, within prescribed limits of accuracy, either the incidence of a given attribute—e.g. height over 6 feet—or the distribution or the mean value of a particular quantitative attribute —e.g. height—in the population to be investigated. Provided some information is available, either from a supplementary source or from the results of a pilot survey, conducted on a random *presample* of the population, there is in neither case any great difficulty in calculating the appropriate size for the main sample.

[1] Some awful warnings of enquiries that went wrong because of the misplaced enthusiasm of certain U.S. Army Officers are given in STOUFFER, S. A., et al. (1950), pp. 710–13.

Incidence of a given attribute. If p is the proportion of units of the given type—e.g. men over 6 feet high—in the whole population, and $q = 1 - p$, or the proportion not of the given type, the *standard error* of the proportion of units of the given type in a random sample of n units (which provides an estimate $\hat{p}$ of p) is given by

$$\text{standard error of } \hat{p} = \sqrt{\frac{pq}{n}}$$

or, if the proportions are expressed as percentages,

$$\text{standard error of } \hat{p}\% = \sqrt{\frac{p\% \cdot q\%}{n}}$$

Thus if 10% of men in a population are more than 6 feet high, the standard error in a sample of 100 is $\sqrt{\frac{10 \times 90}{100}} = 3 \cdot 0\%$.

This does not imply that all determinations by sampling will contain this degree of error. Some samples will be more in error and some less, and it is a matter of chance how much error in the estimate will be introduced by the use of any particular sample. Broadly speaking, however, one-third of the actual *sampling errors* encountered in a succession of random samples will be greater than the standard error, and one-twentieth will be greater than twice the standard error.

Thus, in the example given above, two-thirds of a large number of such samples would provide estimates between 7% and 13%, and nineteen-twentieths would provide estimates between 4% and 16%.

One important point which is revealed by this formula is that the standard error varies inversely with the square root of the size of the sample. In order to halve the standard error it is necessary to quadruple the size of the sample.

Thus in our example, if the size of each sample is raised from 100 to 400, estimates lying between 8·5% and 11·5% will be obtained in two-thirds of such samples, and estimates between 7·0% and 13·0% in nineteen-twentieths of such samples.

Mean value of a given attribute. It is sometimes desired to estimate by sampling the mean value of a particular quantitative attribute (e.g. height, age) in a given population. The standard error of the estimated mean can then be calculated by a process similar to that already described. In such cases an additional factor to be taken into account is the variability among themselves of the values recorded. If a pilot survey of a pre-sample has been conducted, this can be summarised in terms of the *standard deviation* ' s ' of pre-sample values, which provides an estimate of the corresponding standard deviation in the population from which the pre-sample is drawn, and from which it is intended to draw the main sample.

If the pre-sample contains n_1 units which give values for the variate in question of $y_1, y_2, y_3 \ldots y_n$, and if $\bar{y}$ is the mean of these values, the standard deviation of the pre-sample [1]

$$= s = \sqrt{\frac{Sn_1(y_1 - \bar{y})^2}{n_1 - 1}}$$

The next step is to calculate the standard error of the estimate of the mean which will follow the adoption of a main sample of n_2 units. This will be

$$\frac{s}{\sqrt{n_2}} = \sqrt{\frac{Sn_1(y_1 - \bar{y})^2}{n_2(n_1 - 1)}}.$$

As before, the standard error of the estimate of the mean varies inversely as the square root of the size of the sample. In order to halve the standard error it is necessary to quadruple the sample size.

General. These formulæ are adequate when the population is large and normally distributed as to the attribute in question; they also apply only when random sampling has been employed and when the sample is moderately large—i.e. not less than 30–40 sampling units. When any of these conditions is not complied with, the calculation of the standard error, and consequently of the appropriate size of sample in given circumstances, is more complicated, and well beyond the scope of the amateur statistician. It is, however, often possible to determine the appropriate size for a sample along the lines indicated above, and it is clearly better to do so than to make an arbitrary choice of size of

---

[1] Whether or not this is an adequate estimate of the standard deviation in the population as a whole can be gauged by calculating its own standard error. Clearly a very small pre-sample may provide an estimate which is too rough to be useful.

sample which gives results that are either too rough or needlessly accurate.[1]

When a sub-sample—e.g. a certain age-group—will have to be analysed separately, the necessary size of the sub-sample is calculated in the same way. The size necessary for the full sample will then depend on whether or not stratification and a variable sampling fraction are to be adopted.

3. THE PILOT SURVEY

The Pilot Survey is also needed for reasons other than those already mentioned, and it must be admitted that it is sometimes difficult to reconcile all its functions.

The purpose of the pilot survey is quite distinct from that of the main survey. As we have seen, the mass interview or questionnaire properly belongs at the end of a process of elucidation and clarification of a problem. By the time a research programme has reached this stage, the investigator is expected to have decided what is relevant to his hypothesis, and hence what areas he should investigate by further direct questioning. He will still, however, have had no opportunity to discover what are the best means of obtaining the information that he desires. He knows the subject-matter of his questions, but not the most effective form of wording in which to put them. If he is designing a multiple-response form, he will be frustrated by not knowing in advance what responses he will get and how frequently. Finally, unless he is particularly lucky, his field-workers will need intensive training. Until all these preliminaries are complete, it is far more satisfactory if the actual results brought in from the field can be discarded as immature.[2]

If this is to be the aim, the pilot survey should be designed primarily as an exercise in methods of asking questions and in

---

[1] At such stages the subjective skill of the experienced statistician is often worth more than the most painstaking calculations of the amateur. For example, it is sometimes possible progressively to extend the main sample until the desired degree of accuracy is attained, but this technique, sometimes known as 'sequential analysis', requires close collaboration between investigator and statistician.

[2] Mark Abrams (1951, *J. Roy. Statist. Soc.*, **114**, 200) remarked that the carrying out of less than twelve interviews 'was not a fair test of any interviewer, whether trained or untrained. In most large-scale surveys the normal procedure was to regard the first 10, 15 or even 20 interviews turned in by each interviewer as being more or less trial shots; they were still learning the particular approach needed for the survey.'

recording answers. Interviewers should constantly pool their experiences, describing which phrases have proved unintelligible and which issues have aroused interest, and discovering what order of questioning has proved most satisfactory. During this stage experienced interviewers should be free to experiment gently with the wording and order of questions.

In certain types of survey, wording may prove of very great importance. Variations in response due to modifying wording and order can only be determined statistically, and in important investigations, and when the nature of the material demands, it may therefore be necessary—and save time in the end—to interpose an initial statistical inquiry between the exploratory survey and the main survey.[1] This should be designed for the purpose of standardising questions in the form that evokes the most consistent replies.[2]

4. APPROACH TECHNIQUES

The organisation of field-work and the planning and execution of a campaign to win advance attention and approval may be crucial to the success of a survey.

It is therefore necessary that the occasion of the interview should be presented in advance as an important one to those concerned. Care should be taken to perfect each successive preliminary stage. Full co-operation of the leaders and 'representatives' of the group to be interviewed must be won, and it is often necessary to spend much time explaining to them the purpose and methods of the survey. It is virtually certain that these representatives will be approached by individuals who are alarmed at the prospect of being selected for interview, and quite a lot of harm can be done if the representatives give a badly garbled version of the project. Where the population to be interviewed has no natural leaders or representatives, it may be wise to arrange for the setting up of a sponsoring committee of influential citizens. This may be desirable whether or not the interview programme forms part of a wider survey.[3]

[1] The terminology used to describe these different stages varies distressingly. In the United States, the two preliminaries are often known as 'informal interviewing', and the 'pretest'. The Government Social Survey knows them as the 'pre-pilot' and the 'pilot' surveys.
[2] For consideration of the relation between consistency and truth, see p. 241, etc.
[3] See also 'INFLUENCING POTENTATES', pp. 145 seq.

The chances of a flying start can be improved by preparing in advance those individuals selected for the sample. Circumstances vary, but in some cases at least it may be desirable that the informant should be asked in a personal letter to meet the interviewer at a given time, or even that a third party, already known to the informant, should be brought in to effect a more or less formal introduction. This type of 'sales technique' appears to be normal in the United States. It may, however, be contrasted with the approach techniques commonly used in this country, which are characterised by an absence of formality and an emphasis on anonymity, based on the belief that more alarm than confidence is promoted by too much preparation. This is an issue on which it is desirable that preferences for one method or the other should rest on controlled experience, and not on arbitrary *a priori* grounds.[1]

5. THE SETTING AND CONDUCT OF THE INTERVIEW

Some of the early textbooks on applied psychology contain descriptions of the techniques then thought appropriate for ensuring that the consultant maintains an ascendancy over his subject. These provide the source of the celebrated advice to the interviewer that he should place his informant in a lower chair and arrange the light to shine in his eyes.

Such third-degree methods are of course entirely unsuitable for achieving the free and open atmosphere needed for success in the types of interview that we have been discussing. On the contrary, the circumstances should be designed in every way to put the informant at his ease.[2]

The actual material setting is of considerable importance. Complete privacy should be ensured, with no possibility that a third party might overhear the proceedings, and with the minimum of interruption. Interviewer and informant should have similar chairs, in order to stress equality. A supply of cigarettes is a good investment.

Experience shows that the best results are obtained if the informant feels on his home ground. Thus if the informants are factory workers, and the emphasis of the inquiry is on factory

---

[1] It may be noted that in official house-to-house surveys, considerably more than half the interviews have in fact been arranged in advance. See p. 249 fn.
[2] See, for example, OLDFIELD, R. C. (1941), especially Chapter IV.

conditions, it is desirable to conduct the inquiry within the factory, but not in a part of it that the workers will strongly identify with management.[1]

If the householder or the family is the focus of interest, it is preferable, as well as almost unavoidable, to interview at the home. The attentive interviewer then has an opportunity to observe, as well as merely to record answers, and at its lowest this will make it very much easier for him to interpret the informant's responses. In the less fully structured type of interview it will help him to guide the discussion along the most profitable lines. Moreover, the risk of refusals is minimised when the informant, instead of being required to turn up at some unfamiliar office,[2] occupies the position of a host or hostess.

There are corresponding disadvantages. It can be a slow business to find the informants who have been pre-selected by proper sampling methods. Not only is there the time spent in moving from house to house, but also the time spent in revisiting informants who were out or otherwise not available on the first visit. Even those that have been located may be more ready to resent disturbance of their own limited free time than they would be if the interview was taking place in their employer's time. It may be impossible to arrange a confidential interview, as there is often no unoccupied room.[3]

There is also a more subtle difficulty. In recent years there has been a vast proliferation of social-welfare agencies—health visitor, school attendance officer, tuberculosis officer, etc., etc.—and many families are today subjected to a series of visits from officers attached to these agencies. The proper relationship between the informant and these officers is clearly quite different from that

[1] One of the best factory interview rooms which I have managed to secure was normally occupied by the works barber.
[2] Some self-consciousness may occur, however, if there is too great a class difference between interviewer and informant. The solution to this, which has various advantages also, is that the two should as far as possible be matched in respect of class.
[3] John Dollard, whose survey of a colour-conscious town in Alabama has already been mentioned (p. 172), gives a graphic description of his difficulties in finding a suitable place in which to interview negroes. He could not have interviewed them in his lodgings, as that would have embarrassed his hosts. In any case, they would have had to be admitted by the back door. Their own homes were too small and overrun. School and courthouse were impracticable. Finally, he rented an office in a block used by professional people. Even so, he had to let it be known that the door was not locked, for some of his informants were women and ' white men are suspected when they have secret contacts with Negro women '—(*Caste and Class*, pp. 23–5).

between the informant and a social investigator. From visitors of the former type he will be concerned to obtain some concession or to conceal some deficiency. The accent is very directly on action rather than on 'truth'. So the social investigator in his turn must be ready for the customary 'special pleading' and may also be faced with requests for help. His sense of humanity will constrain him to give welfare assistance, or at least advice; this may at times be regarded as inconsistent with his primary purpose of collecting information.[1]

It must be recognised that the interviewer, who has asked for the interview to take place and is assumed to be familiar with what goes on at interviews, holds the initiative and is expected to conduct the proceedings. The friendly atmosphere aimed at in the setting for the interview must also pervade its conduct.

It is bad for an interviewer to adopt a 'next-please' attitude, like a bus conductor or a station hairdresser. While the results of the mass interview will in the end be coldly codified, this is no reason why the relationship between informant and interviewer should be a frigidly impersonal one. Social skill, 'getting on well with people', a genuine interest in others, and a true spirit of equality—all these are essential qualifications of the interviewer, and not in any way incompatible with a scientific approach.

6. NOTE-TAKING AND CARDING

> There is a still more barbarous method, which need not receive more than passing mention. This is simply to register documents in the memory without taking written notes. This method has been used. Historians endowed with excellent memories, and lazy to boot, have indulged this whim, with the result that their quotations and references are mostly inexact. The human memory is a delicate piece of registering apparatus, but it is so little an instrument of precision that such presumption is inexcusable.—LANGLOIS and SEIGNOBOS.

Some form of memorandum is needed to record all types of observation,[2] but in no case is it more important than with interviews.

Apart from purely exploratory occasions, or those confined to free-association techniques, the interviewer will have some idea of the ground that he is expected to cover. Even in the most indirect form of interviewing it is a great help to the analyst if the

[1] The use of social welfare case histories in social research has been discussed on p. 100 seq.
[2] See p. 139.

different topics discussed in each interview are recorded separately and with some uniformity of layout.[1]

At the other extreme we have the detailed questionnaire form or schedule, often with preceded responses, which can only be completed by recording definite answers in fixed positions. There is, of course, no basic difficulty in combining both sorts of question in one interview. The session can first consist of a free form of conversation which allows the informant to express himself without restraint, and then end up with a series of fixed questions—e.g. age, income, occupation. It has been found on the whole better to leave such factual questions to the end of an interview, so as to provide the best chance of a co-operative atmosphere before displaying curiosity about possibly private matters.

There has been much controversy as to whether note-taking should be allowed during the interview, or should be postponed until after the interview. Many authorities have claimed that no note-taking should be visible to the informant, on the grounds that it tends to hold up proceedings, to interrupt his train of thought and to make him conscious that whatever he is saying is being taken down in evidence. Others have treated note-taking as a convenient and unembarrassing activity for the interviewer who is waiting for an informant to express himself freely.

If note-taking is to be abjured during the interview, it is clearly necessary that the earliest opportunity should be given to the interviewer to record in full what was said. Experiments in memorising suggest that even a short lapse of time gives scope for the interviewer's unconscious bias to distort his record.[2] Moreover, from the practical point of view, post-interview note-taking,

---

[1] This advantage is sometimes deliberately renounced, for fear that any kind of uniformity of layout will tend to influence the course of the interview. Indirect interviewing necessitates extended reporting. Roethlisberger and Dickson (op. cit., p. 203) report that the change from semi-structured to indirect interviewing at the Hawthorne Works lengthened each report from an average of two and a half pages to ten single-spaced typewritten pages.

[2] For a comment in favour of simultaneous recording, see KINSEY, A. C. et al. (1948), *Sexual Behavior in the Human Male*, p. 50. Following recommended practice, these investigators initially waited until after their interviews before recording what had transpired. They found, however, that this introduced tremendous error into the records, and after a few months they switched over to direct recording in the presence of the informant. They claim that this involved no loss of rapport, mainly because the use of a code for recording eliminated awkward pauses.

It should be reported, however, that various experienced investigators claim to have developed sufficient mnemonic skill to permit post-recording. See, for example, HADER, J. J., and LINDEMAN, E. C. (1933), p. 146; DOLLARD, J., *Caste and Class*, p. 26.

apart from costing extra time, is often very awkward. Much house-to-house interviewing has to be done during evenings, when housewives have more leisure and earners are at home, and interviewing cannot be confined to fine summer weather. In Britain, interviewers normally travel by bicycle or bus, and an unprotected windy street on a dark winter evening is not a suitable place for writing up what may have been a protracted and complicated discussion. The alternative procedure of returning to some central office after each session is often equally undesirable on the score of time.

It is not surprising, therefore, that the majority of large-scale interview agencies are reconciled to the completion of the interview record sheets in the presence of informants. This is, perhaps, a concession made inherently necessary by the adoption of mass-interview techniques. Moreover, both in the United States and in Great Britain the public is undoubtedly becoming more sophisticated about giving facts and public opinions to relative strangers. Press campaigns against ' Cooper's snoopers ' and their successors have never gained very impressive public support, and increasing familiarity with this form of investigation has undoubtedly made it even more generally acceptable.

Note-taking in the informant's presence can, in one respect at least, be turned to advantage. It should be one of the criteria of success in interviewing that the recorded results are as acceptable to the informant as to the investigator. If the record is made at the time, this criterion can readily be tested, and the informant can be given an opportunity to see and approve its content.[1] It is not inconsistent with this technique to invite the interviewer to record subsequently any comments based on his own observations. One of my former interviewers used to add to the bottom of our sheets a brilliant little pen-picture of each informant; whereas these descriptions were of no value in the statistical analysis of the material, they helped to remind us that the hard facts and predigested fancies noted down were indeed elicited from real individuals.

[1] In any case, few conscious informants are so naïve as not to realise that ' what they say is being taken down in evidence ' whether notes are taken at the time or not. In casually engineered conversations, it is arguable that an informant's readiness to talk will be greater if he does not suspect that what he says is being recorded. But these circumstances belong more with the Formative Interview than in the present context.

The Form of Note-taking. The form in which notes should be taken is a subject which has been well explored, though it is a subject which bores some investigators. Here again we encounter the conflict between the need to amass material suitable for easy analysis and the need to record it in a form sufficiently flexible to avoid distortion of responses by forcing them into over-rigid categories.

Although this basic conflict is inevitable, it is possible to maximise efficiency by forethought. The Webbs, in their *Methods of Social Study*, devote a chapter to ' The Art of Note-taking '; they point out that successful note-taking is not only ' an indispensable instrument in the technique of sociological inquiry ' but is ' in sociology, actually an instrument of discovery '.[1]

This statement can be confirmed by the experience of many investigators. A good system of notes is an important instrument for discovering previously unsuspected connections between different sets of facts, and thus of arriving at unforeseen hypotheses.

Mass-interview and Questionnaire Forms.

Pilot Survey. In the context of the mass interview and the questionnaire, what must be aimed at is a series of identical forms which are easy to fill in, easy to read and free from ambiguity in their wording or lay-out.

The precise nature of each record sheet naturally depends on the interviews to be recorded, and has to be worked out in each case in the light of experience gained during the pilot survey.

In the design of a sheet for a pilot survey itself, it is probably wrong to lay much emphasis upon ease of coding, as any categories tried out at the pilot stage should in any case be provisional. Coding is best left until the pilot material is available.

Some questions—such as the ' standard classification items ' giving age, sex, occupation and so on—will often be pre-determined even on the pilot sheets, and in the interests of neatness these can be given regularly placed boxes, if not pre-coded. The rest of the form should be in accord with the purpose of the pilot inquiry—that is, it should be designed primarily to find out how to get at certain chosen facts, and not to find out what facts to cover. The emphasis is on wording and on the order of questions, and there is little hope of devising a uniform and workable layout

[1] WEBB, S. and B. (1932), p. 83.

that will give adequate scope for experimentation on these points. But as the number of interviews will be relatively small, the task of manual sorting will be quite manageable.

Plenty of space should be left to enable the interviewer to report on any misunderstandings or resistances attributable to the questions, and to give scope for full and unchannelled description of the informant's responses to these questions when any preliminary difficulties have been cleared up. Moreover, as the pilot interviews are essentially exploratory it will almost certainly be necessary to leave space for supplementary questions to be added during the course of the pilot survey.

Main Survey. In the main survey, as the number of separate interviews extends, the need for simplicity of sorting becomes predominant. Very soon—say for more than 100 individual records—multi-sheet forms become difficult and tedious to handle, and single stiff cards are much more convenient. Even if direct recording on such cards is ruled out, it will often be found an ultimate economy in time to transcribe data from the original sheets for the purpose of sorting; it is surprising how much information can be concentrated onto one such card without causing bias through compression.[1]

Paramount Cards. Of particular value at this scale of operation is the Cope-Chat 'Paramount' card, which is surrounded along each of its edges by holes that can be clipped. Each hole is made to correspond with some fact described in writing elsewhere on the card, and all cards used for cases to which this fact applies can be readily separated from the pack by hand, by means of a special needle. Normally all facts likely to be used in the analysis are recorded on one side of the card, leaving the other side free, if required, for more discursive data.

The great advantage of the Paramount card is that it provides a

---

[1] As early as 1897, Langlois and Seignobos felt justified in writing: 'Every one admits nowadays that it is advisable to collect materials on separate cards or slips of paper. . . . The advantages of this artifice are obvious: the detachability of the slips enables us to group them at will in a host of different combinations; if necessary, to change their places: it is easy to bring texts of the same kind together, and to incorporate additions, as they are acquired, in the interior of the groups to which they belong. . . . Moreover, the method of slips is the only one mechanically possible for the purpose of forming, classifying and utilising a collection of documents of any great extent. Statisticians, financiers, and men of letters who observe, have now discovered this as well as scholars.'— LANGLOIS, Ch. V., and SEIGNOBOS, Ch. (Eng. trans. 1898), *Introduction to the Study of History*, p. 103.

visual record of each individual interview and yet is convenient for sorting. When the scale of operation becomes too big, however, manual sorting will be very tedious. The limit is almost certainly reached when 2,000 separate cases have to be analysed, and will be reached much earlier if a large number of cross-tabulations have to be undertaken.

Mechanical Handling. For 2,000 cases or more the method normally adopted is the fully mechanised tabulating process, in which special punched cards are prepared and sorted. The two main systems are Hollerith and Powers-Samas; the former reads the cards electrically and the latter mechanically. Great rivalry between these systems continues; while the Hollerith is generally regarded as the more flexible, the Powers-Samas is used by the General Register Office. Both are now very widely employed in fields in which statistics and accounts are handled on a large scale.[1]

The process involves several stages. The information to be tabulated is first broken down into headings. The maximum possible number of headings or columns on one card is fixed by the size of a given installation; the largest Hollerith card has eighty columns and the largest Powers card has sixty-five columns.[2] *Coding* entails the conversion of the descriptive information that it is desired to tabulate into the appropriate series of code numbers, generally one for each column. Each case (e.g. interview) is thus reduced to a series of up to 80 (or even more) code numbers.

The second stage is *punching*. Punching consists of transferring the coded information on to the special cards, one for each case. Holes can be punched in any of the twelve positions in each column, each of these positions representing a code number or letter. This is generally done by hand machines in both systems, and the punchings are subsequently checked by a rather similar machine, called the *verifier*.

The pack of cards is then accepted as giving a true coded record of the information, and all further operations are performed on

---

[1] There are a number of books and reports devoted to the subject of machine tabulation. For a brief historical survey and an imaginative forecast of future developments, see MANDEVILLE, J. P. (1946), ' Improvements in Methods of Census and Survey Analysis ', *J. Roy. Statist. Soc.*, **109**, 111–29, and for an excellent description of how they work and can be used see YATES, F. (1949), pp. 112–23. Only very experienced users can hope to master all the tricks of these remarkable machines.

[2] By special multiple punching this can be made equivalent to a 130-column card.

them. The simplest operation is that performed by the *sorter*. The sorter operates on one column at a time, and separates cards into twelve boxes, each corresponding with one code number in that column. In this way, for example, cards based on interview data might be divided according to the age of informants. This not only gets the cards into a desired order, but also, with the addition of a counting device, tells the operator how many cards have been sorted into each box.

If, as is normally the case, a permanent record is needed, and particularly when cross-tabulations involving more than one column are desired, a more elaborate machine, called a *tabulator*, may be used. This not only sorts and counts simultaneously on a number of columns but also prints the results; the printing of totals accumulated in the counters is called *tabulation*, and the printing of numbers read from the cards is called *listing*. Various other devices enable the operator to pre-set the machine in many ingenious and useful ways.

Mark-sensing. For a straightforward routine mass-interview or questionnaire, it is worth exploring the possibility of making use of a new system designed for the elimination of the hand-punching stage of punched-card preparation. This system, known as 'mark-sensing', has been extensively used in the United States, both for record purposes and in school examinations. A special Hollerith card is prepared giving a number of pre-coded alternative answers to each question, and the examinee, informant or interviewer, makes a pencil mark against each appropriate reply. Without further transcription these cards are then passed through a machine which picks up the small electric currents that pass along the pencil-marks and punches corresponding holes in orthodox Hollerith cards.

This system appears to have two advantages over the normal punched-card system; one is that the card is slightly more intelligible as a visual record of information than the ordinary punched card, and the other that the manual labour of transcribing can be eliminated. On the other hand, the information that can be fitted on to a punched card is halved, and more skill and care are required of the person who completes the card than are needed to fill up the normal questionnaire or schedule form.[1]

---

[1] In a discussion on Mr. Mandeville's paper at the Royal Statistical Society, Mr. A. Thomas took up the question of mark-sensing. 'He would say that this

Various other suggestions are in the air, and may ultimately lead to the elimination of all intermediate manual operations between the recording and the tabulation of data.

Disadvantages of Mechanical Systems. These machines are invaluable in large-scale social inquiries, particularly in those of a semi-routine nature. Experienced investigators are, however, often reluctant to adopt them in the exploration of fresh fields. This may be partly due to the rather high cost of mechanical tabulation, whether done privately with hired machines or under contract, but it is more probably because their use necessitates pre-coding. The whole process of coding, sorting and tabulation becomes highly elaborate and impersonal, and the punched cards themselves are particularly undescriptive. The result is that the probability is greatly reduced that an unsuspected relationship will be spotted or that a fruitful hypothesis will emerge in the course of analysis. The investigator provides the machine operators with a list of the single classifications and of the cross-tabulations that he wants, and he then loses touch with the proceedings until a number of neat tables are placed on his desk. In one sense it is easy for him to ask for more, because it costs him no personal effort, but this very fact seems to make it less likely that he will do so. Thus what could be the hours of gestation are transformed into sterile delegated industry.

This is one of the dilemmas inherent in large-scale statistical inquiry, but one which may to some extent be overcome if the routine tabulation is preceded by a personal hand-sorting and hand-tabulation of a sample of the final interview material. The pilot survey will have ensured that the questions and the interview technique are properly designed to give manipulable material in the main survey. Next, a batch of the main survey material is put to the test by the investigator himself, who may thereby discover the possibility of a hitherto unsuspected correlation between—shall we say—occupation and frequency of

---

method of recording, although quite efficient in sensing the marks and translating them into holes, was not successful owing to the difficulty of getting people to make proper marks and to put the marks in the right places.

'The mark-sensing was invented [in 1929], and the inventor had met with this difficulty then. When the mark was made with the required thickness of line and in the right place, the device worked, but it was so difficult to get the operators to do this that he continued his development by making a little key-operated machine, just like a punching machine, to make the pencil mark!'
—*J. Roy. Statist. Soc.* (1949), **109**, 124.

attendance at cinemas. He can subsequently put his machine operators on to analysing the whole main sample to discover whether his reasoned hunch is justifiable.

The value of such hypotheses as arise in the course of the analysis cannot be too highly stressed. While it is impossible to estimate how much is lost by delegated tabulation, it appears very likely that much fresh field material is under-employed and that far too much dependence is placed on hypotheses already suggested by other social scientists or originating in the mind of the investigator before he has examined his field material.

This particular problem does not of course arise when a lone investigator conducts all, or a substantial part of, his own interviews. In this case he will be steeped in the problem, and in a position to extract all the goodness out of his recorded material. Such conditions are, however, rare; the scale of organisation required to obtain a statistically adequate sample of interview records generally means that in practice the leader of a research project does no interviewing, and that his report is correspondingly of less value and interest than it might otherwise have been.

Coding. Coding—that is to say, the fixing of categories into which each type of information is divided—is an essential stage in statistical inquiries and one in which it is necessary to follow certain general rules.

These rules may be regarded as a practical application of the principles already discussed, which should guide the use of language.[1] According to these principles, any categories adopted are seen to have no abstract rightness or validity, but to arise solely through the process of collecting the material to fit into them—i.e. in this case to the questions asked—and from the purpose for which the information is being collected. As these will vary in each case there is thus a logical justification for regarding each investigation as an isolated one, and for classifying the fresh survey material from first principles. In practice, although it may ultimately be found necessary to do this, fresh codification should only be attempted after a careful examination of all existing classifications—particularly of those that have been perfected in administrative use—and after a genuine attempt to fit the fresh material into one or other of these.

Unfortunately, but not surprisingly, even official agencies have

[1] pp. 38 seq.

not always found it possible to follow this rule. For example, if it is required to use official statistics for an examination of industrial structure and the distribution of industrial workers, one is faced with the need to attempt a reconciliation of at least three major sources, each of which has its own independent system of coding.[1]

Similarly the endless confusion about the classification of illness and cause of death is only gradually being diminished by international agreement.

Sometimes a single agency which prepares recurrent records of the same data revises its classification in the light of past experience or to meet fresh circumstances. A decision to do so has to be justified by carefully weighing the advantage of a fresh classification, more closely attuned to current needs against the disadvantage of losing comparability with past records. This disadvantage can be minimised, but not eliminated, by undertaking a double analysis—i.e. using both the new and the old classifications, at the time of the change-over.

It is just as important for the unofficial investigator to adopt an existing authoritative classification wherever to do so will not distort his results or prejudice his aims. If, for example, he is undertaking a local survey which involves recording the ages of his informants, his age-group categories can normally without inconvenience follow those employed by the Registrar-General. Whether or not he foresees the need in advance, he may later wish in his report to compare the age-grouping of his sample with that of the whole local population.

Again, if the survey is concerned with social class he may well find it appropriate to use as one of his criteria the Registrar-General's five categories of family class based on the occupation of the principal male earner. This classification is forty years old, and in many ways anomalous, but it is still the most universally adopted in England. There is, of course, nothing to prevent the use of other class categories in addition; these again may already have been used,[2] or may when no alternative exists be of the investigator's own devising.

A second rule is that it is always better to have too many separate categories in the coding system than to start with too few.

---

[1] These three are the Registrar-General's Census of Population material, the Ministry of Labour's statistics on Insured Workers, and the Board of Trade's Censuses of Production. See also p. 46.

[2] See also pp. 52 seq.

Tables can always be simplified, when it is reasonable to do so, by amalgamating the totals of several categories in the raw tabulations, but without going back to the original material it is impossible to split up totals once the tabulation has been made.

The mechanical tabulating systems normally allow twelve positions in each column. It is wise to reserve one of these for N/S (not stated) and often to reserve another for N/A (not applicable).[1] This leaves about ten categories, and it will often be desirable to use them all. Some questions, such as sex and marital status, command only a small number of possible answers. To make the full use of the column, these can either be combined —e.g. male single, male married, etc.—or, in some tabulating systems, double punching of columns is possible.

If 'Paramount' cards, with peripheral holes for hand sorting, are to be used, the total permissible number of individual categories is somewhat limited. At the cost of some extra work in sorting, this can be partly overcome by using some such series as 1, 2, 4, 8. Thus if an item can be classified in fifteen different categories not more than four holes are needed for identification. All cards recording category thirteen, for example, have their holes corresponding with 1, 4 and 8 clipped. These cards can be subsequently identified by a process of elimination by successive needling through the three holes marked 1, 4 and 8.[2]

However carefully the coding has been thought out in advance, and however apparently straightforward the material to be coded, it is never possible to foresee all special cases; a certain amount of judgment is therefore needed in classifying individual particulars. These marginal cases normally constitute only a minor proportion of the total of entries, but it is nevertheless important to make careful decisions about them when they first occur and to ensure that such decisions are followed whenever the same problem occurs.

This is done by compiling a list of *rulings* to be followed by all coders. Some of these rulings can be laid down in advance, as a

---

[1] It is always safer, and more convenient for checking purposes, to require some indication that each usable column has been attended to.

[2] YATES, F. (1949, pp. 111-12) favours the series 0, 1, 2, 4, 7, which has the advantage of being 'self-checking on sorts' if the convention is adopted that 4, 7 denotes 0. In other words, every digit from 0 to 9 is denoted by a pair of holes (4, 7; 0, 1; 0, 2; 1, 2; ... 2, 7) and this simplifies checking.

result of previous experience or knowledge of the material,[1] but others will accumulate as coding proceeds.

Sociometric Diagrams. Some social scientists have found it useful to present their results in diagrammatic form. On occasion, and for certain purposes and certain kinds of analysis, graphic display has proved to be more revealing than immediate reduction to statistical tabulation.

This line of approach is exemplified in a rather sophisticated form in the sociometric diagram. The sociogram was first developed in the 1930s by Dr. J. L. Moreno and has since commended itself to many investigators. Moreno and his followers have used the sociometric test with caution, but its wide popularity may be partly attributed to the simplicity and the graphic qualities of the sociogram. With the aid of some elementary data, a synoptic chart of interpersonal relations can be presented with disarming ease.

Let us assemble a school class, and ask each member of the class to address a Christmas Card to another member. What can we learn from this simple experiment? One schoolchild, or possibly more, will have received a number of cards; this reveals the popular ones, the ' sociometric stars '. Other children will have paired off and addressed cards to each other (' mutual choice '), while some other children (' isolates ') will have been nobody's sociometric choice. If more than one card per child is allowed, other relationships such as ' cliques ' can be shown up.

Conversely, the children can be put through a rejection test. For example, ' In the rejection test the children were asked to imagine a trip to New Brighton—a seaside resort near Liverpool—in a charabanc large enough to convey the whole class with the exception of three children who had to be left behind; ' We want you to put down on a piece of paper—but don't let anyone see—the three children *you* would leave behind; three spoilsports, the nastiest children in the class '.[2]

---

[1] Cf. the list of rulings supplied to enumerators in the Census of Population.
[2] SILBERMAN, L., and SPICE, B. (1950), *Colour and Class in Six Liverpool Schools*, pp. 17-18. Another English programme of sociometric testing is reported in FLEMING, C. M.—Ed. (1951), *Studies in the Social Pscyhology of Adolescence*; this book also contains (pp. 19-26) an instructive brief history of the development of sociometric method, which summarises the very extensive American literature on the subject. The interested reader is referred to two key books by Dr. Moreno—MORENO, J. L. (1934), *Who Shall Survive?* and (1951), *Sociometry, Experimental Method and the Science of Society*; to JENNINGS, H. H. (1943), *Leadership and Isolation*; to the quarterly journal, *Sociometry*, founded in 1937; and to the series of *Sociometry Monographs*.

These relationships may easily be portrayed by putting down the names and drawing appropriate arrows and other symbols between them. Thus, | CASTOR |—| POLLUX | can be used to symbolise ' mutual choice ', while Paris, in the exercise of his judgment, would be something of a ' sociometric star '. The Jolly

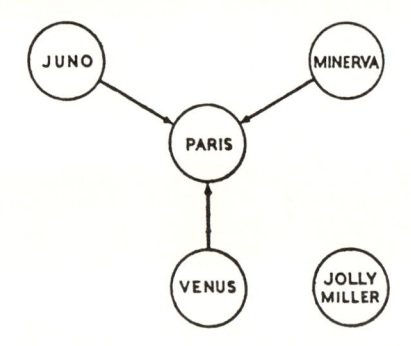

```
      JUNO              MINERVA
          \             /
           \           /
            PARIS
              ↑
              |
          VENUS      JOLLY
                     MILLER
```

Miller, when declaiming ' I care for nobody, no not I, and nobody cares for me ', would be classified as an ' isolate '.

Clearly, sociometric material is least adequate when it is derived from paper-and-pencil exercises such as the dispatch of phoney greetings cards. It becomes increasingly sensible as the situations are made more specific and more meaningful to those taking part. A serious source of data is reported in a later chapter of this book; girls sent to an approved school in New York run by Dr. Moreno in the 1930s were permitted to choose, sociometrically, from among the available ' house mothers ' and ' key girls ' before being placed in one of the cottages in which the inmates lived.[1] Observational material can also be manipulated sociometrically; for example, the interactive behaviour of the men in the Bank Wiring Assembly Room at the Hawthorne Works was noted and described in a series of sociometric diagrams.[2] Furthermore, if real situations are not available, participants can be encouraged to act out their attitudes in a charade or *sociodrama*, which has a therapeutic as well as a diagnostic function.

In some contexts it is found desirable to substitute the *sociomatrix* for the sociogram. This form, which is based on the

[1] See pp. 278–80.
[2] ROETHLISBERGER, F. J., and DICKSON, W. J. (1939), *Management and the Worker*, pp. 495 seq.

notation of matrix algebra, has the merit of completeness in that, if the information is available, the relationship between each pair of individuals can be simultaneously described. On the other hand, material disposed in a sociomatrix is not as easy to grasp in the mind's eye as with the sociogram. Dr. Moreno recommends that the two should be used to supplement each other.

These devices are integral with the active and mature theory of interpersonal relations developed by Moreno, and this theory gives them their distinctive character. But some investigators are tempted to use them out of character, merely as an additional means for assembling empirical material, and even persuade themselves that they are thereby adding to the repertoire of investigational techniques. This minor fallacy is not difficult to avoid.

7. HOW TO MINIMISE BIAS

It has been repeatedly stated as an axiom that informants cannot be regularly expected to give precisely true answers to the questions put to them. This statement will now be considered a little more closely, with special reference to problems encountered in mass interviewing.

Most people accept the fact that answers to personal questions or to those concerned with opinions are liable to be distorted, but they tenaciously hold to the belief that there are certain types of 'objective fact' which can be accepted with complete confidence.

This confidence is reinforced by the form in which statistics are normally presented. If we read that the population of London in 1931 was 8,203,942, we are apt to be impressed by the accuracy of this statement, and to forget not only that it relates to a particular London on a particular day, but also that it can only be made at all because a couple of million householders, assisted by a large number of enumerators, filled in their census forms. And when we think again of the forms that we have filled in, or watched being filled in, and of the inaccuracies and distortions of truth which are constantly being introduced into these forms, we are apt to lose our faith in the exactness even of something as factual as a population count.

There are various ways of dealing with this. The simplest,

and perhaps safest, is to adopt an operational definition. In the case above, for instance, you imply ' Parliament passed a Bill, and the Registrar-General had some forms printed and sent enumerators round with them, and householders filled them up, and Powers-Samas operators added all the answers together and here is the result '. The operational definition is the safeguard normally adopted by the statistician, though he does not necessarily describe it under this name. Thus, Professor Sargant Florence wittily remarks: ' There is an art, for instance, in asking foolproof and shame-proof questions, and in knowing when not to ask questions at all. Each source of data has its own special liability to biased or chance error and falsification, but we shall leave these preliminary difficulties of " authentication " in the care of the antiquarian, the scientific historian, the scholar pursuing the Higher Criticism of his documents, and the immediate observer, recorder, and collector of the material. The data of the statistician, the facts that are given him, we shall take to be authentic, and accurately observed at source and accurately recorded '; and then, in a footnote, ' The statistician should not omit to state the source of his data, the time, place, name of observer, and, where not obvious by inspection, the number of observations made '.[1]

This is clearly the only straightforward way of taking other people's figures. Unlike an election candidate, you cannot demand a recount, so the best alternative is to make it clear that someone else has done the counting.

In the case of a population census, the short time available for each ' interview ' of a householder by an enumerator would probably permit no substantially greater accuracy, even if the census were conducted by specially trained social investigators.

It is well known, however, that the answers given to certain questions can be readily exposed as erratic. For example, informants are not very reliable as a group in stating their ages. For fairly obvious reasons, ages—particularly those of women—tend to be understated, while there is a tendency of people to give their age as a multiple of 5—i.e. to ' round them off '. There is also some detectable, and hardly surprising, inaccuracy in statements to do with marital status.

[1] FLORENCE, P. S. (1929), *The Statistical Method in Economics and Political Science*, p. 50 (text and footnote).

A detailed analysis of the peculiarities of recorded age distribution was included in the Report on the 1911 Census (Volume VII). It was well recognised by that date that the question-and-answer method of fact-finding did not provide 'objective facts' even on such simple issues as these.[1] On the other hand, in the case of the basic census material it is reasonably simple to adjust the raw replies, for example by smoothing the recorded age distributions. Other individual cases of error may, on the investigators' judgment, be regarded as free from bias, and thus assumed to cancel each other out; they are then taken to be relatively harmless in a simple classification, though not necessarily so in a cross-tabulation.

But while it is possible to pass the buck for the accuracy of other people's figures, and particularly perhaps of official statistics, this is ruled out when one is 'the immediate observer, recorder and collector of the material'. In this case the investigator is solely responsible for the authentication of his material.

It is possible to go too far in an opposite direction, and to swing from accepting all informants' statements as true to rejecting them all as irremediably false. While it is difficult to think of any class of fact that no informant would wish to falsify or conceal, it is clear that as the area of study loses its neutrality and becomes emotionally charged, the possibility of bias and the need to safeguard against it increase. For this reason, opinion surveys have been the rallying point for the controversy on reliability, and in them the need for safeguards is pre-eminent. On the other hand, it is by no means safe to assume that no such errors have intruded into factual surveys.

In the interview process, falsification can be admitted at any of several stages. There are, in the first instance, the false data supplied by an informant, irrespective of the impact of the interviewer: this effect will occur even in the case of the self-administered questionnaire. Next come the distortions in the informant's responses caused by the presence of the interviewer and by the manner in which he puts questions or otherwise suggests answers. Finally there are the errors made by the interviewer in reporting what transpired.

There are broadly four ways in which this lack of conclusiveness can be remedied. One is to verify information by finding

[1] See, however, the former Registrar-General's comment, p. 179 fn.

a second source of information. Reliability may also be gauged by internal methods, which may or may not be statistical. The fourth method is to provide optimum conditions for 'truth'.

(a) *Verification by Use of a Second Source of Information*

In many cases, other sources can give demonstrably more reliable information than can be obtained by interview. Thus it is easily shown empirically that a factory pay-office has more accurate figures for weekly earnings than the worker will give at an interview; the figure quoted at an interview is factually unreliable, though it may be of interest in revealing the informant's attitude to his earnings. In a case such as this, unless it is intended to use the material as part of a systematic study of attitudes to earnings, it is better to eliminate the question from the interview.

If all facts could be equally readily collected from a different and more reliable source, and if the survey were purely concerned with facts, there would be no need for interviews. It is probable that in many surveys all the facts are already reliably known and recorded somewhere, but such are the difficulties of gathering from a variety of sources these facts related to specific individuals that the easier course is taken of collecting them afresh by means of *ad hoc* interviews.

Often on many points no fully reliable source of information can be found. In such cases, reasonably consistent answers derived from two distinct sources give some grounds for confidence that the answers are true.[1]

Similarly if the answers to one question agree with those derived from an alternative source, the investigator may be disposed to attach more credence to other statements made in the interview. This is a human reaction, but one which is hard to justify except

[1] Cf. KENDALL and LAZARSFELD in MERTON, R. K., and LAZARSFELD, P. F., *Continuities in Social Research*, pp. 175-6, who are discussing a Research Branch survey into the relation between a soldier's army job and his previous civilian occupation. 'It may not be immediately obvious why we are concerned with the soldiers' descriptions if objective information is available. Why do we ask soldiers whether or not they use their civilian skills if this can be determined by a careful comparison of civilian and Army jobs? The answer is that it is very much easier to rely on the soldiers' descriptions. The authors allude briefly to the tremendous amount of work involved in a matching of civilian and army jobs. We undertake the labour in one study, as a means of checking the descriptions. If they turn out to be reasonably accurate, we rely on them in future studies of comparable populations, and no longer go through the difficult process of actually matching civilian and Army occupations' (p. 176 fn.).

How to Minimise Bias

on the somewhat impressionistic grounds that the witness is a truthful person.[1]

(b) *Statistical Tests for Internal Verification.*

It is generally difficult to determine by internal tests what the ' true ' unbiased answer would be. This is, however, by no means always impossible.

One case in which internal verification was possible occurred in the analysis of the Sickness Survey. The field-work for this was conducted at monthly intervals by the Social Survey, and the informants in each monthly sample were asked to mention all illnesses occurring among adults (16 + years) in their households in the two preceding months. It was believed by some that memories about illnesses occurring as long as three months ago might have seriously faded by the time of the interview, but Stocks,[2] by separate comparison of the three months' illness experiences recorded, was able to show that no advantage would accrue by basing sickness rates on the last month's experience alone, even if the sample size was correspondingly increased.

A more recent example, also based on field material collected by the Social Survey, showed that elderly people were, not surprisingly, much more prone to forget having contracted mumps in childhood than the younger persons interviewed.[3] Even on a subject as full of self-interest as one's own diseases, there is a limit beyond which the memory fails.

There appears to be considerable scope for the adoption of similar tests as a routine procedure in the design and analysis of mass-interviews.

(c) *Assessment of Plausibility*

It is possible to some extent to gauge the plausibility of answers by considering whether the questions asked are such that the informant is likely to be both able and willing to answer them truthfully. It is sometimes necessary to apply this test specifically to certain answers of certain informants.

[1] For the dangers of ' swallowing ground-bait ', and believing a man's second statement because you know his first statement to be true, see THOULESS, R. H. (1936 ed.), *Straight and Crooked Thinking*, p. 117.
[2] STOCKS, P. (1949), *Sickness in England and Wales*, pp. 16–18.
[3] LOGAN, W. P. D. (1951), 'Mumps and Diabetes', *Monthly Bulletin of Ministry of Health*, 10, 140. Cf. KINSEY et al. (1948), pp. 148–50.

As Gottschalk points out,[1] the legal rules of evidence, to which we would naturally turn, are not a very helpful guide, as they are designed more to protect the defendant from the effects of bias in a witness than to arrive at the truth. Legal proof has a distinctive meaning, which involves precautions—such as the exclusion of 'privileged' witnesses—which are not appropriate in social science.

Let us then consider what is involved in *ability* and *willingness* to give truthful answers.

Ability to tell the truth depends on the informant's personal competence and direct knowledge of and interest in the subject at issue. These will all be reflected in the extent and accuracy of his memory.

Personal Competence. The degree of personal competence required will vary with the particular point at issue. A reliable answer to any point does, however, entail a certain minimum level of expertness, health, education, verbal skill and so on. Few informants without special training can be expected to give reliable estimates, for example, of the size of a crowd or of the distance or velocity of an object.

Direct Knowledge. It is normally a waste of time to ask people about things of which they have no direct knowledge. As the Webbs points out, however, knowledge is not synonymous with authority. It is, they write—'almost axiomatic with the experienced investigator that the mind of the subordinate in any organization will yield richer veins of fact than the mind of the principal. This is not merely because the subordinate is usually less on his guard, and less severely conventional in his outlook. The essential superiority lies in the circumstance that the working foreman, managing clerk, or minor official is himself in continuous and intimate contact with the day-by-day activities of his organization ; he is more aware than his employer is of the heterogeneity and changing character of the facts ; and he is less likely to serve up dead generalization, in which all the living detail becomes a blurred mass, or is stereotyped into rigidly confined and perhaps obsolete categories.'[2]

---

[1] GOTTSCHALK, L. (1945), 'The Historian and the Historical Document' in *The Use of Personal Documents in History, Anthropology and Sociology*. The reader is referred to pp. 38-44, which provide the basis of the following treatment.

[2] WEBB, S. and B. (1932), p. 137.

If you want an expert, go to the man who has to do the job. But if you want to sound some men in the street, you have to be prepared to find that they know nothing of the matter in hand. For this reason opinion polls have to be dotted with questions designed to discover if the informant knows at all what he is talking about.[1]

Interest. The subject on which a question is asked must be one which has aroused some interest in the informant, or else it will have failed to capture his attention and will have left his mind a blank. The difficulty is that if he is in any way personally interested, he may desire to convey a misleading impression; in this case he will be able, but unwilling, to tell the truth.

In some such cases, particularly in relation to questions which concern his beliefs and motives, he may be literally unable to tell the truth, because he does not know it or admit it to himself. The justification of the depth or insight interview is just this, that it helps the informant to improve his own skill in knowing the truth, and thus in telling it.

As Gottschalk points out, ' inability to tell the truth leads to errors of omission, rather than commission, because of lack of completeness or lack of balance in observation, recollection, or narrative. Such errors give a picture that is out of perspective because it leaves out some data or over-emphasizes those it does include.'[2]

Willingness to tell the truth. (i) It is axiomatic that the investigator should be on his guard against the *interested witness*. As has been said, most people do not admit the truth about some things, even to themselves; others are quite willing to lie if it suits them. It is often hard to draw the line between conscious and unconscious falsehood, and from the viewpoint of the investigator it may not matter much whether the falsehoods are deliberate or not. In neither case can the investigation provide ' objective facts '; if the intention is to survey the emotional attitudes of informants, different degrees of self-awareness among them may be of secondary importance.

---

[1] Cf. KENDALL, P. L., and LAZARSFELD, P. F. (1950), pp. 170–1.
On two occasions I have found myself a member of a quota sample. One interview began with the question ' Do you know what industrial assurance is ? ' and at the start of the other I was asked to identify a luggage label used by a long-distance airline service. I knew almost nothing about either, but no doubt my opinions served the desired purpose.

[2] GOTTSCHALK, L. (1945), p. 40.

It is necessary, however, to bear constantly in mind that the informant is always liable to twist his answer so that it reflects him in the most favourable light. The investigator who is aware of this will ask himself, in respect of each question, both whether it concerns a subject likely to have a direct bearing on the informant's self-esteem or public standing, and also whether it is of a kind liable to arouse conflicts and anxieties in his mind by its impact on personal beliefs or affiliations. A question has to be very innocuous not to do so.

(ii) Almost everyone likes to dramatise a situation. It is normal, at least in a competitive society, for individuals to try to put themselves over in a big way, to sacrifice truth to art. Moreover, a question is a powerful stimulus, and it is emotionally unsatisfying not only to admit that one does not know the answer, but also to lose an opportunity to give it in the most striking, least qualified, form.

The dictates of literary style in the written word correspond with the desire for self-dramatisation in the interview.

(iii) A tendency for stereotyped thinking is liable to distort evidence.

> Those who count on revolutionaries to be bloodthirsty and conservatives to be gentlemanly, those who expect the young to be irreverent and the old to be crabbed, those who know Germans to be ruthless and Englishmen to lack humor usually find bloodthirsty revolutionaries and gentlemanly conservatives, ruthless Germans and humorless Englishmen. Thus a certain lack of precision is found in such witnesses because their eyes and ears are closed to fair observation; or because, seeking, they find; or because in recollection, they tend to forget or to minimise examples that do not confirm their prejudices and hypotheses.[1]

(iv) Unwillingness to tell the truth can sometimes be traced to the *laws and conventions* which restrict openness of reply. Certain subjects are taboo, and unexceptionable conventional responses may displace honest answers.

Here again the formative interview provides some encouragement to the informant to prise open the mental barriers which normally contain his inmost, publicly inacceptable, thoughts. It is hard to believe, however, that the penetration even at the end of

---

[1] GOTTSCHALK, L. (1945), p. 42. Cf. the quotation from Bertrand Russell, p. 124. For a similar effect in the interview context, see p. 246.

a two- or three-hour 'depth' interview is in any way comparable with the freedom of thought and expression attained at the end of a prolonged course of psychoanalysis.[1]

In general, unwillingness to tell the truth, whether intentional or unconscious, leads to misstatements more often than to omissions. When the same witness is both unable and unwilling to tell the truth, his replies are liable to contain errors both of omission and of commission.[2]

Other Tests for Plausibility. The reader is also referred to an earlier section [3] for a description of five types of circumstance which may encourage the investigator to believe in the truthfulness of statements contained in documents. These are equally applicable to interviews.

(d) *Optimum Conditions for Truth*

Form of Questions. Finally, various measures can be taken with the object of achieving the conditions most likely to evoke truthful answers from informants.

Oldfield states:

In practice there are two principles used to increase the likelihood of reliability. The first is to seek information about matters which have no obvious or direct connection with accepted moral or conventional standards, or with the manifest purpose of the interview. The second is to insist upon a detailed coherent account of concrete events, and not to allow the candidate to gloss over gaps with statements of what he generally does in given circumstances.[4]

It will be remembered that Oldfield is concerned with the use of the interview for assessing candidates for a vacancy. In these circumstances it is easier to keep away from subjects involving ethical judgments than in the research interview, when to do so

---

[1] A precisely opposite solution is advocated by the Kinsey team, who have adopted the method of rapid-fire questioning. This, they claim, not only saves time but 'has the further advantage of forcing the subject to answer spontaneously without too much premeditation. Such a rapid fire of questions provides one of the most effective checks on fabrication, as detectives and other law-enforcement officials well know. It would be practically impossible for a person who was deliberately falsifying to answer the many questions that are asked concerning the details of his activity, when the questions come as rapidly as they do in our interviewing. Looking an individual squarely in the eye, and firing questions at him with maximum speed, are two of the best guarantees against exaggeration.'—KINSEY, A. C. et al. (1948), p. 54.
[2] GOTTSCHALK, L. (1945), p. 42.   [3] See p. 88.
[4] OLDFIELD, R.C. (1941), p. 26.

R

will seriously curtail the area of discussion. It is, however, an important point that some facts, particularly those revealing attitudes or conflicts of attitude, can sometimes only be approached indirectly and as if impersonally.[1]

The second principle mentioned by Oldfield has also proved its value. The technical superiority of framing interview questions in such a form that they elicit specific answers is well established.

If, for example, the point at issue is the frequency of cinema attendance, the question can be put in a variety of ways. Examples are ' How often do you normally go to the cinema ? ', ' When did you last go to the cinema ? ', or ' Did you go to the cinema last week ? '. Of these, the second and third forms, being more specific, will be found to achieve more accurate results, particularly when no great stretch of memory is required. Moreover, if the interviews are evenly spread throughout the week, and if two or even three ways of covering this question are used at each interview, a statistical correspondence between the two sets of answers, if it should be established, helps to confirm the reliability of the material as a statement of the cinema-going behaviour of the sample at the time that the interviews were taking place.[2]

Another source of bias which can be relatively easily corrected is that due to the order of questions and to the order in which the alternative answers are printed. For example, Vernon [3] cites experiments that have shown that in a closed-type questionnaire informants tend to check the answers appearing first on the list of alternatives provided. He therefore recommends that in a large sample survey the order of the answers provided should be altered on a proportion of the questionnaire forms.

A similar precaution, already mentioned, was adopted by the American Institute of Public Opinion (Gallup poll) in 1938.

---

[1] This is another appearance of the ' interviewing variable ' principle, which underlies, *inter alia*, Lazarsfeld's thesis of a latent structure of belief (see pp. 192 seq.). It is not without relevance that current workers in this field are displaying particular interest in the influences which modify questionnaire responses (see e.g. *Am. Journ. Soc.*, **56**, 395–406).

[2] This recalls the requirement of *specificity* in the focused interview. See p. 166.

The use of more than one question to ascertain one fact may be compared with the scalogram analysis of attitudes already discussed (pp. 194 seq.). Clearly neither is proof against the informant who is, consciously or unconsciously, determined to deceive.

[3] VERNON, P. E. (1939), in BARTLETT, F. C. et al.—Eds., p. 206. The author also reminds us that ' some politicians have already realised the advantages of a surname beginning with " A " '.

How to Minimise Bias

Almost all ballots sent out since then have gone out in two forms. In this case the emphasis has been on the wording of questions.

> Wherever there has been any doubt about the wording of a question, the two ballot forms have provided a way to experiment with different question wordings. Since both forms go to comparable national cross-sections, differences in results over and above that which might be expected from sample size could be attributed to the wording of questions.[1]

In the Gallup terminology this is known as the *split-ballot* technique, and the usual procedure is to average the results of the different forms.

Gallup's use of the split-ballot in the 1948 Presidential election is discussed by the authors of the special SSRC Bulletin 60 already alluded to. In their view, the effect of alternating the order of the two candidates in the last seven surveys was sufficient to obscure the trend towards Truman.

> In one split-ballot test of Gallup's data this switch changed the Dewey and Truman figures by about 5 percentage points. About 2 percentage points of this change appeared to reflect differences between the samples to which the two forms of the question were assigned. While the order of the question may not have produced all of the remaining 3 percentage points of change, it undoubtedly had a sufficient influence to affect the interpretation of trends.[2]

A similar variation of result with the question form was observed by Roper.

There are, however, marked divergencies in the amount of variation caused by alterations in order. Thus it is reported [3] that whereas in July 1948 a switch in the order of the candidates produced a poll turnover of 4–5%, a similar switch in July 1944 during the preceding Presidential campaign had no noticeable effect on the poll.

Kendall and Lazarsfeld discuss the use of split-balloting by the Research Branch. The schedules were divided in two different ways. In one form, ' some of the items were slanted in a direction favourable to the Army, and others were anti-Army in wording; on the second form the wording of each item was exactly reversed, usually by the insertion or deletion of " not " '. Of twenty pairs of items, seven gave such different results in the two versions that

[1] GALLUP, G. (2nd ed. 1948), p. 41.
[2] MOSTELLER, F. et al. (1949), p. 166.   [3] *ibid.*, p. 170.

they had to be discarded, while the other thirteen showed only minor differences with no consistent pattern.[1] These divergencies may plausibly be accounted for in terms of the rigidity with which different attitudes are maintained.[2]

Minimising Interaction. We have so far considered the tests which can be applied to a particular statement made by a given informant in the attempt to gauge its likelihood of being truthful. We have also touched on certain general rules as to the form of questioning best adopted for maintaining the quality of interview material. If enough is known about individual informants, both of these can be applied equally readily in the case of the self-administered questionnaire as in the case of the interview.

We next come to the problem of regulating those forms of bias which are a direct consequence of the interaction between interviewer and informant. However self-effacing and free from biasing influences an interviewer may aim to be, the informant is bound to react in some way to his presence. If the two participants get on well, the informant is likely to wish to please the interviewer by giving the answers that he thinks will be most acceptable. Conversely, if the atmosphere is antagonistic, the informant may deliberately set out to displease the interviewer.

This effect is well known, and has recently been more precisely established by a series of studies undertaken by the National Opinion Research Center of the University of Chicago. Hyman reports several relevant inquiries. Thus, samples of Christian respondents in New York City were asked whether Jews in America had too much influence in the business world. Among those who were interviewed by 'Christian' interviewers, 50% said the Jews had too much influence, but among those interviewed by Jewish interviewers only 22% said so. Another study revealed an orderly change in the anti-Semitic opinions expressed, depending on the degree to which the interviewer looked Jewish and emphasised this fact by using a Jewish name.[3]

---

[1] KENDALL, P. L., and LAZARSFELD, P. F. (1950), pp. 176–7. See also STOUFFER, S. A., and TOBY, J. (1951).
[2] See also PAYNE, S. L. (1951), *The Art of Asking Questions*, pp. 129 seq., etc., in which the importance and significance of split-ballot techniques are extensively discussed.
[3] HYMAN, H. (1950), 'Problems in the Collection of Opinion Research Data', *Am. Journ. Soc.*, 55, 366. Other experiments have shown that latent racial prejudice can easily be aroused by an interviewer. See, for example, CHASE, S. (1950), *The Proper Study of Mankind*, p. 164.

A similar effect is known to operate in the case of group interviewing. Experiments have shown that the statements made by individuals singly tend to be more extreme than statements made by the same individuals in the presence of others. When several informants have to express their opinions in the presence of each other, these stated opinions tend to be modified so as to conform with the more moderate views of the group as a whole.

It is clear that no set of answers can be claimed as more truthful than any other set. Each set is truthful within its particular context.

One kind of substitute for truthfulness is obtained by ensuring that the interview contexts are as standardised as human ingenuity can make them. Thus:

> Hamilton, in interviewing two hundred married persons with regard to a wide range of topics having to do with success or failure in the marriage relation, found it necessary to standardise his procedure to a degree which might at first appear preposterous. The questions (over 300 in number) were typed on cards which the interviewee read and answered, Hamilton recording the replies verbatim. Having discovered that the sheer distance between the subject and the interviewer is an important variable, he tied the subject's chair to the wall so that this element could be held constant.[1]

The Social Survey has adopted a regular technique for standardising interviews at their critical moments. Thus, for example, the instruction ' PROMPT ' is placed beside certain questions, such as those in which the informant is required to choose from various possible answers. In these cases the interviewer will read the prompt list aloud to the informant, either straight through (*running prompt*) or pausing for an answer after each item (*individual prompt*). The interviewer may not prompt any questions except those marked.

A technique such as this may be expected to improve the consistency of results obtained. It is arguable, however, that more realistic results would be obtained by allowing the range of interview contexts to recur at random.

Regulating the Interviewer's Beliefs. Interaction effects derive

---

[1] MURPHY, G., MURPHY, L. B., and NEWCOMB, T. M. (1937 ed.), p. 845. The experiment referred to is G. V. Hamilton's *A Research in Marriage* (1929). Strangely enough, this experimenter took no proper steps to select a random sample.

not only from the way in which the informant reacts to the interviewer, but also *vice versa*. Those who interview candidates learn to be on their guard against the so-called 'halo effect', which is displayed in an excessive prejudice in favour of certain candidates. A similar distortion is liable to occur in factual interviewing. There is experimental evidence that the interviewer very soon after encountering an informant for the first time begins to develop certain beliefs about him and to adopt certain expectations about how he will react. These beliefs and expectations cannot fail to influence the interviewer's method of putting questions and recording answers.

Hyman [1] describes such beliefs as of two main types. The first type is due to the adoption of over-simplified stereotypes about the attitudes or forms of behaviour proper to an informant of known status. Thus it has been shown experimentally that a prior belief that a woman would not have a car repaired or that a man would not buy soft furnishings is enough to produce erroneous results.[2]

Hyman describes errors of the second type as 'attitude-structure expectations'. He points out that interviewers, like most human beings, seem to believe that other human beings have a logically consistent and integrated structure of attitudes. They thus tend to infer from informants' initial answers what their later answers will be.

This effect, which it would be hard to dispute, has also been demonstrated experimentally. Two gramophone records were prepared, each purporting to record an interview on the subject of isolationism *v.* internationalism. The general tone of answers of one informant was isolationist, while that of the other informant was internationalist; when these contrasting 'attitude-structure expectations' had been established, a sequence of questions and answers identical in substance was inserted into each record. The records were then played to over a hundred interviewers. On a question whether the United States was spending too much on foreign aid, the answer given by both informants had amounted to

---

[1] HYMAN, H. (1950), *Am. Journ. Soc.*, **55**, 367 seq.
[2] See also HARVEY, S. M. (1938), 'A Preliminary Investigation of the Interview', *Brit. J. Psychol.*, **28**, 263–87, in which the author describes her attempts to induce and measure bias in interviewers. Harvey suggested in advance to the interviewers that different informants would be defective respectively in reliability, sociability, or emotional stability, and up to a point she succeeded in inducing bias in the interviewers' judgment.

' we're spending about the right sum ', but among the interviewers tested only 20% classified the isolationist's answer as ' the right amount ', whereas 75% classified the internationalist's answer as ' the right amount '.[1]

The serious aspect of these two interviewer effects is that both tend unjustifiably towards the confirmation of plausible hypotheses. Results are also liable to conform to what is socially acceptable, owing to the natural reluctance of both interviewer and informant to dwell over tedious, embarrassing and difficult questions.

There is no indication that a breed of interviewers exists, or can be raised, which will be immune from these human limitations. Such evidence as there is gives the impression that neither training nor deliberate self-discipline can be expected to have much effect. Thus the misjudgment on the foreign aid issue mentioned above was virtually independent of the interviewers' own opinions on this issue. Again, a statistical study undertaken under the auspices of the Division of Research Techniques, London School of Economics, has had as its aim a comparison between the performance of experienced professional interviewers and that of students; the evidence failed to support the hypothesis that the inexperience of students led to their recording opinions, preferences or facts significantly different from those recorded by the experienced professional interviewers.[2]

Inquiries such as these are of great importance, and are likely to be greatly extended. At present we can only air the suspicion that good interviewers are born, not made, and that even in the most perfunctory mass-interviews the qualities of social skill and

[1] HYMAN, H. (1950), p. 367.
[2] BOOKER, H. S., and DAVID, S. T. (1952),' Differences in Results Obtained by Experienced and Inexperienced Interviewers ', *J. Roy. Statist. Soc.*, **115**, 232–57. See also DURBIN and STUART (1951).

KINSEY, A. C. et al. (1950), pp. 133–43, give a detailed comparison of the results obtained by the senior investigator and by his two less experienced colleagues. In general, a satisfactory level of correspondence between the three sets of results could be recorded. The results obtained by the senior investigator also showed a remarkable stability over a period of nine years (pp. 143–7).

By way of contrast, MOSTELLER, F. et al. (1949), pp. 122–33, analyse some results collected by Roper's 1948 Presidential Surveys, supplemented by other pools. While based on rather inadequate samples, these suggest that some interviewer variation affects the data on presidential preferences. Moreover, the bias apparently incorporated in the results turned in by any particular interviewer seems to be a consistent feature of the work of that interviewer. Thus, short-run stability is indicated, but it is stability of bias. The persistence of the interviewer in approaching his subject is also shown (p. 130) to have a marked effect on the percentage of ' undecided ' informants.

personal insight, combined with a willingness to follow the rules, are worth more than the most elaborate vocational or theoretical training.

It may be, as Mayo has suggested, that practice as an interviewer ' is immensely effective in the development of maturity of attitude and judgment in the intelligent and sensitive young men and women who give time to it. The subordination of oneself, of one's opinions and ideas, of the very human desire to give gratuitous advice, the subordination of all these to an intelligent effort to help another express ideas and feelings that he cannot easily express is, in itself, a most desirable education '.[1] However complete the instructions prepared by the organiser of a survey, however standardised and codified the questions and answers, the fact cannot be escaped that interviewing is a powerful human experience which leaves its mark on those who have practised it.

8. THE PROBLEM OF NON-RESPONSE

Bias may be introduced not only by faulty sampling, but also by failing to obtain the required information from all designated members of the sample. In social science so much depends on active co-operation of informants that there is virtually always some discrepancy between the proposed sample and the actual sample of informants, and on occasion this can be serious enough to destroy the validity of any results obtained. It is thus of first importance to minimise non-response as a source of bias.

The proportion of the sample lost through non-response is found by experience, and common-sense, to vary broadly with the type of investigation. Thus the questionnaire distributed and returned by post is notoriously defective in this respect, except when there is a statutory obligation to complete and return a questionnaire form ; a response of 70% has often been accepted as reasonably satisfactory. This proportion may clearly be an insecure basis for generalisations, particularly as there are generally plausible grounds for imagining that the non-respondents differ in important respects (e.g. education, means, interest in the issue) from those who have taken the trouble to reply.

Much more complete coverage can be expected with the

[1] MAYO, E. (English ed., 1949), *The Social Problems of an Industrial Civilisation*, p. 75.

interview. Even under satisfactory conditions, however, some losses are probable, and it is often necessary to take special precautions to reduce them.

Those losses arise from two main causes. One is the deliberate refusal of certain members of the sample to be interviewed or to answer questions, and the other is the failure of the interviewer to make contact with some of those selected for interview. It is found that, once contact has been made, refusals are rare in the house-to-house type of interview,[1] but they may be considerable in other circumstances, e.g. in a factory investigation. In either case, once the interview has started, it is relatively infrequent that informants refuse to answer specific questions, provided that the interviewer is skilful.

When either type of failure occurs, it is first necessary to try by all legitimate means to convert the failure into a success. A rather low initial success rate can often be rectified. If the difficulty is one of making contact with a householder, successive visits can be made to the house at different times of the day. If any member of the household can be found, an appointment can be made for some future time likely to be convenient.[2] If it is a case of refusal, an informal contact can sometimes persuade the non-co-operator to change his mind. For postal questionnaires, follow-up letters are generally well rewarded, or the backsliders may sometimes be paid personal visits.[3]

---

[1] GRAY, P. G., and CORLETT, T. (1950) (*J. Roy. Statist. Soc.*, **113**, 1181) report a refusal rate of 2·8% in a sample of 8,000 adult civilians. In this sample, the total failure rate was 10·9%. The authors regard this figure as typical for factual inquiries, but report (p. 183) a refusal rate as high as 60% to a request that subjects should submit to a medical examination. DURBIN, J., and STUART, A. (1951) (*J. Roy. Statist. Soc.*, **114**, 163–205), report a considerably higher refusal rate, particularly in the case of inexperienced student interviewers. Several speakers in the discussion commented that not all inexperienced interviewers are students.

[2] 'For example, while 35% of the sample are interviewed at the first call, 60% of the remainder are interviewed on the second call, the increased productivity of the second round of calls being clearly the result of appointments' (Gray and Corlett, p. 181). Durbin and Stuart found (Table 19, p. 182) that, for experienced and inexperienced interviewers combined, 71% of outstanding interviews were completed at the second call if an appointment had been made at the first visit. If no appointment had been made, the figure dropped to 40% of outstanding interviews. Experienced interviewers proved better at persuading contacts to be interviewed.

[3] GRAY, P. G., and CORLETT, T. (pp. 184–5) report that, as with re-calls on a personally interviewed sample, the first follow-up of a postal inquiry produces a greater proportionate response than the receipt of the questionnaire itself. The first and second reminder together often approximately double the total response rate.

If an abnormally high proportion of refusals is encountered, the first possibility to be considered is that there is something wrong either with the method of approach or with the form of the questions. Investigation may show, for example, that the official approach technique has been faulty, or that certain field-workers are consistently encountering an excessive share of failures. Again, the questions asked may prove to have been too intimate, or the form too long.[1]

In a properly conducted inquiry, faults such as these should have been detected and eliminated during the pilot survey. If this did not happen, it may, under some conditions, be necessary to consider all the work done to date as preparatory, and to start again with a properly adjusted technique.

In most cases those responsible for planning the investigation will reach a point at which they are satisfied that the success rate is as high as can be expected, and that further visits will not substantially augment the proportion of returns. The question then arises as to whether it is better to admit substitute informants or to make the most of information already obtained.

The use of substitutes is never statistically satisfactory, as, however done, it destroys the randomness of the sample.[2] In practice, however, many reputable organisations allow substitution, provided strenuous attempts have been made to contact and interview the original sample. The Social Survey, for example, stipulates a minimum of three attempts to contact members of the original sample before substitution may take place, and it is reported that an appreciable proportion of fourth, or even further calls are made.[3] The interviewer is in this case provided with a

---

[1] 'Free speech works both ways. To be sure, we have the right to ask the questions. The respondent, on the other hand, has every right to refuse to answer them. And sometimes it seems that we do everything we can think of to induce refusals. We approach complete strangers, ask them a battery of impertinent questions, blindfold them, stick strange concoctions under their noses, and refuse to elaborate on the meaning of the questions on the assumption that explaining them might affect the answers. The surprising thing about it all is the small number of turn-downs we receive.'—PAYNE, S. L. (1951), *The Art of Asking Questions*, pp. 114–15.

[2] We are not concerned merely with a theoretical quest for perfection. Houses unoccupied during the day are lived in by families of a type that must be given due representation in the sample. One justifiable use of substitutes is for overcoming the difficulty of the out-of-date frame. If, for example, people included in the sample have left the district, the error lies in the original frame and the substitute list merely increases the sampling fraction of the residual population. It does not, however, improve either the frame or the sample, as newcomers will be omitted from both.

[3] GRAY, P. G., and CORLETT, T. (1950), p. 186.

The Problem of Non-response

random list of substitute informants, and is instructed to select from this list a person of the same sex as that of the uncontacted member, and to try to contact this substitute as strenuously as the original (i.e. again three attempts).

As a further check, interviewers are required to get hold of basic data (e.g. age, occupation and marital status) on every person on the original list whom they fail to interview. These facts are obtained from neighbours or from anyone else who can give them. In factory interview inquiries quite a lot of information—though of varying reliability—may be available in the Personnel Department.

This information can be used for two successive purposes. The non-respondents can be treated as a sub-sample and their known characteristics compared, subject to sampling errors, with those of the main sample. This may reveal that people with a certain set of characteristics—e.g. young married women—are disproportionately represented in the non-response group and are conversely under-represented in the sample of informants.

If comparison reveals no marked difference in respect of these characteristics between the non-respondents and the informants, it may be inferred that little bias has been incurred by failing to interview the former. Often, however, the non-respondents will emerge as a fairly clearly marked type; if so, it may be possible somewhat to improve the accuracy of the results by assuming that if the non-respondents had been interviewed their answers would have been the same as those given by people of similar characteristics (e.g. age, sex, occupation) who did answer. It is evident, however, that this assumption in effect introduces the principle of quota sampling and that any conclusion based on it is vulnerable.

An ingenious form of correction was introduced by Professor Glass in the special 1946 Family Census. The Census was carried out by postal questionnaire. At first, 230,000 forms (17% of the total sample) were not returned, but a second letter sent to the non-respondents elicited 50,000 further replies. The problem was how to estimate for the outstanding 180,000 families. Those who had responded to neither approach were thought likely to have more in common with those who responded after the follow-up than they would have with the whole population. The necessary adjustments were made on this assumption, and gave total birth-rate figures much more in accord with those already known from other sources than the unadjusted figures had given.[1] This is a rather exciting device, which not only permits inherently probable adjustments, but also promises to reduce the need to seek supplementary information about non-contacts, which is sometimes a rather distasteful, snooping task.

If any such adjustments are made, full particulars of their nature will be reported, and both adjusted and non-adjusted results presented. In practice it is often considered better to report the unadjusted results and at the same time to indicate any defects in the sample; the reader is then in a position to exercise his own judgment as to the reliability of any conclusions reached.

9. SUMMARY AND CONCLUSIONS

The advantages and limitations of the mass interview may be summarised as follows:

Advantages. (a) Statistical adequacy. It is relatively easy to collect a large number of records, each of which covers the same chosen points, and which are therefore readily susceptible to statistical tabulation and analysis.

(b) The relatively impersonal rôle of the interviewer and the relatively superficial contact between the interviewer and the informant are likely to ensure, in the case of factual questions with a low emotional content, that information is accumulated without undue trouble. The interview has the merit, not possessed by the questionnaire, of offering an opportunity to explain to the informant, either before or after his initial attempt to answer, any question whose wording is found obscure or misleading. On the other hand, this interpretation may give scope for the interviewer's personal bias or preconceptions and may thus influence the answers given by the informant.

(c) A third advantage of the structured interview is that far less skill is required of the interviewer. Provided that the problem chosen is appropriate to the technique, an interview survey of this nature fulfils a useful subsidiary function in assisting the field education of the social scientist.

Limitations. The main limitations of this type of interview are:

(a) The questions asked relate to what the investigator has in mind, and may completely neglect or distort the issues which seem

---

[1] See YATES, F. (1949), pp. 130–1.

important to the informant. The armchair scientist is able to work out a list of questions which bear no relation to those subjects which mean something to his informants.

The structured interview can thus normally only be safely undertaken after a careful preparatory survey in the course of which the questions to be asked are evolved. At least in its initial stages, this preparatory work should not be carried out by the mass interview technique.

(*b*) The mass interview is most appropriately used when the questions asked are factual and free from emotive content. Full reliability can never be expected, however, even in response to such apparently objective questions as age and marital status. Wide discrepancies in data—e.g. on earnings and expenditure— are sometimes found when replies given at interviews can be compared with facts obtained from other sources.

It is possible in some sense to derive opinions and attitudes by mass interviewing. These are likely to incline towards respectable ' public ' opinions. Devices which have been elaborated to test the consistency of replies given by one informant may still not detect ' private ' opinions. In some cases, such as voting forecasts, however, public attitudes are the main point at issue, and opinion polls can, within sampling limitations, give reasonably accurate forecasts.

Chapter 5

EXPERIMENT

> Students new to social science will be riding the wave of the future, I think, if they become masters of experimental design early in their careers.—S. A. STOUFFER.
>
> The planning process in a democratic society means a continuous series of experiments, tested by public use and acceptance: therefore the function of research is not so much to seek final 'answers' as to guide and clarify this experimentation and render it more effective in terms of individual and public satisfaction.—CATHERINE BAUER.

1. THE SCOPE OF EXPERIMENT

MUCH ink has been spilt in disputes on the feasibility of experiments in social science. Pundits on scientific method are generally agreed that the scientific sequence is incomplete without experimentation; those social investigators who wish to claim admission to the ranks of science have thus naturally been at pains to show that they, too, are in a position to conduct experiments.

Characteristically much of the argument has rotated around the definition of the word experiment. Like so many other words used in the social sciences, the phrase 'social experiment' has a loose and popular connotation. It is already entrenched in common usage to describe procedures which do not qualify as experimental in any precise sense. Thus any new legislative or administrative measure is liable to be described as an experiment even when no systematic attempt is made to determine its consequences. Utopian communities such as those pioneered by Owen and Fourier, the less unrealistic new towns sponsored first by Howard and his followers and later by the State, extensions of the Social Services such as the National Health Service—all these are regularly labelled as experiments, even though they very imperfectly satisfy the criteria of scientific experimentation.

From the early days of social science the need for a definition of social experiment broad enough to admit some actual or conceivable occurrence has been recognised. Thus, Comte conceived of pathological cases as indirect social experiments.

The Scope of Experiment

Whenever the regular course of a phenomenon were to be interfered with in any determinate manner, in his view true experimentation could be said to take place; it was thus unnecessary to postulate a deliberate experimenter.[1] John Stuart Mill elaborated this viewpoint by proposing two different circumstances, both of which could in his opinion be described as experimental. These were the *artificial experiment*, deliberately created by man, and *nature's experiment*, which occurred spontaneously. To him, ' the value of the instance depends on what it is in itself, not on the mode in which it is obtained. . . . There is, in short, no difference in kind, no real logical distinction, between the two processes of investigation.'[2]

In either case the experiment consists, in some form or another, of a comparison between two sets of circumstances, which exactly match each other in all respects except one.

Most accepted facts in the natural sciences have been established by means of artificial experiments.[3] Such experiments have varied greatly in their complexity and in the elaboration of the techniques needed to carry them out, and many of them would have been inconceivable if experimental techniques had not advanced concurrently with scientific knowledge. The natural sciences have also had the advantage, which is important in this context, that, at least until recently, it has been possible to assume with confidence that direct causal relationships do exist in nature and have only to be found. The same initial assumption has appeared to be less justifiable in the case of social science, in which few examples of direct causal relationships have been established. This might be due to man's free will and recurrent illogical and fantastic behaviour, or it might be due to the much greater complexity of social relationships.

John Stuart Mill, who was an unyielding determinist, was so oppressed by the complexities of social phenomena that he despaired of the possibility of experimentation in the social sciences. He was forced to conclude that in social affairs the perfectly equated pair of circumstances, exactly matched in all respects except one, neither occurred in nature nor could be

---

[1] CHAPIN, F. S. (1947), *Experimental Designs in Sociological Research*, p. 2.
[2] MILL, J. S., *A System of Logic*, p. 249.
[3] There are of course important exceptions, of which astronomy—a science built up on the rather exact measurement of angles—offers the most commonly cited example.

created by man.[1] But, as he continued to hold that an hypothesis could only be finally tested by experiment, he had to reconcile himself to defeat in the search for social truth. Mill's pessimistic view was substantially justified in his age, and although modern statistical methods have greatly enlarged the scope of social experimentation, positive achievements in proving social hypotheses of sufficient generality and precision to be useful are not yet impressive.

It is increasingly recognised, however, that the benefits of experiment rest not only in the possibility, which may be remote, of proving something, but also in the direct and intrinsic fact of doing something. One of the first social scientists to apply this was Lewin, who viewed experiment as an essential step in confirming the reality of the social concepts in which he was interested. In a discussion on leadership, for example, he writes:

> As long as the scientist merely describes a leadership form he is open to the criticism that the categories used reflect merely his 'subjective views' and do not correspond to the 'real' properties of the phenomena under consideration. If the scientist experiments with leadership and varies its form, he relies on an 'operational definition' which links the concept of a leadership form to concrete procedures of creating such a leadership form or to the procedures for testing its existence. The 'reality' of that to which the concept refers is established by 'doing something with' rather than 'looking at', and this reality is independent of certain 'subjective' elements of classification.[2]

Lewin correspondingly believed the great virtue of experiment to be that the scientist can successfully manipulate his material even before he fully understands the variables involved. Descriptive techniques break down without full conceptual grasp of the principal variables in operation, whereas the test of an experiment is the simple one of success or failure. Thus, experiment can be both easier and more certain. Moreover, experimental social control mirrors in miniature the practical issues of real life, and bridges the gap between the different ways of looking at social processes that have been built up by the different disciplines. 'Experimentation with groups will therefore lead to a natural

---

[1] MILL, J. S., *A System of Logic*, pp. 573–8. See p. 32.
[2] LEWIN, K. (1947), 'Frontiers in Group Dynamics', *Hum. Rel.*, 1, 9. Reprinted in his (1952) *Field Theory in Social Science*, p. 193.

integration of the social sciences, and it will force the social scientist to recognize as reality the totality of factors which determine group life.'[1]

Lewin claims the support of Cassirir for the view that the experimental approach—that is, the attempt to attain reality by 'doing something with' rather than 'looking at' its subject-matter—has been the major avenue to advance in physics:

> The progress of physics from Archimedes to Einstein shows consecutive steps by which this 'practical' aspect of the experimental procedure has modified and sometimes revolutionized the scientific concepts regarding the physical world by changing the beliefs of the scientists about what is and is not real.[2]

John Dewey also was prepared to make ability to experiment a condition of science.

> It is a complete error to suppose that efforts at social control depend upon the prior existence of a social science. The reverse is the case. The building up of social science, that is, of a body of knowledge in which facts are ascertained in their significant relations, is dependent upon putting social planning into effect. It is at this point that the misconception about physical science, when it is taken as a model for social knowledge, is important. Physical science did not develop because inquirers piled up a mass of facts about observed phenomena. It came into being when men intentionally experimented, on the basis of ideas and hypotheses, with observed phenomena to modify them and disclose new observations. This process is self-corrective and self-developing. Imperfect and even wrong hypotheses, when acted upon, brought to light significant phenomena which made improved ideas and improved experimentations possible. The change from a passive and accumulative attitude into an active and productive one is the secret revealed by the progress of physical inquiry. . . . If we want something to which the name 'social science' may be given, there is only one way to go about it, namely by entering upon the path of social planning and control.[3]

It is not difficult to discern the grounds on which the social scientist has been deterred from attempting to conduct social experiments. Even after *laissez-faire* objections have been overcome, the social scientist still has to storm the prepared defences

---

[1] LEWIN, K. (1947), p. 9. [2] *ibid.*, p. 9.
[3] DEWEY, J. (1931), 'Social Science and Social Control', *New Republic*, 67, 276–7.

of the administrators before he can be allowed directly to influence other men's lives.

It is, for example, widely regarded as insufferable that a man or woman who is eligible for a particular social benefit should be deprived of it because he is needed as a member of the control sample. Chapin writes:

> People resent being chosen to serve as 'guinea-pigs'. Would a government administrator permit admission to a public housing project of some families and exclusion of others equally eligible on the basis of random choice? Most administrators are charged with the responsibility to admit to good housing only the most needy families, other factors being equal. This is the way social reform programs are set up to function because those who sponsor them never question their beneficial effects any more than they ever expect to bring such programs to a scientific test of their effects.[1]

It must be recognised, moreover, that the obstacles to this kind of discrimination are not confined to social science. Some laymen have gained the impression that the controlled experiment can be conducted without difficulty in medical research. Beveridge reminds us that this is not so, and that once a treatment is professionally and popularly accepted as effective it may be too late to find out whether or not it does any good.

> Pasteur's rabies treatment has never been proved by proper experiment to prevent rabies when given to persons after they are bitten and some authorities doubt if it is of any value, but it is impossible now to conduct a trial in which this treatment is withheld from a control group of bitten persons.[2]

In spite of all difficulties, however, persistent social scientists have generally succeeded in finding opportunities for experiment. A few of the results will be described later in the present chapter, but we may here recall that Beatrice Webb as a young woman came to recognise the limitations of unobtrusive observation and determined to use her post as a manager of a benevolent tenement block as a means to social experiment.

> As the managers of Katherine Buildings, my colleague and I could select our tenants according to any principle or prejudice; we could,

[1] CHAPIN, F. S. (1947), p. 168.
[2] BEVERIDGE, W. I. B. (1950), *The Art of Scientific Investigation*, p. 18. See also BRADFORD HILL, A. (3rd ed., 1942), *Principles of Medical Statistics*, p. 7.

The Scope of Experiment

with the consent of the directors, raise or lower rents, permit arrears or ruthlessly put in the broker; and, having chosen a policy, we could watch its results on the number and character of the applicants, the conduct of the tenants, or the profit and loss account of the buildings. ' Experimenting in the lives of other people, how coldblooded! ' I hear some reader object. It is necessary to explain that such ' experimenting ' cannot be avoided; that all administration . . . necessarily amounts to nothing less than ' experimenting in the lives of other people '. What is required [is] to safeguard the community against callousness or carelessness about the human beings concerned . . . And it is essential, if we are to learn from such ' experiments ', that the effect on other persons' lives should be observed and recorded.[1]

The safeguard that Beatrice Webb proposed was ' that the administrator (of a social experiment) should be effectively responsible, for all the results of his administration, to the consumers and producers of the commodities and services concerned and to the community at large '. This condition would effectively restrain irresponsible social experimentation; but it might lead to difficulties, both because it would tend to admit only those experimental changes already established as beneficial and because the identity of administrator and investigator would create a vested interest in the appearance of success. It is at times essential to give scope for an experimental change to be undesirable and even, if not irreversibly so, harmful. In medicine it is possible to enlist the help of volunteers for potentially damaging research; the fact that research into the common cold, for example, is being conducted on volunteers is not regarded as liable seriously to distort results. But in the social sciences there can be no confidence in the representativeness of a group of volunteers, or of their usefulness as material for objective observation. If, therefore, volunteers are to participate in social experiments, their active co-operation must be openly recognised in the experimental design.[2]

[1] WEBB, B. (1926), *My Apprenticeship*, pp. 340–1. Even with the limited scale and scope of present-day social experiment, it is extremely likely that some harm is done to experimental subjects, perhaps particularly to the child victims of certain psychological experiments. There is regrettably little attempt at follow-up in order to determine whether they have suffered any permanent damage.
[2] See pp. 286 seq. The flaw in assuming that volunteers are typical is illustrated by a number of classroom experiments, cited by GREENWOOD, E. (1945), *Experimental Sociology*, p. 98, which were designed to study the influence

Faced with these difficulties in achieving significant experimental results under real-life conditions, the majority of social experimenters have retired to the orthodox locus of experimentation, to the social equivalent of the laboratory. Before the cultural influence on human behaviour was recognised, social psychologists tended to dismiss as immaterial the question of the precise location for their experiments, and the psychological laboratory was used on grounds of convenience. For less elaborate experiments and tests, the public nursery and the classroom were felt to be convenient, and therefore satisfactory. Infants and children have the merit of unself-consciousness, and schools are in any case a useful source of supply of subject-matter, as they make it fairly easy to select two comparable groups of schoolchildren. For similar reasons, many experimenters have used university students.

In this way there has grown up a tradition of atomistic and artificial experimentation in social psychology, in which convenience and accuracy have been emphasised at the expense of realism. At times this may be so much the case that any conclusions reached have no bearing on normal circumstances. Indeed, it has been pointed out, ' the more exact an experiment is—that is the more elementary and isolated the phenomenon, and the more constant the conditions—the greater is its artificiality and the greater its distance from the study of the individual '.[1]

A corollary of artificiality can be almost equally serious. The situations suitable for laboratory experiment are often so simple as to lack significance. Greenwood points out, ' It is quite possible that in trying to achieve control, we would focus attention upon such simple and minute matters, as to sacrifice the significance of our results for the dubious compensation of accuracy ', and agrees with Mannheim that ' we cannot conclude that because a piece of social research is exact, it is therefore worthwhile. Those of us who do so are suffering from an exactitude complex which sanctifies every fact just because it is a fact '.[2]

---

of certain social science courses upon social attitudes. Many of these experiments resulted in the conclusions that such courses produce changes in the direction of liberalism but, as Greenwood remarks, ' those who flock to the social sciences may very well be the ones who are rather critical of the status quo and are liberally inclined to start with '.

[1] Quoted from STERN, W. (3rd ed., 1921), *Differentielle Psychologie*.
[2] GREENWOOD, E. (1945), p. 93. See also Florence Goodenough, quoted on p. 127 fn.

There is the further practical defect in classroom experiments that it is seldom possible entirely to prevent interaction between the experimental group and the control group. The authority of the experimenter normally only operates at certain times, and it is impossible to isolate members of the two groups from each other for the rest of the experimental period. They are often in fact in constant contact with each other for most of the time, and it is merely a polite fiction to suggest that interaction is prevented. As many such experiments are prolonged, lasting for a year or even more, this may be a serious defect in their design.

The task of the social experimenter is thus to steer between two extremes. One extreme to be avoided is the artificial, trivial and exact laboratory test; the other is the realistic, large,[1] important, woolly and totally inconclusive exercise. At the same time there are certain minimum conditions which must be fulfilled before it is useful to describe a social research project as experimental.

These conditions are concrete, rather than abstract, and the rest of this chapter will therefore consist of an annotated outline of a number of such projects which have been claimed with varying justice as experimental.

2. THE CONTROLLED EXPERIMENT

(a) *The Model*

We must take as our starting point the ideal experimental design of many branches of science, which is known as the *controlled experiment*. In one of its simplest forms, the procedure consists of selecting two samples at random from the same population and then exposing one—the experimental sample—to an additional influence. The effect of the fresh influence is determined by comparing the final characteristics of members of the experimental sample with those of members of the control sample which were not so exposed.[2]

[1] It must be repeated that largeness of scale is not necessarily a means to realism. J. S. Mill ruled out the possibility of experiment to decide the controversy between protectionism and free trade. But there are many social interrelationships of great importance which are on quite a small scale and experiments conducted around them will aid mastery over social processes. After all, the test atom bomb in New Mexico was not merely the first atom bomb but equally the culmination of a large succession of experiments in nuclear fission.

[2] The design is unchanged in principle if the comparison to be made is between two or more alternative forms of treatment.

Symbolically, this procedure can be described as follows : [1]

DIAGRAM A

	Before	After	After − Before
Experimental Sample	x_1	x_2	$d = x_2 - x_1$
Control Sample	x'_1	x'_2	$d' = x'_2 - x'_1$

A statistically significant difference between d and d' is interpreted as disposing of the *null hypothesis* [2] that the additional influence brought to bear on the experimental sample has had no discernible effect.

Alternatively, if the two samples have been drawn at random from the same population, conclusions can be based on a direct comparison of x_2 with x'_2. If further precision is required, and if it is difficult to control variations in the two initial samples, the observed characteristics of x_1 and x'_1 can be brought into the analysis by adopting the method of *concomitant observations*; according to Fisher, this enables one to adjust results, by the *analysis of covariance*, so as to afford a final precision, in many cases, almost as great as though complete equalisation had been possible.[3]

It should be noted that in either case it is necessary to provide the means of judging the significance of comparisons between the two samples. It is clearly desirable that the experiment should be self-contained, in that an estimate of error can be derived from the material that it supplies. It is on these grounds that *replication*—i.e. repetition of the comparison within the single experimental

[1] This and following related diagrams are inspired by STOUFFER, S. A. (1950), 'Some Observations on Study Design', *Am. Journ. Soc.*, 55, 355–61.
[2] The concept of *null hypothesis* is basic to modern experimental logic. It was introduced by R. A. Fisher, who writes (*The Design of Experiments*, 1949 ed., pp. 15–16) that the appropriate test of significance is used to distinguish two classes of results—namely, those which show a significant discrepancy from a certain hypothesis and those which show no significant discrepancy from this hypothesis. The hypothesis in question, 'which may or may not be impugned by the result of an experiment, is again characteristic of all experimentation. Much confusion would often be avoided if it were explicitly formulated when the experiment is designed. In relation to any experiment we may speak of this hypothesis as the " null hypothesis ", and it should be noted that the null hypothesis is never proved or established, but is possibly disproved in the course of experimentation. Every experiment may be said to exist only in order to give the facts a chance of disproving the null hypothesis.'
[3] *ibid.*, pp. 161–73.

design—may be seen to be essential. Only by replication, together with random assignment between the alternative samples, can a valid test of significance be guaranteed.[1]

Experimental designs such as these were evolved principally to serve the needs of biological, and more particularly of agricultural, scientists.[2] They have since been adapted for use in the social sciences, mainly in psychology which has built up a tradition of laboratory testing.

As has already been mentioned, in many psychological controlled experiments both the setting and the subjects have been rather artificially selected, and the results obtained may be felt to bear rather remotely on real-life problems.[3] There have, however, been a number of experiments, due to both sociologists and social psychologists, which have been conducted under more or less natural conditions. It is understandable that these should not only be rather simple but should also contain imperfections in design. However, their greater realism adds much to their interest. None of the three experiments described below took place under laboratory conditions, but all will be found relevant to a discussion on experimental design.

(b) *An Experiment in Electioneering Techniques.*[4]

The experimenter was himself a Socialist candidate for political office in a Pennsylvania town. His purpose was to compare the effect of a 'logical' appeal for Socialism with that of an 'emotional' approach, so he prepared two contrasting leaflets.

[1] FISHER, R. A. (1949), pp. 58–62.
[2] In biological and agricultural research, increasing use is being made of *factorial designs* by which several factors are varied simultaneously. This permits economical use of limited experimental material and has various other important statistical advantages. Factorial layouts have hardly penetrated as yet to social science, but there is little doubt that they will increasingly do so (see *ibid.*, especially pp. 91 seq.; YATES, F. (1949), *Sampling Methods for Censuses and Surveys*, p. 105; DURBIN, J., and STUART, A. (1951), *J. Roy. Statist. Soc.*, 114, 169 seq.). Factorial design should not be confused with factor (or factorial) analysis, for which see p. 191.
[3] The best short summary of experiments so far undertaken in social science is contained in GREENWOOD, E. (1945), pp. 56–64. His main source for psychologically inspired experiments was MURPHY, G., MURPHY, L. B., and NEWCOMB, T. M. (1937), *Experimental Social Psychology*, which exhaustively treats this whole field. The list of experiments derived from sociological literature was compiled by Greenwood himself.
[4] HARTMANN, G. W. (1936), 'A Field Experiment on the Comparative Effectiveness of "Emotional" and "Rational" Political Leaflets in Determining Election Results', *J. Abn. and Soc. Psychol.*, 31, 99–114. (Summarised by MURPHY, G., MURPHY, L. B., and NEWCOMB, T. M. (1951), pp. 977–9.)

The rational leaflet contained seven brief statements, to each of which the reader could signify agreement or dissent. For example, one read: 'All banks and insurance companies should be run on a non-profit basis like the school'. At the end, the leaflet read:

> Now go back and count the number of sentences with which you AGREED. Then count the number with which you DISAGREED. If the number of agreements is larger than the number of disagreements, you are at heart a Socialist—whether you know it or not. . . . Why don't you try voting for the things you actually want? . . . VOTE SOCIALIST!

The emotional appeal consisted of a letter addressed to 'Dear Father and Mother' and signed 'Your Sons and Daughters'. It was frankly evocative and sentimental, and ended with the words:

> Our generation cannot enjoy the beauty and justice of the New America if you block our highest desires. There was a time when you were young like us. We beg you in the name of those early memories and spring-time hopes to support the Socialist ticket in the coming elections! . . . VOTE SOCIALIST!

The town had nineteen wards. The emotional appeal was distributed to every family in three wards, the rational appeal to every family in four wards, while the remaining twelve wards served as controls, receiving neither. The distribution of incomes was much the same in the three wards receiving the emotional appeal as in the four wards receiving the rational appeal.

The total vote in the city was one-sixth higher than in the preceding year, but the total Socialist vote—although still small—increased by nearly a third (31%). Increase was sharpest (50%) in the 'emotional' wards, but was also above average (35%) in the 'rational' wards. In the remaining twelve wards which received neither leaflet the increase was only 24%.

The Murphys' comment was:

> It is not 'news', of course, that an emotional appeal is more effective than a rational one. But it is a scientific event of significance when such a common assumption is put to the test of a deliberately devised

experiment having to do with realistic behaviour of run-of-the-min adults in a complex social situation.[1]

(c) *Rural Hygiene in Syria.*[2]

The author set out to discover the relationship between a programme of rural hygiene and the hygienic practices of the families that were supposed to benefit from it. A mobile clinic was trying to instil hygienic behaviour into forty Arab families in the village of Jib Ramli in Syria. It is normally assumed that educational campaigns such as this lower morbidity and mortality, and increase comfort and happiness, but, although millions are spent annually throughout the world on preventive medicine, little attempt has been made to test this assumption.

Dodd's method was to select another village which matched Jib Ramli on nine factors: geographic, demographic, historical, economic, religious, domestic, recreational and in sanitary conditions.[3] This second village was not exposed to the hygienic campaign, and was therefore available as a control.

These two villages were assessed for 'hygienic performance' at the beginning of the experiment and again two years later. The method of assessment was to compile a list of seventy-seven key questions. These questions were retained from an initial list of 270 questions, and together they showed some correlation with objective indices, such as mortality, morbidity and longevity.

It was found at the reassessment, at the end of the two years' experiment, that Jib Ramli's score had increased by 20%. Unfortunately for the normal assumption, however, the hygiene score of the control village in the same period increased nearly as much—i.e. by over 18%. It could therefore not be claimed that the 'null hypothesis'—i.e. that education in hygiene has no effect on hygienic performance—had been disproved by the facts. Either something went wrong with the experiment—for example, hygienic practice may have spread from Jib Ramli to the control village—or else the health programme was a waste of time and money.

[1] MURPHY, G., MURPHY, L. B., and NEWCOMB, T. M. (1937), p. 979.
[2] DODD, S. C. (1934), 'A Controlled Experiment on Rural Hygiene in Syria', American University of Beirut. (Condensed by CHAPIN, F. S. (1947), pp. 55–7.)
[3] There was only one 'survivor' of three villages originally selected as controls. Chapin is in any case doubtful whether the matching was done quantitatively.

(d) *Social Effects of Good Housing.*[1]

This research project, run in conjunction with a rehousing scheme in Minneapolis, is rather too elaborate for adequate condensation here. Description is therefore confined to its strictly relevant features.

In essence it was designed to determine the changes in behaviour introduced when low-income families living in certain slum areas were transferred to a public housing scheme. Scales were used to measure three conditions, which were believed, and to some extent demonstrated, to be valid indices of these changes. The scales, which had all been previously used and validated, related to such points as:

    i. The condition of the living-room, as a measure of social status.[2]

    ii. Use-crowding of dwelling units—i.e. multiple use of rooms designed for a single function, such as living room used also as a bedroom.

    iii. Social participation—i.e. number of clubs made use of by members of family.

The experiment started with a sample of 108 rehoused families and 131 control families, the latter chosen from the waiting list. By the end of the fieldwork a year later the surviving families comprised forty-four rehoused families and thirty-eight waiting-list families. These two groups were matched on ten factors (race of husband and wife, employment of husband and wife, occupational class of husband and wife, size of family, family income, age of wife, years of education of wife). All families surviving into this final sample had by 1940 lived in the same home for twelve months.

The results of the 1940 survey, in which the initial tests were reapplied, were interpreted as disproving the null hypothesis that there had been no significant improvement in social participation, condition of living-room and incidence of use-crowding, such as could be attributed to rehousing.

Our net conclusion is that the residents did change significantly in the social pattern of their response to a change in housing from slum

---

[1] CHAPIN, F. S. (1940), ' An Experiment on the Social Effects of Good Housing ', *Amer. Soc. Rev.* 5, 868–79. See also his (1947), pp. 58–79.
[2] For a brief description of this scale see pp. 140–1.

The Controlled Experiment

living to a public housing project, whereas the control group of families which remained in the same slum dwellings throughout the experimental period of one year changed only to a degree which could occur so frequently as a fluctuation of random sampling as to be insignificant of any real change in their condition.[1]

(e) *Comment and Conclusions*

These descriptions are of three experiments chosen because, in comparison with most experiments in social science, they were well-conducted attempts to operate under the complex conditions of real life. It should not be supposed that the field of choice of suitable examples was large; very few attempts at controlled experiment in social science have in fact been made.

It must also be admitted that the experiments described were disappointingly inconclusive. It will be remarked, for example, that in each of the three cases cited the experiments apparently took place on a ' rising tide '—increasing support of Socialism, higher standards of rural hygiene, improved living habits—and that the control groups differed from the experimental groups only in that the rate of change was slower in their case. This may have been due to chance, but it may also have been due in each case to other causes, such as the imperfect isolation of the two groups, so that the control group was also partially affected by the experimental change.

There remains a still more serious objection: even when the experiments are claimed to have proved something, inspection shows that the logical and statistical grounds for supposing so are extremely slender. In each case there is considerable doubt whether the differences displayed by the experimental and the control sample can be entirely ascribed to the experimental treatment. The suspicion remains that these differences can be accounted for by initial disparities in the two samples.

Mill's doubts on this point, which have already been mentioned,[2] have not been satisfactorily met in the instances quoted. In Experiment A only the simplest possible precautions appear to have been taken to equate the ' rational ' wards with the ' emotional ' wards. In Experiment B attempts at equalisation again seem to have been somewhat rough and ready.

In Experiment C the attempt at matching was far more systematic

[1] CHAPIN, F. S. (1947), p. 73.   [2] See pp. 255–6.

than in the previous two experiments. The method used was a special form of the procedure known (in the United States) by the generic title of *factor equation*.[1]

The precision of different forms of factor equation varies widely from one extreme, called 'frequency distribution control', to the other extreme, which is known as 'precision control'. The former consists only in matching the frequency distribution of certain selected individual factors in the two samples; for example, it may be used to ensure that given races, income groups or occupations are equally represented in each. As already mentioned, this has an affinity with the quota sampling used by opinion pollsters.[2] Precision control, on the other hand, entails a far more rigorous procedure by which the two samples are made up of matched individuals who have been paired according to the factors selected. Thus, if race, occupation and income are three factors to be equated, and if one sample is to contain a Negro mechanic earning $30–40, the other sample must also contain one.

But although precision control is a useful first step, it has still not taken us all the way. All that has been done is to equate the two samples according to a number of characteristics which may be completely irrelevant to the matter in hand. There is clearly no guarantee that the factors which it is easy to discover in advance (such as age, sex, occupation), and which are therefore used for equalisation, will have any bearing on the subject of the experiment. Conversely, there is no safeguard against the existence of a highly relevant but unrecognised factor whose presence may distort one or other sample.

As Fisher has pointed out, it is 'a totally impossible requirement' that the experimental and control samples should match exactly. While known characteristics can at a cost, and should up to a point, be equated, 'the uncontrolled causes which may influence the result are always strictly innumerable'.[3] As additional factors are discovered and isolated, the labour and cost of doing so rise steeply, while the experimenter has no real prospect of arriving at the end of the avenue.

Fortunately we can fall back on *randomisation*, which represents the basic contribution of modern statistical theory to the design of

[1] See CHAPIN, F. S. (1947), p. 74. A similar system is explained by GREENWOOD, E. (1945), pp. 116–17.
[2] See the description of Quota Sampling, p. 212.
[3] FISHER, R. A. (1949 ed.), *The Design of Experiments*, p. 18.

experiments. The procedure starts with the preparation of a double list of individuals paired, by the method of precision control, according to known factors. The next, and vital, step is to construct the two separate samples from this list, making sure that each pair of individuals is assigned at random as between the two samples, so that any individual has an equal chance of being placed in either sample. By this device of randomisation, the validity of the experiment ' may be guaranteed against corruption by the causes of disturbance which have not been eliminated '.[1] It cannot be sufficiently stressed that randomisation is a vital operation in controlled experimental design, and that no design from which randomisation has been excluded can lead to unassailable conclusions.

It will be noted that, while *validity* is safeguarded by randomisation, the *sensitiveness* of an experiment can be improved by pairing. It does not matter how heterogeneous the material is as a whole, provided that the individual items of which it is composed can be divided up into pairs that are reasonably similar in character before the experiment takes place. The experiment virtually comprises a number of identical, and probably simultaneous, experiments in each of which the performance of a member of the experimental sample is compared with the performance of his opposite number in the control sample. But if the individuals to be compared differ inherently too much from each other, it may also be expected that their performance in the course of the experiment will vary so much as to impair sensitiveness, so that a large number of pairs will have to be contrasted before any useful conclusions will emerge. The initial process of pairing is therefore still worth while.

In a single experiment the investigator has the choice of rather exact pairing by a large number of known characteristics or less exact pairing by fewer characteristics. In the case of the former choice, precision control by a large number of known (but not necessarily relevant) factors eliminates a very high proportion of available cases before the experiment begins. Thus in one experiment an initial sample of 1,194 would have been whittled down to forty-six by precision pairing on only six factors.[2] As

[1] FISHER, R. A. (1949 ed.), p. 19.
[2] CHRISTIANSEN, H. F. (1938), *The Relation of School Progress to Subsequent Adjustment* (M.A. thesis constantly discussed by Chapin and Greenwood).

this was regarded as excessive shrinkage, frequency distribution control was substituted, with the result that on six factors the combined experimental and control sample was maintained at 290. The fact that the statistical value of results obtained is thereby sacrificed does not seem to have deterred the author, or to have earned condemnation by the authorities on experimental method. For example, Chapin writes as follows on the use of frequency distribution control in this particular case.

> Its selection and application on grounds of reducing the attenuation of the sample is justified when the results of the experiment are significant. When the results are not significant and no other explanation is reasonable, then it is necessary to resort to the more expensive process of individual matching, but this means repetition of the experiment, or at least increasing the number of cases observed.[1]

Chapin's statement presumes that attenuation is an inevitable consequence of precision control. Fisher shows that this is not the case, and that in fact the experimenter has a chance to display his skill by the wise choice of the moment at which to switch from precision control to randomisation. While it is in the interests of the sensitiveness of the experiment that gross differences between the experimental subject and the control subject should be excluded, equalisation should be carried ' not as far as *possible*, but as far as is practically convenient '.[2] It is highly probable that pairing on a small number of factors chosen for their relevance to the problem in hand, followed by allotment at random to the two samples, would not only replace a statistically vulnerable test for significance by a statistically valid one, but could also provide a more sensitive experiment than any amount of unrandomised precision control.

As no experiment takes place under ideal conditions or is faultlessly conducted, it is also desirable to repeat the experiment under conditions which are planned to reproduce as closely as possible those originally present. This provides a safeguard against errors in procedure, but not against faults in design, which will be

---

[1] CHAPIN, F. S. (1947), p. 102. It can only be repeated that one unalienable condition of tests for significant differences in the comparison of two samples is that these samples should have been selected at random. As this condition is not satisfied in the present case, the use of the word ' significant ' in its statistical sense is not justified.

[2] FISHER, R. A. (1949 ed.), p. 24.

repeated. Statistically the results obtained in successive experiments can be combined, and the aggregate regarded as one enlarged experiment. As Fisher remarks, ' It would clearly be illegitimate, and would rob our calculation of its basis, if the unsuccessful results were not all brought into the account '.[1]

In the natural sciences it is customary for any interesting experiment to be repeated in different laboratories throughout the world,[2] and it provides some measure both of the immaturity of social science and of the difficulties encountered in social experiment that enlargement by repetition under similar conditions has so seldom been attempted.

3. MODIFICATIONS OF THE CONTROLLED EXPERIMENT DESIGN

(a) *The Limits of Post-Factum Analysis*

In cases in which the complete design for a controlled experiment cannot be followed, there are various pseudo-forms which are in common use.

Two of the most widely used forms are illustrated below:

DIAGRAM B

	Before	After
Sample x	x_1	
Sample x'		x'_2

DIAGRAM C

	Before	After
Sample x		x_2
Sample x'		x'_2

In the type of ' experiment ' symbolised in Diagram B the attempt is made to compare one sample at one date with another sample at another date. If these are samples drawn at random from the same population, the design can be used to estimate changes taking place from one date to the next. First developed by Piaget, it finds many applications in social science. Thus, the Sickness Survey was conducted monthly on a sample basis and the results used in order to estimate the incidence of sickness in the

---

[1] FISHER, R. A. (1949 ed.), p. 22.
[2] ' If a scientific theory is important, it will be tested many times, more or less indirectly, by different workers. It is this unlimited repetition and checking that gives science such impersonal validity as it possesses."—ANSCOMBE, F. J. (1948), ' The Validity of Comparative Experiments ', *J. Roy. Statist. Soc.*, III, 196.

adult population as a whole. Pairing was possible, but random allotment between samples was clearly excluded.

Diagram C also represents a design commonly used in the comparison of observational material. It differs from Diagram B in that the two sets of observations are made on the same date, while the populations from which the two samples are taken are designedly different in respect of some particular characteristic. This is a common design for the collection of material destined for correlation analysis: it would be used, for example, to test the theory that convicts tend to be of less than normal intelligence. Some pairing can be introduced—e.g. men of similar ages and backgrounds could be compared—but randomisation is ruled out.

These two designs are in essence incomplete versions of the controlled experiment. In view of the difficulties attached to controlled experiment in social science, an attempt has been made to persuade social scientists that both, and particularly the design represented in Diagram C, are acceptable forms of experiment. In order to bolster up this assertion, the latter procedure has been given the impressive, if rather clumsy, title of the *ex-post-facto experiment*.

The argument for classifying these designs as experimental derives from that earlier suggestion of J. S. Mill that ' the value of the instance depends on what it is in itself, not on the mode in which it is obtained '. The *ex-post-facto* experiment is the latest manifestation of what Mill called ' nature's experiment '.

The controlled experiment is normally designed to test the theory that a given ' cause ' will lead to a given ' effect '. Echoing Mill, Greenwood asserts that the *ex-post-facto* experiment ' can be a two-way affair ',[1] and he correspondingly divides the cases that he cites into those in which the *ex-post-facto* procedure is used to detect the cause of a known effect and those in which it is used to determine the effect of a known cause. He calls these respectively ' effect-to-cause ' and ' cause-to-effect ' experiments.

It will be clear that in logic the two are very different. The effect-to-cause design is derived from an antique theory, and one on which mathematicians and philosophers have argued for centuries. Bayes in the mid-eighteenth century put forward tentatively the first mathematical theory of inverse probability, but

---

[1] GREENWOOD, E. (1945), p. 32 fn.; cf. MILL, J. S., *A System of Logic*, pp. 251 seq.

Modifications of the Controlled Experiment Design 273

in spite of all attempts it has been found impossible to devise a rigorous and generally acceptable technique for distinguishing between the possible causes of a given effect.

Fisher inserts a quotation on this subject in which de Morgan, writing in 1838, contrasts the logic behind effect-to-cause design with that behind cause-to-effect design.

> Given an hypothesis presenting the necessity of one or another out of a certain, and not very large, number of consequences, [investigators] could determine the chance that any given one or other of those consequences should arrive; but given an event as having happened, and which might have been the consequence of either of several different causes, or explicable by either of several different hypotheses, they could not infer the probability with which the happening of the event should cause the different hypotheses to be viewed.[1]

The impossibility of gaining ' compelling evidence ' by means of effect-to-cause arguments has again been stressed by Merton.

> The logical fallacy underlying the *post factum* explanation rests in the fact that there is available a variety of crude hypotheses, each with some measure of confirmation but designed to account for quite contradictory sets of affairs. The method of *post factum* explanation does not lend itself to nullifiability, if only because it is so completely flexible. For example, it may be reported that ' the unemployed tend to read fewer books than they did previously '. This is ' explained ' by the hypothesis that anxiety increases as a consequence of unemployment and, therefore, that any activity requiring concentration, such as reading, becomes difficult. This type of accounting is plausible, since there is some evidence that increased anxiety *may* occur in such situations and since a state of morbid preoccupation does interfere with organised activity. If, however, it is now reported that the original data were erroneous and it is a fact that ' the unemployed read more than previously ' a new *post factum* explanation can at once be invoked. The explanation now holds that the unemployed have more leisure or that they engage in activity intended to increase their personal skills. Consequently, they read more than previously. Thus, whatever the observations, a new interpretation can be found to ' fit the facts '.[2]

[1] FISHER, R. A. (1949 ed.), p. 5.
 In 1859 T. H. Buckle commented ' . . . during the last fifty years an opinion has been gaining ground that the Baconian system has been overrated, and that its favourite idea of proceeding from effects to causes, instead of from causes to effects, will not carry us so far as was supposed by the truly great, though somewhat empirical thinkers of the eighteenth century '. See also pp. 15 seq.
[2] MERTON, R. K. (1945), ' Sociological Theory ', *Am. Journ. Soc.*, **50**, 468. Reprinted in (1949) *Social Theory and Social Structure*, pp. 90–1.

T

Perhaps the author of this last quotation protests too much. It is perfectly legitimate to put forward hypotheses such as the ones he quotes, but no one in his senses—or at least no scientist, we hope—would imagine that the mere fact of having thought up possible explanations completes the process of proof. Up to the point to which Merton pursues the matter, the evidential value is slight. But if, for example, 'reading' and 'anxiety' can be operationally defined and measured and a high inverse correlation between the two is disclosed, then the connection is shown to have some substance.

Even so, a chasm remains between the form of proof implied in an experiment and that implied in a series of observations which are found to be correlated. It therefore appears to be an undesirable and unnecessary extension of the title 'experiment' to include the *ex-post-facto* effect-to-cause design.[1]

This is, however, an appropriate point at which to examine the function of what has been called the *mental experiment*. This concept was originally due to the mid-nineteenth-century Austrian physicist and philosopher, Ernst Mach. As the result of a historical survey of past scientific discoveries, Mach believed that he had isolated the characteristic procedure by which, consciously or otherwise, scientific concepts and laws are elaborated. According to this theory, the first physical experiment is preceded by an imaginary experiment which need not actually take place except in the mind of its formulator. This gives scope for simplification and other devices of idealisation; it also means that the concepts used become tremendously important, for they supply in effect both the instructions and the materials needed for carrying out the imaginary experiment.

We may see here a parallel with the Inverse Deductive Method and with its application to economic analysis,[2] in which the

---

[1] By many authorities, the statistical correlation is regarded as the substitute for experiment in the biological and social sciences. ' No quantity has been more characteristic of biometrical work than the correlation coefficient, and no method has been applied to such various data as the method of correlation. Observational data in particular, in cases where we can observe the occurrence of various possible contributory causes of a phenomenon but cannot control them, has been given by its means an altogether new importance. In experimental work proper its position is much less central; it will be found useful in the exploratory stages of an inquiry, as when two factors which had been thought independent appear to be associated in their occurrence; but it is seldom, with controlled experimental conditions, that it is desired to express our conclusion in the form of a correlation coefficient."—FISHER, R. A. (1950 ed.), *Statistical Methods for Research Workers*, p. 175.   [2] See pp. 68 seq.

instinct of avarice, the desire for material gain, is invoked as a principle according to which a large sector of human activity can be not only explained, but also predicted. Some account is taken in economics of certain antagonistic principles, such as aversion to work, but other considerations—such as those of prestige, power and altruism—are in many cases deliberately excluded.

This one-sided nature of economic analysis has provided an easy target for critics. But no one would deny that in some form or another economic motives permeate a large proportion of social situations; the economist aims to choose for study only those situations in which he believes economic motives to predominate, and proceeds as though, with minor exceptions, no other motives existed. Conclusions drawn from such an Inverse Deductive analysis are openly regarded as approximations; in their proper sphere, however, they often make possible surprisingly accurate predictions.[1]

More ambitiously, but still conforming to the procedure of Inverse Deduction, modern economic theorists have begun to introduce a greater variety of considerations. For ease of conceptualisation, these are combined into a model which represents what is believed by its architect to be a simplified version of reality, in which a limited number of variables are introduced, in a form allowing statistical measurement. The working of this model is then tested experimentally by feeding in empirical facts and determining whether the end-product created by the model corresponds with the empirically ascertained end-product encountered in real life. If there is a regular correspondence between the two, the validity of the model *as a whole* is said to have been established by the facts. If not, the method is tried again with a new combination of variables. And tried again until success is achieved.

This technique, known as econometrics, has been applied with some success to a variety of economic problems; furthermore, it has been claimed that it has thus become possible to confirm the reality of a number of classical economic concepts, such as the demand curve, which had previously been based only on introspection and informal observations.

It is apparent, however, that logically the technique of econometrics represents little more than an elaborated version of the

[1] Cf. MILL, J. S., *A System of Logic*, pp. 588–9.

ex-post-facto effect-to-cause experimental design. Mach's theory was based on experience in natural science, in which the mental experiment is superseded as soon as it is possible to carry out a physical experiment. Unlike econometrics, it is a preparation for experiment, and not a substitute.

Max Weber is one profound thinker who was suspicious of what he called ' the dangerous and uncertain procedure of the imaginary experiment '.[1] He criticises the school of historians who waste time in attempting to weave a web of causality into past events, by speculating on what would have occurred if events had been otherwise.

> Our real problem is, however: by which logical operations do we acquire the insight and how can we demonstrate a causal relationship between these ' essential ' components of the effects and certain components among the infinity of determining factors ? Obviously not by the simple ' observation ' of the course of events. . . . Rather, does the attribution of effects to causes take place through a process of thought which includes a series of *abstractions*. The first and decisive one occurs when we *conceive* of one or a few of the actual causal components as modified in a certain direction and then we ask ourselves whether under the conditions which have been thus changed, the same effect . . . or some other effect ' would be expected '.[2]

Weber goes on to consider how we choose between a number of possible outcomes.

> It involves first the production of—let us say it calmly—' imaginative constructs ' by the disregarding of one or more of those elements of ' reality ' which are actually present, and by the mental construction of a course of events which is altered through modification in one or more ' conditions '. Even the first step towards an historical judgment is thus—this is to be emphasised—a process of *abstraction*. This process proceeds through the analysis and mental isolation of the components of the directly given data—which are to be taken as a complex of possible relations—and should culminate in a synthesis of the ' real ' causal complex. Even this first step thus transforms the given ' reality ' into a ' mental construct ' in order to make it into an historical fact. In Goethe's words, ' theory ' is involved in the ' fact '.[3]

[1] WEBER, M. (translated 1947), *Theory of Social and Economic Organisation*, p. 88.
[2] WEBER, M. (translated 1949), *Methodology of the Social Sciences*, p. 171.
[3] *ibid.*, p. 173. There is an affinity here with Pareto's ' logico-experimental ' method.

Somewhat similar to the pathfinding indulged in by a single mind is the very common dialectical process that may be called *intellectual diplomacy*, by which various individuals thrash out a uniform point of view by a discussion thorough enough to reconcile or submerge any initial differences.[1] This reconciliation of opinions sometimes passes as truth, in spite of the fact that it has not been tested operationally.

The fruitfulness of any such procedures in preparation for an actual experiment is not in doubt.[2] Clearly no efficient experiment can be planned if its instigator has not envisaged the main possible outcomes. But it emphatically does not follow from this that events can be adequately explained in terms of concepts which have not been overtly involved in the prosecution of these events.

Broadly speaking, knowledge is what enables us to envisage the consequences of a course of action. If we follow this course in our imaginations we arrive at hypothetical truths, but it is only after real experimentation that we can genuinely claim knowledge of consequences.

There still remains to be considered the other form of *ex-post-facto* experiment, the so-called cause-to-effect experiment. The conditions under which this takes place are strictly those of the ' nature's experiments ' described by Mill. It has the mark of the controlled experiment in that there are two groups, experimental and control, and that the ' cause ' whose effects it is desired to ascertain is applied only to the experimental group. The initial difference from the controlled experiment is that its conduct is out of the control of the investigator; in consequence, allocation ' in random order ' to the two groups is not possible.

As with previous instances, the potentialities of this design will now be considered by reference to actual investigations in which

[1] MANNHEIM, K. (n.d.), *Man and Society*, pp. 207 seq., etc.
[2] Susan Isaacs sees a link between the make-believe of the child and the imaginative hypothesis of the adult. With implicit reference to Vaihinger's ' As if ' philosophy, she writes (*Intellectual Growth in Young Children*, p. 104), ' The ability to evoke *the past* in imaginative play seems to me to be very closely connected with the growth of the power to evoke *the future* in constructive hypothesis, and to develop the consequences of " ifs ". Imaginative play at its most active may be looked upon as the prototype of " mental experiment " in the sense of Rignano and Mach. . . . The child *recreates* selectively those elements in past situations which can embody this emotional or intellectual need of the present, and he adapts the details movement by movement to the present situation. . . . And in his make-believe, he takes the first step towards that emancipation of meanings from the *here* and *now* of a concrete situation, which makes possible hypotheses and the " as if " consciousness.'

it has been used. As before, the majority of these have been in the field of psychology; the two examples introduced below both happen to have been conducted by psychologists.

(b) *Comparison of Intelligence of Own and Foster Children* [1]

The investigator wished to compare the influence of heredity and upbringing on intelligence and other personality traits. The 'experimental' group consisted of 194 children who had been placed in foster homes when under six months old. At the date of the investigation these children were five to fourteen years old.

The control group was constituted of the true children of these same foster-parents. Each adopted child in the experimental group was *matched* with an 'own' child on such factors as cultural background of true parents and parental school achievement and performance of children and parents in certain personality tests.

The conclusions reached by the author was that I.Q. was only slightly influenced by home environment, but that other personality traits were ' accounted for less by variation in heredity than by variation in environment '.

This was one of a number of psychological studies in the same field. As Blackburn has pointed out,[2] it is necessary to show beyond doubt that prospective foster-parents do not consciously or unconsciously adopt children who match them and their own children in intelligence and other personality traits; if this cannot be proved, the studies are valueless. And the reason why it cannot be proved is the reason why we must be cautious in describing such studies as experiments, that is that the investigator is powerless to allot children *at random* as between the experimental and control groups.

(c) *Who Shall Survive?* [3]

This experiment arose as if by chance out of a continuous programme of social rehabilitation undertaken by Dr. J. L. Moreno and his colleagues at the New York Training School for Girls at Hudson, New York.

---

[1] LEAHY, A. M. (1935), *Nature-Nurture and Intelligence* (Cited by GREENWOOD, E. (1945), p. 67; MURPHY, G., MURPHY, L. B., and NEWCOMB, T. M. (1937), pp. 40, 1081).
[2] BLACKBURN, J. (1947), *The Framework of Human Behaviour*, pp. 33-4.
[3] MORENO, J. L. (1943), *Who Shall Survive?* (Cited by GREENWOOD, E. (1945), p. 66; MURPHY, G., MURPHY, L. B., and NEWCOMB, T. M. (1937), pp. 309-11).

This training school is run along very original lines and includes the special approach to inter-personal relations which Moreno and his colleagues devised, and named *sociometry*.

One feature of sociometric work is to encourage a constant process of adjustment to the wishes of those taking part. This is illustrated by the arrangements at Hudson. The girls are housed in cottages, each holding about twenty-five, and each new girl on arrival meets the ' house-mothers ' and ' key girls ' from those cottages which at the time have vacancies. After a series of private talks, both the new girl and these functionaries express their likes and dislikes and it is mutually decided to which cottage the girl shall go. A house-mother receives no girl who does not like her or whom she does not like. The process is repeated once every six weeks, so a socially maladjusted girl has the chance to find a more congenial ménage.

There is thus normally no opportunity to apply any form of experimental control, as would be needed to assess the value of the sociometric régime. It would be against the principles of those in charge to withdraw from some girls the benefit of choice enjoyed by others. Occasionally, however, illness or accident results in certain girls being placed in a cottage without passing through the regular sociometric procedure, and this was made the pretext for an experimental study.

> [Sixteen girls were regarded as a control group and] compared with two other groups of sixteen each, which had received sociometric placement. One of the latter ' experimental groups ' had been placed under optimal conditions, that is, on entering Hudson they had received their first choices among house-mothers and key girls and had been the same house-mothers' and key girls' first choices. The second experimental group had been sociometrically placed, but mutual first choices had not been possible. Tests repeated every eight weeks over a 32-week period suggest considerably better adjustment in the two experimental groups, as far as general compatibility with their comrades is concerned, than in the control group.[1]

This experiment is not only intrinsically interesting in its subject-matter, but also comes remarkably close in design to a valid ' nature's experiment ' under real-life conditions. Although deliberate randomisation was forsworn on principle, it seems quite

[1] MURPHY, G., MURPHY, L. B., and NEWCOMB, T. M. (1937), p. 311.

possible that the 'illness or accident' which caused a girl's initial placement procedure to be short-circuited may have fallen at random. If this was actually the case—and the onus of proof lies on the investigator—the design appears to have been rather satisfactory.

4. THE EXPERIMENT IN TIME

(a) *Merits and Weaknesses*

Very often in the established sciences it is regarded as unnecessary to reproduce the complete design of the controlled experiment. If, for example, you wish to test the law: ' Pressure times Volume equals (caeteris paribus) a constant', you will hardly bother to set up a second apparatus to show that volume remains constant when nothing else is changed. In many experiments it is customary to start with something, to subject it to certain influences and to note any changes that take place in it.

Diagrammatically, this design can be represented thus:

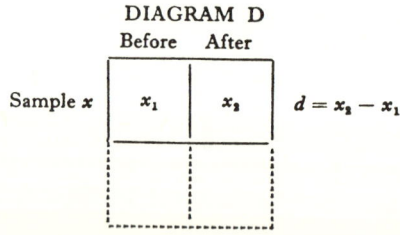

DIAGRAM D

Sample x | x_1 (Before) | x_2 (After) | $d = x_2 - x_1$

This design has many attractions for the social scientist, not least of which is that of greatly simplifying the sampling problem. Apart from wastages in the course of the experiment, the sample remains the same throughout and no problem of pairing is involved.

There are, however, corresponding weaknesses. Fundamentally these are due to the fact that human beings and social groups, unlike gas-filled containers, never approach a condition of static equilibrium. Even if left entirely to themselves they will continue to develop and change in directions which are often unforeseeable. Thus the difference occurring in the course of the experiment is compounded of that due to the experimental influences and of that due to the internal dynamic of the experimental subjects. It is often impossible to disentangle the two or to assess how much is due to each.

Nevertheless, this design is implicit in a very wide range of observational studies, and has been explicitly used as the basis of some rather important experimental investigations.

Most of the latter have been of a psychological nature, conducted under laboratory conditions, and have been concerned with infants or children. Let us consider one typical example.

(b) *Frustration and Regression in Children* [1]

This experiment was designed to test the hypothesis that the behaviour of frustrated children shows regression.

In the first stage thirty nursery-school children aged two and a half to five years were allowed to play, one at a time, for half an hour in a large playroom well equipped with boats, ducks, telephones, ironing-boards, etc. Note was taken of how maturely and constructively the children played, and each child's performance was scored on a ' constructive scale '.

In the second stage each child was in turn shown a fascinating new toy—a large and beautiful toy truck, a new ironing-board with dresses to iron, a pond for the boats, etc. A moment later the child was told that he could not play with these novelties, and was shut in with his old toys.

The observer then carefully noted how each child spent his half-hour with the old toys. It was found that his behaviour was strikingly, though perhaps not surprisingly, less constructive than in his previous play periods. Whereas before being frustrated he might have used the telephone in imaginary conversations, he now tended to bang it about and use it as a rattle. On average, maturity of behaviour of the children declined by about 14 months.

This rather distasteful experiment was more serious than my brief description may suggest, and was designed to test a systematic theory on the processes of learning and growing up. Its design is fairly adequate for the task which the experimenters set themselves.[2] Past experience suggests, however, that the scope

---

[1] BARKER, R., DEMBO, T., and LEWIN, K. (1936), *Experiments on Frustration and Regression in Children.* Paper read at a meeting of the Dynamic Psychologists. (Described by MURPHY, G., MURPHY, L. B., and NEWCOMB, T. M., p. 136, GREENWOOD, E., p. 55.)

[2] In another experiment on children, SOROKIN et al. (1930) tested the effect on work done of individual and pooled payment. The design of this experiment had the merit of allowing for change of behaviour due to experience; this was achieved by repeating experimental and control conditions on alternate days.—(MURPHY, G., MURPHY, L. B., and NEWCOMB, T. M., pp. 482–3).

for work along similar lines is somewhat restricted. If the studies must be confined to children, because they alone can be kept in the dark as to what is going on, or can only be extended to adults if a means can be found of keeping them similarly in ignorance, then the field of application must remain narrow.

There is, however, another possibility to be explored. The techniques of experimentation which have so far been discussed are based on those evolved in the natural sciences. Can it be that a radically different approach is required in social science ? Can the human beings who constitute the subject-matter of social science be regarded, not as objects for experimental manipulation, but as participants in what is being planned ? If this can be so, it requires a transformed attitude towards social experiment. Traditionally, attention is concentrated on the precautions needed to objectify results, and this entails treating the participants as lay figures to be observed before and after subjection to a series of external stimuli. In contrast, the new approach entails the acceptance and encouragement of conscious co-operation by all concerned. There are then no longer an investigator and his passive subjects, but a number of human beings, one of whom is more experienced than the others and has somewhat more complex aims, but all of whom are knowingly collaborating in a research project.

There is nothing mystic in this reorientation. The fundamental change is in the material that the experiment is designed to manipulate. Whereas the orthodox experimental material is a social group, or a bunch of individuals, in this emergent type of experiment the material is a dynamic, or potentially dynamic, social situation. The object of the experiment can quite validly be to discover to what extent, and by what processes, those involved in the situation can adjust themselves to a changed set of external stimuli, and how the last state compares with the first.

(c) *The Hawthorne Experiment* [1]

The most celebrated illustration of this thesis is provided by the series of experiments conducted twenty-five years ago by Professor Elton Mayo and his colleagues at the Western Electric Company's Hawthorne Works at Cicero, Chicago. Of this series of experi-

---

[1] See ROETHLISBERGER, F. J., and DICKSON, W. J. (1939), *Management and the Worker*; MAYO, E. (1945), *The Social Problems of an Industrial Civilisation*.

ments, perhaps the most formative and the most directly relevant to the present context were those conducted in the Relay Assembly Test Room.

In the spring of 1927, Professor Mayo and his associates at Harvard University were asked to conduct some limited tests on a small group of five manual workers, who were to be segregated for the purpose from their normal operating department. These tests were to follow lines orthodox to psychology, and were aimed at discovering the relation between conditions of work and the incidence of fatigue ; with this object, it was intended to vary such things as temperature, humidity and hours of work and sleep under controlled conditions and to note what happened. Results were expected within a year.

The operators selected to take part in the experiment were five girls already skilled in the assembly of small telephone parts called relays. This particular manufacturing process was chosen for the Test Room because it was repetitive, each relay taking around one minute to assemble, and because the speed of the operation was wholly controlled by the operator, there being no conveyor belt or similar device. Each girl's rate of output thus represented her ' natural pace '.

The girls were virtually volunteers. Two experienced operators who were known to be friendly with each other and also cooperative with management were invited to take part and themselves selected the remaining three. There was thus no attempt at random selection, the benefits of which were sacrificed in favour of ensuring willing experimental subjects.

The test room was located some distance away from the regular relay assembly department, in order that the girls should not come into constant contact with the main factory group. In other respects working conditions were similar to those in the regular department, except that special arrangements were made to record output, and a full account of daily happenings was kept by one observer who was stationed in the room.[1] Temperature and humidity were read hourly for several years. Arrangements were made for the periodic physical examination of the girls at a local hospital.

The test was organised into separate periods. The length of these periods varied greatly, but they averaged eight weeks. After

[1] See also pp. 133 seq.

three initial periods which were needed to establish and ascertain a normal rate of working under test-room conditions, the real experiments began. The first point to be investigated was the effect of rest breaks, so four periods were spent in discovering the effect on output of rest breaks of various lengths. In general, the hourly rate of output went up throughout this phase of the enquiry, so much so that although rest breaks reduced total working hours by as much as 5%, the total weekly output of the group was higher at the end of the last period than it had been at the beginning of the first.

This fitted well with the normal hypothesis that rest breaks improve rate of output by reducing fatigue. It was therefore decided to pass on to the next phase of the experiment, which was to reduce the working day while retaining the rest breaks. Results at first were not inconsistent with the orthodox fatigue hypothesis; the fact that hourly output rates did not continue to rise could be explained by a law of diminishing returns.

Towards the end, however, a trial was made of the effects of reverting to working conditions that had already been tested at an earlier stage. If fatigue was the important factor, it was to be expected that output rate would revert to that recorded in the earlier comparable period. In point of fact it did no such thing. Of two periods with identical hours of work, output in the later period was almost 20% higher than it had been in the earlier period. A similar rise occurred as between another pair of ostensibly identical periods.

These results were most unexpected and perplexing to the investigators, who were astonished to find a general upward trend in output irrespective of any particular change in rest breaks or working hours. There appeared to be no simple correlation between working conditions and output.

Five hypotheses were suggested and explored in an attempt to interpret the results. *Hypothesis A* was that the improvement was due to the improved material conditions and methods of work introduced into the test-room. This was never very convincing to the investigators, as earlier experiments in lighting and ventilation had shown that material conditions alone had very little effect on output. It was finally rejected after further experimentation.

Hypothesis B was that the shortening of hours had acted

cumulatively in reducing fatigue. *Hypothesis C* was that it had had the observed effect by reducing the monotony of work.

These two hypotheses were exhaustively examined by studying the variations in output rates of each girl. Effects of fatigue and boredom are known to show themselves in a falling off of output towards the end of each week and towards the late afternoon of each day. But analysis of these records failed to support the cumulative fatigue hypothesis. Blood pressure and other physical tests also gave negative results. The investigators concluded that the operators were at all times working well within their physical capacity.

The tests of the monotony hypothesis were less conclusively negative. It was recognised that monotony in work is primarily a state of mind, and there was—as we shall see—considerable evidence that the attitudes of the girls to their work had changed in a way that might have reduced the sense of monotony.

Hypothesis D was that the operators were responding to a more effective wage incentive. In the main department from which the girls had been drawn, individual wages were tied to the total output of about 200 operators, so that the output of any individual hardly affected her earnings. In the test-room, earnings were tied to the output of the five girls only, so that any girl's output was appreciably reflected in her earnings. This hypothesis was tested by selecting five further girls in the main department and paying these five according to their output rather than according to the output of the whole department.

Results suggested that there was something in the hypothesis. The output of the second test group did increase considerably (in fact by about 12%). It was found difficult, however, to disentangle the direct effect of the wage incentive from the consequent effect that the second test group, like the first, formed themselves into a coherent team of workers and in fact ' had seized upon this test as an opportunity to prove to everyone that they could do as well as the Relay Assembly Test Room operators '. The investigators concluded that there was absolutely no evidence in favour of the hypothesis that the continuous increase in output in the Relay Assembly Test Room during the first two years could be attributed to the wage incentive factor alone.

Finally there was *Hypothesis E*, that the increased output was connected with the noticeably improved attitude in the test-room, and that both were associated with the changes in the method of supervision that had gradually been taking place. According to this theory, the essential change introduced by the experiments had been a social change, and the method of supervision had been the means of gaining the operators' confidence and of establishing effective working relations.

This was by far the most plausible hypothesis. Throughout the experiment, the test-room observer had been in a position to notice how the operators were going about their work, to listen to and join in their conversations, and to smooth their difficulties and relieve their anxieties. As time went on, the change in atmosphere and the growing cohesion of the girls into a team became unmistakable. Much of this change had been due to the observer, who had fostered a kind of relation with the operators that a busy supervisor in a regular department would scarcely have time or opportunity to develop, and would not have been trained to seek.

Furthermore, the investigators gradually came to realise that they were fundamentally changing the character of their experiment. What had been an exercise in orthodox industrial psychology had slowly transformed itself into a co-operative enterprise in which the observer was truly a participant. There was no longer any attempt to test for the effects of single variables, such as an alteration in the length of a rest break. In the place of a controlled experiment in which one variable at a time was adjusted, it was necessary to substitute the notion of a social situation which had to be described and understood as a system of interdependent elements. This situation, moreover, was no longer regarded in terms of certain objective external events but in terms of the meanings which individuals assigned to these events, that is to say their attitudes towards them and their preoccupations about them. The investigators had originally aimed to standardise such ' psychological factors ', but as the experiment developed these very factors came increasingly to dominate the stage.

(d) *Conclusions*

The foregoing experiment is of unique importance, not only because of its scale and of the care with which it was conducted, but also from the manner in which—according to the authors—

the theoretical orientation arose out of the experiment rather than dictating its initial form.

It is, however, such a far cry from the classical laboratory experiment of the natural scientist that many authorities are reluctant to classify it as an experiment at all. Let us therefore briefly examine its claims.

It will be remembered that early in this chapter [1] it was suggested that two functions of the experimental method should be recognised. One merit of experiment rests in the rigour with which it can be used to test hypotheses. The other lies in the direct benefit that the investigator derives from ' doing something with ' his subject-matter rather than merely ' looking at ' it.

Now, in a unique sense, the observer of a social scene has to enter into and become part of what he is observing. In a similar way, the manipulator of a social process cannot avoid entering into and becoming part of whatever he is manipulating. This he cannot do unless he and his experimental subjects enjoy rather full mutual confidence and are generally agreed on aims.

When developed along these lines the experiment tends to submerge its classical objective, the search for proof, and becomes instead a miniature form of social action. If it is found to have desirable social consequences, it will be repeated on an increasing scale until it supplants the previously accepted norm. What the experiment provides is an opportunity to develop the social techniques necessary to bring about an agreed social aim. ' If we have no social technique at all, it is impossible to bring planning and control into being. If we do not have at hand a reasonable amount of technique, then it is by deliberately using what we have that we shall in the end develop a dependable body of social knowledge.[2]

This is all very well, and it is clear that a successful experiment of the type being discussed provides a vivid and exciting human experience for those who take part in it. But what proof have we, the outsiders, that their conclusions were justified by what happened? If the experimenter tells us, for example, that his intervention on the scene made the atmosphere happier, he must in some way be able to demonstrate the correctness of his claims. He must also be able to describe what he did in enough detail to

[1] Page 256.
[2] DEWEY, J. (1931), *Social Science and Social Control*.

enable another social scientist to test his conclusions by repeating the experiment.[1]

The great merit of the Relay Assembly experiment was that the improvement in morale could be measured by the objective index of output. That a change had occurred could not be doubted and, as we have seen, the investigation resolved itself into a series of studies aimed at apportioning responsibility for this change.

On the other hand, there are obvious defects in the experimental design. It was shown that co-operative volunteers under suitable conditions may agglomerate into a team. But what would have happened if five workers had been selected at random and, if necessary under threat of dismissal, ordered off to the test-room? Under what conditions would similar results be achieved if the experiment were to be repeated? How far, in fact, could the Relay Assembly Test Room be accepted as a satisfactory 'pilot plant', ready to be passed for large-scale production?

One would like to think that in natural science a single instance of results as odd as those achieved at Hawthorne would have set scientists throughout the world repeating the experiment until general agreement was reached.[2] But although the Hawthorne

---

[1] There is a parallel here with the status of psychoanalysis, both as a conceptual system and as a therapeutic technique. Although Freud was a practising therapist, his books reveal his intense interest in psychological theory as such. In effect he used his case-histories as material for his brilliant, though often highly speculative, theories about the workings of the mind, whether abnormal or normal. 'It may be asked', he wrote in 1920, 'whether and how far I am myself convinced of the truth of the hypotheses that have been set out in these pages. My answer would be that I am not convinced myself and that I do not seek to persuade other people to believe in them. Or, more precisely, that I do not know how far I believe in them. There is no reason, as it seems to me, why the emotional factor of conviction should enter into this question at all. It is surely possible to throw oneself into a line of thought and to follow it wherever it leads out of simple scientific curiosity.'—FREUD, S. (1950 translation), *Beyond the Pleasure Principle*, p. 81.

As a therapeutic technique, psychoanalysis has now been practised for half a century. With the development of techniques that make it feasible to spread the benefits of psychotherapy to an appreciable number of cases, the question often arises as to whether its value has been demonstrated. Oddly enough, it will be found that very few detached scientific attempts have been made to examine its therapeutic record (see review by WEINBERG, S. K. (1948) in *Am. Journ. Soc.* **53**, 514). As is so often the case with dynamic movements, the influence of psychoanalysis has spread by example and proselytisation, and not by proof.

[2] Experience in natural science has shown this to be very necessary, however simple the point at issue may appear. We laymen may tend to be overimpressed by the exactness of methods in other sciences, but Beveridge (*op. cit.*, pp. 156 seq.) gives many examples of chance successes and failures, and of unrepeatable results.

The Experiment in Time

Experiments began a quarter of a century ago, and are still praised wherever social scientists meet, we have yet to learn of any comparable experiments which have similarly enlarged man's understanding in this particular sphere.[1]

---

[1] Mention has already been made of the highly illuminating study by Trist and Bamforth of the Longwall Method of Coal-Getting. The conceptual perspective of this study is more brilliant than that of the Hawthorne experiment, but it is observational rather than experimental in design and presents an hypothesis rather than a proof.

Chapter 6

THE LIMITS OF SOCIAL SCIENCE

By arrangement with the publishers, I have been enabled to wait until the rest of the book is in type before preparing these final pages. This has allowed me to approach the proofs with a relatively clean palate. But it has also proved to be a rather depressing experience. It has saddened me to find how imperfectly I have succeeded in conveying the lessons that seem to emerge from any survey of social science in action.

It is therefore right that these few final pages should comprise my attempt to summarise what can be learnt from a century's experience in the development of social scientific method.

If we are honest we have to admit that the first century of social science has left us somewhere short of victory. A succession of undeniably talented men and women have fostered high hopes for a social science that will at some unspecified date be worthy to take its place beside the established exact sciences. But no one claims that this millennium has yet arrived, and some explanation of the delay seems to be called for.

Let us first reflect the doubt that today surrounds the paradigm of exactness, whatever the field of knowledge. This ideal of exactness is characteristic of the nineteenth century; in recent decades natural scientists have themselves been adjusting the meaning that they attach to exactness, but there is a real danger that social scientists may continue to strain so busily after an obsolete ideal that they neglect the more pertinent aspects of their task.

At the same time, we must be careful not to lurch to the other extreme by glorifying uncertainty. The quest for exactness cannot lightly be renounced. Laziness and incompetence are obviously not themselves sufficient grounds for imprecision. But those who have followed the argument of this book without rejecting it will be forced into the position that seems to me inescapable, namely that exact truth is both a proper objective and an unattainable one. Exactness is beyond our reach because of the penumbra that surrounds all our observations, and universal truth is not possible because every truth that we adhere to contains within itself some part of our aims, and aims are never unanimous. On both these grounds we have to be content with some residue of uncertainty.

This is not in any way a good thing, but neither is it a pretext for despair. The truth that is powerful in the world is the truth that is sufficiently exact to get things done. To believe this is not to debase the search for ultimate truths but only to recognise that the location of many truths still lies beyond the threshold of science, and cannot in fact be claimed without in turn debasing science. Provided that the scientist has learned to avoid what he does not and cannot know, he has then established himself on firm ground for the explorations that his skills have equipped him to undertake. And above all, the good scientist has the prudence that restrains him from trying to extract more from his material and his procedures than their state of development justifies.

So far, the development of the social sciences has been imperfectly balanced, in that social theory has been more carefully conceived than methods of empirical testing. The result of this, as Comte proclaimed, is that the theory has constantly outstripped the known facts and has acquired a metaphysical flavour. Alchemy, like other early manifestations of natural science, in some respects retarded the growth of science because of its metaphysical basis. At the same time, the empirical techniques developed by alchemists were the origin of many procedures still used today. The desire to explain and to unify social facts, the search for a consistent conceptual framework, these cannot be condemned even by the extreme empiricist, because this desire has motivated much valuable empirical research. But the theoretically inclined social scientist for his part would do well to be more aware of the shadowy nature of his favourite formulations.

The adoption of a mental construct as an aid to understanding is a device common to all the sciences. Just as the physicist conceives an ether or a meson, the social scientist is entitled to his concepts in so far as these concepts help him and his fellow scientists to understand and to 'explain' what they perceive. But far too often the social scientist is content to forge his concepts after the event, and to ignore the crucial criterion of experimental testing—that is that he should put himself and his hypotheses at the mercy of his experiment. The mental experiment is an invaluable dress-rehearsal, but it is no substitute for the real thing. The dependence on experiment is, one may almost state, the distinguishing feature of a mature science, and on this basis the social sciences are not yet adult.

It might be argued that to locate experimentation at the apex of scientific method makes the older, more receptive, techniques redundant. This argument is fallacious. It is not enough to conduct an experiment: the important thing is that it should be the right one. And before we can know what to choose, we have to go through a long process of self-education and of clarification of the concepts that are to become the tools for the purpose in hand. In social science, I suggest in this book, there can often be an orderly progress through search of documents, through observations, through the various forms of questioning, before we are ready for the rigour of experiment. The feature of this progress that requires emphasis is the fact of convergence. What starts as an open field leading in the general direction of an objective ends up as a narrow and a deeply beaten track.

There is one other characteristic of empirical adventure that demands attention. It seems inevitable that the more pragmatic and active the aims of an enquiry the more worldly the concepts will be. When we are viewing in distant perspective the antics of humans we can afford to conceive them at a high level of abstraction. But when we descend to their plane we shall miss many of the nuances of their actions and remarks unless we are prepared to mix with them on terms of equality and to translate our experiences into the language that they have evolved to reflect their own vistas of social reality.

Even this egalitarianism is not enough. In such circumstances a special kind of leadership is required of the social scientist; in no society are all the members equal in experience, and the social scientist is obliged to contribute his special experience—often gained and conceptualised at second hand—to the fund of the social group. In fulfilling his social function he is required to use this experience for the benefit of the group and thus help them to clarify their actions and their aims.

It is sometimes argued that the scientist must take care to avoid final identification with the group, because it is only by a degree of detachment that he can evade taking sides in the intra-group conflicts that rock most societies. The social scientist is therefore advised to join with his colleagues in forming a fresh sub-group whose contribution is valued but whose independence is recognised. This requirement of ultimate detachment is a corollary of another requirement, proposed from the same source, that the social scientist should withdraw in the nick of time from the process of arriving at and of implementing collective decisions. It is felt that to partake would imply a form of social engineering and therefore, by some inference, inconsistent with the scientist's research rôle; his rôle is a transitory one, he is not to be involved in the group experience, his function is catalytic rather than reagent.

This stand is intelligible but not, I think, realistic. It is true that every society is unified at only one level, and that diversities can be discerned at all higher levels. In this sense the band of social scientists, linked by their distinctive backgrounds and specialised interests, will naturally consort together. No one would suggest that they should, even if they wished, submerge their identities, individual or collective. In this they do not differ from the other sub-groups of which any society is formed, but all such groups are involved in the society's collective decisions, if not positively then at least by agreeing to accept them.

To admit the presence of sub-groups is not to deny that different societies vary greatly in the extent of their unification. There are many who believe that there is in the world today a powerful trend towards unification. The abandonment of caste rules, the undermining of all sets of traditional codes of behaviour and belief, the substitution of the 'other-directed' scanning procedure—these are regarded as stages in an irreversible historical process. Certainly we cannot ignore the potency of modern methods of persuasion, nor can we deny the verve with which modern doctrinal and political movements seek to infiltrate into and to dominate all levels of behaviour and belief. The least that we must admit is that perhaps for the first time a unification throughout the world is conceivable, and that the intolerance, the fierce unmasking of ideologies, the brutality, are merely by-products of varied attempts to bring this about.

Those who believe in total unification must face the prospect of a head-on collision between different systems of truth. For them there can survive only one single system. Nor is theirs a minority belief. The hope of some common ground that can unite the human race has sunk so deep into our way of thought that I doubt whether there are many civilised people today who resist it. But there is still a chasm to separate permissive unity, the agreement to differ on all but essentials, from the pervasive dogmas that permit no irrelevancies. On the whole the evidence of history tends to support the view that intolerance and fanaticism are necessary conditions of change, at least in certain of its phases, and that a movement that tolerates incomplete loyalty may be compelled to hand over leadership to a less compromising creed. It is certainly true that no state of mind is as devastating as the inability to believe. As existentialists have declared, the fact of commitment can be the best means to the resolution of doubts. Participation in the acts and beliefs of a movement is, at least to many people, an inescapable step and a condition of sanity.

We have no reason to suppose that social scientists can evade this dilemma that confronts the rest of humanity. Some may attempt to neutralise its power and to postpone the moment of decision by aligning themselves along the endless avenue of factual research, as though they could honestly conceive of a distant age when all the facts have been gathered and all decisions can be spelled out by the operation of some giant calculating machine. But many can find no satisfaction in this standpoint. We can see around us a multitude of practical problems that call for action, and a multitude of people torn by their imperfect understanding of the situations in which they have to act. What they need are not absolute truths and watertight theories but the skills to guide themselves towards realistic and sensible decisions. In this tormented world, the clarifications of which our social science is capable should surely be thrown productively into the scales. Meagre as the contribution still may be, it is potentially great and without doubt is increasing both in effectiveness and in acceptability. And to the extent that improvement continues, both the power and the moral responsibilities of the social scientist will correspondingly expand. He is a person who is elaborating a special kind of skill, but above all he is a human being, and no one but he can decide whether his skills, both in their applications and in their consequences, are to be used for evil or for good.

INDEX OF REFERENCES

Notes (1) Authors appear in the Index of References where full particulars of the work referred to are given. Proper names appearing in the General Index are those to which the above conditions do not apply.

(2) When items are referred to in a sequence of pages, the first page only is indicated in this and the following Index.

(3) Where two dates of publication are given, the former is the date of the first edition and the latter the date of the edition cited.

	PAGE
ABRAMS, MARK, *Social Surveys and Social Action*, London (1951)	17, 180
ABRAMS, MARK, *Contribution to discussion* on paper by DURBIN, J., and STUART, A. (1951)	216
ALBIG, W., *Public Opinion*, New York (1939)	180
ALLPORT, GORDON W., *The Use of Personal Documents in Psychological Science*. Social Science Research Council, Bulletin 49, New York (1942)	84, 104, 114, 172
ANDERSON, NELS, *The Hobo*, Chicago (1923)	133
ANGELL, ROBERT, *A Critical Review of the Development of the Personal Document Method in Sociology, 1920–1940*, in GOTTSCHALK, L., et al. (1945)	84
ANSCOMBE, F. J., 'The Validity of Comparative Experiments', *J. Roy. Statist. Soc.* (1948), **111** (3), 181–211	271
ARCINIEGAS, GERMAN, *Freedom—a Human Right*, in U.N.E.S.C.O. (1951)	56
BAKKE, E. WIGHT, *The Unemployed Man*, London (1933–*1935*)	174
BAMFORTH, K. W. See TRIST, E. L. (1951)	137, 289
BARKER, R., DEMBO, T., LEWIN, K., *Experiments on Frustration and Regression in Children* (Paper read in 1936 to the Dynamic Psychologists; cited by Murphy, Murphy and Newcomb, pp. 136, 1059)	281
BARNARD, CHESTER I., *The Functions of the Executive*, Harvard (1938–*1950*)	31
BARTLETT, SIR FREDERIC C., GINSBERG, M., LINDGREN, E. J., THOULESS, R. H. [Editors], *The Study of Society—Methods and Problems*, London (1939)	25, 69, 95, 101, 138, 191, 242
BARTLETT, SIR FREDERIC C., *Remembering*, Cambridge (1932)	123
BENDIX, REINHARD. See LIPSET, S. M. (1951)	54
BENEDICT, RUTH, *Patterns of Culture*, London (1935)	26
BENEDICT, RUTH, *The Chrysanthemum and the Sword*, Boston (1947)	30, 204
BERELSON, BERNARD, *Content Analysis in Communication Research*, Glencoe (1952)	95, 112
BERELSON, BERNARD. See LAZARSFELD, P. F. (1948)	183, 203
BERNARD, JESSIE, 'The Sources and Methods of Social Psychology', in BERNARD, L. L., *The Fields and Methods of Sociology*, New York (1934)	125
BERNARD, JESSIE, 'Observation and Generalisation in Cultural Anthropology', *Am. Journ. Soc.* (1945) **50**, 284–91	125
BEVERIDGE, W. I. B., *The Art of Scientific Investigation*, London (1950)	142, 258, 288
BLACKBURN, JULIAN M., *Intelligence Tests*, in BARTLETT, F. C., et al. (1939)	191
BLACKBURN, JULIAN M., *Psychology and the Social Pattern*, London (1945)	120, 123

Index of References

BLACKBURN, JULIAN M., *The Framework of Human Behaviour*, London (1947) 278
BLUM, FRED H., ' Max Weber's postulate of " Freedom from Value Judgments ",' *Am. Journ. Soc.* (1944), 50, 46–52 15
BLUMER, HERBERT, *Critiques of Research in the Social Sciences : I. An Appraisal of Thomas and Znaniecki's ' The Polish Peasant '*, Social Science Research Council, Bulletin 44, New York (1939) . . . 84
BLUMER, HERBERT, ' The Problem of the Concept in Social Psychology ', *Am. Journ. Soc.*, 45 (1940), 707–19 . . . . . 50, 130
BOOKER, H. S., and DAVID, S. T., ' Differences in Results Obtained by Experienced and Inexperienced Interviewers ', *J. Roy. Statist. Soc.* (1952), 115 (2), 232–57 247
BOOTH, —, *Charles Booth : A Memoir*, London (1918) 131
BOOTH, CHARLES, *Life and Labour of the People of London*, London (1889) 102
BORN, MAX, *The Restless Universe*, New York (1936) 129
BOWLEY, SIR ARTHUR L., and BURNETT-HURST, A. R., *Livelihood and Poverty*, London (1915) 206
BOWLEY, SIR ARTHUR L., *Elements of Statistics*, London (1901–1937) . 179
BOWLEY, SIR ARTHUR L., *An Elementary Manual of Statistics*, London (1909–1939) 105
BRENTANO, FRANZ, *Psychologie von empirischen Standpunkte*, 1874. See MURPHY, G. (1949), pp. 225 seq. 56
BRIDGMAN, P. W., *The Logic of Modern Physics*, New York (1927) . . 49
BRIDGMAN, P. W., ' The Nature of Some of Our Physical Concepts ', *Brit. Journ. Phil. Sci.* (1951), 1 (4), 257–272 24
BRONOWSKI, J., *The Common Sense of Science*, London (1951). . . 42
BROWN, S. CLEMENT, *The Methods of Social Case Workers*, in BARTLETT, F. C., et al. (1939) 101
BUCKLE, T. H., ' Mill on Liberty ', *Frazers Magazine*, May 1859 (Miscellaneous and Posthumous Works, 1, 75–130) 273
BURGESS, E. W., ' Sociological Research Methods ', *Am. Journ. Soc.* (1945), 50, 474–82 69
BURNETT-HURST, A. R. See BOWLEY, A. L. (1915) 206
BURROW, TRIGANT, *The Social Basis of Consciousness*, London (1927) . 155
BURT, SIR CYRIL L., ' The Trend of National Intelligence ', *Brit. Journ. Soc.* (1950), 1, 154–68 52
BURT, SIR CYRIL L., *Contribution to discussion* in *J. Roy. Statist. Soc.* (1950), B 12 (1), 87–8 191
CANTRIL, HADLEY, *Gauging Public Opinion*, Princeton (1944) . . . 185
CARR, EDWARD HALLETT, *The New Society*, London (1951) . . . 110
CASSIRIR, ERNST, *The Problem of Knowledge*, Yale (1950) . . 110, 116
CAVAN, R. S., HAUSER, P. M., STOUFFER, S. A., ' Note on the Statistical Treatment of Life History Material ', *Soc. Forces* (1930), 9, 200–208 . 114
CENTERS, RICHARD, *The Psychology of Social Classes*, Princeton (1949) . 53
CHAPIN, F. STUART, ' An Experiment on the Social Effects of Good Housing ', *Am. Soc. Rev.* (1940), 5, 868–79 266
CHAPIN, F. STUART, *Experimental Designs in Sociological Research*, New York (1947) 140, 255, 258, 265
CHASE, STUART, *The Proper Study of Mankind*, London (1950). . . 244
CHRISTIANSEN, HELEN F., *The Relation of School Progress to Subsequent Adjustment*, M.A. Thesis (1938), cited by CHAPIN, F. S. (1947), and GREENWOOD, E. (1945) 269

Index of References

CHURCHMAN, C. WEST, *The Theory of Experimental Inference*, New York (1948) 76
CLAUSEN, JOHN A. See STOUFFER, S. A. et al. (1950) 22
COOK, P. H., 'Methods of Field Research', *Austral. Journ. Psych.* (1951) 3 (2), 84–98 . . . . 16, 137
CORLETT, T. See GRAY, P. G. (1950a) . . . 206, 210, 249
CORLETT, T. See GRAY, P. G. (1950b) 210
CRAIK, KENNETH, J. W., *The Nature of Explanation*, Cambridge (1943) 7, 28, 40, 44, 56
CROCKER, LUCY, H. See PEARSE, INNES H. (1943) 137
DAUNT, MARJORIE, 'Language is a Branch of Literature', *Universities Quarterly* (1951), **5**, 239–50 42
DAVID, S. T. See BOOKER, H. S. (1952) 247
DAVIS, ALLISON, and DOLLARD, JOHN, *Children of Bondage*, Washington (1940) 172
DEMBO, T. See BARKER, R., et al. (1936) 281
DEWEY, JOHN, 'Social Science and Social Control', *New Republic* (1931), 67, 276–7 . . . . 257, 287
DICKSON, WILLIAM J. See ROETHLISBERGER, F. (1939) 134, 160, 167, 221, 232
DICTIONARY OF SOCIOLOGY. See FAIRCHILD, H. P. (Ed.) (1944) . . 39
DILTHEY, WILHELM, *Gesammelte Schriften*, Leipzig and Berlin (1914) . 82
DODD, STUART C., *A Controlled Experiment on Rural Hygiene in Syria*, Beirut (1934), cited by CHAPIN, F. S. (1947) 265
DOLLARD, JOHN, *Caste and Class in a Southern Town*, New York (1937–1949) 172, 219, 221
DOLLARD, JOHN, *Criteria for the Life History*, 1st ed., Yale (1935), 2nd ed., New York (*1949*) 169
DOLLARD, JOHN, et al., *Frustration and Aggression*, Yale (1939), London (*1944*) 21
DOLLARD, JOHN, 'Under What Conditions do Opinions Predict Behaviour?' *Public Opinion Quarterly* (1948), **12**, 623–32 . . . 202
DOLLARD, JOHN. See DAVIS, ALLISON (1940) 172
DOUGLAS, J. W. B. See *Maternity in Great Britain* (1948) . . 102, 209
DURBIN, J., and STUART, A., 'Differences in Response Rates of Experienced and Inexperienced Interviewers', *J. Roy. Statist. Soc.* (1951), **114** (2), 163–206 . . . . 247, 249, 263
DURKHEIM, EMILE, *The Rules of Sociological Method* (1895), [8th edition translated by Sarah A. Solovay and John H. Mueller, and edited by George E. G. Catlin], Glencoe (1938) . . . 16, 22, 65, 106
DYMES, MISS D. M. E. [Editor], *Sociology and Education*, Malvern (1943) . 141
EMPSON, WILLIAM, *The Structure of Complex Words*, London (1951) . 43
EVANS-PRITCHARD, E. E., *Social Anthropology*, London (1951) . . 168
EYSENCK, H. J., 'Social Attitude and Social Class', *Brit. Journ. Soc.* (1950), **1**, 56–66 208
FAIRCHILD, H. P. [Editor], *Dictionary of Sociology*, New York (1944) . 39
FARQUHARSON, ALEXANDER, *The Study of Material Culture*, in DYMES, MISS D. M. E. (Ed.), (1943) 141
FERGUSON, L. W., 'The Influence of Individual Attitudes on the Construction of an Attitude Scale', *J. Soc. Psychol.* (1935), **6**, 115–17. . 191
FIRTH, RAYMOND, *We, the Tikopia*, London (1936) 133
FISHER, SIR RONALD A., *Statistical Methods for Research Workers*, Edinburgh (*1925-1950*) 74, 274

Index of References

FISHER, SIR RONALD A., *The Design of Experiments*, Edinburgh (1935–1949) 262, 268, 273
FLEMING, C. M. [Editor], *Studies in the Social Psychology of Adolescence*, London (1951) 231
FLORENCE, P. SARGANT, *The Statistical Method in Economics and Political Science*, London (1929). 64, 234
FLORENCE, P. SARGANT, ' Patterns in Recent Social Research ', *Brit. Journ. Soc.* (1950), **1**, 221–39 138
FOWLER, H. W., and FOWLER, F. G., *The King's English* (1906–1931) . 42
FRANKLAND, P. *See* GRAY, P. G. (1950b) 210
FREUD, SIGMUND, *Beyond the Pleasure Principle* (1920), Translated by James Strachey, London (1950) 16, 288
FREUD, SIGMUND, *Collected Papers* (1924) 155
FREUD, SIGMUND, *Introductory Lectures on Psychoanalysis*, London (1922–1929) 159
FROMM, ERICH, *The Fear of Freedom*, London (1942) . . . 16
GALLUP, GEORGE, *A Guide to Public Opinion Polls*, Princeton (1948) 181, 186, 243
GAUDET, HAZEL. *See* LAZARSFELD, P. F. (1944, *1948*) . . . 183, 203
GEE, WILSON [Editor], *Research in the Social Sciences*, New York (1929) . 86
GINSBERG, MORRIS, *The Problems and Methods of Sociology*, in BARTLETT, F. C., et al. (1939). [Reprinted in GINSBERG, M. (1947)] . . 69
GINSBERG, MORRIS, *Reason and Unreason in Society*, London (1947). . 69
GINSBERG, MORRIS, ' Ethical Relativity and Political Theory ', *Brit. Journ. Soc.* (1951), **2**, 1–11 16
GINSBERG, MORRIS, ' Sociology and Psychoanalysis ', *Brit. Journ. Soc.* (1951), **2**, 76–8 9
GOODENOUGH, FLORENCE L., ' The Observation of Children's Behaviors as a Method in Social Psychology ', *Social Forces* (1937), **15**, 476–9 . 127
GOTTSCHALK, LOUIS; KLUCKHOHN, CLYDE; ANGELL, ROBERT, *The Use of Personal Documents in History, Anthropology and Sociology*, Social Science Research Council, Bulletin 53, New York (1945)   84, 88, 92, 104, 168, 238
GOTTSCHALK, LOUIS, *The Historian and the Historical Document*, in GOTTSCHALK, L., et al. (1945) 84, 88, 92, 104, 238
GRAY, P. G., and CORLETT, T., ' Sampling for the Social Survey ', *J. Roy. Statist. Soc.* (1950a), **113** (2), 150–206 . . . 206, 210, 249
GRAY, P. G., CORLETT, T., FRANKLAND, P., ' The Register of Electors as a Sampling Frame '. Privately circulated, London (1950b) . . 210
GREENWOOD, ERNEST, *Experimental Sociology*, New York (1945) 127, 129, 259, 263, 268, 272, 275, 281
GUTTMANN, LOUIS, ' A Revision of Chapin's Social Status Scale ', *Am. Soc. Rev.* (1942), **7**, 362–9 140
HADER, JOHN J., and LINDEMAN, EDUARD C., *Dynamic Social Research*, London, 1933 . . . . . . 56, 121, 131, 146, 221
HALL, JOHN and JONES, D. CARADOG, ' Social Grading of Occupations ', *Brit. Journ. Soc.* (1950), **1**, 31–55 . . . . . . 54, 191
HARRISSON, TOM. *See* MADGE, CHARLES (1938) . . . 135, 142
HARRISSON, TOM, ' What is Sociology ?', *Pilot Papers* (1947), **2**, 10–25   136, 138
HARTMANN, G. W., ' A Field Experiment on the Comparative Effectiveness of " Emotional " and " Rational " Political Leaflets in Determining Election Results ', *J. Abn. and Soc. Psych.* (1936), **31**, 99–114 . . 263

Index of References

HARVEY, S. M., 'A Preliminary Investigation of the Interview', *Brit. Journ. Psych.* (1938), 28, 263–87 246
HAUSER, P. M. *See* CAVAN, R. S. et al. (1930) 114
HEARNSHAW, F. J. C., *The Science of History*, in ROSE, W. (Ed.) (1931) . 94
HERSCHEL, SIR JOHN, *Discourse on the Study of Natural Philosophy*, cited by NAGEL, E. (1950), p. 170 67
HILL, A. BRADFORD, *Principles of Medical Statistics*, London (1937–1948) 258
HODGES, H. A., *Wilhelm Dilthey : an Introduction*, London (1944) . 58, 82
HOGBEN, LANCELOT, *Mathematics for the Million*, London (1936–1947) . 36
HORNEY, KAREN, *New Ways in Psychoanalysis*, London (1939). . . 155
HYMAN, HERBERT, 'Problems in the Collection of Opinion Research Data ', *Am. Journ. Soc* (1950), 55, 362–70. . . . . 244, 246
HYMAN, HERBERT. *See* MOSTELLER, F., et al. (1949) . 182, 243, 247
ISAACS, SUSAN, *Intellectual Growth in Young Children*, London (1930) . 277
ISAACS, SUSAN, [Editor], *The Cambridge Evacuation Survey*, London (1941) 91
JAMES, WILLIAM, *Pragmatism : a New Name for Some Old Ways of Thinking*, London (1907) 4
JAQUES, ELLIOTT, *The Changing Culture of a Factory*, London (1951)
136, 145, 147
JENNINGS, HELEN H., *Leadership and Isolation*, New York (1943) . . 231
JONES, D. CARADOG. *See* HALL, J. (1950) 54, 191
KAUFMANN, FELIX, *Methodology of the Social Sciences*, New York (1944) 7, 15
KENDALL, MAURICE G. *See* YULE, G. U. (1950) 73
KENDALL, PATRICIA L., and LAZARSFELD, PAUL F., *Problems of Survey Analysis*, in MERTON, R. K., and LAZARSFELD, P. F. [Eds.], (1950)
71, 200, 236, 239, 244
KENDALL, PATRICIA L. *See* MERTON, R. K. (1946) . . 37, 114, 165
KINSEY, ALFRED C., POMEROY, WARDELL, B., MARTIN, CLYDE, E., *Sexual Behaviour in the Human Male*, Philadelphia (1948)
14, 46, 221, 237, 241, 247
KITT, ALICE S. *See* MERTON, R. K. (1950) 72
KLEIN, VIOLA [with Foreword by Karl Mannheim], *The Feminine Character : History of an Ideology*, London (1946) 36
KLUCKHOHN, CLYDE, *The Personal Document in Anthropological Science*, in GOTTSCHALK, L., et al. (1945) 84, 168
KOFFKA, KURT, *The Growth of the Mind*, London (1924–1931) . . 142
LANGLOIS, CH. V., and SEIGNOBOS, CH. [Trans. G. G. Berry], *Introduction to the Study of History*, London (1898) . . . 40, 80, 224
LASSWELL, HAROLD, *The Analysis of Political Behaviour*, London (1948)
113, 131, 154, 164
LAVERS, G. R. *See* ROWNTREE, B. SEEBOHM (1951a) . . . 176
LAVERS, G. R. *See* ROWNTREE, B. SEEBOHM (1951b) . . . 206
LAZARSFELD, PAUL F., 'The Controversy over Detailed Interviews : an Offer for Negotiation ', *Public Opinion Quarterly* (1944), 8, 38–60. . . 187
LAZARSFELD, PAUL F., BERELSON, BERNARD, and GAUDET, HAZEL, *The People's Choice*, New York (1944, 1948) 183, 203
LAZARSFELD, PAUL F. *See* KENDALL, P. L. (1950) . 71, 200, 236, 239, 244
LAZARSFELD, PAUL F. *See* MERTON, R. K., and LAZARSFELD, P. F. [Eds.] (1950) 32, 46, 71, 200, 236, 239, 244

LEAHY, A. M., 'Nature–Nurture and Intelligence', *Genet. Psychol. Monog.* (1935), **17**, 235–308 278
LEVY, HYMAN, *The Universe of Science*, London (1932). . . . 27
LEWIN, KURT, 'Frontiers in Group Dynamics', *Human Relations* (1947), **1**, 5–41 and 143–53 . . . . 9, 24, 256, 257
LEWIN, KURT, *Field Theory in Social Science*, London (1952) . 9, 24, 256, 257
LEWIN, KURT. *See* BARKER, R., et al. (1936) 281
LINDEMAN, EDUARD C., *Social Discovery*, New York (1924) . . . 131
LINDEMAN, EDUARD C. *See* HADER, J. J. (1933) . . 56, 121, 131, 146, 221
LINDGREN, E. J., *The Collection and Analysis of Folk-Lore*, in BARTLETT, F. C., et al. (1939) 95
LIPSET, SEYMOUR M., and BENDIX, REINHARD, 'Social Status and Social Structure: a Re-examintion of Data and Interpretations', *Brit. Journ. Soc.* (1951), **2**, 150–68 and 230–54 54
LOGAN, W. P. D., 'Mumps and Diabetes', *Monthly Bulletin of Ministry of Health* (1951), **10**, 140 237
LUNDBERG, GEORGE A., *Social Research*, New York (1929) 14, 39, 83, 101, 200
LUNDBERG, GEORGE A., *Foundations of Sociology*, New York (1939) . 22, 50
LUNT, PAUL S. *See* WARNER, W. L. (1941) 53, 95
LUNT, PAUL S. *See* WARNER, W. L. (1942) 53
LYND, ROBERT S., *Knowledge for What ?*, Princeton (1939) . 15, 25, 80, 97
MACCURDY, J. T., *The Relation of Psychopathology to Social Psychology*, in BARTLETT, F. C., et al. (1939) 167
MACIVER, R. M., *Community: a Sociological Study*, London (1917–1924) 16, 55
MACRAE, DONALD G., 'Cybernetics and Social Science', *Brit. Journ. Soc.* (1951), **2**, 135–49 203
MADGE, CHARLES, and HARRISSON, TOM [Editors], *First Years Work by Mass-Observation*, London (1938) 135, 142
MALINOWSKI, BRONISLAW, *Argonauts of the Western Pacific*, London, (1922) 132, 168
MALINOWSKI, BRONISLAW, *A Nationwide Intelligence Service*, in MADGE, C., and HARRISSON, T. [Eds.] (1938) 135, 142
MANDEVILLE, JOHN P., 'Improvements in Methods of Census and Survey Analysis', *J. Roy. Statist. Soc.* (1946), **109** (2), 111–29 . . 225
MANNHEIM, KARL, *Ideology and Utopia*, London (1936). . . . 56
MANNHEIM, KARL, *Man and Society*, London (*N.D.*—New York ed., 1940) 154, 277
MANNHEIM, KARL, *Foreword* to KLEIN, V. (1946). 36
MARSHALL, T. H., *Sociology at the Crossroads*, London (1947). . 43, 69
MARTIN, CLYDE E. *See* KINSEY, A. C., et al. (1948) 14, 46, 221, 237, 241, 274
MASS-OBSERVATION, *War Begins at Home*, London (1940) . . . 135
MASS-OBSERVATION, *War Factory*, London (1943) 135
MASS-OBSERVATION. *See* TURNER, W. J. (1947) 135
MATERNITY IN GREAT BRITAIN, *A Survey* undertaken by a Joint Committee of the Royal College of Obstetricians and Gynæcologists and the Population Investigation Committee (1948) 102, 209
MAY, MARK A., *Foreword* to DOLLARD, J., et al. (1944) 21
MAYHEW, HENRY, *London Labour and the London Poor*, 4 vols., London (1851) 174

Index of References

MAYO, ELTON, *Some Notes on the Psychology of Pierre Janet*, Harvard (1948) 142

MAYO, ELTON, *The Social Problems of an Industrial Civilisation*, London (1949) 29, 248, 282

MEAD, MARGARET, *The American Character*, London (1944) . . 24, 141

MERTON, ROBERT K., ' Sociological Theory ', *Am. Journ. Soc.* (1945), **50**, 462–73 . . . . 8, 106, 273

MERTON, ROBERT K., *Social Theory and Social Structure*, Glencoe (1949) 8, 95, 106, 114, 153, 273

MERTON, ROBERT K., and KENDALL, PATRICIA L., ' The Focused Interview ', *Am. Journ. Soc.* (1946), **51**, 541–57 . . 37, 114, 165

MERTON, ROBERT K., and LAZARSFELD, PAUL F. [Editors], *Continuities in Social Research*, Glencoe (1950) . . 32, 46, 72, 200, 236, 239, 242

MERTON, ROBERT K., and KITT, ALICE S., *Contributions to the Theory of Reference Group Behaviour*, in MERTON, R. K., and LAZARSFELD, P. F. [Eds.] (1950) 72

MESS, HENRY A., *Social Structure*, London (1942) 55

MILL, JOHN STUART, *On the Definition of Political Economy and on the Method of Philosophical Investigation in that Science*, London (1836). Reprinted in NAGEL, E. (1950) 2, 41

MILL, JOHN STUART, *A System of Logic*, London (1842–1891) 22, 33, 62, 65, 68, 255, 272, 275

MILL, JOHN STUART, *Examination of Sir W. Hamilton's Philosophy*, London (1867). Extracts reprinted in NAGEL, E. (1950) . . . 59

MOORE, G. E., ' Proof of an External World ', *British Academy Proceedings* (1939), **25**, 273 50

MORENO, J. L., *Sociometry, Experimental Method and the Science of Society*, New York (1951) 231

MORENO, J. L., *Who Shall Survive? A New Approach to the Problems of Human Interrelations*, Washington (1934) . . . 231, 278

MORRIS, CHARLES W., ' Foundations of the Theory of Signs ', *International Encyclopædia of Unified Science*, Chicago (1938), **1** (2), 1–42 . . 38

MOSER, C. A., ' Quota Sampling ', *J. Roy. Statist. Soc.* (1952), **115** (3), 411–23 212

MOSTELLER, FREDERICK, HYMAN, HERBERT, et al., *The Pre-Election Polls of 1948 : Report to the Committee on Analysis of Pre-Election Polls and Forecasts*. Social Science Research Council, Bulletin 60, New York (1949) 182, 243, 247

MURPHY, GARDNER, *Historical Introduction to Modern Psychology*, London (1928–1949) 56, 122, 192

MURPHY, GARDNER, MURPHY, LOIS B. and NEWCOMB, THEODORE, M., *Experimental Social Psychology : an Interpretation of Research upon the Socialization of the Individual*, New York (1931, 1937) 90, 123, 185, 188, 191, 245, 263, 265, 278, 281

MYRDAL, ALVA, *Nation and Family*, London (1945) . . . 111

NADEL, S. F., *The Foundations of Social Anthropology*, London (1951) . 14

NAGEL, ERNEST, *John Stuart Mill's Philosophy of Scientific Method*, New York (1950) 2, 41, 59, 61

NEWCOMB, THEODORE M. See MURPHY, G., et al. (1937) 90, 123, 185, 188, 191, 245, 263, 265, 278, 281

NOTES AND QUERIES ON ANTHROPOLOGY, Royal Anthropological Institute, London (1874—5th ed. *1929*) 179

Index of References

OGDEN, C. K., and RICHARDS, I. A., *The Meaning of Meaning*, London (1923–1930) 38, 40, 43
OLDFIELD, R. C., *The Psychology of the Interview*, London (1941) 144, 218, 241
PARK, ROBERT E., *Sociology*, in GEE, W. [Ed.], (1929) . . . 87, 115
PAYNE, S. L., *The Art of Asking Questions*, Princeton (1951) . . 244, 250
PEAR, T. H., *Some Problems and Topics of Contemporary Social Psychology*, in BARTLETT, F. C., et al. (1939) 199
PEARSE, INNES H., and CROCKER, LUCY H., *The Peckham Experiment*, London (1943) 137
POMEROY, WARDELL B. *See* KINSEY, A. C., et al. (1948)
 14, 46, 221, 237, 241, 247
RECENT SOCIAL TRENDS IN THE UNITED STATES, President's Research Comittee on Social Trends (2 vols.) Vol. I, 1933 112
RICHARDS, AUDREY I., *The Development of Field Work Methods in Social Anthropology*, in BARTLETT, F. C., et al. (1939) . . . 25, 138
RICHARDS, I. A. *See* OGDEN, C. K. (1930) 38, 40, 43
ROETHLISBERGER, FRITZ J., and DICKSON, WILLIAM J., *Management and the Worker*, Harvard (1939) 134, 160, 167, 221, 232, 282
ROGERS, CARL R., *Counseling and Psychotherapy*, New York (1942)
 156, 159, 163
ROGERS, CARL R., 'The Non-directive Method for Social Research', *Am. Journ. Soc.* (1945), 50, 279–83 156
ROSE, WILLIAM [Editor], *An Outline of Modern Knowledge*, London (1931) 94
ROWNTREE, B. SEEBOHM, *Poverty : a Study of Town Life*, London (1901–1902) 206
ROWNTREE, B. SEEBOHM, *Poverty and Progress : a Second Social Survey of York*, London (1941) 206
ROWNTREE, B. SEEBOHM, and LAVERS, G. R., *English Life and Leisure*, London (1951a) 176
ROWNTREE, B. SEEBOHM, and LAVERS, G. R., *Poverty and the Welfare State*, London (1951b) 206
ROYAL COMMISSION ON LABOUR, *Report*, London (1894) . . . 148
ROYAL COMMISSION ON THE POOR LAW, *Report*, London (1909) . . 148
ROYAL COMMISSION ON THE PRESS, *Report*, London (1949) . . . 113
RUSSELL, BERTRAND, *An Outline of Philosophy*, London (1927)
 29, 40, 48, 121, 123
SEIGNOBOS, CH., *Méthode historique appliquée aux sciences sociales*, cited by GOTTSCHALK, L., et al. (1945), p. 3 80
SEIGNOBOS, CH. *See* LANGLOIS, CH. V. (1898) . . . 40, 80, 224
SHILS, E. A., *Primary Groups in the American Army*, in MERTON, R. K., and LAZARSFELD, P. F. [Eds.], (1950) 72
SILBERMAN, LEO, and SPICE, BETTY, *Colour and Class in Six Liverpool Schools*, Liverpool (1950) 231
SOROKIN, PITIRIM A., et al., 'An Experimental Study of Efficiency of Work under Various Specified Conditions', *Am. Journ. Soc.* (1930), 35, 765–82 281
SPICE, BETTY. *See* SILBERMAN, L. (1950) 231
SPENCER, HERBERT, *The Study of Sociology*, London (1873–1884) . . 119
STERN, WILLIAM, *Differentielle Psychologie* (1921), cited by LYND, R. S. (1939) 260

Index of References

STOCKS, PERCY, *Sickness in the Population of England and Wales, 1944–1947*, [Studies on Medical and Population Subjects, No. 2], London (1949) 237

STOUFFER, SAMUEL A., *An Experimental Comparison of Statistical and Case History Methods of Attitude Research*. [Not published, MSS. in University of Chicago Library.] Cited by ALLPORT, G. W. (1942) p. 24 114

STOUFFER, SAMUEL A., et al., *The American Soldier : Vol. I—Adjustment during Army Life ; Vol. II—Combat and its Aftermath*, Princeton (1949) 71

STOUFFER, SAMUEL A., et al., *Measurement and Prediction*, [Vol. 4, in Studies in Social Psychology in World War II], Princeton (1950) 22, 36, 186, 192, 195, 197, 201, 213

STOUFFER, SAMUEL A., *Afterthoughts of a Contributor*, in MERTON, R. K., and LAZARSFELD, P. F. [Eds.] (1950) 32, 46

STOUFFER, SAMUEL A., ' Some Observations on Study Design ', *Am. Journ. Soc.* (1950), **55**, 355–61 . . . . 262 seq.

STOUFFER, SAMUEL A., and TOBY, JACKSON, ' Rôle Conflict and Personality ', *Am. Journ. Soc.* (1951), **56**, 395–406 194

STOUFFER, SAMUEL A. See CAVAN, R. S., et al. (1930) . . . 114

STUART, A. See DURBIN, J. (1951) 247, 249, 263

SUMNER, WILLIAM GRAHAM, *Folkways : a Study of the Sociological Importance of Usages, Manners, Customs, Moves and Morals*, Boston (1907) 95

THOMAS, A., *Contribution to discussion* on paper by MANDEVILLE, J. P. (1946) 226

THOMAS, DOROTHY SWAINE, et al., *Observational Studies of Social Behaviour*, New Haven (1933) 126

THOMAS, WILLIAM I., and ZNANIECKI, FLORIAN, *The Polish Peasant in Europe and America*, New York (1919) 82, 91

THOMPSON, G. P., Review in *New Statesman and Nation* (1950), **40**, 466 . 32

THOMSON, SIR GODFREY H., *The Factorial Analysis of Human Ability*, London (1939, *1948*) 191

THRASHER, FREDERIC M., *The Gang*, Chicago (1927–1936) . . 91

THOULESS, ROBERT H., *Straight and Crooked Thinking*, London (1930–1936) 237

THURSTONE, LOUIS L., ' Attitudes Can Be Measured ', *Am. Journ. Soc.* (1928), **33**, 544 seq. 190

TITMUSS, RICHARD M., *History of the Second World War : Problems of Social Policy*, London (1950) 94

TOBY, JACKSON. See STOUFFER, S. A. (1951) 194

TURNER, W. J., and MASS-OBSERVATION, *Exmoor Village*, London (1947) . 135

TRIST, ERIC L., and BAMFORTH, K. W., ' Some Social and Psychological Consequences of the Longwall Method of Coal-Getting ', *Human Relations* (1951), **4** (1), 3–38 . . . . . . 137, 289

U.N.E.S.C.O., *Freedom and Culture*, London (1951) . . . 56

VERNON, P. E., *Questionnaires, Attitude Tests and Rating Scales*, in BARTLETT, F. C., et al. (1939) 242

VIVIAN, SIR SYLVANUS, *Contribution to discussion* on paper by KYD, J. G., *J. Roy. Statist. Soc.* (1947), **110** (4), 317 179

WARNER, W. LLOYD, and LUNT, PAUL S., *The Social Life of a Modern Community*, Yankee City Series, Vol. I, New Haven (1941) . 53, 95

WARNER, W. LLOYD, and LUNT, PAUL S., *The Status System of a Modern Community*, Yankee City Series, Vol. II, New Haven (1942) . . 53

WEBB, BEATRICE, *My Apprenticeship*, London (1926) . . 27, 96, 210, 259

Index of References

WEBB, BEATRICE, *Our Partnership*, London (1948) 149
WEBB, SIDNEY and BEATRICE, *Methods of Social Study*, London (1932)
    92, 99, 104, 118, 148, 223, 238
WEBER, MAX [Trans. by Shils and Finch], *The Methodology of the Social Sciences*, Glencoe (1949) 15, 276
WEBER, MAX [Trans. by Talcott Parsons], *Theory of Social and Economic Organisation*, London (1947) 276
WEINBERG, S. K., *Review* in *Am. Journ. Soc.* (1948), 53, 514 . . . 288
WEISS, ALFRED PAUL, *A Theoretical Basis of Human Behaviour*, New York (1921) 50
WIRTH, LOUIS, *Foreword* to MANNHEIM, K. (1936) 128
YATES, FRANK, *Sampling Methods for Censuses and Surveys*, London (1949)
    138, 206, 225, 230, 252, 263
YOUNG, PAULINE V., *Scientific Social Surveys and Research*, New York (1939, *1949*) 140
YULE, G. UDNY [and, in recent editions, KENDALL, M. G.], *An Introduction to the Theory of Statistics* (1911–*1950*) 73
ZNANIECKI, FLORIAN. *See* THOMAS, W. I. (1919) . . . 82, 91
ZWEIG, FERDINAND, *Labour, Life and Poverty*, London (1948) . . 175

GENERAL INDEX

ACCOUNTING for results, 76
Action Research, 136, 289, 292
Adler, A., 154
Administration, facts used in, 46, 70
Agreement, Method of, 61
Aims, agreement on, 5, 287
Alchemy, 20, 291
Animism, 22
Anthropology, 25, 169
  cultural, 26, 33, 37
  functional, 132, 135
A priori truths, 3, 66
Aristotle, 59
Art,
  and science, 7, 27
  works of, 95
Artificiality, 128, 260
'As if', 277
Attitude-structure expectations, 246
Attitude studies, 187
Authentication, 103
Autobiography, 36, 82, 86, 114, 167

Bacon, F., 60
Band-waggon effect, 203
Bedeutung, 58
Behaviour, overt, 14, 34, 51, 83, 129
  verbal, 34, 38, 129, 138
Behaviourism, 14, 33, 51, 83, 124, 129
Booth, C., 17, 102, 131, 150
Boyle's Law, 23, 280
Buckle, T. H., 109

Case histories, 100, 174
Cattell, R. B., 122
Causality, 21, 79
Causes, Plurality of, 65, 72, 272
Census, 92, 207, 209
  tracts, 211
Chi-square, 73
Ciné-camera records, 125, 139
Class, definitions of, 52, 229
Clausen, J. A., 22
Coding, 225
Commitment of investigator, 6, 119, 294
Complexity, 20, 24, 31, 33, 119
Comte, A., 1, 17, 21, 81, 109, 254, 291
Concepts, 8, 20, 69
Concomitant observations, 262
  Variations, Method of, 64
Consensus, 5, 130, 136

Content analysis, 112
Convergence, as scientific principle, 12, 21, 37, 292
Correlation analysis, 74, 274
Counselling, 153
Covariance, analysis of, 262
Craik, K., 7
Criterion situation, 202
Croce, B., 109
Cross-examination, 149, 241
Culture, 26
Curle, A., 136
Cutting point, 195
Cybernetics, 7, 203

Deduction and induction, 59
Definitions, exact, 39
  by minute description, 44
  operational, 46, 56, 234, 256
  primitive total meanings, 43, 57
  taxonomic, 44
Determinism, 21
Diagnosis, fashions in, 102
Diagrams, sociometric, 35, 231
  topological, 24
Diaries, 82, 87
Dictionary, sociological, 39
Difference, Method of, 61
Dilthey, W., 110
Direct recording, 221
Discourse, universe of, 42
Distortion by informant, 85, 87, 234
  by investigator, 89, 119, 244
Documents, availability of, 90, 95
  historical, 80
  primary and secondary, 92, 96
  personal, 81, 114
Droysen, J. G., 110
Durkheim, E., 7, 77

Ecological studies, 211
Econometrics, 275
Economics, 69, 274
Effects, Intermixture of, 65, 72
Election forecasting, 181
Electoral Register, 210
Emotional *v.* rational appeals, 263
Empiricism, 60
Engels, F., 4
Error, due to bias, 207
  sampling, 207
Ethical neutrality, 14
Ethology, 68

305

General Index

Euclid, 59
Evidence, oral, 148
Evolution, 16
Experiment, 9, 32, 62, 66, 72, 79, 254, 291
  artificial, 255
  controlled, 261
  co-operative, 282
  crucial, 32
  ex-post-facto, 272
  imaginary, 276
  in time, 280
  laboratory, 260, 287
  mental, 274, 291
  nature's, 255
  so-called social, 254
  validity of, 269
Explanations, 8, 76

Fact and opinion, 152, 179, 204
Factor analysis, 191
  equation, 268
Factorial design, 263
Field theory, 23
Folklore, 95
Frame, 210
Freewill, 21
Frequency distribution, control by, 268, 270
  normal, 46, 215
Freud, S., 154

Geddes, P., 17
General Register Office, 210, 229, 234
Generalisation, 90, 98
Gestalt, 24, 121, 124
Good listening, 158, 162
Government Social Survey, 206, 210, 217, 237, 245, 249
Group, limits to size of working, 31
  small, 32

Halo effect, 246
Hart, H., 112
Harvey, W., 60
Hawthorne works, 114, 133, 160, 282
Health Visitors, 102
Herschel, Sir J., 61, 64, 67
Historians, 70, 91, 108
Hollerith, 225
Human guinea-pigs, 258
Hume, D., 60
Hygienic performance, 265
Hypothesis, 8, 37, 71, 89, 118, 141
  null, 262, 265

Ideology, 4, 16
Idiographic description, 199
Indirect approach, 161
Industrial psychology, 133, 160

Inference in all observation, 122
Instruments of measurement, 125
Intellectual diplomacy, 277
Intelligence, 36, 47, 51, 187, 278
Interaction, 120, 127, 245, 261
Interested witness, 239
Interpretation, 77, 89, 108
Intervening variables, 77, 191, 242
Interview, and journalism, 174
  depth, 152
  focused, 89, 114, 164, 187
  formative, 153
  informal, 173
  mass, 151, 177
  motivating, 146
  non-directive, 153, 165
  open-ended, 184
  point-blank, 187
  rapid-fire, 241
  semi-structured, 165, 184
  structured, 165
  unstructured, 165
Interviewer, rôle of, 163, 247
Introspection, 83, 111
Inverse Deductive Method, 67, 274
Inverse Probability, 272

James, W., 4
Joint Method of Agreement and Difference, 63
Jung, C. G., 154

Kant, I., 3, 60
Kendall, P. L., 184
Knowledge, sociology of, 4
  as end in itself, 2, 8

Language, 38, 147
Lasswell, H., 113
Latent structure analysis, 191
Laws, natural, 3
  social, 8
Leites, N., 113
Le Play, F., 17, 131
Letters, 82, 87
Lewin, K., 24
Life History, 82, 167
Listing, 226
Locke, J., 60
Logic, 58
  inductive, 61
Lynd, R. S. and H. M., 133

Mach, E., 274
Maintenance register, 210
Manifest and latent content, 162
Mannheim, K., 4
Mark-sensing, 226
Marxism, 4, 16, 52
Mass-interview, 36, 151, 177
  -observation, 95, 135, 175

General Index

Material culture, 140
 inventories, 139
Mathematics, 6, 59
Measurement of attitudes, 187
Memorandum, 220
Merton, R. K., 184
Metaphysics, 1
Methods of Experimental Inquiry, 61
Mill, J. S., 3, 32, 61
Minute description, definition by, 44
Motives and personal documents, 85
Moving observer, principle of, 138
Multiple questioning, 188

Names, unimportance of, 56
Newspapers, 93
Nightingale, F., 77
Nomothetic generalisation, 199
Non-response, 248
Normality, 16, 46, 51
Note-taking, 143, 220
Novelists, 27, 33

Objectifying devices, 125
Objectivity, 3, 10, 28, 52, 109, 111, 120, 126, 130, 178, 233
Observation, 10, 117
 acquired skill in, 141
 participant, 130
Occam's razor, 7
Opinions, private and public, 185, 200
Orientations, general, 8
Origin situation, 202
Overheards, 137

Panel technique, 78, 183
Paramount cards, 224, 230
Park, R. E., 133
Pearson, K., 73
Peirce, C. S., 4
Persistence forecasting, 182
Personal document, 81, 114
Phenomenology, dogmatic, 83
Pilot survey, 216, 223
Plausibility, 88, 237
Poincaré, H., 7
Point-blank questioning, 187
Pool, I. de S., 113
Porter, E. H., 159, 162
Post-factum analysis, 271
Powers-Samas, 225, 234
Pragmatism, 4, 16
Precision, 7, 40, 112, 290
 control, 268
Pre-coding, 184
Prediction, 22, 88, 182, 201
Preference rules, 7
Pre-pilot survey, 217
Pre-sample, 213
Presuppositions, 3, 6, 60, 111
Pretest, 217

Primary material, 91, 96, 117
Primitive society, 31, 132, 169
Probability, 74, 207
 inverse, 272
Projective tests, 123, 169
Prompting, 245
Protectionism v. free trade, 33, 67, 261
Psychoanalysis, 16, 89, 111, 136, 154, 167, 170, 172, 288
Psychology, 26, 33, 77, 83, 120, 133, 160, 246, 260
Psychological levels, 167
 tests, 123, 169, 202
Psychotherapy, 85, 154, 159, 288
Public opinion polling, 36, 180
Punching, 225

Quantitative methods, 13
Quasi-scale, 198
Questionnaire, 36, 115, 150, 177, 221, 248
 omnibus, 185
Quintamensional Plan, 186
Quota Sampling, 182, 212, 239, 268

Randomisation, 207, 262, 268, 270
Rank, O., 155
Rapid-fire questioning, 241
Rating records, 211
Rationalism, 3, 16
Reality, 24, 31
Records, 92
 gramophone, 125, 246
Reference, frame of, 124
Refusals, 249
Rejection test, 231
Relay Assembly Test Room, 134, 160, 283
Relevance, 11, 89, 97, 111, 292
Repetition, 271, 288
Replication, 262
Reports, 93
Reproducibility, coefficient of, 195, 197
Research and therapy, 103, 136, 164, 167
Residues, Method of, 64
Rorschach test, 123, 169, 202
Royal Commissions and the like, 148
Rules, preference, 7
Rulings, 230
Russell, B., 59

Sampling, 35, 73, 205
 analytical, 208
 error, 206, 213
 fraction, 208
 geographical, 211
 multi-phase, 209
 multi-stage, 208
 random, 207
 unit, 210

General Index

Scalability, 196
Scalogram, analysis, 186, 194
Schedules, observational, 126, 139
Science, applied, 12
Secondary sources, 91, 96, 117
Self-consciousness, 128, 260
Semi-autobiography, 168
Semiotics, 38
Sense organs, 10, 120
Sensitiveness of experiment, 269
Sequential analysis, 216
Shifts in attitude, 183, 193
Significance, tests for, 74, 270
Sinnott, E. W., 25
Size of sample, 213
Skill, social, 28, 150, 248
   verbal, 51, 202, 238
Social accounting, 11
   class, 52, 229
   control, 257
   distance, 188
   engineering, 6, 11, 17, 258, 287
   studies, 100
   survey, 17, 206
   welfare, 100, 219
Social Science,
   complexity of, 21, 33, 119
   practical function of, 8
Sociodrama, 232
Sociogram, 35, 231
Sociology of knowledge, 4
Sociomatrix, 232
Sociometric scales, 266
Sociometric Star, 231
Sociometrics, 231, 278
Socrates, 111
   mortality of, 59
Specialisation, 25
Specification, 78
Spencer, H., 3, 21
Split-ballot, 243
Spurious factors, 76
Standard classification items, 221, 223
   deviation, 215
   error, 213

Statistics, 35, 72, 205
   interpretation of, 105
   official, 93
Stereotypes, 240, 246
Stouffer, S. A., 79
Stratification, 208
Substitutes, 250
Suicide, 77
Syllogism, 59, 110
Symbols, 6, 38

Tabulation, 226
Taine, H., 109
Tavistock Institute of Human Relations, 136, 289
Taxonomy, 44, 55
Test situation, 202
Theoretician, 11, 72
Theory, 1, 8, 70, 118, 290
Thucydides, 109
Thurstone scales, 189
Transcendentalism, 60
Truth, 3, 76
   by compromise, 149, 277

Uncertainty, 22, 290
Understanding, 58, 110
Uniqueness, 30
Utility, 16

Validity of experiment, 269
Value judgment, freedom from, 17
Values, 14
Variables, intervening, 78, 106, 191
Verbs, substitution for nouns, 56
Verification, 11, 236
   external, 87, 104
   internal, 88
Verifier, 225

Webb, S. and B., 81
Weber, M., 15
Whitehead, A. N., 59
Will, freedom of, 21
Wirth, L., 128

Yankee City Series, 53, 133

TITLES IN THIS SERIES

1. Harry Elmer Barnes. *Historical Sociology: Its Origins and Development.* 1948.
2. Jacob Burckhardt. *Judgments on History and Historians.* 1958.
3. Herbert Butterfield. *Herbert Butterfield on History.*
    Christianity and History. 1949.
    The Discontinuities between the Generations in History. 1971.
    The Present State of Historical Scholarship. 1965.
4. Courtland Canby, Nancy E. Gross, eds. *The World of History.* 1954.
5. G. Kitson Clark. *The Critical Historian.* 1967. bound with *Guide For Research Students Working on Historical Subjects.* 1958.
6. Robin G. Collingwood. *Essays in the Philosophy of History.* 1965.
7. Henry Steele Commager. *The Nature and the Study of History.* 1965.
8. L. P. Curtis, Jr., ed. *The Historians Workshop: Original Essays by Sixteen Historians.* 1970.
9. Folke Dovring. *History as a Social Science.* 1960.
10. Martin Duberman. *The Uncompleted Past.* 1969.
11. Mircea Eliade. *Cosmos and History: The Myth of the Eternal Return.* 1954.

12   G. R. Elton. *Political History: Principles and Practices.* 1970.
13   Martin Feldman, Eli Seifman, eds. *The Social Studies: Structure, Models, and Strategies.* 1969.
14   John A. Garraty. *The Nature of Biography.* 1957.
15   John Higham, Leonard Krieger, Felix Gilbert. *History.* 1965.
16   H. Stuart Hughes. *History as Art and as Science.* 1964.
17   Paul Murray Kendall. *The Art of Biography.* 1965.
18   William Leo Lucey. *History: Methods and Interpretation.* 1958.
19   Raymond G. McInnis, James W. Scott, eds. *Social Science and Research Handbook.* 1974.
20   John Madge. *The Tools of Social Science.* 1953.
21   Arthur Marwick. *The Nature of History.* 1981.
22   Hans Meyerhoff, ed. *The Philosophy of History in Our Time.* 1959.
23   A. D. Momigliano. *Studies in Historiography.* 1966.
24   Herbert J. Muller. *The Uses of the Past.* 1953.
25   Allan Nevins. *The Gateway to History.* 1938.
26   Roy Pascal. *Design and Truth in Autobiography.* 1960.
27   A. L. Rowse. *The Use of History.* 1946.
28   Robert Allen Skotheim, ed. *The Historian and the Climate of Opinion.* 1969.
29   Robert Stover. *The Nature of Historical Thinking.* 1967.
30   Pardon E. Tillinghast. *The Specious Past: Historians and Others.* 1972.
31   Ludwig von Mises. *Theory and History.* 1957.